Real World

ADOBE®
Illustrator® CS5

MORDY GOLDING

Peachpit Press

Real World Adobe Illustrator CS5
Mordy Golding

Peachpit Press
1249 Eighth Street
Berkeley, CA 94710
510/524-2178
Fax: 510/524-2221

Find us on the web at www.peachpit.com.
To report errors, please send a note to errata@peachpit.com.
Peachpit Press is a division of Pearson Education.

Project Editor: Rebecca Freed
Production Coordinator: Cory Borman
Copy Editor: Kim Saccio-Kent
Proofreaders: Liz Welch
Composition: Myrna Vladic, David Van Ness
Indexer: James Minkin
Cover Design: Charlene Charles-Will
Cover Illustration: Von R. Glitschka

ISBN-13: 978-0-321-71306-3
ISBN-10:   0-321-71306-0

9 8 7 6 5 4 3 2

Printed and bound in the United States of America

This book is dedicated to my wife, Batsheva,
who continues to support me in everything I do.

The words in this book belong to her
just as much as they do to me.

Acknowledgments

While this certainly isn't the first book that I've written, I am still amazed by how much work is required to produce such a high-quality product. I am indebted to the team at Peachpit Press for once again making me look great in print. Thanks to Nancy Ruenzel, Charlene Charles-Will, Sara Jane Todd, Glenn Bisignani, Christine Yarrow, and all the folks at Adobe Press. I want to personally thank Kim Saccio-Kent for copyediting this book and Cory Borman, Myrna Vladic, and David Van Ness for their work on its production. A man is lucky to have an editor, but for this book I've been blessed with two. Karyn Johnson is a friend first and an editor second, and Rebecca Freed has expertly navigated this book from start to finish. I want to thank you both for continuing to trust in me and for always being there with a gentle, yet firm command.

Any book that covers technology needs a great technical editor, and I consider myself lucky to work closely with one of the most knowledgeable minds in the design and print world, Jean-Claude Tremblay. Many of the tips throughout this volume come from JC's suggestions.

While writing a book is hard, I can assure you that writing and producing a powerful graphics application like Illustrator is a Herculean task. In my own opinion, Illustrator CS5 stands as one of the best versions we've seen. Special thanks go to the entire Illustrator team for their concerted efforts, and specifically to David Macy, Terry Hemphill, Teri Pettit, Anil Ahuja, Preeti Shukla, and Brenda Sutherland for their personal assistance and advice. I'd also like to thank John Nack, Whitney McCleary, Jill Paley, Rachel Luxemburg, Liz Frederick, Jane Brady, and the always-entertaining Russell Brown for their continued friendship.

I'm lucky enough to count a number of professional authors and educators among my friends. Thanks to David Blatner, Deke McClelland, Bert Monroy, Claudia McCue, Michael Murphy, Scott Citron, Brian Wood, Matthew Richmond, and the awesome Michael Ninness, who continue to share advice, support, and funny anecdotes over the occasional drink.

I reserve a personal note of appreciation for my friend Von Glitschka, who continues to blow me away with incredible artwork, including the colorful illustration that is featured on the front cover of this book.

Finally, I want to thank my entire family for their encouragement and support. Your collective words, smiles, and hugs help me keep my focus on the most important things in life. Speaking of important things, Simcha, go get your Gemara—let's learn.

Table of Contents

Introduction

Because I've been the product manager of Adobe Illustrator, people frequently approach me who, prior to attending a demo or workshop on Illustrator, either thought they had no need for the program or were under the impression it is used only for designing logos.

The truth is, Illustrator is essential to a broad range of professionals and hobbyists, and it has an incredible number of uses—so many that it's hard to define exactly what Illustrator does. Features such as transparency, 3D, Live Trace, Live Paint, gradient mesh, live effects, professional typography, Flash animation, and now multiple artboards and the Blob Brush tool have all redefined how people use Illustrator every day. It's certainly not the same program it was 10 years ago.

My goal with this book is threefold: to teach new users how to take advantage of the technology, to help experienced users learn about features that have changed, and to give power users the understanding they need to push themselves and still produce reliable files. I love showing people all the cool and productive things you can do with the product, and nothing makes me happier than seeing a designer crank out a totally awesome design using Illustrator. Throughout this book, I share my thoughts, experiences, and knowledge about Illustrator so that you can have fun with it, sharpen your skills, and make it work for you.

The Many Uses of Illustrator

Look all around you.

Billboards along the side of the highway, packages for cereal and other gro-ceries at the supermarket, navigation icons on a website, posters announc-ing an exhibit at a museum, advertisements throughout magazines and newspapers, logos and artwork on T-shirts and sportswear, animated car-toons and feature films, user interfaces on your computer and cell phones... all of these and more are created with the help of Illustrator.

Illustrator is used by individuals who want to express their creativity in print, on the web, in video, and on wireless devices. Illustrator is distributed in many different languages, and you can find millions of users across the globe. Of course, with such a diverse user base, Illustrator is applied in many ways. To get an idea of what I mean, look at how some creative professionals use Illustrator and how this book can help them.

Creative Genius: The World of Graphic Design

It's difficult to define the job of a graphic designer because the title encompasses so many different types of design. For the most part, these professionals specialize in a particular field of design such as corporate, advertising, direct mail, or even typography. Graphic designers work on a variety of projects and usually have experience with several programs, including Adobe Photoshop and Adobe InDesign or QuarkXPress.

For these kinds of users, Illustrator serves as a creative springboard for designs such as logos and type treatments, ad storyboards and campaigns, spot illustrations, maps, and general design elements.

If you're a graphic designer, you'll find the following chapters most help-ful as you read this book: Chapter 1, "Creating and Managing Documents" (page 1); Chapter 4, "Creative Drawing" (page 105); Chapter 6, "Coloring Art-work" (page 177); Chapter 7, "Working with Live Effects" (page 237); Chapter 8, "Working with Typography" (page 265); and Chapter 10, "Working with Images" (page 333).

Telling a Story: Illustration and Animation

To an illustrator or animator, Illustrator is an empty canvas waiting to come alive. In a world of animated feature films and TV shows, it's easy to understand the benefits of drawing characters and animations directly on a computer. Its ability to repurpose art for almost any need makes Illustrator the perfect environment for creating animations and illustrations.

Adobe didn't name its product Illustrator without reason. Artists create illustrations for children's books, magazine covers and articles, packages, and a variety of other products, and they use Illustrator to take advantage of the high quality and precision available in the program. A variety of tools, such as gradient meshes, blends, and even 3D, allow illustrators to translate the images they see in their minds into reality.

If you're an animator or an illustrator, you'll find the following chapters most helpful as you read this book: Chapter 2, "Selecting and Editing Artwork" (page 27); Chapter 3, "Technical Drawing" (page 69); Chapter 4, "Creative Drawing" (page 105); Chapter 6, "Coloring Artwork" (page 177); Chapter 10, "Working with Images" (page 333); and Chapter 11, "Web Design" (page 371).

Interactive Experience: Interface and Web Design

Web designers have a language all their own, which includes acronyms such as HTML, XML, FXG, SWF, GIF, JPEG, PNG, and CSS. Illustrator supports these and other web-specific technologies, giving web designers access to the formats in which they need to deliver their designs. Taking advantage of Illustrator's object-based design environment, web designers can lay out precise navigation elements, buttons, and entire pages.

In today's fast-paced world, everyone needs a presence on the web. However, businesses find that they also need to provide content in print format. By creating art in Illustrator, web designers can easily use that art for both web and print layouts, thus reducing the need to re-create art for each medium.

If you're a web or interface designer, you'll find the following chapters most helpful as you read this book: Chapter 2, "Selecting and Editing Artwork" (page 27); Chapter 5, "Organizing Your Drawing" (page 145); Chapter 7, "Working with Live Effects" (page 237); Chapter 9, "Drawing with Efficiency" (page 299); Chapter 10, "Working with Images" (page 333); and Chapter 11, "Web Design" (page 371).

Tomorrow's Trends: Fashion and Apparel Design

If you're thinking about bathing suits while it's snowing outside, either you're dreaming about going on vacation or you're a fashion designer. What type of clothes you design may directly correlate to the seasons of the year, but designing apparel is also a highly creative field that demands the most of a designer. The object-based approach to design in Illustrator makes it easier to work with body shapes, apparel guidelines, and product labels.

Fashion designers can create symbol libraries of repeating objects such as motifs, buttons, buckles, and zippers. With Illustrator, designers can also create pattern fills and use transparency effects to simulate shading and add realism.

If you're a fashion designer, you'll find the following chapters most helpful as you read this book: Chapter 2, "Selecting and Editing Artwork" (page 27); Chapter 3, "Technical Drawing" (page 69); Chapter 4, "Creative Drawing" (page 105); Chapter 6, "Coloring Artwork" (page 177); Chapter 9, "Drawing with Efficiency" (page 299); and Chapter 10, "Working with Images" (page 333).

Thinking Outside the Box: Package Design

If you're good at reading upside-down text, you just might be a package designer. That's because most package designs are created flat on one sheet, with different panels facing different directions. Once printed, the entire package is folded up so it appears visually correct. Package designers use Illustrator to define spot colors, place images from Photoshop, and apply trapping settings—all in an effort to grab a potential buyer's attention.

Because of production requirements, package designers often need to be able to make minute adjustments to colors and artwork. By building files in Illustrator, these designers can control nearly every aspect of the file and meet their deadlines at the same time.

If you're a package designer, you'll find the following chapters most helpful as you read this book: Chapter 2, "Selecting and Editing Artwork" (page 27);

Chapter 6, "Coloring Artwork" (page 177); Chapter 8, "Working with Typography" (page 265); Chapter 9, "Drawing with Efficiency" (page 299); Chapter 10, "Working with Images" (page 333); and Chapter 13, "Prepress and Printing" (page 445).

The Science of Design: Art and Print Production

Production artists are a separate breed (I would know—I'm one of them). To them, everything in a file matters. Illustrator allows production artists to dig deep into graphics files and make the edits and changes that are necessary to print a file correctly. Whether for producing or using spot colors, using overprint commands, using transparency flattening, or generally cleaning up paths and shapes, production artists have come to rely on Illustrator. Because they can use it to open and edit EPS and PDF files (and many other file formats), Illustrator has become a required tool for art production.

If you cringe at the thought of an RGB file with overprints, transparencies, and spot colors, then you're certainly a production artist. You might not care much about how to create nice brush strokes, but you care about simplifying paths so that they print faster.

If you're a production artist, you'll find the following chapters most helpful as you read this book: Chapter 1, "Creating and Managing Documents" (page 1); Chapter 5, "Organizing Your Drawing" (page 145); Chapter 6, "Coloring Artwork" (page 177); Chapter 9, "Drawing with Efficiency" (page 299); Chapter 10, "Working with Images" (page 333); Chapter 12, "Saving and Exporting Files" (page 401); and Chapter 13, "Prepress and Printing" (page 445).

Frame by Frame: Motion Graphics

In an industry where the term *indie* doesn't refer to InDesign, the art of producing movies and motion graphics lives by its own set of rules. And although that is certainly true, Illustrator still plays a huge part in generating graphics that can help jazz up a corporate promotional video or create an intricate opening or credits sequence for a big-budget film.

Illustrator's artwork may be vector, but that allows for more options when used in a pixel-based video workflow. Used with applications such as Adobe After Effects, Adobe Premiere Pro, Apple Final Cut Pro, or even

Apple iMovie, Illustrator adds an entire dimension to the motion graphics workflow.

If you're into motion graphics or video production, you'll find the following chapters most helpful as you read this book: Chapter 1, "Creating and Managing Documents" (page 1); Chapter 5, "Organizing Your Drawing" (page 145); Chapter 8, "Working with Typography" (page 265); Chapter 9, "Drawing with Efficiency" (page 299); Chapter 10, "Working with Images" (page 333); and Chapter 11, "Web Design" (page 371).

The Melting Pot of Design: Creativity for Everyone

If you didn't identify with any of the titles I've listed so far, that's okay. In fact, it's nearly impossible to list all the kinds of people who use Illustrator every day. Because Illustrator has so many uses, the people who use it are very diverse. They may include doctors, lawyers, architects, signage and environmental designers, video and film specialists, or even a restaurant owner who is designing a menu cover.

Just realize that Illustrator is for everyone who wants to express their creativity, and that makes for one big happy family!

Where Did Illustrator Come From?

Our past is what helps define our future. Whether you're new to Illustrator or a veteran who has been using it for years, it helps to better understand the history behind a product that helped redefine the graphics industry.

In the 1980s, during a time when the personal computer was beginning to take the world by storm, Apple Computer introduced the Macintosh with an "affordable" laser printer called the Apple LaserWriter. What made the LaserWriter so remarkable wasn't so much the price (about $7,000 at that time) as the technology that was hidden inside it—Adobe PostScript, a computer language that enabled the LaserWriter to print beautiful graphics.

John Warnock, one of the founders of Adobe Systems, invented PostScript and was trying to find a way to make more money selling it. Although PostScript was cool, graphics still had to be created by entering line after line of computer code. John needed a way for people to create PostScript files visually, and that's how Illustrator was born. In early 1987, using the Bézier curve as the basis for vector graphics, Adobe introduced Illustrator 1.1 with much success. Now, nearly 25 years later, Illustrator continues to thrive and help those in the design community innovate.

When Should You Use Illustrator?

Good designers have many tools at their disposal. Especially in an environment where most designers have other powerful graphics applications, it can be difficult to choose which one to use for a particular task. For example, a designer can apply soft drop shadows in Photoshop, Illustrator, and InDesign—is one application any better than the others for this?

How do you know when to use Illustrator? To answer the question directly, "Use Illustrator when it's the right tool for the job."

In reality, using the right tool for the job is what this book is all about. When you understand the strengths (and weaknesses) of each program, you also understand when it's best to use (or not to use) a particular application. As would be expected, every design or production task you are called upon to do will require a different technique, method, or feature. When you are comfortable with Illustrator, you'll easily be able to look at any project and know how to go about implementing it.

What's New in Adobe Illustrator CS5?

Every time Adobe ships a new version of Illustrator, users get that mixed emotion of yearning for new cool and timesaving features while also worrying about what Adobe has changed about their favorite graphics program.

Overall, you'll find that Adobe has made many changes throughout. I cover all the new CS5 features in the context of this book—you can read the book, learn the techniques, and use the knowledge that you've learned to quickly master Illustrator CS5. However, if you're looking for a head start on learning about the new big features in CS5, here's a list that will point you to where you will find more detailed information in the book:

- **Perspective Drawing.** Illustrator CS5 gives you the ability to define perspective grids with vanishing points, and to then snap artwork to automatically appear in the correct perspective. Read about drawing artwork in perspective in Chapter 3, "Technical Drawing."

- **Adjustable Strokes.** Illustrator CS5 breathes new life into strokes by allowing to you use variable widths, align dashes perfectly, and specify arrowheads. Read about the all-new stroke features in Chapter 6, "Working with Color."

- **Expressive Brushes.** Illustrator CS5 introduces the Bristle brush, which gives you the ability to simulate real paintbrush strokes. In addition, both Art and Pattern brushes are enhanced. Read about these brush features in Chapter 4, "Creative Drawing."

- **Enhanced Drawing Functions.** Illustrator CS5 introduces several features to make drawing artwork more efficient. A new Shape Builder tool lets you easily combine multiple shapes to create art, and new drawing modes allow you to draw behind objects and even inside other objects. You can learn about the Shape Builder tool in Chapter 2, "Selecting and Editing Artwork," and you can read up on the new drawing modes in Chapter 9, "Drawing with Efficiency."

- **Symbols Improvements.** Symbols in Illustrator CS5 get some welcome enhancements that include support for 9-slice scaling, registration points, and even layers. Read about improved symbols in Chapter 9, "Drawing with Efficiency."

- **Multiple Artboards Improvements.** Illustrator CS4 introduced multiple artboards, but Illustrator CS5 makes them better with the ability to easily name, reorder, and rearrange artboards. A new Artboards panel is added as well. You can read about all this in Chapter 1, "Creating and Managing Documents."

- **New Web Design Features.** Illustrator CS5 can help you create pixel-perfect web graphics with new control over art and text antialiasing settings. In addition, exporting slices is faster and more efficient. Read about improved web design workflows in Chapter 11, "Web Design."

How This Book Is Organized

Unlike most other books on Illustrator, this text isn't formatted to systematically cover each menu, tool, panel, and feature. Rather, it is organized based on my years of personal experience teaching Illustrator. In this way, you'll understand the important aspects behind the features before you actually use them. The way I see it, it's like taking a class on skydiving—you spend a few hours on the ground learning all about the physics of the jump, and then you get on the plane. Once you've already jumped, it's a bit too late to start learning.

Sprinkled throughout the book are recurring elements that help you with your learning experience:

Sidebars. Most chapters in this book contain sidebars that discuss conceptual or physical differences between Illustrator's features and technologies. These are meant to give you a deeper understanding of the tools you have at hand, and they will assist you in choosing the right tools or functions for the right tasks.

Keyboard shortcuts. When keyboard shortcuts are included for Illustrator commands, the Mac OS shortcut appears first, followed by the Windows shortcut in parentheses.

Appendixes. You'll also find an appendix toward the end of this book covering application preferences, which serves as a great reference in case you ever need to know what a particular preference setting is. You'll find two more chapters online at the book's registration page (www.peachpit.com/rwillcs5). These chapters, "Drawing with Data" and "Exploring the World

NOTE Notes appear in the margin, providing additional information on the topic.

TIP Tips appear throughout the book to offer bite-sized nuggets of information and resources where appropriate.

of 3D," include details on using the Graphs feature and the 3D Live Effect feature. Also on the book's registration page you'll find a link to additional materials and updates.

See the Pretty Art!

Being this is a full-color edition, and even more so, being that the title of this book includes the words *real world*, it is a perfect opportunity to use actual, real-world art to help illustrate the features and functionality of Illustrator. Even though I dabble a bit here and there in the world of illustration, my background has always been firmly seated in art production, not creative illustration. So, I turned to the creative source I've come to embrace as the ultimate design resource: iStockphoto. Yes, I know the word *photo* appears in the name, but iStockphoto (www.istockphoto.com) sells royalty-free stock art that includes photographs, illustrations, Flash animations, and even video content.

What's great about iStockphoto is that it's a collaborative resource—anyone around the world can create art and sell it on iStockphoto. And as such, I've come to discover some incredibly talented artists and illustrators from all over the world. I've had the pleasure of actually meeting some of these artists, and iStockphoto also maintains some pretty sweet discussion forums on its website where many like-minded creative pros exchange ideas not just on technical issues such as how to best take advantage of the Gradient Mesh feature in Illustrator but also on how to drive creative inspiration.

Most of the chapters throughout this book feature art from various iStockphoto members. If you like a piece of artwork or an illustration that you see in the book, you can head over to iStockphoto and purchase it or even contact the artist directly. Here's a listing of the chapters and the artists featured throughout the book (the artist's iStockphoto member name appears in parentheses):

- Chapter 1, "Creating and Managing Documents": Julie Felton (jfelton)
- Chapter 2, "Selecting and Editing Artwork": Simon Oxley (simonox)
- Chapter 3, "Technical Drawing": John Woodcock (johnwoodcock)
- Chapter 4, "Creative Drawing": Cheryl Graham (freetransform)
- Chapter 5, "Organizing Your Drawing": Diane Labombarbe (diane555)
- Chapter 6, "Coloring Artwork": Kemie Guaida Ortega (kemie)

- Chapter 7, "Working with Live Effects": Che McPherson (chemc)
- Chapter 9, "Drawing with Efficiency": Jennifer Borton (bortonia)
- Chapter 11, "Web and Mobile Design": Fanelie Rosier (absolutely_frenchy)
- Chapter 13, "Prepress and Printing": Sam Posnick (sposnick)

Additional Resources

This book is jam-packed with information about using Illustrator, but there's always more to learn (I still learn new things all the time). With that in mind, here's a collection of additional resources you will find helpful in your quest to master Illustrator:

- **The Real World Illustrator blog.** An up-to-date companion to this book, the Real World Illustrator blog offers insights, tutorials, and interesting information about the use of Illustrator and other Adobe applications. Readers of the blog (and book) are welcome to submit questions and participate via commenting on the blog or by emailing rwillustrator@ gmail.com. You can find the Real World Illustrator blog at http:// rwillustrator.blogspot.com.

- **Adobe Community Help.** With the release of Adobe Creative Suite 5, Adobe has created a separate AIR-based application called Adobe Community Help. You can launch this application by choosing Illustrator Help from the Help menu in Illustrator. You can also access Adobe Community Help directly on the Web at http://community.adobe.com/ help/illustrator/. The Adobe Community Help search engine will return results on the requested topic from internal Adobe documentation as well as third-party information in the form of published articles, blogs, and tutorials. These resources are moderated (I happen to be a moderator for the Illustrator content) and are constantly updated to offer the most useful and accurate information.

- **Adobe Illustrator user-to-user forum.** An extremely valuable resource, Adobe's user-to-user forum is a great place to ask questions, get advice from other Illustrator users, and share your own knowledge. The forum has a search function that is a tremendous resource as well. You can find the forums for Illustrator (and all other Adobe applications) at www.adobeforums.com.

- **Lynda.com.** Although reading the written word is a fantastic way to learn new material, seeing something in action can also be a wonderful way to learn new techniques. I currently have several video training titles on Adobe Illustrator at www.lynda.com that present yet another dimension in learning how to make the most of Illustrator. You can sign up for a free seven-day trial at http://www.lynda.com/freepass/mordy.

- **Fridays with Mordy.** Each week, I do a free screen share from my desk on a topic about Illustrator. It's a great opportunity to chat with friends, talk about Illustrator and design technology in general, and to ask questions. Each week is recorded, so you can view past episodes as well. For more information, visit the website at http://fridays.mordy.com.

Creating and Managing Documents 1

An artist can have a collection of the best paints and brushes, but those tools aren't worth much unless the artist has a canvas to paint on. Likewise, all the powerful tools and functions in Adobe Illustrator are meaningless until you have a document open on your screen. In the traditional sense, you can choose different types of paper to paint or draw on, all of which affect the overall appearance of the final result. With Illustrator, the settings you specify for your document also control your final result.

With the multiple artboards feature in Illustrator, creating and managing documents takes on new meaning. No longer limited to a single "page" metaphor, Illustrator documents can now manage overall concepts or even entire campaigns. Even more so than in previous versions, you have to strategize in advance to plan the best way to set up your document—a little bit of planning or forethought before you get started can have a huge impact later in your workflow. So, before learning how to use all the powerful drawing features in Illustrator, you'll learn everything you need to know about setting up and managing your documents.

The artwork featured throughout this chapter comes from Julie Felton (iStockphoto; username: jfelton).

Exploring the Welcome Screen

Upon launching Illustrator, you can choose Help > Welcome Screen, where you'll see a variety of options to quickly get started in Illustrator (**Figure 1.1**). You can either choose to open files you've recently worked on or choose to quickly create new documents by clicking a variety of new document profiles that are already set up for certain workflows (you'll learn more about document profiles in just a bit). At the bottom of the welcome screen, you'll find a collection of helpful links. The bottom-right corner of the welcome screen is dynamic, and if you're connected to the web, the content displayed there will vary.

Figure 1.1 *The Illustrator welcome screen gives you several useful options, including the ability to open recent documents and learn about new features.*

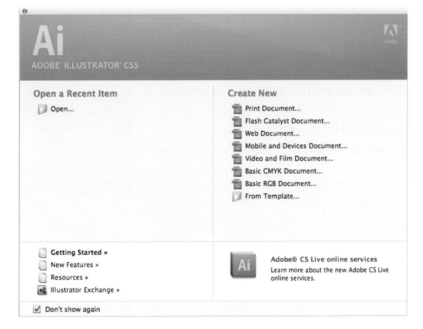

The "Don't show again" check box in the lower-left corner controls whether the welcome screen is visible every time you open Illustrator.

When it was first introduced several versions ago, the welcome screen wasn't too useful. However, with the ability to quickly access recently used documents and the capability to add your own custom new document profiles, the welcome screen actually serves as a wonderful time-saver to just about any workflow.

Creating New Documents

You can create a new document by clicking any of the new document pro-files that appear in the Create New section of the welcome screen. A *new document profile* stores several important document attributes, artboards, size, orientation, measurement units, color mode, raster effects, and Pre-view mode, making it easy to get started working on a new document for a specific workflow with one click of the mouse. Most importantly, new docu-ment profiles can also contain custom content, such as swatches, brushes, symbols, and graphic styles.

In addition to basic CMYK and RGB profiles, Illustrator features five new document profiles:

- **Print.** The Print profile is optimized for quickly creating artwork that will be used for print purposes. The Color Mode option is set to CMYK, and the Raster Effects option is set to 300 ppi.

- **Web.** The Web profile, optimized for web graphics, has Color Mode set to RGB, Raster Effects set to 72 ppi, the Align to Pixel Grid setting turned on, and Units set to pixels.

- **Mobile and Devices.** The Mobile and Devices profile is optimized for developing content that will appear on cell phones and handheld devices. Color Mode is set to RGB, Raster Effects is set to 72 ppi, and Units is set to pixels.

- **Video and Film.** The Video and Film profile, used for creating docu-ments that will be used in video and film applications, includes an addi-tional option to set Illustrator's transparency grid. This makes it easier to preview the alpha settings. This profile sets Color Mode to RGB, Ras-ter Effects to 72 ppi, and Units to pixels.

- **Flash Catalyst.** The Flash Catalyst profile, meant for content that you intend to eventually bring into Adobe Flash Catalyst, contains color swatches that match across the two applications. It is similar to the Web profile otherwise.

When you choose a new document profile from the welcome screen, Illustra-tor presents you with the New Document dialog box (**Figure 1.2**, on the next page). You can also bypass the welcome screen altogether and create a new document simply by choosing File > New or by pressing the keyboard shortcut Command-N (Ctrl-N). Clicking the Advanced arrow button reveals additional options that you can set as you create your new document. Although choosing

TIP Hold the Option (Alt) key when choos-ing a new document profile to quickly create a new file, skip-ping the New Document dialog box altogether. Alternatively, press Command-Option-N (Ctrl-Alt-N) to quickly create a new document based on the same settings as the last document created.

The New Document dialog box is "sticky," which means it remembers the last settings you used. So if you create an RGB file to create a web graphic, the next time you create a new document, the dialog box will be set to RGB.

a new document profile will automatically adjust some of these settings as necessary, you can always change them to suit your particular needs.

Figure 1.2 *Clicking the arrow button next to Advanced lets you set additional options in the New Document dialog box.*

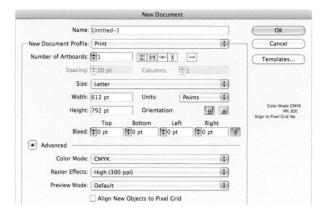

Although you can adjust any of the settings you find in the New Document dialog box even after you've already created a document, it's always better to get them right before you get started. Here's an overview of what each setting means:

- **Name.** The Name field simply lets you name your file before you even create it. Note that this setting doesn't save your file yet but merely saves you one step later.

- **New Document Profile.** The New Document Profile pop-up menu allows you to choose from a variety of preset profiles. Choosing a setting can serve as a starting point to adjust other settings in the New Document dialog box.

- **Number of Artboards.** The Number of Artboards setting allows you to specify how many artboards your document will contain. A single Illustrator document may contain up to 100 artboards. A row of icons that appears to the right of this setting also allows you to control how artboards appear within your document (you'll learn more about artboards and their specific settings later in this chapter).

- **Spacing.** The Spacing setting is available only when you have chosen to create more than one artboard; it determines the amount of space that is added between each artboard on the overall canvas.

- **Rows.** The Rows setting allows you to specify the number of rows your artboards have. This setting is available only when specifying more than one document and using a setup option that uses rows.

- **Size.** The Size pop-up menu is populated with standard sizes that are appropriate for the chosen new document profile.

- **Width, Height, and Orientation.** The Width and Height settings allow you to customize the size of the document's artboard. You can also choose between portrait (tall) and landscape (wide) orientations.

- **Units.** The Units setting determines the default general measurement system used in the document. You can choose to use points, picas, inches, millimeters, centimeters, or pixels.

- **Bleed.** The Bleed setting allows you to specify an area to extend artwork beyond the artboard boundary where necessary. Bleed settings are applied universally to all artboards in a single document (two artboards within a single Illustrator document cannot have two different bleed settings).

- **Color Mode.** Illustrator supports two color modes: CMYK, which is used for artwork that will appear on the printed page, and RGB, which is used for artwork that is destined to be displayed on a TV or computer screen. Refer to the "CMYK or RGB?" sidebar in this chapter for important information on the differences between these two color modes.

- **Raster Effects.** The Raster Effects setting controls the resolution used when applying special effects such as soft drop shadows, glows, and Photoshop filters (such as the Gaussian Blur filter). Although you can change this setting within your document at any time, it's important to understand the consequences of doing so. For detailed information about the Raster Effects setting, refer to the "Massaging Pixels in Illustrator" section in Chapter 7, "Working with Live Effects."

- **Transparency Grid.** The Transparency Grid setting is available only when you choose the Video and Film new document profile. The grid is a checkerboard pattern that appears on your artboard to help you better identify the Opacity values of objects in your document. This makes it easier to understand how artwork in Illustrator will composite with other art or video content later in your workflow. Refer to the section "Setting Up Your Document" later in this chapter for more information.

- **Preview Mode.** The Preview Mode setting lets you to specify the initial preview setting that Illustrator uses when the new document is created. You can leave it set to Default (which is Illustrator's normal preview setting), Pixel (for better representation of web and video graphics), or Overprint (for better representation of print graphics and spot colors).

- **Align New Objects to Pixel Grid.** The Align New Objects to Pixel Grid setting, used when designing graphics for web or video, helps ensure that artwork displays clear and sharp on a computer screen. Refer to Chapter 11, "Web Design," for more information.

The New Document dialog box also has a Templates button. Clicking this button will direct you to a folder containing all the prebuilt templates that come with Illustrator. For more information on templates, refer to the section "Working with Templates" later in this chapter.

CMYK or RGB?

CMYK stands for *cyan, magenta, yellow, and black* (black is called K because some printers refer to the black plate as the *key plate*). Mixing these colors creates a gamut (range) of colors. It's easier to think of colors in CMYK because the mode seems to follow the rules we all learned in preschool. Mixing cyan and magenta (blue and red) makes purple, mixing yellow and magenta makes orange, and so on. Today's printing presses use the four CMYK inks to produce printed material in color. For jobs you want printed, you should choose the CMYK color mode.

RGB stands for *red, green, and blue* and is used to display color on TV screens, computer monitors, and other electronic devices such as digital cameras. Unlike CMYK where you start out with a white sheet of paper and then add colors to get to black, RGB works in reverse. For instance, when your TV screen is off, it's dark, and when you turn it on and add red, green, and blue, the cumulative effect is white. The RGB color mode has a significantly larger gamut of colors than CMYK does, especially in the area of bright fluorescent colors. For jobs you want displayed on the web or in video, RGB is the color mode you should choose.

When creating a new document in Illustrator, you can choose between the two color modes in the New Document dialog box. Illustrator conveniently indicates the document's color mode in the Document title bar. Since version 9, the artboard in all Illustrator documents is restricted to the use of only one color mode (previous versions allowed both CMYK and RGB elements to appear on the same artboard). For example, if you copy and paste an object from an RGB document into a CMYK document, Illustrator will convert the object to CMYK as soon as you paste it onto the artboard.

In contrast, panels in Illustrator (Swatches, Color, Symbols, Brushes, Styles, and so on) can contain both CMYK and RGB content. Content from a new document profile is copied into each new file you create, so if you create a new web document, your Swatches panel will be filled with RGB colors. Although you can switch color modes at any time by choosing File > Document Color Mode, it's important to realize you're changing the color mode only of the document artboard—not the content that already exists in your Swatches or Symbols panel.

CMYK or RGB? *(continued)*

In a real-world workflow, it's possible that you may create an RGB document but convert the document to CMYK at a later point in time. If that happens, each time you apply a swatch color from your Swatch panel (which still contains RGB colors), Illustrator will be converting that RGB swatch to CMYK. If you ever see CMYK percentages with odd decimal values instead of whole numbers (**Figure 1.3**), there's a good chance that your document either is set to RGB or started out as RGB and was converted to CMYK. Remember that each time you make a color conversion, color shifts can occur.

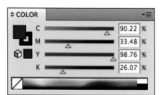

Figure 1.3 *Odd CMYK breakdowns are almost always the result of an RGB conversion.*

When opening Macromedia FreeHand files or older Illustrator files, you might see a dialog box telling you the file contains mixed color modes (**Figure 1.4**), and you can choose what color mode to convert to when opening the file.

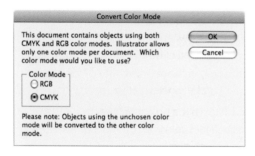

Figure 1.4 *Illustrator alerts you when opening a file that contains mixed color modes and asks you to choose the color mode to which you want to convert the file.*

Creating Your Own New Document Profiles

The profiles in Illustrator are quite generic, so you may find it useful to create your own new document profiles to suit your own needs. The good news is that it's easy to do—just follow these steps:

1. Create a document using an existing new document profile. If you want your profile to include the Transparency Grid setting, make sure you start with the Video and Film profile.

2. Once the new file is open, adjust your document settings to match your desired profile. For example, use the View menu to choose the Preview setting, choose Effect > Document Raster Effects Settings to adjust the Raster Effects value, and use the Artboard tool to adjust your artboard(s).

3. Add any desired content to the Swatches, Brushes, Symbols, or Graphic Styles panels. You can also remove content you don't want or need from these panels.

4. Choose File > Save, choose Format > Adobe Illustrator, and save the file in the following location on your computer (for U.S. English versions of Illustrator):

   Mac: *Username*/Library/Application Support/Adobe/Adobe Illustrator CS5/en_US/New Document Profiles

   Windows: C:\Documents and Settings*Username*\Application Data\ Adobe\Adobe Illustrator CS5 Settings\en_US\New Document Profiles

New document profiles work on all platforms and can be easily distributed among an entire design group or company.

Setting Up Your Document

NOTE In previous versions, changing settings for the artboard, such as portrait and landscape, were found in the Document Setup dialog box. Those settings are now changed with the Artboard tool.

There was a time when the Document Setup dialog box was accessed quite frequently, but since most of the page and printing settings have been moved to the Print dialog box or into the Artboard tool itself, you don't have to go to Document Setup nearly as often. That being said, it's still helpful to know what options you have when working with a document. The Document Setup dialog box (**Figure 1.5**), which you can access by choosing File > Document Setup or by clicking the Document Setup button that appears in the Control panel when there is no active selection, is split into three groups of settings.

Bleed and View Options. This pane allows you to change some of the settings you saw in the New Document dialog box, such as measurement units and bleed. To make changes to individual artboards, you can click the Edit Artboards button, which closes the Document Setup dialog box and puts you into Artboard Edit mode (see the section "Using Multiple Artboards" later in this chapter). Additionally, there's a setting for how raster-based images appear when you're in Outline mode. By default, images appear only as empty boxes in Outline mode for performance reasons, but with the Show

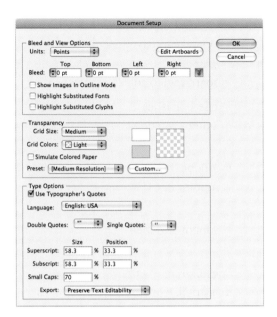

Figure 1.5 *The Document Setup dialog box displays bleed, view, transparency, and type options at a glance.*

Images In Outline Mode option activated, raster images are visible (in black and white) in Outline mode.

You can choose to have Illustrator highlight substituted fonts or glyphs, which can be helpful when opening files that other designers created. With these options activated, Illustrator highlights missing fonts in pink and missing glyphs in yellow so that you can quickly find where these problem areas are in a file.

Transparency. This pane allows you to specify settings for the transparency grid (which you can turn on by choosing View > Show Transparency Grid). Similar to the transparency grid found in Photoshop, this checkerboard pattern makes it easy to identify transparent areas in a file. If your file is going to be printed on colored paper, you can also have Illustrator simulate that color onscreen by using the Simulate Colored Paper option.

In Chapter 13, "Prepress and Printing," you'll learn more about transparency and how it prints. For now, it's important to know that a process called *transparency flattening* has to occur to correctly process artwork with transparency in it. This flattening process has many different options, all controlled by choosing from several different presets. Specifying a preset in the Transparency section sets a default preset for your document that you use when copying art with transparency to the clipboard or when exporting files to formats that don't support transparency.

Type Options. This pane contains several important settings for how text is used in Illustrator. You can specify the language for the file and how double and single quote marks should appear when you type them in your document. There's also an option to use typographer quotes, which means the correct curly quotes are automatically used instead of straight marks. Illustrator also allows you to define the size and position percentages for creating superscript, subscript, and small-cap characters. However, if you're using OpenType fonts, you can take advantage of the built-in support for these specific features, which we'll cover extensively in Chapter 8, "Working with Typography."

The final option in the Type Options pane is for specifying how text is exported when you are saving to legacy file formats (any version prior to Illustrator CS). When you choose the Preserve Text Editability option, text is broken up into individual type objects. When you choose the Preserve Text Appearance option, all type objects are converted to vector outlines.

Using Multiple Artboards

Before we get into the details of how to use multiple artboards, it's important to get a grasp of the capabilities and limitations of multiple artboards within Illustrator:

- Every Illustrator document consists of an overall canvas, measuring 227.54 inches square. Up to 100 artboards can live anywhere within this canvas area.

- Each artboard in a document can be named and by default, maintains its own rulers, origin point, and coordinates.

- Each individual artboard can be of any size (within the limits of the overall canvas) or orientation (portrait or landscape).

- Artboards can be moved and positioned anywhere within the canvas and can also overlap each other.

- You can choose to print and export any specific artboard or a range of artboards. You can also instruct Illustrator to "ignore artboards," treating all artboards as a single cumulative large one.

- Illustrator does not feature master pages, although you could use symbols to manage repeating artwork across multiple artboards.

- Each Illustrator document supports a single color mode (RGB or CMYK). You cannot have some artboards that use CMYK and others that use RGB.

A single Illustrator document can contain up to 100 artboards, but only one artboard can be *active* at any one time. To make it easier to navigate within your documents, you'll notice the overall canvas is shaded a very light gray and that each artboard features a white background and a small drop shadow. Artboards are outlined with a gray border, and the active artboard can be easily identified with a black border (**Figure 1.6**).

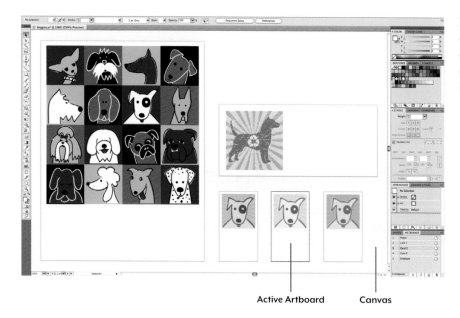

Active Artboard   Canvas

Figure 1.6 *The active artboard is identified with a black border. Other artboards display a gray border.*

Although it's important to understand that there's a concept of an active artboard, you don't really have to do anything specifically to make an artboard active, simply because Illustrator handles that for you. Whenever you click within the boundary of an artboard (or for example, when you click to select an object that sits on an artboard), that artboard automatically becomes active.

Having a single active artboard is necessary in order for some core Illustrator functions to work as you might expect them to. For example, when you choose Window > Fit Artboard in Window (or press Command-0 [Ctrl-0]), Illustrator adjusts the zoom level so that the active artboard fills the screen. Likewise, when you choose File > Save for Web & Devices, just the artwork on the active artboard is exported.

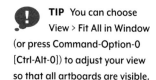

TIP You can choose View > Fit All in Window (or press Command-Option-0 [Ctrl-Alt-0]) to adjust your view so that all artboards are visible.

Modifying Artboards

Although you can specify the number of artboards at the time you create a new document, you can also modify the number, the position, the name, and the size of artboards at any time with the use of the Artboard tool (Shift-O). When the Artboard tool is active, Illustrator switches into Artboard Edit mode.

By default, artboards are highlighted, the rest of the canvas is darkened in Artboard Edit mode, and the active artboard appears with a dashed outline. Each artboard is identified with a number and a name, found in the upper-left corner of the artboard (**Figure 1.7**). Numbers are automatically assigned to artboards in the order in which you create them, although they can be changed easily enough with the Artboards panel, which we'll learn more about in just a bit.

Figure 1.7 *You can add, remove, and modify artboards when you're in Artboard Edit mode.*

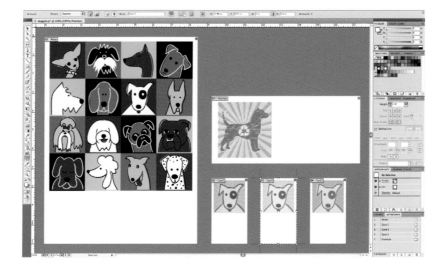

NOTE The artboard number is used when navigating within a document, when printing, and also when placing native Illustrator content into other applications, including InDesign, Flash Catalyst, and Flash Professional.

When you're in Artboard Edit mode, you can modify the active artboard by moving it or by resizing it using any of the handles that appear along its perimeter. Add new artboards by clicking and dragging any empty area on the artboard, or hold the Shift key while dragging to create a new artboard within the boundaries of an existing one. As with regular objects in Illustrator, you can also hold the Option (Alt) key while dragging an existing artboard to duplicate it. To delete an active artboard, simply press Delete on your keyboard.

In Artboard Edit mode, the Control panel offers a range of settings to help you modify the artboards on the canvas. One of the most important settings is the Move/Copy Artwork with Artboard option (**Figure 1.8**). With this setting turned on (which is the default), any artwork that appears within the bounds of an artboard will move along with the artboard. Likewise, if you duplicate an artboard, the new artboard will also contain a copy of the associated artwork. Turning the Move/Copy Artwork with Artboard option off lets you reposition artboards on the canvas without moving any artwork.

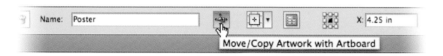

Figure 1.8 *When Move/Copy Artwork with Artboard is on, any artwork that falls within the boundaries of an artboard will move when the artboard is moved while in Artboard Edit mode.*

Another important setting in the Control panel is the Artboard Options button, which opens the Artboard Options dialog box (**Figure 1.9**, on the next page). The following settings are present in this dialog box:

- **Name.** Naming an artboard helps you quickly identify it. Artboard names are also preserved when using Illustrator files with other applications, such as Flash Catalyst.

- **Preset.** The Preset pane of the Artboard Options dialog box allows you to choose from a list of preset artboard sizes (unfortunately, the list isn't customizable), including the ability to automatically generate an artboard size to match the artwork bounds of all art within the document or the bounds of any currently selected art. In addition, you can adjust the width, height, or orientation of the active artboard.

- **Position.** The Position pane of the Artboard Options dialog box enables you to specify the x and y coordinates for the active artboard. You can use the 9-point proxy to control the artboard location with precision.

- **Display.** The Display pane of the Artboard Options dialog box enables you to hide or show an artboard's center mark, crosshairs, and video safe areas. In addition, you can set a ruler pixel aspect ratio. These settings are useful if you're working in video workflows.

- **Global.** The Global pane of the Artboard Options dialog box enables you to choose whether the canvas turns a dark gray when you're in Artboard Edit mode and whether artboards are highlighted in a lighter color while you're dragging them around on the canvas.

WARNING If artwork is locked or hidden, that artwork will *not* move with its artboard, even if you have the Move/Copy Artwork with Artboard option turned on.

Figure 1.9 *The Artboard Options dialog box provides additional settings for each artboard.*

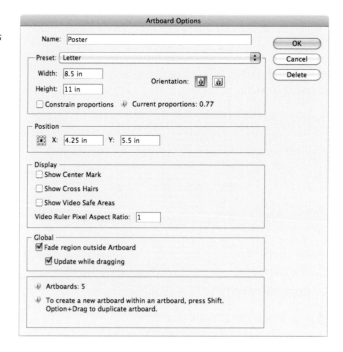

TIP You may find it easier to skip the Artboard tool altogether. Use the Transform panel to accurately position regular rectangles, select the shapes, and choose Object > Convert to Artboards.

TIP To copy and paste artwork from one artboard to another while maintaining precise positioning, choose Edit > Paste in Place or Edit > Paste on All Artboards.

Figure 1.10 *The Artboards panel gives you a quick and always accessible way to manage the artboards in your document.*

Some of the options in the Artboard Options dialog box are also listed directly in the Control panel when Illustrator is in Artboard Edit mode. Keep in mind that the x and y coordinates, as well as the Width and Height values, all represent the single point of the artboard that is indicated by the selected point in the 9-point proxy. You can also use the arrow keys on your keyboard to nudge an artboard's position.

To exit Artboard Edit mode, simply press the Escape key on the keyboard or select any tool other than the Artboard tool.

You can also modify the artboards in your document using the Artboards panel (**Figure 1.10**) which you can open by choosing Window > Artboards. With the Artboards panel, you can do the following:

- Click the name of an artboard to make it the active artboard.

- Double-click the name of an artboard to make it active and to fit it into the document window.

- Double-click the orientation icon to the far right of the artboard name, to bring up the Artboard Options dialog for that artboard.

- Click the Up and Down arrow icons that appear at the bottom of the Artboards panel to reorder the artboards. Alternatively, you can drag the name of an artboard to adjust its position in the order.

- Drag the name of an artboard onto the New Artboard icon that appears at the bottom of the Artboards panel to create a duplicate.

- Choose Rearrange Artboards from the Artboards panel menu to clean up the layout of all the artboards within a single document (**Figure 1.11**).

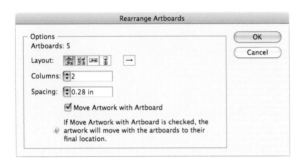

Figure 1.11 *You can use the Rearrange Artboards function to neatly line up all the artboards in your document.*

Adding Bleed

To print art all the way to the edge of a sheet, also known as *bleeding*, a printer uses a larger-sized sheet than the finish size (trim size), and after printing, the printer cuts the paper down to size. Printers can't print all the way to the edge of a page because a certain amount of space is needed for *gripper space* (space for the printing press to grab the sheet of paper). Additionally, if this space weren't there, the ink could run off the sheet and onto the press, causing smudging on other sheets.

When a printer trims the paper to the final size, the paper may shift while being cut, and if your image comes only up to the border of the trim size, you might end up seeing a bit of white near the edge of the paper. To avoid this, printers need *bleed*, or extra image space. If the artwork extends beyond the edges of the trim size, even if the cutter is off a bit, you'll still get color all the way to the edge of your sheet.

As a designer, it's important to leave enough room when you're cropping photos or backgrounds to allow for bleed (**Figure 1.12**). You should speak to your printer if you have questions, but most printers ask for anywhere from .125 to .25 inch of bleed. If printers don't have enough image space to add bleed, they may need to trim the paper to a slightly smaller size.

The Bleed setting is a document-wide setting and is not artboard-specific. In other words, all artboards within a single file all share the same bleed setting—individual artboards cannot feature different bleed settings. You can adjust a document's bleed settings by choosing File > Document Setup or by using the New Document dialog box when creating a new file. Bleed settings are honored when printing from Illustrator or when saving and exporting most file types.

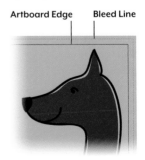

Artboard Edge   Bleed Line

Figure 1.12 *When a bleed value is specified, Illustrator identifies the bleed area with a red border.*

Navigating Within a Document

You might find yourself struggling to navigate across many artboards within a single document. Fortunately, you can quickly move from one artboard to another in several ways:

- Choose Window > Artboards to open the Artboards panel. In the Artboards panel, double-click the name of any artboard to make it the active one. Illustrator also sets the view to Fit Artboard in Window for the chosen artboard.

- At the bottom of the document window, just to the left of the status bar, is an Artboard Navigation pop-up menu, which lists each artboard in the document (**Figure 1.13**). You can either choose to jump directly to an artboard or use the First, Previous, Next, and Last buttons to move between artboards. When using any of these methods, Illustrator automatically changes the zoom level to Fit Artboard in Window and makes the requested artboard active.

Figure 1.13 *The Artboard Navigation pop-up menu gives you quick access to any artboard in your file.*

- Choose Window > Navigator to open the Navigator panel (**Figure 1.14**). In the Navigator panel, you can drag the red box around to quickly pan around the entire document. You can also adjust the zoom slider at the bottom of the panel to zoom in and out. The Navigator panel gives you a great bird's-eye view of all the artboards on your canvas and even displays the active artboard with a black outline.

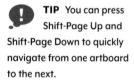

TIP You can press Shift-Page Up and Shift-Page Down to quickly navigate from one artboard to the next.

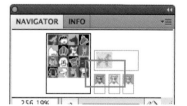

Figure 1.14 *The Navigator panel provides a bird's-eye view of the canvas and gives you the ability to quickly move from one spot to another.*

Naturally, you can always use the Hand and Zoom tools to navigate within your document. You can also use custom views in Illustrator to save and return to specific zoom settings. The custom views feature is covered later in this chapter.

Handling Artboards and Legacy Workflows

Illustrator CS4 was the first version to support multiple artboards, and in previous versions of Illustrator, designers employed a variety of work-arounds to simulate multiple pages. For example, many designers used the Page Tiling feature in the Print dialog box to simulate multiple pages in Illustrator. Some also used FreeHand, which has had support for multiple pages for the longest time. Wouldn't it be nice if Illustrator could open all of those FreeHand and Illustrator files (Adobe refers to older Illustrator files as *legacy* files) and convert them to multiple artboards? Great news—that's exactly what Illustrator does.

If Illustrator senses any kind of multiple page–compatible setting when opening legacy Illustrator files, the Convert to Artboards dialog box appears (**Figure 1.15**), offering the following options:

- **Legacy Artboard.** The artboard from the legacy document is converted to a single artboard.

- **Crop Area(s).** Any crop area defined in the file is converted to an artboard. If the file is an Illustrator CS3 file and multiple crop areas are present in the file, each crop area is converted to an artboard.

- **Artwork Bounding Box.** The bounding box of the artwork in the file is converted to a single artboard.

- **Page Tiles.** If the document has page tiles defined, each page tile is converted to an artboard.

Illustrator disables those options that aren't applicable to the file you are opening, so you may find that not all four options are available for every file.

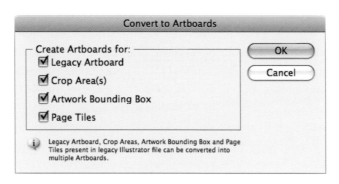

Figure 1.15 *You can use the Rearrange Artboards function to neatly line up all the artboards in your document.*

Multiple Artboard Strategies

Just because an Illustrator document *can* contain up to 100 artboards doesn't mean it *should*. Taking a few moments to think about your task or project before you start will always help you make the right choice about how to build your document in the most efficient manner. Now that you have a strong understanding of the multiple artboards feature in Illustrator, you can make informed decisions about when it's best to work on a project in Illustrator and when it might be better to look toward a dedicated page layout application, such as InDesign.

Overall, two main factors will come into play when you decide how to best choose how to build your documents. Illustrator supports artboards that can be of any size or orientation. If you're working on a project that requires assets of multiple sizes, Illustrator might be the right choice. On the other hand, InDesign maintains a *significant* edge in the form of performance and long-document features, especially with text-heavy layouts. Remember that it's always beneficial to think of ways to use all the tools at your disposal to get your work done—you don't always have to force one application to do everything.

Viewing Documents

As you're working in Illustrator, you can choose to view your artwork in different ways, each offering different benefits. The most common view mode, Preview mode, allows you to create and edit art while seeing a close representation of what your art will look like when printed. In Outline mode, Illustrator hides all the pretty colors and effects and shows you just the vector geometry of the shapes in your document. Although it may be difficult to visualize what your file is going to look like when actually printed, Outline mode gives you the ability to easily see whether shapes are aligned correctly, and it gives you a better idea of the structure of the file (**Figure 1.16**). Think of Outline mode as an X-ray film that a doctor reads. Although just black and white, an X ray reveals what's going on behind the scenes. Just like a doctor reads an X ray, an experienced Illustrator user can sometimes get a better idea of how an Illustrator file is constructed when in Outline mode. You can toggle between Preview and Outline modes by pressing Command-Y (Ctrl-Y).

Figure 1.16 *The same artwork viewed in Preview mode (left) and Outline mode (right).*

Using Overprint Preview

For those in the print business, Illustrator has a special preview mode called Overprint Preview that you can access by choosing View > Overprint Preview. Overprinting is a process you use when creating color separations to control how certain colors interact with each other (we'll cover overprinting in detail in Chapter 13, "Prepress and Printing"). Because overprinting is an attribute applied only in the print process, designers traditionally struggle with proofing files that specify overprints. Illustrator's Overprint Preview mode simulates overprints so that you can see how they will print (**Figure 1.17**). In truth, Overprint Preview is far more accurate than the regular Preview mode in Illustrator, especially when your file uses spot colors (you'll learn more about that in Chapter 6, "Coloring Artwork"). While Overprint Preview gives you the best possible representation of what your final art is going to look like when printed, it is slower in redraw performance than normal Preview mode.

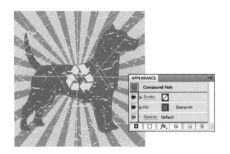 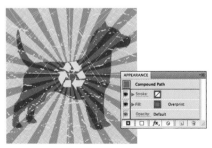

Figure 1.17 *On the left, the vector shape's fill is set to Overprint, as shown in the Appearance panel. On the right, with Overprint Preview turned on, you can see the effects of the overprint.*

Using Pixel Preview

Not to leave web designers out in the cold, Illustrator has another preview mode called Pixel Preview, which you can also access via the View menu. Illustrator, as a vector-based application, produces resolution-independent art. Most of today's printers have high-resolution settings, and modern imagesetters use resolutions upward of 2500 dots per inch (dpi). For that reason, print designers aren't worried about how good their artwork looks on their screen, because they know when output at high resolution, everything will be perfect. Web designers, however, care very much about how their artwork appears on a computer screen because that's exactly how other people view their designs. Pixel Preview renders artwork to the screen as pixels and shows how antialiasing affects the art (**Figure 1.18**). We'll cover Pixel Preview and these web-specific issues in Chapter 11, "Web Design."

Figure 1.18 *In Pixel Preview mode, Illustrator displays artwork as it would display in a browser. Zooming in on your artwork reveals the actual pixels and the effects of antialiasing.*

NOTE Each artboard maintains its own rulers and coordinates. The rulers display the values for the artboard that is currently active. Choosing Change to Global Rulers from the ruler's contextual menu treats the entire canvas as a single artboard.

Using Rulers and Guides

Even though you can scale Illustrator artwork to virtually any size, it's still important to be able to create artwork using exact and precise measurements. Package designers and technical illustrators are always careful about creating artwork to scale, and even designers need to know what size a logo or an illustration has to be.

Choose View > Rulers > Show Rulers to display vertical and horizontal rulers along the left and top edges of your document window. You can Control-click (right-click) a ruler to change its measurement system (**Figure 1.19**).

Although the rulers can help identify the coordinates of objects that appear in a document, rulers also serve another function. You can click a ruler and drag a guide onto your artboard. A *guide* is a line that's visible on your screen but not on the printed or exported art. Guides have "magnetic personalities," and objects that are moved or drawn near them stick to them, helping align objects and create consistent art and layouts. Hold the Option (Alt) key while dragging to toggle between horizontal and vertical guides, and hold the Shift key to have a guide snap to the tick marks that appear on the ruler.

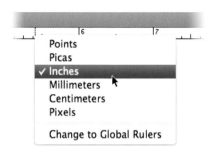

Figure 1.19 *The ruler's contextual menu lets you specify any of the measurement systems that Illustrator supports.*

You can lock and unlock guides by choosing View > Guides. Unlocked guides act just like regular objects do, and you can reposition them to your liking. You can even use the x and y coordinates in the Control panel to precisely position guides. In addition, you can convert any path into a guide by choosing View > Guides > Make Guides (or by pressing Command-5 [Ctrl-5]).

Using Smart Guides

In addition to normal guides, Illustrator has a useful feature called *smart guides*; these guides, which are turned on by default, offer a variety of onscreen feedback options while you work. You can toggle smart guides on and off by choosing View > Smart Guides (or by pressing Command-U [Ctrl-U]). As you move your cursor around on the screen and as you create and modify artwork, different smart guides appear and assist you as you work.

Illustrator features six types of smart guides, and each offers assistance in a specific way (**Figure 1.20**, on the next page). Admittedly, when all six smart guides are being used, the "information overload" may be distracting or too much to bear. Thankfully, Illustrator allows you to keep things in your control via a dedicated Preferences panel that you can find by choosing Illustrator > Preferences > Smart Guides (Edit > Preferences > Smart Guides).

TIP By default, guides span the entire canvas. If you drag out a guide while in Artboard Edit mode and move your cursor within the bounds of the active artboard, the guide will span just that artboard.

Figure 1.20 *The six types of smart guides (left to right): alignment guides, object highlighting, transform tools, construction guides, anchor/path labels, and measurement labels.*

TIP When smart guides are active with the Alignment Guides option turned on, object bounds snap to guides and to other objects, making it easier to position objects precisely.

Smart guides work just about everywhere in Illustrator—even in Artboard Edit mode. As you get used to smart guides, you'll get a better feel for which of the six types are more important for the kind of work you do most often. Remember that you can always quickly toggle the feature on and off as you need it. The six kinds of smart guides in Illustrator are as follows:

- **Alignment guides.** Alignment guides appear when you move your cursor, helping you align objects in context while drawing, moving, or editing objects. In this way, you don't have to perform additional align functions.

- **Object highlighting.** Object highlighting identifies the underlying Bézier paths or original text or artwork when you mouse over objects that have live effects or envelopes applied to them.

- **Transform tools.** Transform tools are guides that appear when using any of Illustrator's transform functions, such as Rotate or Scale.

- **Construction guides.** Construction guides appear as you're drawing new shapes and identifying similar planes or angles with other objects. You can specify which angles are identified using the pop-up menu, or you can choose Custom Angles and specify up to six custom angles.

- **Anchor/path labels.** Anchor/path labels identify anchor points and paths as you mouse over them.

- **Measurement labels.** Measurement labels help you identify the dimensions of objects as you draw or modify them. They also identify an anchor point's coordinates, if the Anchor/Path Labels option is also on.

Defining Custom Views

Sometimes you work on a document and then never see it again. Other documents contain artwork you constantly revisit. If those documents are complex or have many layers, you may find you're constantly panning and zooming to different parts of the document or that you're always hiding and showing layers.

To navigate more easily, you can define *custom views*, which allow you to save the view state of a document. To do so, use your Hand and Zoom tools to adjust your document to the desired view. Then, toggle the visibility of the layers to your liking. Finally, choose View > New View. Assign a name to the view, and click OK. You can repeat this as many times as you'd like to add multiple view settings to your document (**Figure 1.21**). Each view you create will appear listed at the very bottom of the View menu, and you can quickly "jump" to a view by choosing it from that menu.

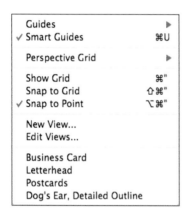

Figure 1.21 *Creating a new view makes it easy to quickly return to a specified state of a document. In this example, several custom views have already been defined.*

Custom views are saved with the document, so they will be available even after you've saved, closed, and reopened the document. Likewise, those views will also be available to anyone else who opens the file on their own computer.

Working with Templates

For repetitive work, use templates that allow you to set up a file with certain settings and attributes—even actual artwork and layers—to create more consistent files in less time. Illustrator templates are really just regular Illustrator files with one difference—you can't save them. You can only perform a Save As function with them (so you don't overwrite the template).

To create a template file, start by creating a new Illustrator document. Draw guides, add content, place artwork on the artboard, add layers, and adjust your document settings as you'd like them to appear in the template. When you're ready to save your template, choose File > Save As, and specify the Illustrator Template (AIT) format in the dialog box. Template files contain a flag in them so that when they are reopened in Illustrator, they open as untitled documents.

NOTE If you're a professional designer, you might not want to use any of Illustrator's prefab templates, but it's helpful to open the files and explore them to see how they were created. One of the best ways to learn is by reverse-engineering what someone else has done. One of the techniques you'll learn in this book is how to pick apart an Illustrator file; Illustrator's template files are perfect for this because they employ many different features and techniques.

Illustrator actually ships with hundreds of professionally designed templates, which you can access by choosing File > New from Template. The templates are stored in the Adobe Illustrator CS5/Cool Extras/en_US/Templates folder. You can also browse the template files using Adobe Bridge (choose File > Browse in Bridge) so you can see previews of what the templates contain. Before you wrinkle your nose about using "clip art," you'll be happy to know that Illustrator also includes an entire folder of blank templates. These blank templates have everything you need to quickly create print- or web-ready work.

New Document Profiles or Templates?

When you create a new Illustrator file, you'll notice that several swatches, symbols, brushes, and graphic styles are already present in the file. How did they get there? The answer is that they were copied from the file used to define the new document profile you chose when you created the file.

This means if you use certain swatches or symbols frequently, you can simply edit these new document profiles (or create your own custom ones), and you never have to load another library again. Although this is true, the more content you have in your new document profile, the more content you will have in every file you create, making for larger files (which also take longer to open).

Templates, on the other hand, can also contain content. Additionally, template files are really full Illustrator files that can contain paragraph and character styles, artwork on the artboard, crop marks, layers, and more—something new document profiles can't do. It may be more efficient to keep a small startup file but have a set of rich templates that you can open at any time to get a running start on your design work.

If you ever do edit your new document profiles (instead of creating your own new ones), be sure to first create and save a backup of the existing files (save them somewhere where you can find them and not accidentally delete them). This way, if you end up doing something crazy, you still have a way to return to the original default files. You can also simply delete a profile from its folder, and Illustrator will automatically generate a new one in its place.

Creating Meaningful Metadata

If you go to any popular stock photo website, you can enter a keyword or a description for the kind of image you're looking for and instantly see a list of images matching your criteria. Have you ever wondered how this works? How does a search engine know what the contents of a photograph are? The answer is metadata.

Metadata is information that describes a file, and it can be just about anything. The creation date, author, creation application, keywords, and copyright information are all examples of metadata. Adobe applications use an XML-based standard called Extensible Metadata Platform (XMP) to store this metadata inside files. The metadata resides in an XML header at the top of each file, and Adobe applications can read this data.

In Illustrator, you can choose File > File Info to open the File Info dialog box, where you can enter a variety of metadata for your file (**Figure 1.22**). When you save the file, the metadata is embedded within the file.

Illustrator takes metadata a step further, because certain information is automatically added to each file as you save it. For example, each time you save your file, Illustrator adds a list of fonts, swatches, color groups, and color separation plates in the file's metadata for you.

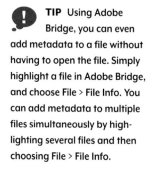

TIP Using Adobe Bridge, you can even add metadata to a file without having to open the file. Simply highlight a file in Adobe Bridge, and choose File > File Info. You can add metadata to multiple files simultaneously by highlighting several files and then choosing File > File Info.

Figure 1.22 *The File Info dialog box in Illustrator stores keywords and other metadata using the XML-based XMP standard.*

Selecting and Editing Artwork 2

The tools you will employ most often when using Illustrator on a day-to-day basis are the selection tools. The power of Illustrator lies not just in creating graphics but more so in editing and manipulating them. To perform just about any function in Illustrator (or nearly any computer graphics program, for that matter), you need to *select* something first. Without selections, Illustrator has no idea which of the objects in your document you want to modify.

Speaking of modifications, this chapter is full of them, in the form of tools and functions that affect vector paths. Experienced illustrators know that often the best way to create a complex shape is to start with a few simple shapes first. A few quick edits will get you to your final result much faster (and often with better results as well).

The artwork featured throughout this chapter comes from Simon Oxley (iStockphoto; username: simonox).

Selecting Objects

If you've used Illustrator before, you're familiar with the twins: the *Selection tool* and the *Direct Selection tool* (**Figure 2.1**). These tools have been given a variety of alternative names over the years, including the "black and white arrows" or the "solid and hollow arrows." There's also a third tool called the *Group Selection tool*, although it doesn't get much exposure because of a certain keyboard shortcut that we'll talk about shortly.

Figure 2.1 *The dynamic duo, the Selection and Direct Selection tools, are also referred to as the black and white arrow tools.*

Making Selections

Before we talk about the tools themselves, the reason why there are two different selection tools, and when to use one over the other, let's first see how you can make a selection in Illustrator:

- **The click method.** To select an object, just click it with any of the selection tools. To select multiple objects, you can click a second object while holding the Shift key to add the second object to your selection. Shift-clicking an object that is *already* selected will *deselect* it.

- **The marquee method.** Another way to make selections is by creating a *marquee*, which is similar to drawing a rectangle, only with a selection tool instead of a shape tool. You start by clicking and dragging the pointer to specify a rectangular area, called a *marquee*. When you release the mouse button, any objects that fall within the boundaries of the marquee become selected (**Figure 2.2**).

Keep in mind that you can use a combination of both methods to make more efficient selections. For example, say you want to select all the objects in a certain area except for one. You can use the marquee method to first select all the objects and then Shift-click the object you don't want in order to deselect just that object.

NOTE In reality, the selection tools do more than just select objects. You can use them to move selected objects as well. Moving an object in Illustrator is actually considered a transform function, so we'll be talking about the Selection and Direct Selection tools later in this chapter as well.

NOTE The keyboard shortcut to quickly select all objects in a document is Command-A (Ctrl-A). You can also select all objects within the active artboard by pressing Command-Option-A (Ctrl-Alt-A).

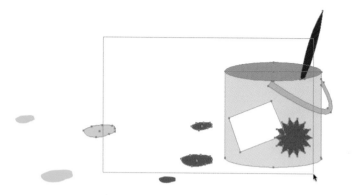

Figure 2.2 *Selecting multiple objects using the marquee method keeps you from having to Shift-click multiple shapes to select all of them.*

Sometimes, you don't want the ability to select an object at all. Especially in complex files with many overlapping objects, it can be easy to accidentally select objects without realizing what you've done (until it's too late, of course). Illustrator allows you to select an object and choose Object > Lock > Selection, which makes the object unavailable for editing. Learning the keyboard shortcuts to lock (Command-2) [Ctrl-2] and unlock (Command-Option-2) [Ctrl-Alt-2] is a good idea.

New in Illustrator CS5, you can select "through" overlapping objects to reach objects behind in the stacking order by holding the Command [Ctrl] key while clicking repeatedly with the Selection tool. Each time you click, Illustrator selects the next object below in the stacking order. Alternatively, you can right-click an object and choose Select > Next Object Below from the context menu (**Figure 2.3**).

NOTE The ability to isolate individual groups and objects in Illustrator makes it easier to select and work with complex illustrations. Chapter 5, "Organizing Your Drawing," covers isolation in more detail.

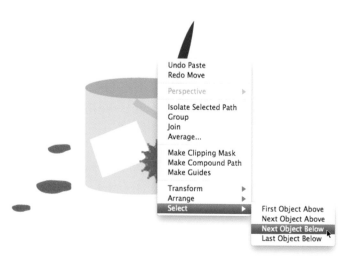

Figure 2.3 *It's a bit clunky, but you can use a context menu to select objects that appear beneath others in the stacking order.*

Setting Your Selection and Anchor Display Preferences

When it comes to making selections, Illustrator offers a few ways to help you make selections through the Selection & Anchor Display panel in Preferences (**Figure 2.4**). You can find a description for each of the settings in the Appendix, "Application Preferences."

Figure 2.4 *The Selection & Anchor Display panel in Preferences gives you greater control over how you make selections.*

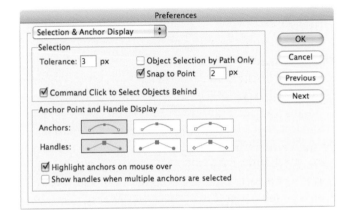

Here are a few options you can set in the Selection & Anchor Display panel in Preferences:

- You can set a tolerance for how close your cursor has to be in order to select an anchor point or an object. A higher pixel value will make it easier to select objects quickly, but a lower pixel value will give you far more accurate results, making it easier to select anchor points that appear very close to each other.

- The Object Selection by Path Only setting restricts Illustrator to select objects only when clicking their vector paths (not their fills).

- The Snap to Point setting determines the distance at which your cursor snaps to other objects or guides.

- You can control the size of anchor points and control handles. On high-resolution monitors, anchor points and control handles appear very small and are difficult to grab with the selection tools. Preference settings allow you to choose from three different sizes for both anchor points and control handles, making it easier on your eyes (and your sanity).

NOTE By default, the Object Selection by Path Only setting in Preferences is off, which allows you to select an object by clicking its path or anywhere within its fill area (if it has a fill attribute applied). Although this is convenient, sometimes—especially when you are working with complex artwork—this behavior makes it difficult to select objects. Turning this preference on allows you to select objects only by clicking their vector paths, not their fill areas.

- With the Direct Selection tool, Illustrator will highlight anchor points as you move the pointer over them. This can help you identify where the anchor points are and, more importantly, can make it easier to identify what you're editing. You can set this behavior by selecting the "Highlight anchors on mouse over" check box.

Using the Direct Selection Tool

If there's one aspect that confuses people most about Illustrator, it's that it has two selection tools (the Pen tool doesn't *confuse* people nearly as much is it *frustrates* them). Fear not, though, there's a method to the madness—and once you understand it, you'll breathe easier. The good news is that whatever you learn here will apply to InDesign, Photoshop, Fireworks, Flash Professional, and Flash Catalyst as well, because they use similar selection tools.

When you are using the Direct Selection tool, clicking the fill area of an object selects the entire object (unless the object's fill is set to None or unless Object Selection by Path Only is turned on in Preferences). Clicking the vector path either selects a segment of the path (if you click between two anchor points) or selects the anchor point that you click.

If you hold the Option (Alt) key while clicking either the fill or the path of an object with the Direct Selection tool, it selects the entire object—just as the Selection tool does. So, with a single keyboard shortcut, you can make the Direct Selection tool act like its twin. If you are working with a group of objects, holding down Option (Alt) and clicking an object's path once with the Direct Selection tool selects the entire object. Holding down Option (Alt) and clicking a second time selects all the objects in the group. If there are nested groups (groups within other groups), each additional Option (Alt) click results in the next level up in the hierarchy of the group being selected. If you ever want to select an entire group with one click, press the Command (Ctrl) key to temporarily switch to the Selection tool.

Once you master this method of using the Direct Selection tool while using the keyboard shortcuts, you'll never think twice about the two selection tools again.

TIP If you have an object that is already selected, you can use the Direct Selection tool to click and release any anchor point to select it. You don't need to deselect the entire object first and then reselect just the desired anchor point.

Selection Tool vs. Direct Selection Tool

On a basic level, the Selection tool (the black, or solid, arrow) is used to select entire objects and groups. The Direct Selection tool, however, is used to select parts of objects or individual objects within a group. For example, if you draw a star shape and click it with the Selection tool, the entire star becomes selected. In contrast, if you click one of the points of the star with the Direct Selection tool, only that point becomes selected (**Figure 2.5**).

At first, it sounds like life in Illustrator is all about constantly switching between these two tools. To make things a bit easier, when you have one selection tool active, you can press the Command (Ctrl) key to temporarily switch to the other selection tool. To make life even easier than that, you can learn how power users utilize modifier keys with the Direct Selection tool efficiently; this practice practically negates the need for both the Selection tool and the Group Selection tool.

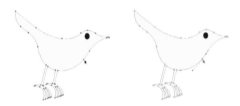

Figure 2.5 *The object on the left is selected with the Selection tool. The object on the right is selected with the Direct Selection tool.*

Using the Group Selection Tool

In reality, Illustrator has *three* core selection tools: the Selection tool, the Direct Selection tool, and the Group Selection tool. The Group Selection tool is useful for selecting groups of objects. As you will learn in Chapter 5, groups can be nested (meaning you can have groups within groups). Using the Group Selection tool, clicking an object once selects the object. Clicking the same object a second time selects the entire group to which the object belongs. Each successive click selects the next level up in the hierarchy.

Earlier we referred to Illustrator as having two selection tools because the Group Selection tool is rarely chosen. Why? It's because of the keyboard shortcut that we mentioned. When the Direct Selection tool is active, pressing the Option (Alt) key toggles to the Group Selection tool, which is why you can then select entire objects.

Using Alternative Selection Techniques

Although most of the selections you make will incorporate the use of the Selection tool or the Direct Selection tool, sometimes you might need a more specialized selection tool. Illustrator can offer a helping hand in a variety of ways.

Using the Lasso and Magic Wand Tools

The Lasso tool and the Magic Wand tool first appeared in Photoshop, but both made their way into the Illustrator toolset. Although they're similar in concept to those found in Photoshop, remember that Illustrator is an object-based program, so these tools select objects, not pixels.

The Lasso tool in Illustrator acts much like the Direct Selection tool in that it can select individual anchor points. Whereas a marquee is always limited to a rectangular shape, the specialty of the Lasso tool is that you can draw a marquee in any free-form shape. Where you have many objects in close proximity to each other, the Lasso tool allows you to draw a custom marquee shape to select just the objects—or anchor points—you need (**Figure 2.6**).

> **NOTE** If you're a production artist, the Magic Wand tool is invaluable. By setting a tolerance of .25 point for the stroke weight and clicking a path with a .25-point stroke on your artboard, you can select all paths in your document with a stroke weight between 0 and .5 point, making it easy to set consistent hairline stroke widths.

Figure 2.6 *Drawing a free-form marquee with the Lasso tool can be helpful when you are trying to make complex selections with art that is in close proximity to other art.*

If you have several similarly styled objects in your document and you need to select them all, it can be tedious to manually select them using the click method. If they are scattered throughout the document, the marquee method won't work for you either. In such cases, the Magic Wand tool allows you to click one object; when you do, any other objects in your file that have the same attributes as the object you clicked become selected as well. Not bad for one click, right? If you double-click the Magic Wand tool in the Tools panel, the Magic Wand panel appears; here you can specify which specific

> **NOTE** Unlike the Selection and Direct Selection tools, the Lasso and Magic Wand tools can't move objects; they can only select them.

attributes you want the Magic Wand tool to pay attention to (**Figure 2.7**). The true power of the Magic Wand tool is that you can set a tolerance for each attribute. So if your document contains several objects colored a variety of shades of a color, you can still select them all with the Magic Wand tool by clicking a single object (**Figure 2.8**).

Figure 2.7 *You can use the Magic Wand panel to specify tolerance levels for different attributes.*

Figure 2.8 *With the Magic Wand tool, you can easily select a range of objects that share similar colors.*

Selecting Similar Objects

Illustrator has a Select menu that contains a variety of selection-based functions. You'll find some of the most useful ones in the Select > Same menu and the Select > Object menu. To use the *Same* functions, first make a selection on the artboard with any of the selection tools in Illustrator. Then choose from the list of attributes to select objects based on that attribute (**Figure 2.9**). At any time, you can use the *Object* functions to select a certain kind of object in your file. You don't need to have any objects selected first in order to use the Select > Object functions.

Figure 2.9 *The Control panel also contains a button that allows you to select similar objects. The button is available whenever you have an object selected.*

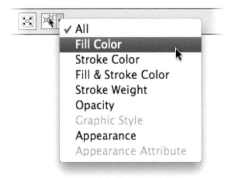

Saving Selections

Making complex selections can take time, and it can be tedious having to constantly make selections on objects as you are working on a design. To make life just a tad easier, you can save your selections and retrieve them later. Once you have made a selection using any of the methods mentioned earlier, choose Selection > Save, and give your selection a name. That selection then appears at the bottom of the Select menu, which you can access, or *load*, at any time. Because selections in Illustrator are object-based, a saved selection remembers objects even after they've been moved or modified.

Making Transformations

Drawing objects in Illustrator is only part of the design process. Once art is created, you can manipulate it in a myriad of ways. In Illustrator, the process of changing or manipulating a path is called a *transformation*, and transformations can include anything from simply moving an object to changing its size or rotation.

When you move a file, its x,y coordinates change, and Illustrator considers that a transformation. You can also move selected objects precisely by changing the x,y coordinates in the Control or Transform panel. Alternatively, double-click the Selection tool to open the Move dialog box, where you can specify values numerically as well (**Figure 2.10**). Clicking the Copy button in the Move dialog box leaves the original shape in place and moves a copy of it.

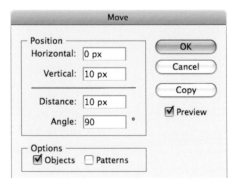

Figure 2.10 *The Move dialog box remembers the last move transform made, so you can move an object on your artboard and then open the Move dialog box to see how far you moved it.*

Of course, you can use the Selection tool to click and drag an object to reposition it manually. If you press and hold the Option (Alt) key while dragging, Illustrator moves a copy of the selection. If an object is filled with a pattern, pressing and holding the tilde (~) key while dragging adjusts the positioning of the pattern without moving the object.

Using the Bounding Box

The bounding box allows you to perform several common transform functions; you can do this by simply clicking an object using just the Selection tool. Once you've made a selection, you can click an object to move it, or you can click any of the eight *handles* that appear on the perimeter of the bounding box to scale or resize the selection (**Figure 2.11**). Holding the Shift key while resizing constrains the proportion. If you place your pointer just outside the edge of a handle, you can rotate your selection. Hold the Shift key to constrain the rotation angle to increments of 45 degrees.

Figure 2.11 *The bounding box makes simple transforms, such as scale and rotate, quick and painless.*

By default, Illustrator has the bounding box setting turned on. To turn it off, choose View > Hide Bounding Box (Command-Shift-B) [Ctrl-Shift-B].

TIP If you do turn off the bounding box function, you can still access similar functionality by using the Free Transform tool.

The bounding box appears only when you select objects with the Selection tool. Although the bounding box is certainly useful, it can get in the way as well. Illustrator has a Snap to Point setting that lets you drag an object by an anchor point and easily align it to an anchor point in a different object. As your pointer approaches an anchor point, the object you are dragging snaps to it. When the bounding box is turned on, you can't always grab an object by the anchor point because doing so allows you to scale the object instead. Your alternative is to either turn off the bounding box or use the Direct Selection tool (which many Illustrator users do anyway). An easy way to access the Direct Selection tool is to press and hold the Command (Ctrl) key when the regular Selection tool is active. Doing this will also make the bounding box temporarily disappear (until you release the Command [Ctrl] key).

Living by the Numbers with the Transform Panel

The Transform panel, which you can access by choosing Window > Transform, is a production artist's best friend. In reality, it's a panel that can be helpful to anyone. The Transform panel provides numeric feedback on the exact specifications of a selection. This includes x,y coordinates, width and height measurements, and rotate and shear values. You can also use the panel to make numeric changes to selected objects.

You can enter values using any measurement system, and you can even specify math functions. For example, you can change the x coordinate of an object by adding +.125 to the end of the value and pressing Return (Enter) or Tab. You can even mix different measurement systems, such as subtracting points from millimeters. Use the asterisk for multiplication functions and the slash for division. If you hold the Option (Alt) key while pressing Return (Enter) for a value, you'll create a copy.

At the far left of the Transform panel is a 9-point proxy that corresponds to the 8 points of an object's bounding box and its center (**Figure 2.12**). The point you click is extremely important—not only for the Transform panel but for all transform functions. If you click the center point, the x,y coordinates you see in the Transform panel refer to the center point of your selection. Clicking a different point reveals the coordinates for that point of the selection. When specifying transformations such as width or height settings or rotation or skew values, the point you choose becomes the *origin point*—the point from which the transformation originates. Rotating an object from its lower-left corner yields very different results from that same rotation applied from its center point.

NOTE The Transform panel can also help ensure that web graphics appear crisp and sharp with the new Align to Pixel Grid option, covered in detail in Chapter 11, "Web Design."

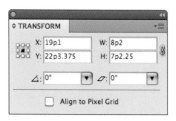

Figure 2.12 *The 9-point proxy in the Transform panel enables you to set an origin point for a transformation. You can find the proxy (also called a* reference point*) in transform dialog boxes and in the Control panel as well.*

TIP To lock the proportion of width and height
values, click the link icon at the
far right of the Transform
panel. This allows you to specify just the height or the width
of a selected object, and Illustrator scales the other value
proportionally.

If you want to transform strokes and effects, choose the Scale Strokes &
Effects option from the Transform panel menu, which stays on until you
turn it off. From the same panel menu, you can also choose to flip objects
on their horizontal or vertical axis.

Using Preview Bounds

One of the benefits of using Illustrator is that you can be extremely precise
when drawing objects. The Control, Transform, and Information panels in
Illustrator all provide exact feedback on coordinates, positioning, sizing,
and more. By default, these panels use the actual vector path to determine
these numbers, not the visual boundaries of the object. For example, you
may have a shape that has a thick stroke or a scale effect applied to it that
is not represented in the value you see in the Transform panel. When the Use
Preview Bounds preference is turned on in the General panel in Preferences,
all panels use the visual boundary of a file as the value, not the underlying
vector path.

Working with the Transformation Tools

Illustrator contains specific tools for performing scale, rotation, reflection
(mirroring), and shearing (skewing). These tools allow you to perform transformation with precision and with more power than the bounding box or
even the Control panel.

The four transformation tools—Scale, Rotate, Reflect, and Shear—all work the
same way. Here, we'll discuss the Rotate tool specifically; you can apply the
same techniques to the other tools.

To rotate an object, select it and choose the Rotate tool (R). Take a look at
the selection on your screen, and you'll see a special icon that appears at its
center. This icon, which looks like a small crosshairs, is your origin point
(**Figure 2.13**). To perform a rotation, position your pointer a fair amount of
space away from the origin point, and click and drag in a circular motion.
You don't have to click the object itself to perform the rotation. If you click
too close to the origin point, you'll find that it is difficult to control the rotation. The farther away you move your pointer from the origin point before
dragging, the more leverage and control you have (**Figure 2.14**).

Figure 2.13 *The crosshairs cursor indicates the precise location of the transformation origin point.*

Figure 2.14 *When using the Rotate tool, clicking away from the origin point gives you better leverage, or control, for rotating your selection.*

While dragging with the Rotate tool, press the Shift key to constrain the rotation to 45-degree increments, press the Option (Alt) key to create a copy, and press the tilde (~) key if your object is filled with a pattern and you want to rotate the pattern only.

The powerful part of using a transformation tool is that you have control over the exact placement of the origin point. For example, if you select an object and then switch to the Rotate tool, you'll see the origin point, as we discussed earlier. At that time, you can click once anywhere on your screen to redefine that point elsewhere. If you then click and drag, Illustrator uses the repositioned origin point for the rotation. Alternatively, you can simply click and drag the origin point itself to any location on your screen.

The ability to reposition the origin point arbitrarily means you can specify an origin point that's outside the boundaries of your object. When using the Transform panel, you can choose from only one of the nine preset options using the 9-point proxy.

You can also specify transformations numerically with any of the four transformation tools (Scale, Rotate, Reflect, and Sheer) by making a selection and double-clicking the desired transformation tool. One of the powerful features of opening the dialog box for a specific transformation tool is that when you enter a value, the next time you open the dialog box, that same value remains. Additionally, the dialog boxes for each transformation tool record the last transformation you performed with the tool. For example, if you use the Scale tool to manually resize an object, you can then open the Scale dialog box to see the exact percentage to which you scaled the object.

TIP With the Transform Tools option turned on in the Smart Guides preferences, Smart Guides will display the rotation angle in real time as you apply the transformation.

TIP You can bring up a Transform tool's dialog box by selecting the tool and pressing the Enter key while an object is selected.

Transforming Multiple Objects at Once

When you select several objects, Illustrator performs all transformations based on a single origin point. This behavior is certainly fine for some needs, but sometimes you want to have transformations applied to a range of objects, and you want those transformations to be applied using individual origin points. For example, if you have several shapes selected and you want them each to rotate 45 degrees, you want each selected shape to rotate around its own center. For example, when you have several individual (ungrouped) shapes (**Figure 2.15**, left), selecting them all and rotating them forces all objects to share a single origin point (**Figure 2.15**, center). With the Transform Each function, you can then rotate the multiple objects around their own individual origin points (**Figure 2.15**, right).

Figure 2.15 *With the Transform Each function, you can rotate multiple objects around their own individual origin points.*

The Transform Each function was designed specifically for applying transformations across a range of objects, where each object maintains its own origin point. As an added bonus, the feature also contains something no other transformation tool has—a randomize function.

> **TIP** Even though the Transform Each function was created for applying transformations to multiple objects at once, it's a great tool to use on single objects as well. This is especially true since the Transform Each dialog box allows you to specify multiple transformations in one step.

To use this feature, select a range of objects—even grouped objects—and choose Object > Transform > Transform Each to open the Transform Each dialog box. Selecting the Preview check box allows you to see the effects of the transformation before you apply it. Specify Scale, Move, Rotate, and Reflect settings, and if you'd like, click the Random button so that each object gets a slight variation of the settings you specify.

By far, the most important setting you need to specify in the Transform Each dialog box is the origin point. Select a point from the 9-point proxy to define the origin point for each selected object. Click OK to apply the transformations, or click the Copy button to create copies.

Exploring the Power of the Transform Again Feature

The Transform Again feature builds on the power of the transformation tools you've learned. Illustrator always remembers the last transformation you applied, so choosing Object > Transform > Transform Again simply reapplies that transformation, even if you've selected a different object. The keyboard shortcut for this feature is Command-D (Ctrl-D); it's a good idea to memorize it, because you'll use it often.

This example illustrates the power of this feature. Draw a rectangle on your artboard. Choose the Selection tool, and drag the rectangle to the right while holding the Option (Alt) key, which creates a copy of the rectangle beside the original. Now apply the Transform Again command. Illustrator now repeats the last transformation, leaving you with three rectangles, evenly spaced.

The Transform Each dialog box allows you to apply multiple transformations in one step. Applying a Transform Again command after applying a Transform Each function simply duplicates those settings. The power to transform is now within you. Use it wisely.

The Art of Building Artwork

The basic drawing tools in Illustrator (i.e., Rectangle, Ellipse) are great on their own, but you'll often need to create shapes that are a *bit* more complex. Many times, it's far easier to combine basic primitive shapes to create more complex ones. It can also be easier to edit existing shapes using new simple shapes rather than trying to adjust the anchor points of individual paths.

As a general concept, visualize what you want to draw, and try to break it down into rectangles, ovals, and lines. After creating these basic objects, you can use a variety of tools and functions—such as the Shape Builder tool and the Pathfinder commands—to complete your artwork. In other words, if you think about *building* artwork in Illustrator instead of thinking about *drawing* artwork, you'll be far more successful. Not only will you be able to create artwork more quickly, but you'll also be able to create artwork that is more precise and easier to work with.

Using the Shape Builder tool

At first glance, the Shape Builder tool (M) helps you build artwork by quickly adding and subtracting overlapping objects. However, the tool contains useful settings and can even be used to apply color attributes as well.

To use the Shape Builder tool, two or more objects must first be selected on your artboard. Then, you can perform one of two basic functions:

- Click and drag across your artwork with the Shape Builder tool. A line appears as you drag the cursor across your artwork, and any region that the line touches becomes highlighted. Release the mouse and all highlighted regions become joined into one new object (**Figure 2.16**).

NOTE Pressing the Shift key while dragging with the Shape Builder tool will replace the line with a marquee rectangle, making it easier to add or subtract larger areas of artwork at once.

- Press and hold the Option (Alt) key while you click and drag across your artwork with the Shape Builder tool. A line appears as you drag the cursor across your artwork, and any region that the line touches becomes highlighted. Release the mouse and all highlighted regions are removed from your artwork (**Figure 2.17**).

Figure 2.16 *You can use the Shape Builder tool to combine overlapping regions into one fused shape.*

Figure 2.17 *The Shape Builder tool can also easily remove unwanted regions from your artwork.*

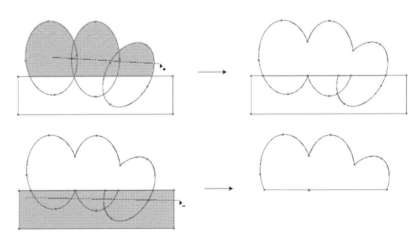

Double-clicking the Shape Builder tool in the Tools panel brings up the Shape Builder Tool Options dialog box (**Figure 2.18**), which includes the following options:

- **Gap Detection.** Each overlapping area in your artwork, or region, is defined by an area that is fully enclosed by intersecting paths. With Gap Detection active, small gaps in the paths may be considered closed, resulting in regions that can still be combined or removed. More details on Gap Detection can be found in the "Drawing with Live Paint" section in Chapter 4.

Figure 2.18 *The Shape Builder tool features options that are similar to those found in the Live Paint feature.*

- **Options.** The Shape Builder tool can apply fill color at the same time you are building your artwork. This prevents you from having to first build shapes and then apply color afterwards. In the Pick Color From pop-up menu you can choose from two settings: Color Swatches and Artwork. With Color Swatches active, you can choose a color from the Swatches panel, which will be applied to artwork as you build it. Selecting the Cursor Swatch Preview check box will allow you to select colors by pressing the left and right arrow keys on your keyboard as you use the Shape Builder tool (more details on the Cursor Swatch Preview setting can be found in the "Drawing with Live Paint" section in Chapter 4). With the Artwork setting active, Illustrator will take the fill color from the first region you click with the Shape Builder tool and apply it to the result.

- **Highlight.** You can control how artwork is highlighted when you mouse over it with the Shape Builder tool, including the color used for the highlighting.

Exploring the Pathfinder Panel

The Pathfinder panel, which you can open by choosing Window > Pathfinder, contains two horizontal rows of buttons, each offering a different type of function. The top row, *shape modes*, offers functions used to combine multiple selected shapes (**Figure 2.19**, on the next page). The bottom row, *pathfinders*, consists of functions that are used to split shapes apart in a variety of ways (**Figure 2.20**, on the next page).

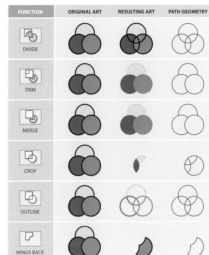

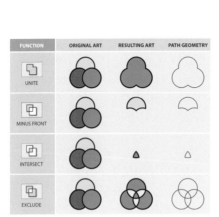

Figure 2.19 *The shape mode functions.*

Figure 2.20 *The pathfinder functions.*

Combining Shapes with Shape Modes

To use any of the shape modes, select two or more objects in your document, and click any of the shape mode buttons in the Pathfinder panel. To create the cute clouds in **Figure 2.21**, for example, start with three ovals and a rectangle (A), use Unite to combine the three ovals (B), and then use Minus Front with the rectangle to complete the shape (C). Add sky for an added touch (D).

Figure 2.21 *With shape modes, you don't have to know how to draw complex art in order to create it.*

The following are the four shape mode functions in the Pathfinder panel:

- **Unite.** The Unite shape mode combines all the selected shapes and gives the appearance they were all joined together.

- **Minus Front.** The Minus Front shape mode combines all the selected shapes and then takes the top objects and removes them from the bottommost object.

- **Intersect.** The Intersect shape mode combines all the selected shapes and displays only the areas in which all the objects overlap with each other.

- **Exclude.** The Exclude shape mode combines all the selected shapes and removes the areas in which the objects overlap each other.

By default, when you use any of the shape modes in the Pathfinder panel, the resulting object is a new single path. But there's some "hidden" functionality that allows you to use the shape modes to create something called a *compound shape*. A compound shape has the appearance of a single path, but the original paths that were used to create the final shape are still present in the final result (**Figure 2.22**). To create a compound shape, hold the Option (Alt) key while applying any of the shape mode functions from the Pathfinder panel.

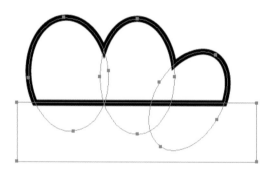

Figure 2.22 *Even though the cloud has the appearance of a single path, the individual shapes that were used to create the shape are still editable.*

Compound shapes offer several significant benefits over the default shape mode paths:

- Compound shapes are "live," and each of the individual components can be edited independently.

- Compound shapes can be nested, much in the same way as groups can.

- Compound shapes can be applied to live text, symbols, and other complex objects.

- Compound shapes are compatible with the Shape Layers feature in Photoshop (see the sidebar "Illustrator Shape Modes and Photoshop Shape Layers").

Once you've created a compound shape, you can "flatten" it and reduce it to a path object by clicking Expand in the Pathfinder panel. Additionally, you can release a compound shape by choosing Release Compound Shape from the Pathfinder panel menu. Releasing compound shapes returns the objects to their individual states and appearances.

 CAUTION The default behavior of the shape modes in the Pathfinder panel changed in Illustrator CS4. In previous versions, compound shapes were created by default, and you were required to use the Option (Alt) key to create expanded paths. As of Illustrator CS4, Adobe reversed the behavior so that now expanded paths are created by default, and you are required to use the Option (Alt) key to create compound shapes.

Illustrator Shape Modes and Photoshop Shape Layers

If you've used Photoshop, you might be familiar with vector shape layers, which allow you to create vector-based masks. Although Photoshop is primarily a pixel-based program, these *shape layers*, as Photoshop refers to them, allow you to create vector shapes within your Photoshop document. Upon close inspection, you'll find that to create more complex shapes, you can create shape layers in Photoshop using a variety of modes, including Add, Subtract, Intersect, and Exclude—the same functions (with similar names) in the Pathfinder panel in Illustrator.

These objects are interchangeable between Illustrator and Photoshop, and they retain their shape mode settings in the process as well. Create a compound shape in Illustrator, copy and paste it into Photoshop, and the compound shape becomes an editable vector shape layer. The same applies in reverse.

Changing Paths with Pathfinders

To use any of the pathfinder functions, select two or more objects in your document, and click any of the pathfinder buttons in the Pathfinder panel. The following are the six pathfinder functions in the Pathfinder panel:

- **Divide.** One of the most often-used pathfinders, Divide takes all selected objects and breaks them apart into individual shapes based on their overlapping parts. Open paths act like knives and slice paths that intersect with them.

- **Trim.** The Trim pathfinder removes all overlapping areas from the selected paths.

- **Merge.** The Merge pathfinder removes all overlapping areas from the selected paths and joins all areas of the same color.

- **Crop.** The Crop pathfinder takes the topmost selected object and removes all objects and areas beneath it that fall outside its path. Unfortunately, this pathfinder works on vector objects only, and you can't use it to crop a raster image (you'll need Photoshop for that). This function ignores strokes on objects, so it's best to perform an Outline Path function before applying the Crop pathfinder.

- **Outline.** The Outline pathfinder converts the selected shapes to outlines and divides the lines where they intersect.

- **Minus Back.** The Minus Back pathfinder is similar to the Minus Front shape mode, but instead of using the top object to define the subtracted area, the function uses the bottom object.

Once you've applied a pathfinder function, you can choose Repeat Pathfinder from the Pathfinder panel menu to apply the same effect again. In reality, it takes longer to access the panel menu than it does to just click the icon in the panel, so it pays to memorize the Command-4 (Ctrl-4) keyboard shortcut.

From the Pathfinder panel menu, you can choose Pathfinder Options to open the Pathfinder Options dialog box (**Figure 2.23**), where you can set the level of precision to use when applying pathfinder functions (lower numbers may result in more complex paths). You can also specify that Illustrator should remove redundant points (always a good idea) and unpainted artwork when performing Divide or Outline functions.

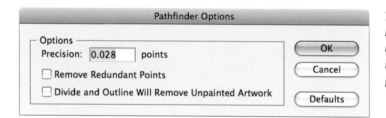

Figure 2.23 *The Pathfinder Options dialog box offers the ability to remove redundant anchor points.*

Aligning Objects

When working with a range of objects or anchor points, you will often want to align them evenly or distribute them across a specified distance. Rather than being forced to figure out the math on your own and then manually move each object, you can apply the variety of functions that the Align panel contains to a range of objects in order to both align and distribute objects precisely (**Figure 2.24**). You can open the Align panel by choosing Window > Align.

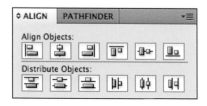

Figure 2.24 *The Align panel features plenty of options in the form of teeny icons.*

TIP By default, the align functions use the actual path of an object for calculating alignment. If you want Illustrator to factor in the appearance of the object (for example, the stroke width), choose Use Preview Bounds from the Align panel menu.

To align a range of objects or anchor points, select them, and click one of the Align Objects icons in the Align panel. Admittedly, these small icons can be hard to decipher, but if you move your pointer over them for a second, a tool tip pops up identifying the name of the function. The Align Objects functions also appear in the Control panel.

One thing that is somewhat vague when it comes to aligning objects, though, is, what exactly are you aligning your objects *to*? Illustrator offers three distinct options:

- **Align to Selection.** The Align to Selection option, which is the default setting, automatically takes one object from your selection and aligns all other objects in your selection to that object. Illustrator chooses an object based on the specific align function you apply. For example, if you use the Align Vertical Top function, Illustrator aligns all objects in your selection to the object that is at the top (**Figure 2.25**).

Figure 2.25 *The original selection (left) and the objects after they've been aligned with the Vertical Align Top option (right).*

- **Align to Key Object.** The Align to Key Object feature was present in previous versions of Illustrator, but it required a "secret handshake" because there was no specific user interface for its use. You would use the Align to Key Object option when you wanted to align your objects to a specific object, within a selection, that you chose. Start by selecting your artwork (including the object that you want to align everything else to) with the Selection tool. Then, click the object once that you want all the other objects to align to (don't Shift-click because this will deselect that object). A heavy blue outline identifies the object as a key object (**Figure 2.26**). You can also change the key object simply by clicking any other object in your selection. Then, apply the desired align function from the Align or Control panel.

Figure 2.26 *A heavy blue outline clearly identifies the key object you've chosen.*

- **Align to Artboard.** The Align to Artboard option will align all your selected artwork to the active artboard. This function also works when you have just one object selected. To activate the Align to Artboard option, use the pop-up widget in the Align or Control panel (**Figure 2.27**).

Figure 2.27 *You can quickly choose options for aligning objects directly from the Control panel.*

The align functions treat a group of objects as a single object, so performing an align function on a group won't do anything unless you're aligning it to the artboard. Of course, you can select multiple groups and align them as if each group were a single object.

Distributing Objects

The Align panel in Illustrator can do more than just align objects—it can also distribute objects. In fact, when it comes to distribution, Illustrator allows you to distribute the objects in your selection (Distribute Objects) or distribute the spacing that appears between each object (Distribute Spacing). Yes, there's a difference. To take advantage of all that the Align panel has to offer, choose Show Options from the panel menu (**Figure 2.28**).

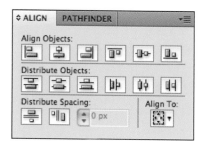

Figure 2.28 *The fully expanded Align panel displays the Distribute Spacing options.*

Distribute Objects

The six buttons in the Distribute Objects section of the Align panel allow you to evenly distribute objects within a specified area. But what *is* the specified area? In the case of alignment, you are always aligning objects to another single key object (whether you define one or not) or an artboard. But in order to distribute objects evenly, you need *two* key objects. By default, Illustrator picks the two objects that are the farthest apart from each other and uses those as key objects. The remaining objects within the selection are then evenly distributed between the two key objects. In **Figure 2.29**, for example, the dashed lines indicate the center of each object in their original location (left). After applying the Horizontal Distribute Center command, the objects on the far left and right remained in place, while the objects in between moved so that their centers were distributed evenly (right). The amount of space between the *centers* of all the objects is now consistent.

Figure 2.29 *An object before (left) and after (right) aligning with the Horizontal Distribute Center command.*

When using the Distribute Objects functions, you have no control over the distance between each object. If you find you need to adjust the amount of space between the objects, you will have to adjust the position of the outermost two objects and try again. If you're concerned about the amount of space that appears between the distributed objects (for example, you need .25" between each object), then you'll want to learn how to use the Distribute Spacing functions.

Distribute Spacing

As any good designer knows, white space isn't just an abstract—it actually exists—and to better understand what the Distribute Spacing functions do, you need to think about white space. That's because the two Distribute Spacing functions in the Align panel apply an even amount of white space *between* each object in your selection (**Figure 2.30**).

Figure 2.30 *After applying the Horizontal Distribute Space command to the original objects (left), the amount of white space that appears between the objects is consistent (right).*

By default, Illustrator defines the outermost two objects in your selection as key objects and then evenly distributes the white space between each of the objects. If you want to specify the exact amount of white space that should appear between each object, you must first manually define a key object. Just like when using the align functions, you can define a key object by clicking an object with the Selection tool after you've made your selection. Once a key object is active, you can specify a value in the field in the Distribute Objects section of the Align panel.

TIP Once you define a key object, you can specify a Distribute Spacing value of 0, which will automatically "kiss fit" your objects to each other.

Working with Tools of Mass Distortion

Illustrator has a plethora of tools that can help you create crisp, clean paths with extreme precision. But at times a design calls for something less perfect, and it is also appropriate to bend or stretch artwork to achieve a distorted effect. That's where the distortion tools come into play.

Painting with Distortion: The Liquify Tools

In your average box of classic toys, you'd surely find an Etch A Sketch, a Slinky, a collection of Tinkertoy parts, and, undoubtedly, a plastic egg filled with Silly Putty. For those not familiar with the popular toy, Silly Putty is this gooey plastic substance that looks much like a wad of chewing gum. Once you've flattened the plastic, you can press it firmly on newsprint (we always used the comics section) to transfer the images or text to the plastic surface. Then the fun begins; you can pull and twist and stretch the plastic to distort the pictures or words.

If you've missed out on all the fun over the years, fear not—you can perform the same distortion to your artwork using the suite of Liquify distortion tools in Illustrator (although your hands won't smell of Silly Putty afterward). The

Liquify toolset includes the Warp, Twirl, Pucker, Bloat, Scallop, Crystallize, and Wrinkle tools (**Figure 2.31**). Each of these tools allows you to "paint" with distortion effects by simply clicking and dragging over vector art. The tools feature a brush size, which helps determine how large of an area is distorted (**Figure 2.32**). You can change the brush size for any of the Liquify tools interactively by holding the Option (Alt) key while dragging with the tool. Adding the Shift key while dragging constrains the brush size to a perfect circle.

Figure 2.31 *The Liquify tools appear grouped together in the Tools panel and offer a wide range of distortion effects.*

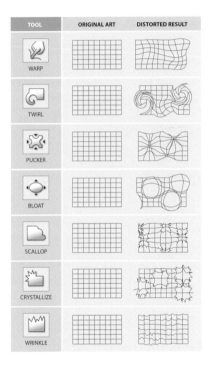

Figure 2.32 *Changing the size of a Liquify brush allows you to control how much of a selection becomes distorted with each drag of the mouse.*

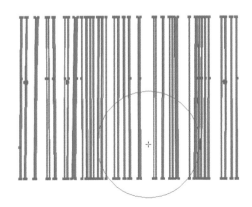

You'll have to be careful when using the Liquify tools, because they exhibit different behavior based on your selection. If you have artwork selected before you start dragging with a Liquify tool, only the selected art becomes distorted. However, if you have not made a selection, clicking and dragging with a Liquify tool distorts any path you touch.

The Liquify tools don't work on live text (you'll need to convert text to outlines first), but they do work on embedded images. As you drag a Liquify tool over an embedded image, Illustrator creates a mesh that is used to distort the image beneath it. In fact, if you've created a gradient mesh object, using the Liquify tools on the mesh object produces interesting effects as well.

Double-clicking any of the Liquify tools in the Tools panel opens a dialog box offering a variety of settings (**Figure 2.33**). The top half of the dialog box features Global Brush Dimensions settings, which control the size (width and height), angle, and intensity of the tools. In addition, if you are using a pressure-sensitive tablet, you can choose to control the intensity with pen pressure by selecting the Use Pressure Pen check box. Any changes you make to the Global Brush Dimensions settings are applied to all the Liquify tools.

The bottom half of the dialog box offers options for the specific tool that you double-clicked. Most tools offer Detail and Simplify settings, although the Wrinkle tool offers many additional options as well. The changes you make to each of these tool-specific settings affect only the tool you double-clicked.

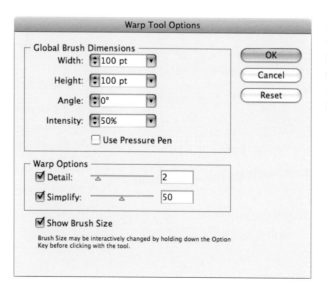

Figure 2.33 *If you have a pressure-sensitive tablet, you can achieve greater control over the Liquify tools by selecting the Use Pressure Pen setting.*

Getting Into Shape: Envelope Distortion

Ever see those cartoons where one of the characters gets his head stuck in a glass jar? And remember that when he pulls his head out of the jar, his head is in the shape of the jar? Wouldn't it be cool if you could do the same thing with your artwork? Well, you can, using the enveloping features in Illustrator.

An *envelope* is a regular vector shape that can contain other artwork. And any artwork that is contained inside the envelope becomes distorted to take on the shape of the envelope. As you will soon learn, envelopes use the mesh technology in Illustrator to distort artwork. In fact, these *envelope meshes*, as they are called, are identical to the gradient meshes you will learn about in Chapter 4, "Creative Drawing."

You can create an Envelope distortion in Illustrator in three ways, and naturally, each offers a slightly different approach and warrants its own benefits. As you learn about these three different types of envelopes, you will understand when it's best to use them for a specific project or desired result. You can find these three methods in the Object > Envelope Distort menu; they are named Make with Top Object, Make with Mesh, and Make with Warp.

Using Method 1: Make with Top Object

A commonly used Envelope distortion technique in Illustrator is the Make with Top Object method. Creating an Envelope distortion using the Make with Top Object method is similar to creating a mask. A regular vector shape at the top of the stacking order acts as the envelope, and all selected artwork that appears beneath the envelope becomes distorted to fit within the envelope shape. Here are the steps you'll need to follow to perform this technique:

1. Select the shape you will be using as the envelope. You can use any vector object consisting of a single path as an envelope.

2. Choose Object > Arrange > Bring to Front. This ensures that the envelope is at the top of the stacking order.

3. Select both the artwork you want to distort and the vector shape that will become the envelope.

4. Choose Object > Envelope Distort > Make with Top Object. The selected artwork becomes distorted to fit within the envelope shape (**Figure 2.34**).

Figure 2.34 *The Make with Top Object command makes it easy to distort artwork to quickly add perspective.*

Once you've created an Envelope distortion, you can edit the envelope shape using your Direct Selection tool—just as you'd do with any other vector shape. As you adjust the shape of the envelope, the distorted artwork updates to match the edited shape (**Figure 2.35**). Pay close attention to the position of the control handles that appear on the anchor points of your envelope path, because they also affect how art within the envelope shape is distorted.

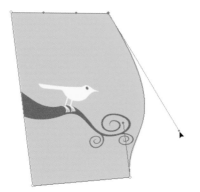

Figure 2.35 *Changing the shape of the envelope after you've applied the distortion makes it easy to tweak your distortion to perfection.*

Using a distinct custom shape as a distortion envelope is useful for times when you need artwork to fit within the confines of a specific shape. However, you'll notice that although you can easily adjust the outside path to change the overall shape of the distortion, you have little control over how the artwork inside the envelope is distorted. To control distortion across the entire object, not just the edges, you need to employ one of the next two methods: Make with Mesh or Make with Warp.

TIP You can also use the Mesh tool to add mesh points to envelopes you created using the Make with Top Object method.

Using Method 2: Make with Mesh

When using the Make with Mesh method, Illustrator creates the envelope shape for you, so you don't need to create a shape first. The shape that Illustrator creates is a rectangle, so no immediate distortion is visible when you apply this kind of envelope. Once the envelope is created, you can edit the mesh points to control how the distortion affects the artwork. Editing an envelope mesh is identical to editing a gradient mesh.

To create an Envelope distortion using the Make with Mesh method, perform the following steps:

1. Select any artwork on your artboard. You can select multiple objects, and although you aren't required to group them, you may want to do so to ensure easier editing later.

2. Choose Object > Envelope Distort > Make with Mesh.

3. In the Envelope Mesh dialog box, specify how many rows and columns you want the mesh to be initially created with (**Figure 2.36**). It doesn't matter whether you aren't sure of the exact number of rows and columns at this point, because you are able to add mesh points later as needed. Click OK to apply the Envelope distortion.

Figure 2.36 *The Envelope Mesh dialog box gives you the ability to set how many mesh points appear initially in the envelope. Creating more rows and columns gives you additional control over the amount of distortion you can apply.*

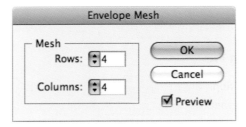

4. Using the Mesh tool or the Direct Selection tool, move the individual mesh points and their control handles to apply distortion to your artwork (**Figure 2.37**).

Figure 2.37 *Similar to working with a gradient mesh, adjusting the position and control handles of mesh points in an envelope mesh controls the distortion of the artwork.*

If you want to add mesh points to your envelope, select the Mesh tool, and click anywhere within the selected envelope. Hold down the Option (Alt) key while clicking with the Mesh tool to remove mesh points.

Although you start with a rectangle mesh shape, moving the individual mesh points on the envelope gives you control over not just the outer edge of the distortion but also any points within the envelope shape. However, this method is harder to use because you aren't starting with a distorted shape, just a grid of mesh points.

Using Method 3: Make with Warp

The Make with Warp method of applying Envelope distortion is nearly identical to the Make with Mesh method—only with a twist (sorry, couldn't resist). Instead of starting with a rectangular-shaped mesh, Illustrator gives you the option of choosing from several preset shapes. Actually, they are the same presets as those found in the Warp effect.

Follow these steps to apply an Envelope distortion using the Make with Warp method:

1. Select any artwork on your artboard. You can select multiple objects, and although you aren't required to group them, you may want to do so to ensure easier editing later.

2. Choose Object > Envelope Distort > Make with Warp.

TIP When you select art you've enveloped with a warp, you can adjust the warp settings directly from the Control panel.

3. In the Warp Options dialog box that appears, choose a Warp style, and adjust the settings as necessary. Click OK to apply the Envelope distortion (**Figure 2.38**).

Figure 2.38 *Starting an Envelope distortion with a warp gives you a head start in getting the look you need.*

4. Using the Mesh tool or the Direct Selection tool, move the individual mesh points and their control handles to apply distortion to your artwork (**Figure 2.39**).

Figure 2.39 *Although the envelope starts out as a warp, you can add mesh points as needed to adjust the distortion to your liking.*

TIP When a point type object is selected, you can quickly apply the Envelope Make with Warp and/or Make with Mesh function by clicking the icon that appears in the Control panel.

Overall, this third method of creating an envelope mesh is a combination of the first two. You start with an initial distortion using a warp, and then you complete the distortion by editing the envelope as a mesh object. This method is useful for times when you want to use a warp shape but need the ability to tweak the distortion a bit—something that isn't possible with the Warp effect. Refer to the sidebar "Envelopes vs. the Warp Effect" for an in-depth comparison of the Envelope and Warp effect distortion features.

Adjusting Envelope Distortion Settings

By default, Illustrator tries to create Envelope distortions as quickly as possible. Artwork that takes longer to distort, such as live effects, gradients, or patterns, is not distorted at all, and images or other complex artwork may not fit perfectly within the envelope shape. Don't assume that the Envelope distortion in Illustrator is below par; rather, select your envelope, and choose Object > Envelope Distort > Envelope Options. Alternatively, you can click the Envelope Options button that appears in the Control panel. This opens the Envelope Options dialog box, where you can adjust the settings that Illustrator uses to create Envelope distortions (**Figure 2.40**).

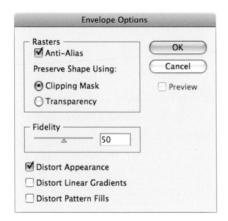

Figure 2.40 *The Envelope Options dialog box gives you control over how Illustrator distorts artwork within envelopes.*

The following are the options you can set in the Envelope Options dialog box:

- **Rasters.** If your envelope contains a raster image, you can choose to turn antialiasing on or off. With antialiasing turned on, Illustrator produces smoother and nicer-looking art, at the expense of longer calculations and render times. When nonrectangular shapes are used as an envelope (as is usually the case), you can choose to have any raster art enclosed by a clipping mask or a transparency alpha channel.

- **Fidelity.** When Illustrator performs an Envelope distortion, it has to stretch or squeeze artwork to fit within another shape. During this process, Illustrator may make small adjustments to the art so that it doesn't become overly complex. A higher-fidelity setting forces Illustrator to preserve the integrity of the artwork as much as possible, which may produce more anchor points but results in final distorted art that closely matches the original. A lower-fidelity setting gives Illustrator more wiggle room to create files that print and save faster.

- **Distort Appearance.** If the artwork you're placing into an envelope contains live effects or multiple fill or stroke attributes, those appearances become distorted by the envelope shape by default. You must deselect the Distort Appearance option if you want the Envelope distortion to be applied just to the vector paths.

- **Distort Linear Gradients.** If the artwork you're placing into an envelope contains linear gradients, the gradient does not become distorted by the envelope shape by default. You must select the Distort Linear Gradients option if you want the Envelope distortion to affect the gradient fill.

- **Distort Pattern Fills.** If the artwork you're placing into an envelope contains a pattern fill, that fill does not become distorted by the envelope shape by default. You must select the Distort Pattern Fills option if you want the Envelope distortion to affect the pattern.

Editing Envelopes and Their Contents

It is certainly no coincidence that many of the features in Illustrator exhibit live functionality, thus allowing you to perform edits without having to re-create art. Live effects, symbols, Live Trace, Live Paint, and Compound Shape modes are all examples of effects that are live and can be edited at any stage of the workflow. Envelope distortion is no exception. Once you apply an Envelope distortion using any of the three methods described earlier, you can continue to adjust either the envelope itself or the artwork it contains.

Illustrator manages the process of editing envelopes and their contents by giving you two distinct modes in which to work. At any one time, you can work with the envelope shape, or you can change modes and edit the contents of the envelope. Unfortunately, Illustrator doesn't clearly identify the difference between these two modes, so we'll take a closer look at how you can edit Envelope distortions and the artwork within them.

When you first create a new Envelope distortion, Illustrator is in the Edit Envelope mode. In this mode, you can select and edit the shape of the envelope, but you have no way to access the art that is distorted within the envelope. If you look at the Layers panel, you'll notice an object named Envelope, but you won't find the distorted artwork listed anywhere (**Figure 2.41**).

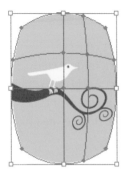
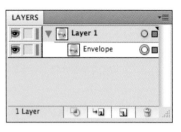

Figure 2.41 *The Layers panel lists only one object on Layer 1—the Envelope object.*

To edit the contents of an envelope, select it on your artboard, and choose Object > Envelope Distort > Edit Contents, or press Command-Shift-V (Ctrl-Shift-V). Doing so puts Illustrator into the Edit Contents mode, where you can select the artwork and edit it as normal. In the Edit Contents mode, you cannot adjust, or even select, the envelope. If you look at the Layers panel, you'll see that the Envelope object now contains a triangle to the left of its name, which you can click to reveal the objects contained within the envelope (**Figure 2.42**). This triangle is your only clue as to which mode you are in. If you see the disclosure triangle, you're in Edit Contents mode; if you don't, then you are in Edit Envelope mode. If you are in Edit Contents mode and want to return to Edit Envelope mode, use the same keyboard shortcut mentioned earlier, or choose Object > Envelope Distort > Edit Envelope.

TIP When you're editing the contents of an envelope, you might find it easier to make edits to your art with Smart Guides turned on. The Object Highlighting feature of Smart Guides allows you to quickly find and see the art you are editing.

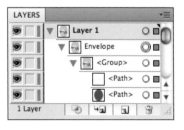

Figure 2.42 *When you're in Edit Contents mode, Illustrator reveals the artwork within the Envelope object on Layer 1.*

NOTE You can toggle between editing an envelope and its contents by clicking the Edit Envelope and Edit Contents buttons that appear in the Control panel. Alternatively, you can double-click an envelope with the Selection tool to toggle between the two editing modes.

Keep in mind that Illustrator maintains each Envelope distortion in your file as a separate entity. Therefore, it's entirely possible to have one envelope in Edit Envelope mode and have another envelope in Edit Contents mode.

Releasing and Expanding Envelopes

At any time, you can select an existing envelope and choose Object > Envelope Distort > Release, which returns the artwork to an undistorted state. In addition, you can choose Object > Envelope Distort > Expand, which applies the Envelope distortion to the artwork itself. You can then edit the distorted paths freely, although you won't be able to edit or change the Envelope distortion after this point.

Envelopes vs. the Warp Effect

After learning how to apply some of the Envelope distortion features—especially the Make with Warp method—you may wonder how these kinds of distortions differ from the Warp effect distortions covered in Chapter 7, "Working with Live Effects."

Although it's true that both the Warp effect and Envelope distortions are live in that you can edit them after you've applied them, they don't behave the same way. The Warp effect, which appears in the Effect menu, exhibits the same behavior as any other live effect. That means you can apply the Warp effect to any object, to any group, or even to an entire layer. Because live effects appear listed in the Appearance panel, you can apply warps to individual parts of an object (that is, just to the stroke). In addition, you can save a warp in a graphic style so you can easily apply it to other objects.

Envelope distortions give you complete control over the shape of your overall distortion, and using mesh points, you can even control how the interior artwork is distorted. Overall, envelopes offer a level of control that is simply not possible with the Warp effect. After all, the Warp effect contains only 15 shapes to choose from, and these cannot address every design need. Generally, the Warp effects are great for quick adjustments to artwork, whereas envelopes excel at distortions that require individual attention.

Creating Transitions with Blends

By definition, a *blend* is the result of two or more items that are combined. In Illustrator, a blend is a set of at least two objects that morph into each other. In an example where you are blending two objects, Illustrator generates new shapes that appear between the two objects, making it seem like one of the objects is turning into the other. The iterations that are created between the two main objects (also referred to as *key objects*) are called *steps*, and as you'll learn shortly, Illustrator gives you control over how many steps make up each blend (**Figure 2.43**).

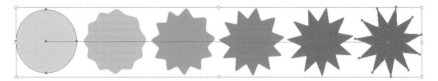

Figure 2.43 *A blend in Illustrator consists of key objects and blend steps. A straight line, called the* spine, *connects the key objects.*

Although at first glance it may seem like creating blends is something reserved for highly specialized tasks, the reality is that you can use blends for many different reasons. In fact, back in the day, before gradients were introduced to Illustrator, blends were the only way you could create color gradations. Here's a list of some other common uses for blends in Illustrator:

- **Creating shading effects.** You can use blends to create photorealistic shading effects. Because blends can be created using any vector shape, you can create customized gradations not only in color but in shape as well (**Figure 2.44**). This gives blends a distinct advantage over gradients.

Figure 2.44 *By blending two shapes, you can get realistic shading in a way that is not possible with linear or radial gradients.*

- **Creating animations.** When creating animations in Illustrator, you can use a blend to *tween* steps between objects, saving you from having to create the necessary keyframes yourself (**Figure 2.45** on the following page). *Tweening* is a term used in animation to define the steps that appear when showing movement or one object morphing into another.

In Chapter 11, "Web Design," you will learn how to export animated SWF (Flash) files directly from Illustrator.

Figure 2.45 *By blending two symbols with different opacity levels, Illustrator creates the necessary steps to create an animation.*

- **Distributing objects.** If you need to repeat art across an area or along the curve of a path, you can use a blend to evenly distribute a specific number of steps.

You can't blend images or Area Type objects (text enclosed within a shape), but you can blend just about anything else—including symbols and groups. In fact, you can even blend between objects that have different live effects settings; Illustrator blends the settings of those effects as well. Blends are pretty powerful, but don't worry, they are easy to work with.

Creating a Blend

If there were always just one way to perform a particular function in Illustrator, there would be less of a need for books like this one. But as you've seen up to this point in this book, Illustrator offers a variety of ways to perform tasks, each of which offers specific benefits. In the case of blends, Illustrator allows you to generate a blend from a menu item, or you can achieve finer control over the result of your blend using the Blend tool.

Using Method 1: Using the Blend Menu

Creating a blend using the Make command is the quickest way. You simply select at least two objects and choose Object > Blend > Make (Command-Option-B) [Ctrl-Alt-B]. Using this method, Illustrator takes the bottommost object in your selection and creates a blend with the next object up in the stacking order.

Using Method 2: Using the Blend Tool

Creating a blend using the Blend tool takes a few extra clicks of the mouse but gives you the ability to control the blend in ways that the menu command can't. You begin by selecting the objects you want to blend, and then you choose the Blend tool (W) from the Tools panel. Then, click an anchor point once in the first object to define where you want the blend to start, and click an anchor point in the second object where you want the blend to end. If you have more than two objects to blend, keep selecting an anchor point in each object until the blend is created.

Unlike the first method where Illustrator created the blend based on stacking order, this method allows you to control the order in which key objects appear in the blend. Additionally, if you click an anchor point near the top of one object and then choose an anchor point toward the bottom of the next key object, Illustrator rotates and modifies the intermediate steps of the blend to match the orientation of the anchor points.

Editing a Blend

Once you've created a blend, you can edit it in a variety of ways. It should come as no surprise to you at this point to learn that blends are live in Illustrator, meaning you can adjust them even after you apply the blend. To do so, using the Direct Selection tool, click a key object, and change its color, shape, position, attributes—whatever. When you do, Illustrator simply redraws the blend to incorporate the change.

You will notice that you can't select or edit the intermediate steps that Illustrator creates to form the blend. This is an attribute of the live functionality of the blend—you can access the steps only by expanding the blend (see "Releasing and Expanding Blends" later in this chapter). However, you can control how Illustrator draws blend steps by selecting a blend and choosing Object > Blend > Blend Options.

In the Blend Options dialog box, you have two general settings:

- **Spacing.** The Spacing setting determines the number of blend steps that are created. When you choose Smooth Color, Illustrator creates as many steps as are necessary to display a smooth and gradual transition between key objects (**Figure 2.46** on the following page). The Specified Steps setting allows you to define exactly how many blend steps

NOTE In case you're ever playing something like the Adobe edition of Trivial Pursuit, you'll find this information helpful: The 3D effect in Illustrator uses blends to create lighting and shading effects.

NOTE Illustrator can have a maximum of 256 steps in a blend. The number of steps that appear in a blend has a direct impact on screen redraw speed, print performance, and file size.

Illustrator creates. Using a higher number of steps results in a smoother transition, whereas a lower number allows you to see the individual steps in the blend. The Specified Distance setting allows you to specify how far apart each step appears from the next. When you want to create shading techniques using blends, the Smooth Color option provides the best results. When creating steps for a Flash animation, specifying fewer steps will help playback performance.

Figure 2.46 *The Blend Options dialog box offers spacing and orientation options for blending.*

- **Orientation.** The Orientation setting controls the baseline angle of each step in your blend. With the Align to Page setting, each blend step aligns parallel to the bottom of the page, even if the path is curved or diagonal. With this setting, all blends steps share the same orientation. In contrast, the Align to Path setting aligns the baseline of each blend step to the angle of the path. With this setting, you'll see that each blend step has a different orientation (**Figure 2.47**).

Figure 2.47 *On the left, the blend is set to the Align to Page option. The blend on the right is set to the Align to Path orientation option.*

Replacing the Spine of a Blend

As we briefly mentioned earlier, you'll notice a straight path that connects the key objects in a blend. This path is referred to as the *spine* of the blend. The individual steps that are created in a blend follow along the spine as they connect the two outer objects. The spine is an editable path, and you can use the Pen tool and the Direct Selection tool to edit the path if you want to alter the direction of the blend steps. In fact, the position of the control handles on a spine can control how the individual steps are distributed along the spine.

Additionally, you can perform a delicate operation—a spine transplant. You can draw any vector path, open or closed, and use it as the spine for an existing blend. To perform this surgery, select both the blend and the path you've created, and then choose Object > Blend > Replace Spine. Illustrator then uses the path you created as the spine for the blend, allowing you to customize how blend steps appear.

Reversing Blends

With a blend selected, you can choose Object > Blend > Reverse Spine to reverse the order of the key objects in your blend. This function is helpful when you want to flip the blend so that it travels in the opposite direction.

You can reverse the stacking order of the key objects in a blend by selecting the blend and choosing Object > Blend > Reverse Front to Back. This setting is especially useful for when you are using blends to create animations, which always travel in one direction. To have your animation play in reverse, you use this feature.

Releasing and Expanding Blends

As with Envelope distortions, you can select an existing blend and choose Object > Blend > Release, which removes the blend steps and returns the artwork to its original state (just the two original objects). In addition, you can choose Object > Blend > Expand, which applies the blend to the artwork itself, leaving the individual blend steps visible and available for editing. Once a blend has been expanded, it is no longer updated when the original two objects are edited.

There is yet another way to release a blend that is useful, especially when you're creating frames for animations either that will be exported directly from Illustrator as SWF (Flash) files or that will be imported into video software such as Adobe After Effects, Adobe Premiere Pro, or Apple Final Cut Pro. This method actually expands the blend into its individual steps and then places each step on its own layer. To release a blend in this way, you must follow these steps:

1.   If it isn't already open, choose Window > Layers to open your Layers panel.

2.   In the Layers panel, highlight the blend object you want to release by clicking it once (**Figure 2.48**).

Figure 2.48 *The Release to Layers command is a feature of the Layers panel, so selecting the blend on the artboard won't help. You have to highlight the blend in the Layers panel.*

3.   From the Layers panel menu (**Figure 2.49**), choose Release to Layers (Sequence), or choose Release to Layers (Build).

Figure 2.49 *Illustrator supports the ability to release artwork to layers using the Sequence or Build method.*

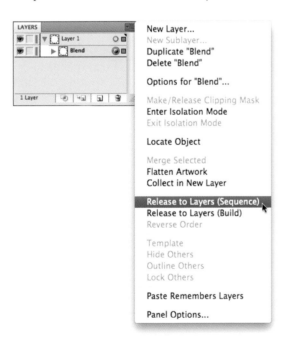

You should use the Sequence option when you want each layer to contain only one step, and you should use the Build option when you want to produce layers that add steps cumulatively to each layer that is created.

Technical Drawing

3

Some people seem to "get" the concept of vector drawing immediately. Terms such as *anchor points*, *control handles*, and *compound paths* all make perfect sense to these folks, and the Pen tool in Illustrator is a natural extension of their imagination and creativity. They spend as much time in Outline view as they do in Preview mode. These "people of the path," if you will, possess an analytical view, and they can visualize the vector "building blocks" that make up an overall graphic.

In this chapter, we'll focus on the paths and anchor points that make up a vector shape, and we'll get a grasp of all the tools you can use to create and modify these paths. The good news is that Illustrator has plenty of tools and functions that can help you create your masterpiece—or just a rectangle if that's what you need.

The artwork featured throughout this chapter comes from John Woodcock (iStockphoto; username: johnwoodcock).

Drawing Primitive Vector Shapes

Illustrator contains a healthy set of primitive vector drawing tools. In this case, *primitive* doesn't mean "something simple" as much as it means "acting as a basis from which something else is derived." Artists are taught to sketch using primitive shapes, such as rectangles and ovals, so that they can build structure; you can certainly apply similar techniques to drawing with vector shapes in Illustrator. Instead of trying to draw complex shapes, try to visualize how you can combine simple shapes in a variety of ways to create more complex ones (**Figure 3.1**).

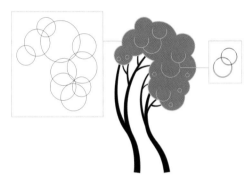

Figure 3.1 *Rather than draw complex elements from scratch, you can draw elements from a tree, for example, from basic circles. You can make the overall shape by adding multiple circles to each other (left), and you can create the detail by subtracting circles from each other (right).*

The primitive drawing tools in Illustrator are split up between those that create closed-path vector objects and those that create open-path vector objects. Additionally, these tools are interactive in that you can specify or control certain settings while drawing shapes. To take advantage of this functionality, you choose a tool and begin drawing. As you hold down the mouse button, you're able to make changes to the shape you're creating, but once you release the mouse button, you commit to the shape. Let's explore how this works.

NOTE Shape tools may not sound very exciting, but they are incredibly useful when combined with the Shape Builder tool. See "The Art of Building Artwork" in Chapter 2 for more details.

Using Closed-Path Shape Tools

The closed-path tools in Illustrator comprise the Rectangle, Rounded Rectangle, Ellipse, Polygon, and Star tools, and they are all grouped together in the Tools panel (**Figure 3.2**). To create any of these shapes, choose the desired tool, click the artboard, and drag outward. While dragging the pointer, you can add commands to adjust the shape interactively. See **Table 3.1** for a list of these interactive commands.

Figure 3.2 *The closed-path shape tools are all grouped with the Rectangle tool in the Tools panel.*

Table 3.1 *Drawing with Closed-Path Shape Tools*

Interactive Command	Rectangle Tool	Rounded Rectangle Tool	Ellipse Tool	Polygon Tool	Star Tool
Keyboard Shortcut	M	N/A	L	N/A	N/A
Shift	Constrains all sides to be equal, resulting in a perfect square.	Constrains all sides to be equal, resulting in a perfect square with rounded corners.	Constrains all arc segments to be equal, resulting in a perfect circle.	Constrains the bottom side to be parallel to the constrain angle.	Constrains the bottom two points to be parallel to the constrain angle.
Option (Alt)	Draws the shape out from its center point instead of its corner.	Draws the shape out from its center point instead of its corner.	Draws the shape out from its center point instead of its corner.	N/A	N/A
Command (Ctrl)	N/A	N/A	N/A	N/A	Adjusts the inner radius of the shape.
Spacebar	Allows you to reposition the shape on the artboard.	Allows you to reposition the shape on the artboard.	Allows you to reposition the shape on the artboard.	Allows you to reposition the shape on the artboard.	Allows you to reposition the shape on the artboard.
Tilde (~)	Creates multiple copies of the shape.	Creates multiple copies of the shape.	Creates multiple copies of the shape.	Creates multiple copies of the shape.	Creates multiple copies of the shape.
Up Arrow	N/A	Increases the corner radius value.	N/A	Increases the number of sides.	Increases the number of points.
Down Arrow	N/A	Decreases the corner radius value.	N/A	Decreases the number of sides.	Decreases the number of points.
Right Arrow	N/A	Turns on the rounded corners.	N/A	N/A	N/A
Left Arrow	N/A	Turns off the rounded corners.	N/A	N/A	N/A
Moving the Mouse	N/A	N/A	N/A	Moving the mouse in a circular motion rotates the shape.	Moving the mouse in a circular motion rotates the shape.

Using Open-Path Shape Tools

NOTE Even though they are grouped with the open-path tools, the Rectangular Grid and Polar Grid tools create a combination of both open and closed paths.

The open-path tools in Illustrator comprise the Line Segment, Arc, Spiral, Rectangular Grid, and Polar Grid tools, and they are all grouped together in the Tools panel (**Figure 3.3**). To create any of these shapes, choose the desired tool, click the artboard, and drag outward. While dragging the pointer, you can add commands to adjust the shape interactively. See **Table 3.2** for a list of these interactive commands.

Figure 3.3 *The open-path shape tools are all grouped with the Line tool in the Tools panel.*

Table 3.2 *Drawing with Open-Path Shape Tools*

Interactive Command	Line Segment Tool	Arc Tool	Spiral Tool	Rectangular Grid Tool	Polar Grid Tool
Keyboard Shortcut	\ (backslash)	N/A	N/A	N/A	N/A
Shift	Constrains the path to angles in 45-degree increments.	Constrains the X and Y axes, creating a perfect quarter circle.	Constrains the path to angles in 45-degree increments.	Constrains the grid to a perfect square.	Constrains the grid to a perfect circle.
Option (Alt)	N/A	Draws the arc out from its center point instead of its corner.	Increases the length of the path.	Draws the grid out from its center instead of its corner.	Draws the grid out from its center instead of its corner.
Command (Ctrl)	N/A	N/A	Adjusts the decay of the path (making the winds of the spiral more drastic).	N/A	N/A
Spacebar	Allows you to reposition the path on the artboard.	Allows you to reposition the path on the artboard.	Allows you to reposition the path on the artboard.	Allows you to reposition the path on the artboard.	Allows you to reposition the path on the artboard.
Tilde (~)	Creates multiple copies of the path.	Creates multiple copies of the path.	Creates multiple copies of the path.	Creates multiple copies of the path.	Creates multiple copies of the path.
Up Arrow	N/A	Increases the slope of the curve to make it more convex.	Increases the number of segments in the spiral.	Increases the number of rows in the grid.	Increases the number of concentric dividers.

Table 3.2 *Drawing with Open-Path Shape Tools (continued)*

Interactive Command	Line Segment Tool	Arc Tool	Spiral Tool	Rectangular Grid Tool	Polar Grid Tool
Down Arrow	N/A	Decreases the slope of the curve to make it more concave.	Decreases the number of segments in the spiral.	Decreases the number of rows in the grid.	Decreases the number of concentric dividers.
Right Arrow	N/A	N/A	N/A	Increases the number of columns in the grid.	Increases the number of radial dividers.
Left Arrow	N/A	N/A	N/A	Decreases the number of columns in the grid.	Decreases the number of radial dividers.
Moving the Mouse	N/A	N/A	Moving the mouse in a circular motion rotates the path.	N/A	N/A
C and X Keys	N/A	C draws the arc as a closed shape instead of an open path.	N/A	C skews the columns in the grid to the left; X skews the columns in the grid to the right.	C skews the concentric dividers toward the center; X skews away from the center.
F and V Keys	N/A	F flips the X and Y axes of the path.	N/A	F skews the rows in the grid to the top; V skews the rows in the grid to the bottom.	F skews the radial dividers toward the left; V skews them to the right.

Drawing by Numbers

If you're an aspiring artist, you can buy a paint-by-number kit that uses numbers to indicate where colors are supposed to go, taking the guesswork out of the design process. Although being free to create is certainly a good thing, you don't want to be guessing when you've been asked to create a shape that's an exact size. The methods of drawing we've discussed to this point are purely for those in a creative state of mind. As you create each shape, your mind is saying, "Yeah, that's about right." However, sometimes you are required to specify exact dimensions for shapes, and Illustrator can be precise up to four decimal places.

To create any shape numerically, select the tool you need, click the artboard once, and immediately release the mouse button. A dialog box appears, letting you specify exact values for the shape or path you want to create (**Figure 3.4**, on the next page). For most shapes, this action uses the point where you clicked the artboard as the upper-left corner of the shape. To draw a shape with its center point at the place you click, press the Option (Alt) key while clicking, and then drag.

Figure 3.4 *Clicking the artboard with a shape tool allows you to specify numeric values and create a shape precisely.*

In Chapter 2, "Selecting and Editing Artwork," we discussed how you can use the Control panel or the Transform panel to change an existing object's dimensions numerically as well.

Drawing and Editing Free-Form Vectors

Strip away the cool effects. Forget all the fancy tools. Ignore the endless range of gradients and colors. Look past the veneer of both print and web graphics. What you're left with is the basis of all things vector—the anchor point. You can learn to master every shape tool in Illustrator, but if you don't have the ability to create and edit individual anchor points, you'll find it difficult to design freely.

Illustrator contains a range of tools that you can use to fine-tune paths and edit anchor points. At first, it might seem like these all perform the same functions, but upon closer inspection, you'll find each has its use.

Mastering the Pen Tool

TIP When drawing new paths with the Pen tool, it's best to set your fill to None and your stroke to black. Otherwise, Illustrator will fill the path as you create it, making it difficult to see your work.

Just the mention of the Pen tool sends shivers down the spines of designers throughout the world. Traditionally, the Illustrator Pen tool has frustrated many users who have tried their hand at creating vector paths. In fact, when the Pen tool was introduced in the first version of Illustrator in 1987, word had it that John Warnock, the brain and developer behind Illustrator, was the only one who really knew how to use it. In truth, the Pen tool feels more like an engineer's tool than an artist's tool.

But don't let this prevent you from learning to use it.

Learning how to use the Pen tool reaps numerous rewards. Although the Pen tool first appeared in Illustrator, you'll find it in Photoshop, InDesign, Flash Professional, Fireworks, and even After Effects; if you know how to use it in Illustrator, you can use it in all the other applications as well. You can use the Pen tool to tweak any vector path to create the exact shape you need, at any time. Additionally, if you give yourself a chance, you'll see that there's a method to the madness. After learning a few simple concepts, you'll quickly realize that anyone can use the Pen tool.

Usually, when new users select the Pen tool and try to draw with it, they click and drag it the same way they might use a normal pen on paper. They are surprised when a path does not appear onscreen; instead, several handles appear. At this point, they click again and drag; now a path appears, but it is totally not where they expect it to appear. This experience is sort of like grabbing a hammer by its head and trying to drive a nail by whacking it with the handle—it's the right tool, but it's being used in the wrong way.

While we're discussing hammers, let's consider their function in producing string art. When you create a piece of string art, you first start with a piece of wood, and then you hammer nails part of the way into it, leaving each nail sticking out a bit. Then you take colored thread and wrap it around the exposed nail heads, thus creating your art. The design you create consists of the strands of colored thread, but the thread is held and shaped by the nails. In fact, you can say that the nails are like anchors for the threads.

When you're using the Pen tool in Illustrator, imagine you're hammering those little nails into the wood. In this situation, you aren't drawing the shape itself; instead, you're creating the anchors for the shape—the Bézier anchor points. Illustrator draws the thread—the path—for you. If you think about drawing in this way, using the Pen tool isn't complicated at all. The hard part is just figuring out where you need to position the anchors to get the shape you need. Learning to position the anchors correctly comes with experience, but you can get started by learning how to draw simple shapes (**Figure 3.5**).

TIP Holding the Shift key while you click with the Pen tool constrains paths to 45-degree increments. Additionally, you can choose View > Smart Guides to have Illustrator display helpful guides and hints as you move the pointer (see Chapter 1, "Creating and Managing Documents," for more information about smart guides).

Figure 3.5 *Even though it may appear complex at first glance, this skyline is made up of of straight paths, curved paths, and combination paths—which consist of both straight lines and curves.*

Anatomy of a Vector Object

To truly comprehend how vectors work, you need a solid understanding of the terminology. Otherwise, the words are meaningless and don't make sense when you try to apply techniques that use these terms. Overall, when working in Illustrator, there are two parts of an object that you're concerned with. The vector *path* defines the object in a mathematical way using anchor points. This path doesn't print. The *appearance* of a path determines how it will look when printed and is defined with attributes such as fills and strokes (**Figure 3.6**).

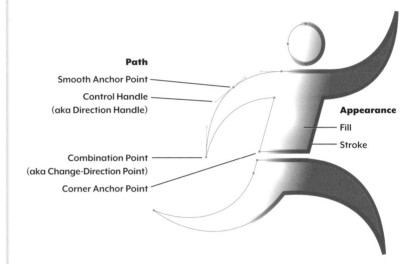

Path
Smooth Anchor Point
Control Handle
(aka Direction Handle)
Combination Point
(aka Change-Direction Point)
Corner Anchor Point
Appearance
Fill
Stroke

Figure 3.6 *Vector graphics are composed of paths and appearances.*

Drawing Objects with Straight Paths

Follow these steps to use the Pen tool to draw a straight path:

1. Select the Pen tool, and click the artboard once—do not click and drag.

   Clicking once with the Pen tool creates a *corner anchor point*. This anchor point is the start point of your path.

2. Now, move your pointer to where you want the end point of your path (**Figure 3.7**); click again to define a second corner anchor point.

Figure 3.7 *After you've clicked once to create the first anchor point, move your pointer to the location where you want the second anchor point.*

■

Once you create this second point, Illustrator automatically connects the two anchor points with a straight path, completing the line (**Figure 3.8**).

Figure 3.8 *Clicking a second time creates the path between the two anchor points.*

For now, the *first concept* becomes clear: When you're using the Pen tool, clicking—not dragging—is what defines a corner anchor point.

At this point, with your Pen tool still selected, Illustrator assumes you want to add points to your path. By clicking again, you can create a third corner anchor point, and if you do, Illustrator draws a path to connect the second anchor point to the newly created one (**Figure 3.9**).

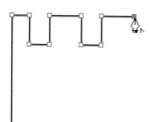

Figure 3.9 *Each successive click with the Pen tool continues to create additional path segments.*

Admittedly, this behavior may prove confusing because you may have been expecting to start a new path rather than add to the existing one. To start a new path, you first have to deselect the current path.

Ending a Path

The easiest way to end a path is to click a blank area on the artboard while pressing the Command (Ctrl) key, which temporarily changes your tool to the Selection tool. Once you've deselected the path and released the Command (Ctrl) key, you can click with the Pen tool to start drawing a new path.

So, now you understand the *second concept*: When drawing an open path with the Pen tool, each click adds another anchor point to the path until you deselect the path, which is how you indicate to Illustrator you've finished that path.

Drawing a Closed Path

You can indicate that you've finished drawing a path in another way—by drawing a closed path. Until now, you've been creating open paths, but now you can try to create a closed shape—in this case, a triangle, such as one that might indicate the roof of a building:

1. With nothing selected, select the Pen tool, and click once to define the first anchor point of the triangle.

2. Move the pointer to another part of the artboard, and click again to define the second point.

3. Now move the pointer once more, and click to define a third anchor point (**Figure 3.10**).

   A triangle has three sides, so you have all the anchor points you need, but at the moment, the object you've drawn is an open path.

4. To complete the shape, move the pointer so it rests directly on the first anchor point that you defined, and click once to close the path (**Figure 3.11**).

   At this point, if you click again elsewhere on the artboard, the Pen tool starts drawing a new path.

This brings you to the *third concept*: When you've created a closed path, the next click with the Pen tool starts a new path.

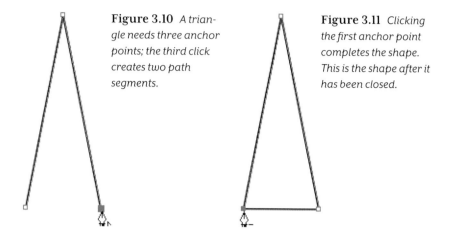

Figure 3.10 *A triangle needs three anchor points; the third click creates two path segments.*

Figure 3.11 *Clicking the first anchor point completes the shape. This is the shape after it has been closed.*

If this sounds confusing, try it once or twice, which should help—especially if you pay attention to your Pen tool pointer. When you're using the Pen tool, the pointer changes as you draw, helping you understand the three concepts you've just learned. When the Pen tool is going to start creating a new path, a small *x* appears at the lower right of the icon; when the Pen tool is going to add anchor points to an existing selected open path, no icon appears next to it; and when the Pen tool is going to close a path, a small *o* appears at the lower right of the icon (**Figure 3.12**).

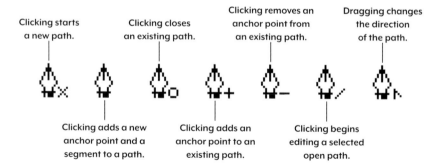

Clicking starts a new path.

Clicking closes an existing path.

Clicking removes an anchor point from an existing path.

Dragging changes the direction of the path.

Clicking adds a new anchor point and a segment to a path.

Clicking adds an anchor point to an existing path.

Clicking begins editing a selected open path.

Figure 3.12 *The Pen tool subtly indicates which function it will perform.*

Drawing Objects with Curved Paths

The paths you've drawn up until this point were all made up of corner anchor points, which are connected with straight lines. Of course, you'll also need to create paths with curved lines, like those used to define the trees that appear in the skyline artwork; this section explains what you need to know.

NOTE By now, you understand the statement we made earlier about how drawing the path is the easy part of using the Pen tool. The hard part is trying to figure out where to place the anchor points to get the path you want.

Curves are defined with *direction handles* that control how the paths between anchor points are drawn. When you want to draw a curved path, you follow the same basic concepts you learned for creating straight paths, with one additional step that defines the direction handles.

1. To draw a curved path, select the Pen tool, and make sure an existing path isn't selected. Position your pointer where you want to begin your path, and then click and drag outward before releasing the mouse button (**Figure 3.13**).

Figure 3.13 *Clicking and dragging with the Pen tool defines the smooth anchor point and, at the same time, lets you position the direction handles.*

This action creates a *smooth anchor point* where you first clicked and defines direction handles at the point where you released the mouse.

2. Now position your pointer where you want the next anchor point to be, and click and drag once again (**Figure 3.14**).

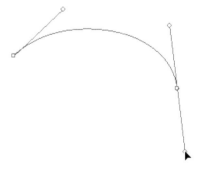

Figure 3.14 *Clicking and dragging a second time completes a curved path segment between the first two anchor points and defines the next curve that will be drawn.*

Using the direction handles as guidance, Illustrator draws a curved path connecting the two smooth anchor points.

3. Move your pointer to another location on your artboard, and click and drag to create a third smooth anchor point.

4. Click and drag the first anchor point to close the path (**Figure 3.15**).

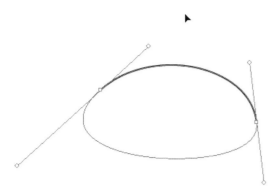

Figure 3.15 *Clicking and dragging the first anchor point completes the curved shape.*

We can now define a *fourth concept*: Clicking and dragging with the Pen tool creates a smooth anchor point and defines its direction handles.

Learning to anticipate how the placement of direction handles creates the path you want takes time, but you don't have to get it right the first time. Once you create a smooth anchor point, you can switch to the Direct Selection tool and click and drag the anchor point to reposition it (**Figure 3.16**). Additionally, when you select a smooth anchor point at any time, the direction handles become visible for that anchor point, and you can use the Direct Selection tool to reposition those as well.

> **TIP** Even the most experienced Illustrator artists need to switch to the Direct Selection tool to tweak the curves they create, which can be time-consuming. To get around this, you can press the Command (Ctrl) key while the Pen tool is active to temporarily access the last-used selection tool. While the Selection tool is active, click and drag the anchor points or direction handles to adjust the path, and then release the key to continue creating more points with the Pen tool.

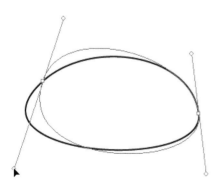

Figure 3.16 *Using the Direct Selection tool, you can change the position of anchor points and direction handles to adjust a curved path.*

Drawing Objects with Both Straight and Curved Paths

In the real-design world, shapes consist of both straight and curved lines. You can use the knowledge you've gained up to this point to create paths that contain a mixture of both corner and smooth anchor points. Basically, you know that clicking with the Pen tool produces a corner anchor point and a straight line, and you know that dragging with the Pen tool produces a smooth anchor point and a curved line.

Try drawing a path with both types of anchor points:

1. Select the Pen tool, and make sure you don't have an existing path selected (look for the small *x* icon on the Pen tool pointer). Click once to create a corner anchor point.

2. Move your pointer, and click again to create a straight line (**Figure 3.17**).

Figure 3.17 *You can begin a new path by creating two corner anchor points to make a straight line.*

3. Move your pointer, and click and drag to create a smooth anchor point.

   You now have a single path that consists of both a straight line and a curve (**Figure 3.18**).

Figure 3.18 *Adding a smooth anchor point creates a single path with both straight and curved path segments.*

You can use the Convert Anchor Point tool to convert a corner anchor point to a smooth anchor point, and vice versa. To do so, choose the Convert Anchor Point tool (which is grouped with the Pen tool), and apply the same concepts you've learned. Click an existing anchor point once to convert it to a corner anchor point, and then click and drag an existing anchor point to pull out direction handles and convert it to a smooth anchor point.

Changing Direction on a Path

As you were creating smooth anchor points, you may have noticed that when you are creating or editing direction handles, a mirror effect occurs. On a smooth anchor point, the direction points are always opposite each other, and editing one seems to affect the other. Remember that the direction handles control how the path passes through the anchor point, so the direction handles are always tangential to the curve (**Figure 3.19**).

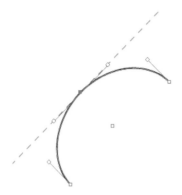

Figure 3.19 *With a smooth anchor point, the direction handles are always tangential to the curve of the path.*

Creating a Combination Point

You can, however, change the direction of a path as it passes through an anchor point:

1. Use the Direct Selection tool to select a smooth anchor point.

2. Switch to the Convert Anchor Point tool, and click and drag one of the *direction handles* (not the anchor point).

    In essence, this creates a combination point that you can then continue to edit with the Direct Selection tool (**Figure 3.20**).

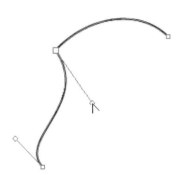

Figure 3.20 *Clicking and dragging a direction handle with the Convert Anchor Point tool creates a combination anchor point.*

Creating a Combination Point as You Draw

To make life easier, you can create combination points as you draw with the Pen tool:

1. Start by clicking and dragging to create a smooth anchor point.

2. Move your pointer to a different position, and click and drag again to create another smooth anchor point and, hence, a curved path.

3. Now, position your pointer directly on the second anchor point you just created. You'll notice that the Pen tool icon shows a small inverted v in its icon.

4. Click and drag the anchor point while holding the Option (Alt) key to drag out a single direction handle (**Figure 3.21**).

Figure 3.21 *As you're drawing a path with the Pen tool, you can create a combination point by clicking and dragging the last anchor point of the path while holding the Option (Alt) key.*

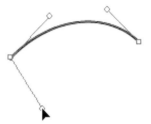

5. Move your pointer to another location, and click again; you'll see that you've created a combination point.

Converting Type to Outlines

Overall, using the Pen tool takes some getting used to, and if you're going to use Illustrator often, it's best to practice. One of the best ways to learn is to reverse-engineer artwork that has already been created. You might find it useful to convert some type to outlines (select a type object and choose Type > Create Outlines) to see how the anchor points are positioned in those shapes. Try to re-create them on your own, and get a feel for when you need a corner anchor point and when you need a smooth anchor point. The more you use the Pen tool, the easier it will be to use.

Adding and Deleting Anchor Points

Because anchor points are used to define paths, you must add and delete points from a path to achieve the shapes you need. You may think you can select an anchor point with the Direct Selection tool and simply press the Delete key on your keyboard, but doing this deletes a portion of the path (**Figure 3.22**). Although this may be useful at times, what you really want is to keep the path but remove the anchor point.

Figure 3.22 *Using the Direct Selection tool to select and delete an anchor point (left) also deletes the connecting path segments (center). The Delete Anchor Point tool keeps the path closed but removes the anchor point (right).*

To delete an anchor point from a path without deleting the path, select the Delete Anchor Point tool, and click the anchor point once that you want to remove. Likewise, you can switch to the Add Anchor Point tool and click a selected path anywhere to add a new anchor point to the path (**Figure 3.23**). As an alternative, you can click the Remove Selected Anchor Points button in the Control panel. Note that this button will not appear when *all* anchor points of a path are selected.

Figure 3.23 *The Add Anchor Point tool enables you to add new anchor points to an existing path.*

Illustrator tries its best to help you get your work done, but sometimes its over-zealousness gets in the way. By default, when you move your pointer over an existing path with the Pen tool, Illustrator, thinking you want to add a point to the existing path, conveniently switches to the Add Anchor Point tool. Likewise, when you move your pointer over an existing anchor point, Illustrator switches to the Delete Anchor Point tool, thinking you want to remove that anchor point. This is great, unless you wanted to start drawing a new path with the Pen tool on top of an existing selected path. You can turn this feature off by selecting the Disable Auto Add/Delete option in the General panel in Preferences, which politely tells Illustrator, "Thanks, but no thanks."

Using the Reshape Tool

Using the Direct Selection tool to select individual points on a path results in some anchor points moving while others remain stationary. In most kinds of path editing, this is the desired behavior, although it can result in paths that appear distorted. At times, you may want to stretch a path by moving selected points, but you may also want other points to move as necessary to maintain a nondistorted path appearance. The Reshape tool (**Figure 3.24**) is perfect for this task.

Figure 3.24 *The Reshape tool is grouped with the Scale tool in the Tools panel.*

1. Select a path using the Selection tool, and then select the Reshape tool.

2. Click an anchor point or part of a path that you want to act as a focus point when you stretch the path. This way, you'll have the most control over how this focused point is moved.

    You can also hold the Shift key and select additional focus points (as well as drag to marquee-select additional anchor points).

3. Once you've selected your focus points, click and drag one of the focus points to reshape the path.

    You'll notice that as the points that are in focus move, other points in the path move as well to keep the general proportion of the path (**Figure 3.25**).

Figure 3.25 *When some anchor points on a path are selected (left), dragging with the Direct Selection tool moves all the anchor points as a single unit (center). With the Reshape tool, the selected anchor points move in a proportionate manner (right).*

The Reshape tool also comes in handy when you want to quickly turn a straight path segment into a curved one. To do so, select the Reshape tool, and click and drag any straight line segment (**Figure 3.26**).

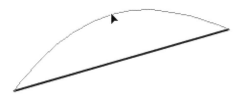

Figure 3.26 *The Reshape tool lets you "pull out" a curve from a straight line segment.*

NOTE You can also use the Reshape tool across multiple selected paths.

Cutting Paths with the Scissors and Knife Tools

When editing paths, you might find you need to cut or split a path at a certain point. With the Scissors tool selected, you can click any topmost vector path (selected or not) to cut the path. In essence, you create two anchor points by doing this. The Scissors tool can cut only one path at a time.

The Knife tool is much like the Scissors tool, but you cut or split a path by dragging the pointer across a path instead of clicking it. Whereas using the Scissors tool results in an open path, using the Knife tool results in at least two closed paths. The Knife tool cuts through multiple paths when nothing is selected but cuts through only objects that are selected (even if those selected objects appear beneath other objects).

Using the Scissors or Knife tool is unwieldy at best, and you may find that if you're doing a lot of path editing, you'll get better results by using the Shape Builder tool, the Pathfinder functions, or the Live Paint feature (Live Paint is covered in Chapter 4, "Creative Drawing.")

TIP If you find you need to cut through multiple paths at once, you should look into Rick Johnson's Hatchet tool that is part of his Cutting Tools plug-in (http://rj-graffix.com/software/plugins.html).

TIP Holding the Option (Alt) key while dragging with the Knife tool constrains the tool so that it draws straight lines only.

Creating Compound Paths

A *compound path* is a single path that consists of more than one path. That sounds like an oxymoron, no? Think of the letter *o* in the alphabet. It appears to be a large circle with a smaller circle cut out from its center. How is such a shape created with Illustrator? The answer is by drawing two circles and combining them to become a single compound path. You do this by choosing Object > Compound Path > Create. The result is a shape with a hole cut out of the middle (**Figure 3.27**, on the next page). Compound paths are treated as one entity, and therefore, both paths that make up this compound path take on the attributes of the bottommost path. If your compound path consists of multiple shapes, Illustrator does its best to figure out which paths become hollow and which appear solid.

Figure 3.27 *An example of a compound path. The outer shape of the eye allows objects that appear behind it (the yellow rays) to be visible.*

Compound Path

NOTE When a path reverses direction in a shape such as in a figure eight, it can never be all clockwise or counterclockwise. In such a case, the direction of the region(s) with the largest total area is what defines the result.

Illustrator uses one of two methods to decide which paths of a compound shape are hollow and which are solid. The default method is the Non-Zero Winding Fill Rule method; Illustrator can also use another method, the Even-Odd Fill Rule method. You'll find both of these buttons in the Attributes panel, and you can click them when a compound path is selected on the artboard. By default, Illustrator uses Non-Zero Winding Fill Rule and makes the bottommost path clockwise and all the other selected paths counterclockwise. For a detailed explanation of these rules, refer to the sidebar "How Fill Rules Work."

When you create a compound path and click Non-Zero Winding Fill Rule, you can manually reverse the path direction to control whether a shape is hollow or solid. Use the Direct Selection tool to select the path you need, and click the appropriate button in the Attributes panel (**Figure 3.28**).

Figure 3.28 *When using the Non-Zero Winding Fill Rule method for a compound path, you can also click Reverse Path Direction On or Reverse Path Direction Off to control which parts of a shape are solid or hollow.*

Reverse Path Direction On
Reverse Path Direction Off
Non-Zero Winding Fill Rule
Even-Odd Fill Rule

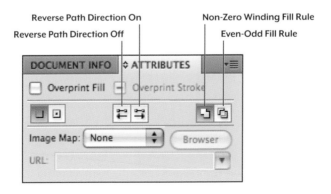

How Fill Rules Work

More math! When you compare them to each other, Even-Odd Fill Rule seems more intuitive than the Non-Zero Winding Fill Rule, and it is easier to predict which areas will be filled and which areas will be hollow. Although you have more flexibility with Non-Zero Winding Fill Rule—because you can manually control the result—this rule is more difficult to understand, and the result is harder to predict.

With Even-Odd Fill Rule, every area inside an even number of enclosed areas becomes hollow, and every region inside an odd number of enclosed areas becomes solid (**Figure 3.29**). An *enclosed* area refers to an area enclosed by another path (or the loop of a path in a self-intersecting shape). The outermost enclosed area is always 1, and therefore a regular path is filled (it is enclosed by a single area, which is an odd number).

 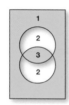

Figure 3.29 *When using the Even-Odd Fill Rule method, Illustrator labels areas using odd and even numbers to determine hollow and solid areas.*

In contrast, the Non-Zero Winding Fill Rule method takes into account the direction of a path: An area enclosed by a clockwise loop counts as +1, and an area enclosed by a counterclockwise loop counts as –1. When the sum of these counts is zero, that area becomes hollow. When it is anything else, that area becomes solid (**Figure 3.30**). Because you can manipulate the path direction to get different results from the same shapes, Non-Zero Winding Fill Rule is more flexible, but it's an exercise of trial and error since you can't see the direction of a path on the artboard.

 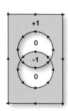

Figure 3.30 *When using Non-Zero Winding Fill Rule, Illustrator takes into account the direction of the path when it determines the hollow and solid areas of a compound path. The arrows indicate path direction.*

Although the results in most cases are the same whether you use the Non-Zero Winding Fill Rule or Even-Odd Fill Rule setting, sometimes the result is different (**Figure 3.31**).

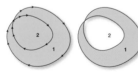 

Figure 3.31 *Some compound paths appear different, depending on the fill rule specified, especially with self-intersecting paths.*

—*Special thanks to Teri Pettit of the Adobe Illustrator team for helping explain these rules.*

Performing Advanced Path Editing

Editing paths by hand can be tedious, but it doesn't always have to be. Many times, you'll need to perform certain edits on vector paths, such as removing extra anchor points from a complex path or splitting larger shapes into smaller ones of equal size. Other times, you may need to create outlines of strokes, create duplicate paths at larger or smaller sizes, or simply clean up loose paths and objects in your file. The good news is that Illustrator has a variety of useful path functions you can use to perform these kinds of tasks.

You can find the functions covered here in the Object > Path menu.

Working with the Join and Average Commands

NOTE With Illustrator CS5, it is now possible to join more than two anchor points at once. Previous versions required that only two anchor points be selected before using the Join command.

If you have separate paths and want to connect their anchor points to create a single continuous path, you can use Illustrator's Join command. Either select the two anchor points you want to join together, or select the paths themselves, and then choose Object > Path > Join. The Join command won't work if you're trying to join paths from different groups or paths that are within a graph object, however.

NOTE Older versions of Illustrator allow you to use the Average command to easily align point text objects. Unfortunately, that functionality is no longer available in Illustrator.

In addition, the Average function (Object > Path > Average) allows you to select at least two anchor points and reposition them by evenly dividing the space between them. You can average anchor points horizontally, vertically, or both horizontally and vertically. There is no limit to how many anchor points you can average at once.

You can also select two anchor points and press Command-Option-Shift-J (Ctrl-Alt-Shift-J) to perform a combined Average and Join function in one step (**Figure 3.32**).

Figure 3.32 *If anchor points are not overlapping each other, you can choose to average their position and join them.*

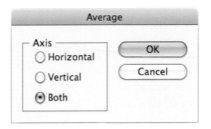

Using the Outline Stroke Command

The stroke of a path adds thickness to the appearance of the path, but it's an attribute you can't physically select and manipulate on the artboard. However, you can select a path with a stroke and choose Object > Path > Outline Stroke; when you do, the stroke of that path expands to become a filled shape that you can then edit with the Pen tool. This allows you to tweak the path to make it appear as if the "stroke" is thinner and thicker in different places.

Sometimes you might want to convert a stroke to an outline for production reasons. If you have a final version of a logo, converting all strokes to filled paths assures that it will scale properly under all circumstances, because users may forget to turn on the Scale Strokes & Effects setting.

Similar to what happens with patterns, when you apply transformations to objects that have strokes or effects applied, the default behavior is that only the shape is transformed, not the strokes or the effects. Selecting the Scale Strokes & Effects option in the General panel of Preferences changes the default behavior so that strokes and effects are transformed as well. You can also find this setting in the Scale Options dialog box.

Exploring the Offset Path Function

One of the most useful path functions in Illustrator is Offset Path. This function creates a new vector path that is offset a user-specified amount from the selected object(s). The original selected path is not affected. If you think about it, it's like a scaling function—you can offset paths to be larger or smaller. But if you've ever tried to scale objects that aren't a perfect circle or a square, you'll know that doing so creates a shape of a different proportion. If you want to create an object that is the same but that has its edges enlarged evenly across the entire object, choose Object > Path > Offset Path (**Figure 3.33**).

TIP You can use Offset Path with negative values as well, which allows you to create paths that are offset inside existing paths.

Figure 3.33 *Scaling an object (left) just makes a shape larger in size, but using Offset Path (right) gives a different result. The gray area indicates the result of the function in each case.*

Offset Path always creates a new closed path, so when the function is applied to an open path, a new closed path appears. If your intention is to have just an offset path along one side of your path, you'll have to manually delete the parts of the new offset path as needed (**Figure 3.34**).

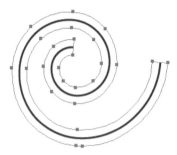

Figure 3.34 *When applied to an open path, the Offset Path command creates a new closed path.*

Simplifying Vector Paths

Earlier in this chapter, you learned how to use the Remove Anchor Point tool to delete existing anchor points from a path. Although that tool is useful for removing a point or two from a path here or there, it's quite another story when you're trying to remove a lot of anchor points from a path.

You may find that some vector paths contain unnecessary anchor points. By *unnecessary*, we mean you might be able to create the same path with fewer anchor points. Too many unnecessary anchor points on a path translates into more complex files that take longer to print and that are more difficult to edit.

You'll often come across this problem when you're importing files from CAD or 3D applications, or when you're using vector tracing programs such as Adobe Streamline (the Live Trace feature in Illustrator, covered in Chapter 10, "Working with Images," does not suffer nearly as much from this problem).

To reduce the number of anchor points on a path, select the path, and choose Object > Path > Simplify. You can use the Preview option to see the results as you change the settings. The Simplify dialog box also gives you real-time feedback on the number of anchor points on the original path and the number of points using the current Simplify settings (**Figure 3.35**).

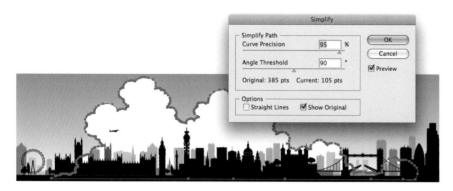

Figure 3.35 *When using the Simplify function, you can see real-time feedback on the number of reduced anchor points and the integrity of the shape of the path.*

The Simplify dialog box offers the following settings:

- **Curve Precision.** This controls how closely the simplified path matches the curves of the original selected path. A higher Curve Precision setting results in a path that more closely matches the original but that has fewer anchor points.

- **Angle Threshold.** The Angle Threshold setting determines the smoothness of corners. If the angle of a corner point is less than the Angle Threshold setting, the corner point is not changed to a smooth anchor point.

- **Straight Lines.** This setting forces the simplified path to use only corner anchor points, resulting in a path that is far less complex. Of course, the path may not match the original that well, but this option may be useful in a creative mind-set.

- **Show Original.** With the Show Original option selected, Illustrator displays both the original path and the simplified result, allowing you to preview the difference between the two.

Using the Split Into Grid Feature

The Rectangular Grid tool is great for creating quick grids for illustration purposes, but with it you lack fine control, especially if you want to create gutters—space that appears between columns and rows. The Split Into Grid feature in Illustrator takes an existing shape and splits it into a specified number of equal-sized rectangles.

TIP The Split Into Grid feature is wonderful for creating layout grids and for creating columns you might use to create tables.

With any vector object selected, choose Object > Path > Split Into Grid to open the dialog box. Select the Preview check box so you can see the results as you enter the values. Add rows and columns as needed, and also specify a value for the gutter. Illustrator automatically calculates the width and height values for you as you change the other values. At the bottom of the dialog box is an Add Guides check box, which draws guides at the borders of the rows and the columns.

Removing Unnecessary Elements with the Clean Up Feature

While working on revision after revision of a file, your document may become littered with stray anchor points, empty text objects, or unpainted objects (those that have neither a fill nor a stroke applied). Having these objects present in a file can be problematic for a variety of reasons. Empty text objects may contain references to fonts, and you, thinking that those fonts aren't there, may forget to include them when you send your source files to prepress. Additionally, stray points in a file can cause files to export with unexpected size boundaries and could lead to corrupted files.

Choose Object > Path > Clean Up, and select which of these elements you want to automatically remove from a file. Be aware that, to Illustrator, a stray point is a single anchor point with no path. Some designers use the Paint-brush tool to click just once to place a single instance of a brush. Running the Clean Up command to delete stray points deletes these brush objects from a file as well. In reality, it's better to use symbols rather than brushes for these types of tasks, something we'll discuss in Chapter 9, "Drawing with Efficiency."

Drawing in Perspective

Sometimes an illustration needs to be drawn in perspective. In these cases, the artwork is distorted to appear as if it is fading into the distance; some parts appear closer and other parts further away. Traditionally, artists would accomplish this by first defining vanishing points and then drawing a series of guides that they could use to help them create their artwork. But with the Perspective Grid feature in Illustrator, drawing artwork in perspective is less of a hassle (**Figure 3.36**).

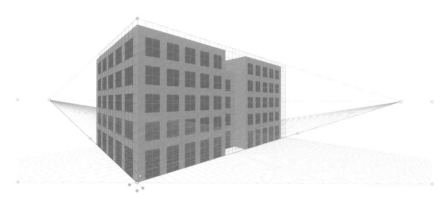

Figure 3.36 *With the perspective grid feature in Illustrator, you can quickly create art that appears to vanish into the distance.*

Before learning how to use the Perspective Grid, it's important to keep a few basic points in mind:

- **This isn't 3D.** The perspective grid helps you create two-dimensional flat art that automatically distorts towards vanishing points. However, the feature isn't real 3D—you can't expect to rotate artwork to view it from various angles. The artwork appears at the angle and perspective in which you draw it.

- **One document, one grid.** While Illustrator can support multiple artboards within a single document, you can specify only one perspective grid per document. If you need to create artwork at different perspective angles or views, you'll need to create a separate document for each piece of artwork.

- **One, two, or three points.** You can define grids in one-, two-, or three-point perspective. In other words, perspective grids can feature one, two, or three vanishing points.

- **There are some limits.** Perspective grids make it easy to distort artwork, but there are some kinds of artwork or types of attributes that won't work with the Perspective Grid feature, including strokes, patterns, graphs, and raster images.

- **Get it right the first time.** You can modify a perspective grid at any time, but artwork won't update to match the newer grid settings. It's always best to take the time to get your grid set up correctly from the beginning, ensuring you won't have to redo your artwork.

- **Use Smart Guides.** When using the Perspective Grid feature in Illustrator, it is best to turn Smart Guides on. Hints and values will appear as you move your cursor across the grid, helping you to easily align artwork in perspective.

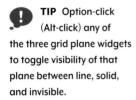

TIP Option-click (Alt-click) any of the three grid plane widgets to toggle visibility of that plane between line, solid, and invisible.

Defining a Perspective Grid

The first step to drawing in perspective in Illustrator is to set up your grid so that your artwork will snap correctly to the angles you specify. You can activate the perspective grid simply by choosing the Perspective Grid tool in the Tools panel (**Figure 3.37**). By default, Illustrator displays a two-point perspective grid in the center of your document.

Figure 3.37 *The Perspective Grid tool allows you to activate and modify the perspective grid in your document.*

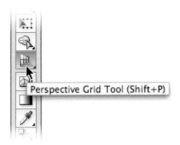

With the Perspective Grid tool active, widgets appear in various places on the perspective grid (**Figure 3.38**), and you can begin to adjust the grid to your liking:

Figure 3.38 *With the Perspective Grid tool active, a variety of widgets appear directly on the perspective grid, enabling you to adjust the grid settings.*

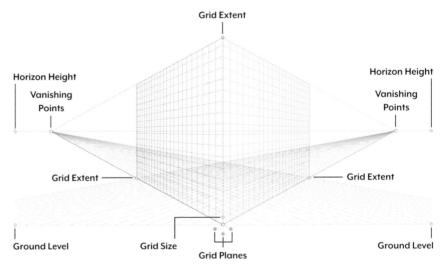

- **Grid Planes.** In the case of a two-point perspective grid, there are three grid planes: Left, Horizontal (sometimes referred to as the floor, or ground), and Right. The left and right grid plane widgets can be moved left and right, while the horizontal grid plane widget can be moved up and down.

- **Vanishing Points.** A two-point perspective grid contains two vanishing points, which are the points at which the lines in the grid are no longer visible. These points meet the horizon line.

- **Grid Extent.** The hollow diamond-shaped Grid Extent widgets control how much of the perspective grid is visible on each grid plane. If the lines of the grid would be too close together (such as those that are closer to the vanishing point), Illustrator hides them (though they reappear at higher zoom levels).

- **Grid Size.** The Grid Size widget simply controls the number of parallel grid lines that are drawn on the grid. While this has no effect on the kind of art you can create in perspective, more guides mean you have more places to snap art to.

- **Horizon Height.** The Horizon Height is sometimes also referred to as the horizon level, or the eye level. It defines the point at which art is no longer visible.

- **Ground Level.** The Ground Level defines the point that the perspective grid rests on. If you position the horizon height line below the ground level line, you'd appear to be looking down at your artwork. If you position the horizon line above the ground level line, you would see your artwork as though you were standing in front of it, looking upward.

Modifying Grid Settings

While you can use the widgets on the perspective grid to modify its settings, you can also make certain adjustments numerically for more precise control. Since the perspective grid is akin to guides or grids in Illustrator, you'll find many of the perspective grid settings listed in the View menu.

You can toggle the visibility of the perspective grid by choosing View > Perspective Grid > Hide Grid or Show Grid, or use the keyboard shortcut Command-Shift-I (Ctrl-Shift-I). In the same submenu, you can also choose to lock the entire grid, or to lock just the station point, which is the point where

TIP If you're trying to match a specific perspective angle, say from a photograph, you can place the photo in Illustrator and then adjust the perspective grid to match the image.

the grid planes meet each other. You'll notice that when the station point is locked, moving one vanishing point moves them all, allowing to you easily adjust the viewing angle of the grid.

Choosing View > Perspective Grid > Define Grid brings up the Define Perspective Grid dialog box, where you can make precise adjustments to your perspective grid (**Figure 3.39**). You can also adjust the appearance of the grid, including settings its opacity. A lower opacity setting will make it easier to see your artwork as you draw.

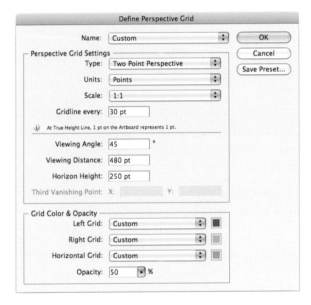

Figure 3.39 *The Define Perspective Grid dialog box gives you the ability to adjust the opacity of the grid, and to save presets.*

You can also save your grid settings as a Grid Preset, which you can then easily apply from within other documents.

Understanding Perspective Planes

Before you start drawing artwork in perspective, there are three important points to keep in mind. Understanding these concepts now will help you as you start to use the perspective grid feature.

On the artboard, the perspective grid helps you visually position the various grid planes. However, you don't need to draw artwork on the visual grid itself. In fact, once you've defined a perspective grid, your *entire document* is now in perspective. This concept will make more sense once you understand the next concept—that of active planes.

A two-point perspective grid contains three different grid planes (right, horizontal, and left). At any one time, however, only one of those three grid planes can be active—so it's not much different than the multiple artboards feature. In other words, when the right grid plane is active, all artwork that you create, *anywhere in your document*, will snap to the right grid plane. This can be confusing as you start working with perspective grids, because you can easily forget which grid plane is active at any one time. This leads us to the third concept: the Active Plane widget.

When the perspective grid is visible in your document, you'll notice a teardrop-shaped icon in the upper left corner of your document window (**Figure 3.40**). This icon is the *active plane widget,* and it performs two basic functions: It lets you know which grid plane is currently active, and it lets you change the active plane. While the active plane widget is visible when the perspective grid is visible, you can interact with the widget only when the Perspective Grid tool, the Perspective Selection tool, or any of the supported drawing tools (listed in the following section) is active.

Figure 3.40 *The colors in the active plane widget match the colors of the individual grid planes on the perspective grid that's on the artboard.*

Now that you understand these concepts, you're ready to start drawing in perspective.

Drawing and Editing Artwork in Perspective

Once you've defined a perspective grid in your document, you've got choices. There are two methods that you can use to create artwork in perspective:

- **Draw new art directly onto the perspective grid.** This option is available only for the following drawing tools: Rectangle, Rounded Rectangle, Ellipse, Polygon, Star, Line Segment, Arc, Spiral, Rectangular Grid, and Polar Grid.

- **Attach existing art onto the perspective grid.** To create artwork in perspective with other creation tools—including the Text, Pen, or Paintbrush tools—or to add perspective to any other kind of artwork (with the exception of images or gradient mesh objects, which are not supported), you must create the artwork off the perspective grid. You can then attach it to one of the grid planes with the help of the Perspective Selection tool.

NOTE You can choose to have the active plane widget appear in any of the four corners of your document window by double-clicking the Perspective Grid tool in the Tools panel.

TIP Once you've added artwork to the perspective grid, you can use the Perspective Selection tool to apply transformations to artwork (move, copy, etc.) while still keeping the art locked to the perspective grid.

Drawing New Art Directly onto the Perspective Grid

As we discussed earlier, even though you have multiple grid planes in your document, only one can be active at any one time. So before you start drawing, you have to choose which grid plane you want your art to snap to. To make this choice, you will use the active plane widget:

1. Select the Rectangle tool.

2. Click one of the sides of the cube in the active plane widget to choose the active grid plane.

3. Click and drag on the artboard to create a rectangle. As you drag, the rectangle will automatically snap to the proper perspective.

To draw a rectangle on a different grid plane, use the active plane widget to choose a different plane, and then draw a new rectangle. If you want to draw a new shape that is not in perspective, click in the circle that appears just outside the cube in the active plane widget. This sets the active plane to No Active Grid, allowing you to draw nondistorted artwork (**Figure 3.41**).

Figure 3.41 *Setting the active plane widget to No Active Grid will allow you to create artwork that does not snap into perspective as you draw it.*

In reality, having to constantly use the active plane widget to change the active plane is tedious. The good news is that you can use a few simple keyboard shortcuts to manage the process far more efficiently.

Along the top left of your keyboard, the numbers 1-4 help you choose an active plane in your document:

*   1 = Makes left grid plane active

*   2 = Makes horizontal grid plane active

*   3 = Makes right grid plane active

*   4 = Deactivates the grid plane so that you can draw nondistorted shapes

Using the keyboard shortcuts, you'll find that drawing in perspective is faster and more intuitive:

1. Select the Rectangle tool.

2. Press the 1, 2, 3, or 4 key to choose the active grid plane.

TIP Learning the keyboard shortcuts for the active plane widget is really important because it not only makes drawing in perspective easier, but it also allows you to perform advanced techniques such as moving artwork from one grid and attaching it to another.

3. Click and drag on the artboard to create a rectangle. As you are dragging with the rectangle tool, you can decide to switch grid planes by pressing the 1-4 keys on your keyboard.

Now that you know how to draw artwork directly onto the perspective grid, let's take a look at how you can attach artwork that already exists onto a perspective grid.

Attaching Existing Art onto the Perspective Grid

You already know that only a handful of Illustrator's drawing tools will draw in perspective. For all other artwork that needs to snap into the correct perspective, you'll need to first create the artwork in a flat, nondistorted manner, and then attach it to the perspective grid. In reality, this isn't so bad, because it's difficult to draw complex artwork directly in perspective—especially if you're drawing artwork with any kind of precision.

You can attach any artwork to a perspective grid, including text and symbols, with the exception of raster-based content (embedded images are not supported either). To do so, you'll use the Perspective Selection tool (**Figure 3.42**):

Figure 3.42 *The Perspective Selection tool is grouped with the Perspective Grid tool.*

1. Choose the Perspective Selection tool (Shift-V).

2. Press the 1, 2, or 3 key to choose the active grid plane.

3. Click any object and start dragging it. As you do so, it will snap to the correct perspective for the active grid plane. As you drag the artwork, you can also press any of the keyboard shortcuts to change the active grid plane and the artwork will adjust as you do so.

If you want to edit text or symbols that have been attached to a perspective grid, simply double-click the object to enter isolation mode. Alternatively, you can toggle between the two Edit buttons that appear in the Control panel. You'll be able to see the art in a nondistorted form, making it easier to perform the edit. Once you complete the edit, press Esc or double-click on a blank area to exit isolation mode, which will cause the artwork to snap back into the proper perspective (**Figure 3.43**). This ability to isolate artwork for quick and easy editing is reason enough to consider turning complex artwork into symbols before attaching it to a perspective grid. It's also a way to ensure that you can always go back to a nondistorted version of your artwork. Once you attach a regular path to a perspective grid, however, you can no longer return it to its original form.

Figure 3.43 *When a text object is attached to a perspective grid, it may appear that it is converted to outlines, but the text is still live and editable when you double-click it.*

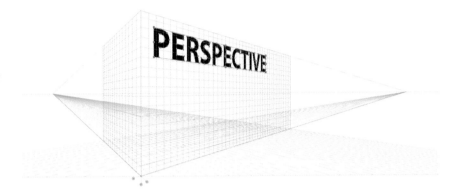

Modifying Artwork that Is Already in Perspective

The Perspective Selection tool really proves its use when you're working with artwork that is already attached to a perspective grid. When you use the Perspective Selection tool to move or transform such artwork, those edits will happen in perspective. You can move an object while holding Option (Alt) to create a copy in perspective, and if you have the Bounding Box option turned on (View > Show Bounding Box), you can scale artwork in perspective as well.

In addition, you can use the Object > Transform > Transform command to create repeated artwork in perspective, and you can even create blends in which the intermediate steps of the blend match the perspective.

If you have artwork that is attached to one grid plane, and you want to have that artwork attached to a different grid plane (you want to move an object from the right grid plane to the left grid plane, for example), you can do so by following these steps:

1. Choose the Perspective Selection tool and select the artwork you want to move.

2. Click and drag to start moving the artwork. While you are still dragging, press the 1, 2, or 3 key to select the desired grid plane.

Normally, the Perspective Selection tool will slide your artwork along the active grid plane. However, there may be times where you want to move the artwork perpendicular to the active grid plane, to give the illusion of depth. To do so, press and hold the 5 on your keyboard as you drag the artwork with the Perspective Selection tool (**Figure 3.44**).

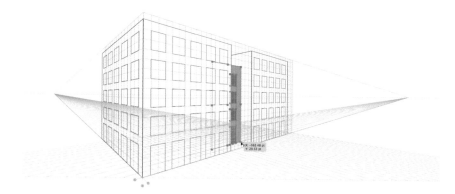

Figure 3.44 *Perpendicular movement makes it easy to keep the middle section of the building aligned to the right grid, while making it appear inset from the rest of the building.*

If you use the Perspective Grid tool to make adjustments to the perspective grid after you've already attached artwork to the grid, your artwork will not update to match the new grid settings. This is why it's really important to get your grid set up correctly before starting to draw your art. However, there is one exception to this, as you can make one kind of edit to a perspective grid where your art will update to match the new setting:

1. Select the Perspective Grid tool.

2. Press and hold the Shift key while clicking and dragging on the grid plane widget to activate the plane that you want to edit. Holding down the Option (Alt) key will duplicate the art at the same time.

Alternatively, you can double-click one of the grid plane widgets for precise control over how much you want the grid plane to move, and whether you want the objects to move or copy as well.

Keeping It All in Perspective

It's obvious that the perspective grid feature in Illustrator is powerful, and even fun to use. At the same time, sitting down to work on a project that requires its functions could potentially result in much confusion. There are some tools that work in perspective, and some that don't. In addition, you have to constantly switch between active planes by clicking the widget, and you have to use a variety of keyboard shortcuts to get the desired result.

Perhaps even more confusing, however, is the requirement to use a special selection tool, the Perspective Selection tool, when moving art in perspective. If you're experienced in using Illustrator, your instinct will always be to use the regular Selection tool—but this could lead to problems within your artwork when you're working in perspective. For example, you can use the regular Selection tool to select an object that is currently attached to a grid, and you can move that object. Illustrator provides no visual cue to let you know that the selected object is attached to a grid, however, and moving the object with the regular Selection tool moves it without snapping to the perspective grid. In other words, you've moved your artwork off the grid, and it now no longer conforms to the proper perspective.

So as you work with the new perspective grid, be careful to use the right tool as you work. This will prevent a situation where you create artwork that does not appear to be correct.

Creative Drawing

4

In the previous chapter, we discussed technical drawing. On the other side of the spectrum is creative drawing, where the focus is on the appearance of the path. In creative drawing, you couldn't care less about anchor points and control handles. The importance here is color, composition, texture, and feel.

Unfortunately, many people get caught up in the technical drawing aspect of Illustrator. After experiencing frustration in the attempt to grasp the concept of the underlying vector graphics structure, they never realize there's an entirely different side of Illustrator—a side that not only can be fun to use but that can also be rather addictive.

The Live Paint feature adds an entirely new dimension to drawing and editing in Illustrator, and the new Bristle brush helps you create truly expressive artwork. So put on your creative hat and come inside—this chapter has something for everyone.

The artwork featured throughout this chapter comes from Cheryl Graham (iStockphoto; username: freetransform).

Drawing with Live Paint

Although you can appreciate the power and precision that vector graphics have to offer, you can also appreciate how easy it is to use pixel-based paint programs such as Photoshop or Corel Painter to easily apply color to artwork. In a paint program, you can perform flood fills, in which you choose a color and use a paint bucket–like tool to fill areas with color. When working with vectors, you have to create distinct paths and shapes in order to apply a fill to add color. In other words, you can't just apply a fill to any arbitrary area on your artboard; rather, you need to select a distinct object to which to apply the fill. This need to create distinct objects can make drawing in Illustrator seem nonintuitive or time-consuming at best.

Live Paint introduces a new concept of working with vector paths, where you can colorize vectors and edit them without having to follow the traditional vector rules we've been covering up to this point. This feature makes it a lot easier to draw (and edit) in Illustrator. Let's take a closer look.

Using Live Paint to Color Paths

First let's draw something using Live Paint so you can get a feel for what the feature is all about. Then we'll discuss how the feature works, and at that point, you'll better understand how to use it in a meaningful way. The art itself may not be that exciting to look at, but the concepts you learn will be priceless.

1. Using the Line Segment tool, draw two parallel vertical lines and two parallel horizontal lines to create a rough outline of a rectangle. It doesn't matter if the lines or spacing aren't perfect; for this exercise, you just want to make sure the lines cross each other (**Figure 4.1**).

Figure 4.1 *Using the Line Segment tool, you can create a simple tic-tac-toe graphic.*

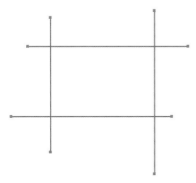

2. Select the four lines, and select the Live Paint Bucket tool (it's grouped with the Shape Builder tool in the Tools panel). As you move your pointer over the four paths, the paths become highlighted (**Figure 4.2**).

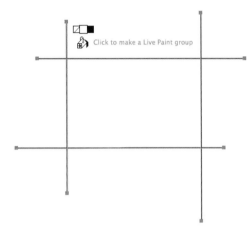

Figure 4.2 *If you have the Live Paint Bucket tool selected, Illustrator shows a tool tip to create a Live Paint group when your pointer passes over a valid selection.*

3. Click once to create a Live Paint group.

4. Pick a fill color (a solid color, gradient, or pattern) from the Control or Swatches panel, and move your pointer over the center area of the four paths.

    The enclosed area in the middle becomes highlighted in red, which indicates an area that you can fill with color (**Figure 4.3**).

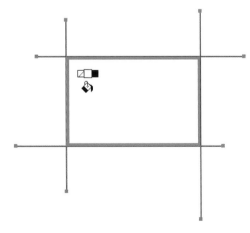

Figure 4.3 *Illustrator's Live Paint Bucket tool highlights areas that can be filled as your pointer moves over them, even if the Live Paint groups aren't selected.*

5. Click once with the Live Paint Bucket tool to fill the highlighted area (**Figure 4.4**).

Figure 4.4 *With one click of the Live Paint Bucket tool, you can fill areas that appear to be enclosed, even though there isn't an actual vector object there.*

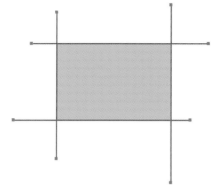

The resulting behavior is very "Photoshopesque"—you've filled an *area* that *looks like* it is enclosed on all sides, but you didn't apply a fill to an actual *object*.

6. Select the Direct Selection tool, then select one of the anchor points on one of the paths, and move it just a bit.

Notice that the color in the area updates to fill the center (**Figure 4.5**). If you move one of the paths far enough so that it no longer touches the other paths, you'll find that the fill color disappears, because there is no longer an enclosed area to fill (**Figure 4.6**).

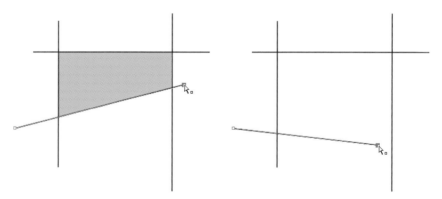

Figure 4.5 *The fill areas in a Live Paint group update automatically when you're moving the paths with the Direct Selection tool.*

Figure 4.6 *When editing the paths in a Live Paint group, creating an opened area results in the loss of the fill.*

Understanding Live Paint groups

Let's take a moment to understand how Live Paint works. When you select several overlapping paths or shapes and click them with the Live Paint Bucket tool, you are creating a *Live Paint group*. This is a special kind of group in which the object stacking order is thrown out the window. All objects in a Live Paint group are seemingly combined onto a single flat world, and any enclosed area acts as a closed shape that can be filled with color.

Although clicking several selected paths with the Live Paint Bucket tool (K) is the easiest way to create a Live Paint group, you can also select several paths and choose Object > Live Paint > Make (or press Command-Option-X [Ctrl-Alt-X]) to create a Live Paint group. Once you've created a Live Paint group, however, you may find that you want to add paths or shapes to the group. To do so, draw the new paths, and use the Selection tool to select the existing Live Paint group and the new paths. Then choose Object > Live Paint > Add Paths. The new paths will become part of the group, and any intersecting areas will act as individual areas that you can fill with color.

Live Paint groups can also use the isolation mode feature that enables you to draw objects directly in existing groups. Using the Selection tool, double-click an existing Live Paint group to enter isolation mode, indicated by a gray bar that appears across the top of the document window. Now switch to any shape or path tool to add paths directly to the Live Paint group (**Figure 4.7**). This ability to add paths directly to a Live Paint group is extremely powerful because it allows you to define regions for color in just a few quick steps. Exit isolation mode by pressing the Esc key.

TIP If you move a path so that an enclosed painted area becomes unpainted, Illustrator doesn't remember that the region was filled with a color prior to the edit. Moving the path to its original position will not bring back the fill; you'll need to reapply the fill color.

TIP You can use the Live Paint Bucket tool to color multiple regions with a single color in one step by clicking one region and dragging the pointer across additional contiguous regions.

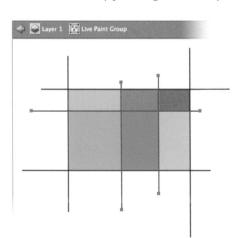

Figure 4.7 *In group isolation mode, you can draw new paths in an existing Live Paint group to instantly create additional regions that can be filled with color.*

TIP When using the Live Paint Bucket tool, you can press the Shift key to toggle between painting the fill and painting the stroke.

It's important to understand that the geometry of the paths themselves define the paintable regions. So if you wanted, you could set the stroke attributes for the additional paths to none (**Figure 4.8**).

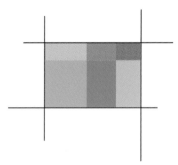

Figure 4.8 *Even though the strokes aren't visible, they still allow you to fill the areas they define.*

NOTE Unfortunately, the Live Paint feature doesn't work with paths that have brush attributes or width profiles applied. If you do try to turn paths with brushes into a Live Paint group, the appearance of the brush or profile will disappear, leaving just the appearance of the stroke. The exception to this rule is Illustrator's Blob Brush, covered later in this chapter.

In the Tools panel, double-click the Live Paint Bucket tool to change its behavior. By default, the Live Paint Bucket tool affects only the fill of a path, but you can also set the tool to apply color to strokes as well (**Figure 4.9**). The Cursor Swatch Preview option refers to the three boxes that float above the Live Paint Bucket tool pointer (**Figure 4.10**). These boxes represent swatches that appear in the Swatches panel, and when the Live Paint Bucket tool is active, you can press the arrow keys on your keyboard to select a color swatch. This allows you to choose colors and quickly fill areas without having to return to the Swatches panel. Additionally, you can specify the color that the Live Paint tool uses to highlight closed regions.

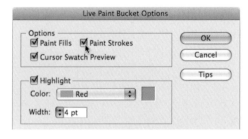

Figure 4.9 *You can set the Live Paint Bucket tool to apply color to strokes in a Live Paint group as well.*

Figure 4.10 *The three colors that appear above the Live Paint Bucket tool represent the selected color in the Swatches panel and each swatch immediately to the left and right of that swatch.*

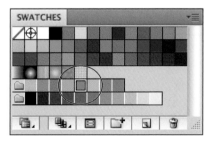

Dealing with Gaps in Your Artwork

Until now, all the regions you were filling with color were completely closed. But what happens if your paths don't exactly meet each other? That's where the Gap Detection feature can really make a difference. You need to choose Object > Live Paint > Gap Options to control the settings for this feature (**Figure 4.11**). If you don't have any Live Paint groups selected when you choose this option, the settings you pick become the default settings for all new Live Paint groups. You can specify different gap options for each selected Live Paint group in a document as well.

TIP If you want to see where gaps occur in your artwork, you can choose View > Show Live Paint Gaps, and Illustrator will preview those areas in red.

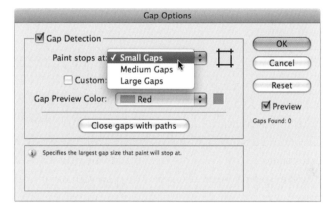

Figure 4.11 *The Gap Options dialog box makes it possible to fill areas in a Live Paint group even if they aren't completely enclosed.*

With Gap Detection turned on, you can specify that paint will fill areas containing small, medium, or large gaps (**Figure 4.12**). Additionally, you can specify an exact amount for how big a gap can be before Live Paint considers it an open area instead of a closed one. Illustrator previews gaps in the selected color, and you can also have Illustrator fill any gaps in an object with physical paths (Illustrator always uses straight paths to do so).

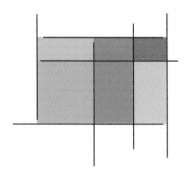

Figure 4.12 *Even though the paths don't actually enclose the areas completely, you can still fill the areas with the Gap Detection feature.*

Releasing and Expanding Live Paint Groups

NOTE The Live Trace feature in Illustrator can quickly convert traced vector art into Live Paint groups for easy coloring. Refer to Chapter 10, "Working with Images," for more information.

Live Paint groups can be expanded, at which time they behave like ordinary vector paths. The appearance of an expanded Live Paint group remains identical to the original, but it is split into multiple objects for both fills and strokes. This is similar in concept to expanding live effects. To expand a selected Live Paint group, either click the Expand button in the Control panel or choose Object > Live Paint > Expand.

From a production standpoint, you don't need to expand Live Paint groups in order to prepare a file for print. Live Paint groups print perfectly, because Illustrator performs the necessary expansion of paths at print time (similar to live effects).

Additionally, you can choose Object > Live Paint > Release to return a Live Paint group to the original paths used to create it. Whereas expanding a Live Paint group results in objects being broken up in order to preserve appearance, releasing such a group preserves the geometry of the original paths, but the appearance or colors are lost.

Merging Live Paint Groups

If you have several separate Live Paint groups, you may want to combine them to edit them as one entire group. You can do so easily by selecting the different groups and clicking Merge Live Paint in the Control panel. Alternatively, you can choose Object > Live Paint > Merge. Just note that for Live Paint groups that consist of many complex paths, the Gap Detection feature impedes performance. You may experience better performance by splitting very large Live Paint groups into several smaller ones or by turning off Gap Detection.

Using Live Paint to Edit Paths

TIP When working with Live Paint groups, you can use both the Direct Selection tool to edit the individual paths and the Live Paint Selection tool to edit, giving you the best of both worlds.

Live Paint allows you to apply attributes—such as fills and strokes—to paths based on their appearance as opposed to their actual makeup. It would be even nicer if you could actually edit your paths based on appearance as well, don't you think? Adobe was apparently reading your mind and added another tool to the mix—the Live Paint Selection tool (Shift-L)—that enables you to select portions of objects based on their appearance (**Figure 4.13**).

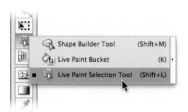

Figure 4.13 *With the Live Paint Selection tool you can make selections based on the appearance of artwork, not the underlying vector construction of it.*

Let's work through an example:

1.   Use the Line Segment tool to draw two perpendicular lines, creating an *x*.

2.   Select both paths, and press Command-Option-X (Ctrl-Alt-X) or choose Object > Live Paint > Make to convert the two paths into a Live Paint group.

3.   Select the Live Paint Selection tool, and click one of the paths.

    You'll notice that you can select each segment of the line individually. What were two paths before are now four line segments (**Figure 4.14**).

Figure 4.14 *Using the Live Paint Selection tool, you can select visual segments of a path.*

4.   With one segment selected, press the Delete key to remove that segment from the path.

5.   Select another segment, and change its stroke (**Figure 4.15**).

Figure 4.15 *In a Live Paint group, you can easily apply different strokes to the segments of a path.*

The Live Paint Selection tool can also select Live Paint areas (fills). If you have two overlapping shapes in a Live Paint group, you can select the overlap and delete it (**Figure 4.16** on the following page). You can also double-click to select continuous areas of similar attributes and triple-click to select similar attributes across the entire Live Paint group.

Figure 4.16 *The Live Paint Selection tool enables you to select any area of a Live Paint group.*

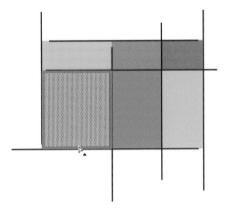

At the end of the day, Live Paint adds a more flexible way to color and edit paths, and it also adds more value to the Pencil tool, because complete closed paths aren't required. The important point to remember is that a Live Paint group is a group, and anything you can do with a group in Illustrator you can do with Live Paint groups as well. For example, you can add attributes such as strokes to the Live Paint group for interesting effects. Experimenting with the Live Paint feature certainly helps you when you're editing paths, and the good news is that it's fun to use.

Drawing with the Pencil Tool

To draw with the Pencil tool, simply click and drag on the artboard. As you drag, you'll see a light path trail the movement of your pointer (**Figure 4.17**). After you release the mouse button, Illustrator creates the anchor points necessary and creates a vector path for you (**Figure 4.18**).

Figure 4.17 *As you drag with the Pencil tool, a faint line traces the path of your pointer.*

Figure 4.18 *After you release the mouse button, Illustrator creates anchor points as necessary and displays the drawn path. Depending on how well you control the mouse (or pressure-sensitive pen), the path may have a jittery appearance.*

Because drawing with the Pencil tool relies on how steadily you handle your mouse or tablet pen, you can employ several tools and settings to help create better-looking paths.

You can use the Smooth tool, which you'll find grouped with the Pencil tool in the Tools panel, to iron out the wrinkles of any vector path. Select any vector path, and click and drag over it with the Smooth tool. Doing this repeatedly makes the vector path smoother and smoother. The angles in the path become smoother, and the path modifies to match the contour of the direction in which you drag with the Smooth tool (**Figure 4.19**).

TIP Pressing the Option (Alt) key with the Pencil tool selected will temporarily switch to the Smooth tool.

Figure 4.19 *Using the Smooth tool on a path can enhance its appearance.*

Double-clicking the Pencil tool or the Smooth tool opens the Pencil Tool Options dialog box, allowing you to specify that tool's behavior (**Figure 4.20** on the following page).

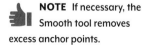

NOTE If necessary, the Smooth tool removes excess anchor points.

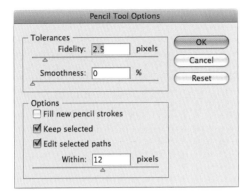

Figure 4.20 *Selecting the "Edit selected paths" option allows you to easily reshape or adjust existing paths.*

The Pencil Tool Options dialog box offers the following settings:

- **Fidelity and Smoothness.** Available for both the Pencil and Smooth tools, the Fidelity setting determines how close the vector path is drawn in relation to the movement of your mouse or input pen. A lower Fidelity setting results in a path that more closely matches the exact movement of your mouse. A higher Fidelity setting results in a path that is smoother and less jittery but that may not match your stroke exactly. If you're good with handling the mouse or if you're using an input pen, you might go with a lower setting. If you have trouble controlling the mouse or pen precisely, you might benefit from a higher Fidelity setting. The Smoothness setting refers to how much smoothing Illustrator applies to paths as you draw them. The higher the Smoothness setting, the fewer anchor points you'll see on your paths. If you're looking for more fluid strokes, increasing the Smoothness setting will help.

- **Fill new pencil strokes.** By default, Illustrator creates paths drawn with the Pencil tool as paths with a stroke but no fill. Selecting this option gives you the ability to choose a fill color and create filled paths as you draw them with the Pencil tool. This setting is available for the Pencil tool only, not for the Smooth tool.

- **Keep selected and Edit selected paths.** With Illustrator's default behavior, when you draw a path with the Pencil tool, the path becomes selected as soon as you complete it. You can change this behavior by deselecting the "Keep selected" option. When the "Edit selected paths" option is selected and your pointer is within the specified number of pixels from an existing selected path, Illustrator allows you to modify the selected path by simply drawing over it with the Pencil tool. This can be helpful because it allows you to tweak a path to perfection as you are drawing it, almost as if you were using the Smooth tool. Where this gets

TIP The preferences for the Pencil and Smooth tools are saved when you quit Illustrator so that you don't have to set these for each new file you create or each time you launch Illustrator. If you trash your preferences file, however, you'll need to reset these preferences to your liking.

TIP Remember that you can use the Smooth and Path Eraser tools on any vector path in Illustrator—even those that were not created with the Pencil tool.

in the way, however, is when you intend to draw a new path but inadvertently end up editing a path that is selected instead. This can happen often if you have the "Keep selected" option selected. Many designers prefer to deselect the "Keep selected" option but leave the "Edit selected paths" option selected. This way, if they do need to edit a path, they can Command-click (Ctrl-click) a path to select it; at this point, the "Edit selected paths" option lets them draw over it.

Pen Tool vs. Pencil Tool

In contrast to the Pen tool, the process of drawing with the Pencil tool mimics that of drawing with a real pen on paper. In reality, the Pencil tool is the exact opposite of the Pen tool. With the Pen tool, you define the anchor points, and Illustrator completes the paths. With the Pencil tool, you draw the path, and Illustrator creates the anchor points for you.

If using the Pencil tool to draw paths sounds a lot easier than creating anchor points with the Pen tool, remember that the mouse isn't the easiest tool to control when you're trying to draw. Although the Pencil tool is easier to use to create paths, it's not as easy to create exact or precise paths with it. However, if you have a pressure-sensitive tablet available, the Pencil tool is a bit easier to control.

For technical drawing and precise illustration work, including logo creation and letterforms, you'll most likely find that the Pen tool offers the fine control you need. You'll find the Pencil tool useful when you're working with creative illustrations, cartoons, and projects that require a more natural feel.

Unleashing the Power of Brushes

Each version of Illustrator brings new features and tools to the hands of designers. Some are cool effects, and some add useful functionality. And every once in a while, a feature is introduced that is so unique and powerful that it changes everything. The brushes in Illustrator are such a feature.

The concept is simple: Instead of drawing a predictable, boring line using the Pencil tool, the Paintbrush tool can create flourishes, lines with tapered ends, and artsy elements that mimic the strokes you can create with Speedball or calligraphy pens. More powerful than you might think, brushes support pressure-sensitive tablets and can even distribute art and patterns along a drawn path. By using brushes, you can streamline your work by creating complex artwork with just a few paths. Brushes are also easy to modify.

Under the hood, the Paintbrush tool functions exactly like the Pencil tool and allows you to click and drag to create a vector path. The difference is in the appearance of the path it creates. The Paintbrush tool applies vector artwork to the paths you draw. When using a pressure-sensitive tablet, you can also control how the artwork is applied to the vector paths.

Exploring the Illustrator Brush Quintet

Illustrator has five kinds of brushes; each offers a different kind of behavior in which art is applied to a path:

- **Calligraphic brush.** The Calligraphic brush allows you to define a *nib*, or tip, of a pen. The art that is drawn with a Calligraphic brush takes into account the angle and shape of the nib, resulting in natural thicks and thins and variable thickness (**Figure 4.21**).

Figure 4.21 *With the help of a pressure-sensitive tablet, the Calligraphic brush can create strokes with natural thicks and thins to achieve a hand-drawn look and feel, as in this illustration of a skier.*

- **Scatter brush.** The Scatter brush allows you to define any vector art as a brush (except the ones listed in the sidebar "What's in a Brush?"). The art that is drawn with a Scatter brush consists of copies of the art, scattered across the vector path. You can control the way art is scattered in each brush's settings (**Figure 4.22**).

Figure 4.22 *You can use a Scatter brush to create consistent borders or to quickly fill an illustration with random art, such as the sparkles in this illustration.*

- **Art brush.** The Art brush allows you to define any vector art as a brush (except the ones listed in the sidebar "What's in a Brush?"). The art drawn with an Art brush is stretched across the entire length of the path, resulting in the controlled distortion of art along a vector path (**Figure 4.23**).

Figure 4.23 *You can use an Art brush to apply artistic brush strokes or to stretch art along a path.*

- **Bristle brush.** The Bristle brush allows you to simulate real paintbrush strokes. Using a variety of brush tip shapes and fine-tuned bristle controls, the Bristle brush can create painterly artwork in various styles from watercolor textures to Japanese calligraphy (**Figure 4.24**).

Figure 4.24 *With the powerful Bristle brush settings, you can simulate a wide range of natural media. In this example, both the textured leaves and the painterly sky were created with the Bristle brush.*

- **Pattern brush.** The Pattern brush allows you to specify up to five pre-defined patterns as a brush. The art that is drawn with a Pattern brush is distributed along a vector path based on the brush's settings, resulting in perfect corners and art that is contoured to the vector path (**Figure 4.25**).

Figure 4.25 *A Pattern brush can bend art to match the curve of a path and can also contain a variety of settings that change based on the makeup of the path.*

What's in a Brush?

When you're creating artwork that will be used to define a brush, be aware that brushes cannot understand all kinds of vector objects. Brushes cannot contain gradients, mesh objects, bitmap images, graphs, placed files, or masks. For Art and Pattern brushes specifically, the artwork also cannot contain editable type objects. If you want to include these kinds of objects, you either need to expand them or convert them to outlines first.

Applying Brush Strokes

NOTE If you double-click the Paintbrush tool, you'll find that the preferences are identical to those of the Pencil tool.

To paint with a brush, choose the Paintbrush tool in the Tools panel, and then select a brush from the Brushes panel. You create brush strokes the same way you create paths with the Pencil tool, so once you've selected a brush to use, click and drag on the artboard to define a path. When you release the mouse button, Illustrator applies the brush stroke to the newly created vector path (**Figure 4.26**). Illustrator also indicates the applied brush stroke in the Appearance panel, making it easy to identify when a particular brush has been used (**Figure 4.27**).

Figure 4.26 *When you create a brush stroke, a single vector path is defined, and the appearance of that path displays the brush art.*

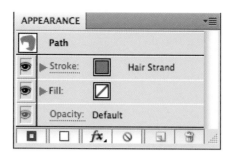

Figure 4.27 *By identifying the brush applied to a path, the Appearance panel gives yet another reason for why it should always be open and visible on your screen.*

You don't have to use the Paintbrush tool to apply a brush stroke to a vector path. Simply selecting a vector path and clicking a brush in the Brushes panel applies the brush to the selected path. The only benefit you gain by using the Paintbrush tool is the ability to define a brush shape using a pressure-sensitive tablet (see the sidebar "Can You Handle the Pressure?").

Can You Handle the Pressure?

Illustrator has full support for pressure-sensitive pen tablets such as the line of Wacom tablets. You can set Calligraphic or Scatter brushes to use variable settings based on pressure, thus enabling you to easily draw lines of varying thickness or to apply different scatter settings. For the Bristle brush, Illustrator automatically senses whether you're using a tablet, making it possible to simulate realistic brush motion and technique.

The natural lines you can achieve with a Calligraphic brush and a Wacom tablet are perfect for sketching or drawing in Illustrator. It would seem that the next logical step after creating a sketch with the Paintbrush tool is to convert the art to a Live Paint group to quickly colorize the art. Unfortunately, the Live Paint feature doesn't support brushes, and converting a brushed path to a Live Paint group results in the loss of the appearance of the brush. Instead, you might try using the Blob Brush tool, covered later in this chapter.

When using the Bristle, Calligraphic, or Scatter brushes, Illustrator also supports Wacom's 6D Art pen. You can find a library of 6D Art pen brushes that is filled with 18 Calligraphic and 6 Scatter brushes by choosing Window > Brush Libraries > Wacom 6D Brushes > 6D Art Pen Brushes.

Defining a Calligraphic Brush

To define a new Calligraphic brush, click the New Brush icon in the Brushes panel, or choose New Brush from the Brushes panel menu. Select New Calligraphic Brush in the New Brush dialog box, and click OK to open the Calligraphic Brush Options dialog box (**Figure 4.28** on the following page).

Figure 4.28 *The Calligraphic Brush Options dialog box lets you click and drag the nib shape in the preview area to define its settings.*

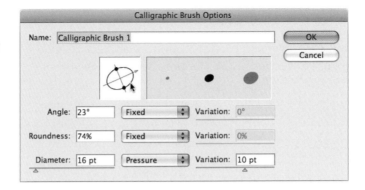

The Calligraphic Brush Options dialog box allows you to specify the shape and behavior of the nib using three settings:

- **Angle.** You can set the angle of a Calligraphic brush to a fixed angle or to a random number. When the Roundness setting is set to 100%, the Angle setting does not produce any noticeable change in the shape of the brush. With pressure-sensitive tablets, you can set the angle to change based on pressure, stylus wheel, tilt, bearing, or rotation. When you're not using the Fixed option, the Variation slider allows you to specify a range that the angle can change, which you can also see in the preview area of the dialog box.

- **Roundness.** You can set the roundness of a Calligraphic brush to a fixed or random number. When the roundness is set closer to 100%, the tip of the nib becomes circular in shape (like a traditional ink pen). When the roundness is set closer to 0%, the tip of the nib becomes flat (like a traditional calligraphy pen). With pressure-sensitive tablets, you can set the roundness to change based on pressure, stylus wheel, tilt, bearing, or rotation. When you're not using the Fixed option, the Variation slider lets you specify a range that the roundness can change, which you can also see in the preview area of the dialog box.

- **Diameter.** You can set the diameter, or size, of a Calligraphic brush to a fixed or random number. With pressure-sensitive tablets, you can set the diameter to change based on pressure, stylus wheel, tilt, bearing, or rotation. When you're not using the Fixed option, the Variation slider allows you to specify a range that the diameter can change, which you can also see in the preview area of the dialog box.

TIP When you're using a pressure-sensitive tablet, giving the Diameter setting a variation based on pressure enables you to create strokes that appear thicker as you press harder. If you have Wacom's 6D Art pen, it makes sense to set the angle to the pen's Rotation attribute.

Defining a Scatter Brush

To define a new Scatter brush, start by creating the art for the brush on the artboard. Once it is complete, drag the artwork directly to the Brushes panel. Alternatively, you can select the art and click the New Brush icon in the Brushes panel or choose New Brush from the Brushes panel menu. Select New Scatter Brush in the New Brush dialog box, and click OK to open the Scatter Brush Options dialog box (**Figure 4.29**).

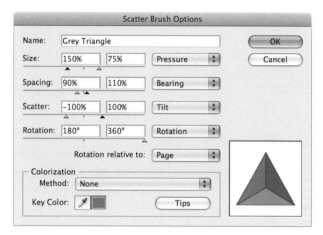

Figure 4.29 *The Scatter Brush Options dialog box presents a plethora of settings you can use to create a wide variety of results.*

You can fine-tune the Scatter brush with the following settings:

- **Size.** The Size setting can be a fixed or random number; this setting determines how big or small the art is drawn on the path, relative to the actual size of the art used to define the brush. For example, if you create a design that is 1 inch tall and use it to define a Scatter brush, a Size setting of 50% results in a Scatter brush that creates designs that are .5 inches tall. With pressure-sensitive tablets, you can set the size to change based on pressure, stylus wheel, tilt, bearing, or rotation. When you are not using the Fixed option, the two values determine the range that the size can change.

- **Spacing.** The Spacing setting can be a fixed or random number; this setting determines the amount of space that appears between each instance of art that is drawn on the path. Higher values add more space between each copy of the art, and lower values make the copies of art appear closer together. With pressure-sensitive tablets, you can set the spacing to change based on pressure, stylus wheel, tilt, bearing, or rotation. When you're not using the Fixed option, the two values determine the range that the spacing can change.

- **Scatter.** The Scatter setting can be a fixed or random number; this setting determines how far away each instance of art that is drawn deviates from the path. Negative values shift art lower and to the left of the path; positive values shift art higher and to the right of the path. With pressure-sensitive tablets, you can set the scatter to change based on pressure, stylus wheel, tilt, bearing, or rotation. When you're not using the Fixed option, the two values determine the range that the scatter can change.

- **Rotation.** The Rotation setting can be a fixed or random number; this setting determines the angle that each instance of art is drawn on the path. With pressure-sensitive tablets, you can set the rotation to change based on pressure, stylus wheel, tilt, bearing, or rotation. When you're not using the Fixed option, the two values determine the range that the rotation can change.

- **Rotation relative to.** You can set the rotation so that it is relative either to the page, in which case all instances of the art appear consistent, or to the path, in which case all instances of the art rotate in accordance with the direction of the path (**Figure 4.30**).

Figure 4.30 *Depending on your desired result, you can specify art to rotate in relation to the page (top) or the path (bottom).*

- **Colorization.** The Colorization option lets you choose from one of four settings. If you choose the None setting, the Scatter brush creates art in the same color that is used to define it. If you choose the Tints setting, the Scatter brush creates art in varying tints of the current stroke color. If you choose the Tints and Shades setting, the Scatter brush creates art in varying tints of the current stroke color while preserving black objects. If you choose the Hue Shift setting, the Scatter brush creates art and changes the key color of the art to the current stroke color. To define a key color, click the Eyedropper icon in the dialog box, and click part of the art in the preview area.

Defining an Art Brush

To define a new Art brush, start by creating the art for the brush on the artboard. Once it's complete, drag the artwork directly into the Brushes panel. Alternatively, you can select the art and click the New Brush icon in the Brushes panel or choose New Brush from the Brushes panel menu. Select New Art Brush in the New Brush dialog box, and click OK to open the Art Brush Options dialog box (**Figure 4.31**).

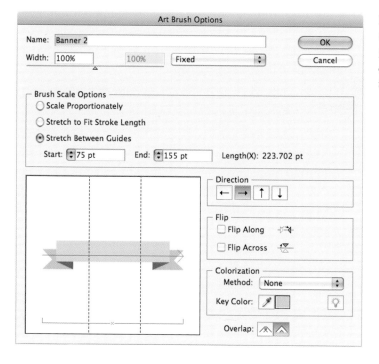

Figure 4.31 *The Art Brush Options dialog box gives you a visual preview of the direction of the art in relation to the path.*

You can fine-tune the Art brush with the following settings:

- **Width.** The Width setting determines how big or small the art is drawn on the path relative to the actual size of the art that was used to define the brush. For example, if you create a design that is 1 inch tall and use it to define an Art brush, a Size setting of 50% results in an Art brush that creates designs .5 inches tall. If you're using a pressure-sensitive tablet, you can specify a variable width setting by choosing any option other than Fixed from the pop-up menu.

- **Brush Scale Options.** The Brush Scale Option offers three ways to control how the brush artwork is distributed along the path. Scale Proportionately will enlarge or reduce the entire artwork in proportion along the path; Stretch to Fit Stroke Length will scale the artwork horizontally along the entire path; and Stretch Between Guides will intelligently stretch the artwork according to your specification. When Stretch Between Guides is selected, you can drag the two guides that appear in the preview window to control how the artwork will scale along the path. The segment of the art that appears between the guides will scale, whereas the artwork that appears to the left and right of the guides will not scale.

- **Direction.** The Direction setting determines the orientation of the art with respect to the path to which the brush is applied. A blue arrow appears in the preview area, allowing you to visually understand how the art will be drawn on a path.

- **Flip.** The Flip Along and Flip Across options enable you to reflect the artwork on both the horizontal and vertical axes.

- **Colorization.** The Colorization option lets you choose from one of four settings. When you choose None, the Art brush creates art in the same color that is used to define it. If you choose Tints, the Art brush creates art in varying tints of the current stroke color. If you choose Tints and Shades, the Art brush creates art in varying tints of the current stroke color while preserving black objects. If you choose Hue Shift, the Art brush creates art and changes the key color of the art to the current stroke color. To define a key color, click the Eyedropper icon in the dialog box and click part of the art in the preview area.

- **Overlap.** The Overlap setting lets you specify whether you want Illustrator to try to adjust the artwork for the best appearance when the underlying path contains acute angles or complex geometry.

Defining a Bristle Brush

The Bristle brush is arguably one of the most innovative features you'll find in Illustrator. Unlike other brushes that apply predefined artwork along a path, the Bristle brush uses a physics engine to simulate the bristles of an artist's paintbrush as you paint with the tool. Each brush can be defined with different tip shapes, and you can precisely adjust the characteristics of the bristles themselves.

To define a new Bristle brush, click the New Brush icon in the Brushes panel, or choose New Brush from the Brushes panel menu. Select Bristle Brush in the New Brush dialog box, and click OK to open the Bristle Brush Options dialog box (**Figure 4.32**).

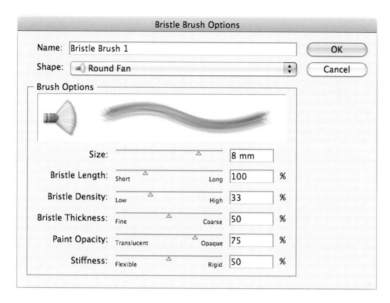

Figure 4.32 *The Bristle Brush Options dialog box provides a helpful preview that displays a sample stroke so that you can visualize the result as you adjust the bristle settings.*

Once you've named your brush, you can modify its settings in any of the following ways:

• **Shape.** Illustrator can simulate up to five different brush tip shapes (point, blunt, curve, angle, and fan) for both round and flat brushes, for a total of ten possible tip shapes. If you are using a pressure-sensitive tablet, you'll be able to see the shape of the bristles on your screen as you move the cursor around your document (**Figure 4.33**).

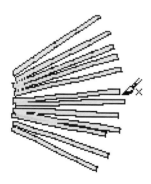

Figure 4.33 *Using a pressure-sensitive tablet, you can preview how the bristles of your brush will align to the page as you paint strokes with the Paintbrush tool.*

- **Size.** You can set the size of your brush anywhere from 1mm to 10mm, although you can also increase and decrease the size of your brush as you're painting strokes on the artboard by pressing the square bracket keys on your keyboard (similar to adjusting brush size in Photoshop).

- **Bristle Length.** Increasing the length of the bristles in a brush will allow the brush to meet more surface area on the artboard when pressure is applied. While longer bristles might work well when trying to simulate brushes used for Japanese calligraphy, shorter bristles will add more texture.

- **Bristle Density.** A high bristle density means there's less space between each bristle, while a low bristle density translates to bristles that are spread further apart. With a really low bristle density setting, you'll be able to distinguish bristle texture as you paint with the brush.

- **Bristle Thickness.** Coarse bristles will result in heavier appearances in your strokes, while fine bristles will produce subtle textures in your artwork.

- **Paint Opacity.** Bristle brush strokes are vector, and simulating wet paint isn't possible. Illustrator uses opacity settings to simulate the appearance of bristle textures. When different-colored strokes overlap on your artboard, the appearance of mixed ink colors becomes possible. With an Opacity setting of 100 percent, Bristle brush does not use any transparency in the brush stroke, resulting in artwork that prints without requiring transparency flattening. See "Expanding Brush Art" later in this chapter for more detail.

- **Stiffness.** Flexible bristles create more surface area when pressure is applied, while rigid bristles usually result in brush strokes with individual bristles that are more noticeable in your artwork.

TIP You can increase and decrease paint opacity as you're painting strokes on the artboard by pressing any of the number keys across the top of your keyboard (1=10 percent, 2=20 percent, and so on. Pressing 0 sets the brush to 100 percent paint opacity).

TIP It's always a good idea to learn from existing examples, and that goes for Pattern brushes too. You can find a wide variety of Pattern brushes in the Window > Brushes menu.

Defining a Pattern Brush

To define a new Pattern brush, it's easier to first define the pattern swatches that will be used in the brush (defining pattern swatches is covered in Chapter 6, "Coloring Artwork"). A Pattern brush can contain up to five different pattern tiles, which are used for different parts of a path (see the "Pattern tiles" bullet in the following list). Once you've defined the necessary pattern swatches, click the New Brush icon in the Brushes panel, or choose New Brush from the Brushes panel menu. Select New Pattern Brush in the New

Brush dialog box, and click OK to open the Pattern Brush Options dialog box
(**Figure 4.34**).

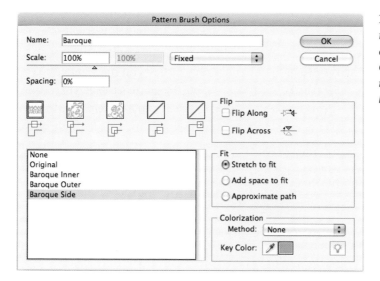

*Figure 4.34 Though it
might appear complicated
at first, the Pattern Brush
Options dialog box makes
it easy to define powerful
Pattern brushes.*

The various settings of the Pattern Brush Options dialog box are as follows:

•   **Scale.** The Scale setting determines how big or small the pattern swatch
    is drawn on the path, relative to the actual size of the art that was used
    to define the pattern (by default, a Pattern brush applies art at the size
    the art was originally created). For example, if you create art that is 1
    inch tall and use it to define a pattern swatch, a Scale setting of 50%
    results in a Pattern brush that creates tiles that are .5 inches tall. If you
    have a pressure-sensitive tablet, you can set a variable width based on
    one of the tablet attributes, such as pressure.

•   **Spacing.** The Spacing setting determines the amount of space that
    appears between each pattern tile that is drawn on the path. By default,
    all pattern tiles touch each other, and specifying higher values adds
    more space between them.

•   **Pattern tiles.** A Pattern brush can use up to five pattern tiles for the dif-
    ferent parts of a drawn path. The side tile is used along the middle of
    the path, the outer and inner corner tiles are used whenever the path
    encounters a corner anchor point at 90 degrees, and the start and end
    tiles are used at the beginning and end of an open path. We'll cover each
    tile type in detail later in this chapter. To set a tile, click the preview box
    above each tile, and choose from the list of defined pattern swatches

that appears. Only pattern swatches from the current document appear in the list. It is not necessary to assign a pattern swatch to every tile in order to define a Pattern brush. For example, some Pattern brushes do not have start or end tiles defined.

- **Flip.** The Flip Along and Flip Across settings enable you to reflect the pattern tiles on both the horizontal and vertical axes.

- **Fit.** The Fit setting, arguably one of most powerful settings among all the brushes, allows you to specify how pattern tiles are drawn on a path. The "Stretch to fit" option modifies the brush's Scale setting to ensure a perfect fit across the entire path, with no spaces between tiles. The "Add space to fit" option modifies the brush's Spacing setting to ensure the tiles fit evenly across an entire path. The "Approximate path" option actually changes the size of the path so that it fits to the size of the pattern tiles.

- **Colorization.** The Colorization option lets you choose from one of four settings. When you choose None, the Pattern brush creates tiles in the same color used when the pattern swatches are defined. If you choose Tints, the Pattern brush creates tiles in varying tints of the current stroke color. If you choose Tints and Shades, the Pattern brush creates tiles in varying tints of the current stroke color while preserving black objects. When you choose Hue Shift, the Pattern brush creates tiles and changes the key color of the tiles to the current stroke color. To define a key color, click the Eyedropper icon in the dialog box, and click part of the tile in the preview area (which is extremely difficult considering how small the previews for each tile are).

> **NOTE** Most of the information about Pattern brushes here comes from the genius mind of Teri Pettit, one of the engineers on the Illustrator team at Adobe. You can find more detailed information from Teri on a variety of topics on her website at http://tpettit.best.vwh.net/adobe/.

These next options let you define the five parts of a Pattern brush. Pattern brushes comprise up to five different individual pattern tiles: side, outer corner, inner corner, start, and end. It's rare you would define a single Pattern brush with all five of these types of tiles, though, because the corner tiles are mostly beneficial when creating borders, which are closed paths and therefore have no need for start or end tiles. Likewise, Pattern brushes with start and end tiles are generally applied to open paths that may not require corner tiles.

- **Side tiles.** The most common type of tile used, the side tile simply repeats itself along the path to which it is applied (**Figure 4.35**).

Figure 4.35 *This is a Pattern brush comprised of just a side tile (inset) to simulate stitching as it might appear on a baseball. The stitches follow the contour of the path and appear seamless.*

- **Outer corner and inner corner tiles.** The terms *inner* corner and *outer* corner refer to the corners of a clockwise path. On such a path, the corners that point outward will use the outer corner tile, and the corners that point inward will use the inner corner tile. On counterclockwise paths, these roles will be reversed.

  If a rectangle is created by dragging it from top left to bottom right, or vice versa, the top of the rectangle runs from left to right, and all corners will use the outer corner tile. If the rectangle is drawn by dragging between the top-right and bottom-left corners, then the bottom of the rectangle runs from left to right. Thus, the brush pattern as displayed along the top of the rectangle will be upside down, and all corners will use the inner corner tile (**Figure 4.36**).

NOTE If a brush doesn't have inner or outer corner tiles defined, those sections of the path will appear blank.

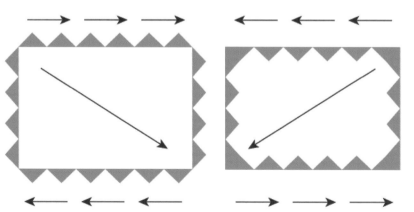
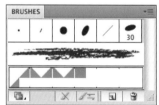

Figure 4.36 *The arrows that appear within the rectangles indicate the direction in which they were drawn, whereas the arrows that appear along the outside of the rectangles indicate the direction the paths run in. The rectangle on the left runs clockwise and uses the outer corner tile, whereas the rectangle on the right runs counterclockwise and uses the inner corner tile.*

- **Start and end tiles.** Start and end tiles appear, respectively, at the beginning and end of an open path. If a brush does not have start or end tiles defined, then the side tile will be used instead.

A few things are somewhat confusing with regard to how Illustrator displays pattern tiles in the user interface. For example, the tiles appear in one particular order when listed in the Pattern Brush Options dialog box (**Figure 4.37**), yet they appear listed in a completely different order when viewed in the Brushes panel (**Figure 4.38**). Although the order doesn't really make a difference, it's easy to get confused when you're assigning patterns to each tile.

Figure 4.37 *The order in which Pattern brushes appear within the Pattern Brush Options dialog box. A diagonal line (slash) means there is no pattern specified for that tile.*

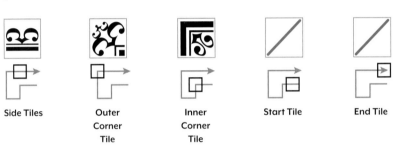

Side Tiles   Outer Corner Tile   Inner Corner Tile   Start Tile   End Tile

Figure 4.38 *The order in which Pattern brush tiles appear within the Brushes panel.*

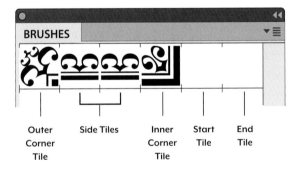

Outer Corner Tile   Side Tiles   Inner Corner Tile   Start Tile   End Tile

In addition, because of the way inner corner tiles are drawn along paths, they are flipped (or reflected) –45 degrees, which means you need to compensate for that when defining the artwork for such tiles. It gets confusing because the Brushes panel shows a preview of the tile as though it appears correct, but the same tile appears reflected when viewed in the Pattern Brush Options dialog box (**Figure 4.39**). So that you remain sane, it's best to draw your pattern art normally and simply reflect it 45 degrees before defining it as a pattern.

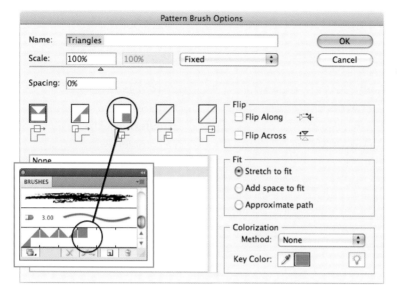

Figure 4.39 *In the Pattern Brush Options dialog box, the inner corner tile appears flipped, compared to the same tile that appears in the Brushes panel (inset).*

Modifying Brush Strokes

Double-click any brush in the Brushes panel to specify or change its settings. Alternatively, you can hold the Option (Alt) key while dragging vector art from the artboard onto an existing Art or Scatter brush to modify or replace the brush. When you do, a thick black line appears around the brush icon indicating that you are about to modify it.

When you're about to modify a brush, Illustrator checks to see whether the existing brush has already been applied to objects in your document. If it finds such objects, Illustrator asks whether you want the existing paths to now take on the appearance of the modified brush or whether you want to leave them intact (**Figure 4.40**). If you want to leave them intact, Illustrator makes the change just to the selected objects.

TIP If you want to modify only a single brush stroke within an entire document, you can do so either by selecting the path and clicking the Options of Selected Object button in the Brushes panel or by double-clicking the name of the brush in the Appearance panel.

Figure 4.40 *Always watching what you're doing, Illustrator alerts you if your edits will affect objects that have already been drawn.*

You can delete brushes from a document by dragging them to the trash can icon in the Brushes panel.

Expanding Brush Art

When you apply a brush stroke to a path, only the vector path is editable. The art that makes up the brush stroke cannot be edited or otherwise tinkered with. However, you can easily reduce any brush stroke to editable vector art by choosing Object > Expand Appearance. Doing so removes the link to the brush, and the path no longer updates if the brush swatch is updated (**Figure 4.41**).

Additionally, you can always access the original art that was used to create an Art, Scatter, or Pattern brush by dragging the brush from the Brushes panel to a blank area on the artboard.

Figure 4.41 *When viewed in Outline mode, brush strokes appear as open paths (left). Once expanded, the paths form closed shapes that can be edited as needed (center). In Preview mode, however, live and expanded brush strokes appear identical (right).*

Certain Bristle brush artwork (where Paint Opacity is set to anything other than 100 percent) can create complex images that could result in extremely long print and save times. This is mainly due to the number of objects that are generated when transparency flattening is applied (refer to Chapter 13, "Prepress and Printing," for detailed information on when this is necessary). Adobe suggests that in such cases it makes sense to rasterize your artwork before printing or saving (**Figure 4.42**). You can do this either of two ways: Select the artwork and choose Object > Rasterize, or select the artwork and choose Effect > Rasterize. By using an Effect, you can keep the Bristle brush artwork editable in Illustrator, but it will print or export as a raster image at the resolution that you specify.

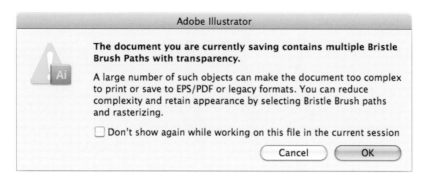

The document you are currently saving contains multiple Bristle Brush Paths with transparency.

A large number of such objects can make the document too complex to print or save to EPS/PDF or legacy formats. You can reduce complexity and retain appearance by selecting Bristle Brush paths and rasterizing.

☐ Don't show again while working on this file in the current session

Cancel OK

Figure 4.42 *If Illustrator senses there are enough Bristle brush strokes in your document to cause printing issues, you'll see this message.*

Drawing and Erasing with Ease

The brush types we've discussed to this point—Calligraphic, Art, Scatter, Bristle, and Pattern—all work in the same way, in that they are applied as appearances along a path. You can apply these brushes directly with the Paintbrush tool and can even apply them to existing paths. If you make an adjustment to an underlying path, the appearance of the brush updates accordingly. Although this "live" behavior has many benefits, you don't have access to the actual art that these brushes create until you expand them.

For certain types of illustration, the ability to fine-tune and edit brush strokes is very important. In fact, many illustrators in the past have used a variety of Calligraphic and Art brushes to create their art, only to expand the brushes and combine them with Pathfinder commands so that they could edit the art more effectively. It's easy to see how tedious this process can be. But more importantly, it breaks the flow of creativity from the designer.

The Blob Brush tool—added in Illustrator CS4—gives designers the freedom to express their creativity without getting lost in the technical details. At a basic level, the Blob Brush tool draws art that appears no different from that drawn with the Calligraphic brush. However, behind the scenes, the Blob Brush tool automatically expands the brush strokes as you draw them (**Figure 4.43** on the following page). At the same time, the Blob Brush tool intelligently combines your brush strokes with underlying objects into single, easy-to-edit shapes—shapes that can easily be adjusted or modified with the Eraser tool (**Figure 4.44** on the following page).

TIP Although "live" brushes in Illustrator don't work with Live Paint (the brush appearance is lost when they are converted to Live Paint groups), objects drawn with the Blob Brush tool work extremely well with Live Paint.

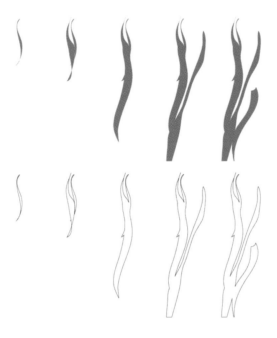

Figure 4.43 *This figure illustrates how the Blob Brush tool can be used to create these strands of hair. As each brush stroke is added (left to right), the artwork is shown in Preview mode (top) and the resulting path geometry (bottom).*

Figure 4.44 *As a closed and filled path, the shape is easily modified with the Eraser tool.*

Using the Blob Brush Tool

Drawing with the Blob Brush tool is easy and fun. Start by selecting the Blob Brush tool (Shift-B) from the Tools panel (**Figure 4.45**), and then specify a *stroke* color (the Blob Brush tool paints using the stroke, not the fill, as you might think). Then, click and drag on the artboard. By default, as you over-lap brush strokes, they automatically combine to create a single, unified shape. To better qualify that statement, brush strokes are automatically com-bined only if their attributes are alike. For example, if you're painting with a specific shade of brown, only underlying objects that are also filled with that same color will be merged. Objects filled with other colors, however, are left untouched (**Figure 4.46**). This makes it easy to modify shapes with the Blob Brush tool, because you can draw over existing objects that have the same color attributes. Most important, this makes it possible for artists to make quick edits and adjustments without having to constantly lock and unlock complex overlapping objects.

Figure 4.45 *The Blob Brush tool may have a funny name, but it's a serious drawing tool.*

Figure 4.46 *As you draw with the Blob Brush tool, your stroke color deter-mines which objects your brush strokes merge with, enabling you to perform edits on one shade of color without affecting other objects with dif-ferent colors.*

You can easily adjust the size of the Blob Brush tool by pressing the open and closed bracket keys, just as you might adjust a brush size in Photoshop. While the Blob Brush tool is selected, you can also press the Option (Alt) key to acti-vate the Smooth tool, which you can use to smooth out the edges of selected shapes as you draw them. Using the Smooth tool to fine-tune paths drawn with the Blob Brush tool is important because the expanding and merging that happens behind the scenes as you draw with the Blob Brush can result in paths with many anchor points. Remember that you can quickly select an object by pressing the Command (Ctrl) key to temporarily activate the last-used Selection tool.

NOTE Interestingly, the Blob Brush tool uses the stroke attribute to determine the color it paints with, but once you've painted a shape, the result is an object that is filled with that color and has no stroke.

NOTE How does the Blob Brush tool work? As you paint with it, Illustrator applies the Expand command and performs a Pathfinder Unite function with any overlapping paths that have similar attributes.

To control the behavior of the Blob Brush tool, double-click the tool in the Tools panel to open the Blob Brush Tool Options dialog box (**Figure 4.47**). The bottom half of the dialog box looks exactly like the Calligraphic Brush Options dialog box—which is not a coincidence. In fact, as mentioned earlier, the Blob Brush tool is based on the functionality of the Calligraphic brush (you can even select a saved Calligraphic brush in the Brushes panel and use it to paint with the Blob Brush tool).

Figure 4.47 *The Blob Brush Tool Options dialog box gives you complete control over the behavior of the Blob Brush tool.*

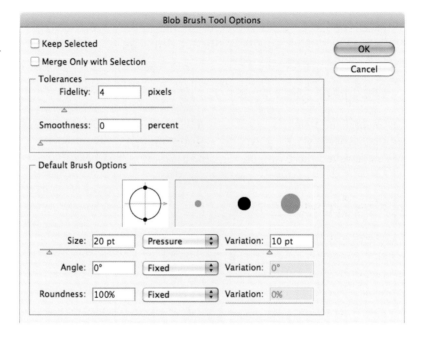

The top of the dialog box offers the following settings:

- **Keep Selected.** With this option deselected (the default setting), paths that you draw with the Blob brush tool will become deselected after you've released the mouse button or input pen. By selecting this option, the object will remain selected after you've drawn it, which would make it easier to immediately adjust the shape with the Smooth tool. In addition, the Keep Selected option could be useful when used in tandem with the Merge Only with Selection setting.

- **Merge Only with Selection.** As you've learned, the Blob Brush tool automatically merges new brush strokes with existing overlapping objects if those objects have similar attributes. For further control, the Merge Only with Selection option will allow the Blob Brush to merge new brush strokes only if the underlying objects have similar attributes *and* they are selected. Objects that are not selected, even if they share the same attributes of the brush, are not merged. In this way, you have further control over which brush strokes are merged and which are not.

- **Tolerances.** The Fidelity setting determines how close the vector path is drawn in relation to the movement of your mouse or input pen. A lower Fidelity setting results in a path that more closely matches the exact movement of your mouse. A higher Fidelity setting results in a path that is smoother and less jittery but that may not match your stroke exactly. If you're good with handling the mouse or if you're using an input pen, you might go with a lower setting. If you have trouble controlling the mouse or pen precisely, you might benefit from a higher Fidelity setting. The Smoothness setting refers to how much smoothing Illustrator applies to paths as you draw them. The higher the Smoothness setting, the fewer anchor points you'll see on your paths. If you're looking for more fluid strokes, increasing the Smoothness setting will help.

Using the Eraser Tool

The perfect companion to the Blob Brush tool is the Eraser tool (Shift-E). In fact, you'll find the Eraser tool right next to the Blob Brush tool, grouped with the Scissors and Knife tools (**Figure 4.48**). To use the Eraser tool, select it, and then click and drag over any object (or objects). If nothing is selected, the Eraser tool will erase all objects across all layers in your document, with the exception of locked objects and layers, of course. For more control, you can make a selection first and then use the Eraser tool (**Figure 4.49** on the following page), at which time the tool will erase only those objects that are selected (leaving all other objects intact).

Figure 4.48 *The Eraser tool (not to be confused with the Path Eraser tool) is grouped with other tools that cut or sever paths.*

Figure 4.49 *By selecting an object, you can quickly erase parts of one path without affecting other paths. This illustration is also a great example of how you might use the Eraser tool in a creative way, by editing shapes and colored regions.*

TIP If you have a large area to erase, press the Option (Alt) key while dragging with the Eraser tool to create a marquee area. Anything that falls within the boundaries of the marquee will be erased.

It's important to realize that although the Eraser tool makes it seem effortless to quickly remove parts of an illustration, the tool still must abide by the general rules of how vector objects are drawn. This means if you try to erase part of a single closed path, the result will be two closed paths, not open ones. It's easiest to see this when attempting to erase paths that contain strokes (**Figure 4.50**). In addition, although you can certainly use the Eraser tool to erase portions of a stroke, the stroke attribute for each segment of the resulting path is reapplied (**Figure 4.51**). In the latter case, you can get around this by first choosing the Object > Path > Outline Stroke command before using the Eraser tool. The same applies when trying to erase paths with Calligraphic, Art, Scatter, Bristle, and Pattern brushes applied. In fact, this behavior is why the Eraser tool and the Blob Brush go so well together—the Blob Brush tool creates expanded paths that can be erased easily with the Eraser tool.

Figure 4.50 *Although you may initially expect the Eraser tool to simply remove an area from an object (left), the result will actually be two closed shapes (right).*

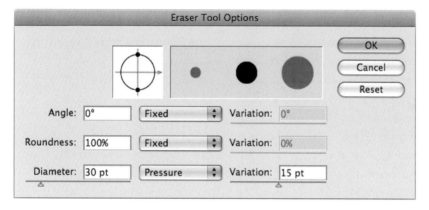

Figure 4.51 *If a stroke has the Round Cap option specified, the Eraser tool may appear to create a clean break while you're using it (left), but the result will be two paths, each with its own respective round cap appearance (right).*

Once you get used to the behavior of the Eraser tool, it becomes a useful (and fun!) tool to use. Just as with the Blob Brush tool, you can adjust the size of the eraser by tapping the bracket keys on your keyboard. You can also double-click the Eraser tool in the Tools panel to open the Eraser Tool Options dialog box (**Figure 4.52**). You can manually adjust the numerical values for the angle and roundness of the Eraser tool, or you can click and drag the black dots and the arrow in the preview near the top of the dialog box to adjust those values visually. You can adjust the size of the diameter of the eraser as well.

Figure 4.52 *The Eraser Tool Options dialog box offers similar controls to that found for the Blob Brush tool and the Calligraphic brush.*

By default, all the values are fixed, meaning they remain consistent as you use the Eraser tool. However, you can choose to make the values random and select a variation for each setting. Even better, if you have a pressure-sensitive tablet, you can choose other variables, including Pressure. For example, setting Diameter to Pressure with a high Variation value gives you the ability to erase with more control and flexibility.

TIP If you have a Wacom tablet, you can take advantage of a natural drawing workflow. When drawing with the Blob Brush tool, you can flip the pen over to have Illustrator automatically switch to the Eraser tool. Flip the pen back again, and you're back to drawing with the Blob Brush tool.

Using Gradient Mesh

Gradients, which are covered in detail in Chapter 6, allow you to fill an object with gradations of color that blend into each other. Although these gradients are certainly useful, they are limited from a creative standpoint because they can be used only in linear or radial forms. In Illustrator 8, Adobe introduced a radical new feature called Gradient Mesh, an incredible tool that allows you to create gradients in any shape. The result is artwork that looks as if it had come right from Photoshop—yet it is all in vector form using the Gradient Mesh tool (**Figure 4.53**). And if you can achieve the appearance you're looking for while keeping your file in vector form, you can keep your art completely scalable and editable throughout the design process. For example, changing one color in a gradient mesh is far easier than trying to replace a color that's used in a Photoshop file.

Figure 4.53 *Illustrator Cheryl Graham uses the Gradient Mesh feature to create photorealistic clouds that are scalable to virtually any size.*

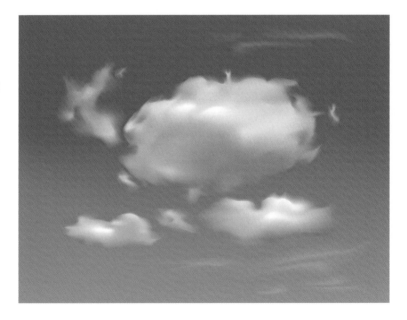

TIP If you converted a path to a mesh object and then want to get the path back, you can select the mesh object and use the Offset Path function with a setting of 0. This creates a new path that you can edit and color as you want.

However, the Gradient Mesh tool (U) isn't the easiest feature to understand. Many people would like to use the feature, but they can't figure out any consistent way to explain its behavior. This section will help you understand what a gradient mesh is and how it works.

Before you learn how to apply a gradient mesh, let's talk about what a mesh is. A *mesh* is a grid consisting of multiple *mesh points* that act much like smooth anchor points (**Figure 4.54**). You can adjust each of these points (and their control handles) to control the shape of the mesh. A mesh is really a special kind of construct or object in Illustrator, and it does not act like a regular path does. Mesh objects do not have normal fill or stroke attributes and can't display certain kinds of live effects. Rather, you use mesh objects to contain two kinds of attributes in Illustrator: gradients and envelopes (envelopes were covered in Chapter 2, "Selecting and Editing Artwork"). When you're using a mesh to define a gradient, each mesh point determines a change in color, and the control handles for each point determine the way in which that color blends into other nearby colors.

Mesh Points

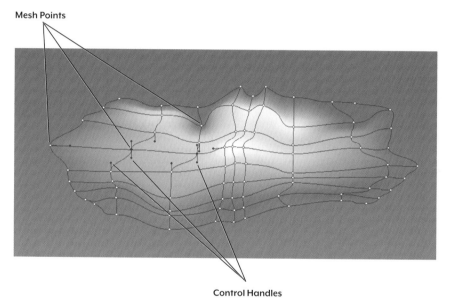

Control Handles

Figure 4.54 *A mesh is a grid that consists of mesh points and control handles.*

NOTE When you expand an object that is filled with a gradient (using the Object > Expand command), you can choose to convert the gradient into a mesh.

You can create a gradient mesh object in Illustrator in two basic ways, and in both cases, you start by first drawing a regular vector object. You don't draw gradient mesh objects from scratch in Illustrator; you convert existing vector shapes to mesh objects. With a vector object selected, do one of the following:

NOTE You can use both process and spot colors in a gradient mesh, and the file will separate correctly when printed.

• Choose Object > Create Gradient Mesh. This opens the Create Gradient Mesh dialog box, giving you the ability to specify the number of rows and columns in your mesh (**Figure 4.55**, on the next page). If your original object already has a color applied to it, you can use the Appearance and Highlight options to shade the object with white.

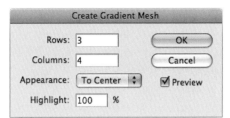

Figure 4.55 *Choosing the number of rows and columns determines the number of mesh points in your mesh. You can always add or remove mesh points later.*

- Select the Mesh tool from the Tools panel, and click anywhere within your vector path. Each click with the Mesh tool adds mesh points to the mesh object. You'll also notice that as you add mesh points to an object, the paths connecting the mesh points match the contours of the object.

Once you have mesh points defined, you can switch to the Direct Selection tool and select each individual mesh point to adjust its position and its direction handles. With a mesh point selected, you can choose a color from the Swatches or Color panel to define the color for that point. You can also change the opacity of a selected mesh point using the Transparency or Control panels. As needed, you can switch back to the Mesh tool and click to add mesh points. To remove a mesh point from a mesh object, hold the Option (Alt) key while clicking a point with the Mesh tool.

Organizing Your Drawing

5

Some people have clean, organized desks, whereas others have desks that are quite messy. Likewise, some designers organize their Illustrator files using groups and layers, while many do not. And just as there are benefits to keeping an orderly desk, there are advantages to using groups and layers for adding structure to your files. In Illustrator, not only do groups and layers offer a convenient way to manage objects in a file, but they can also control the appearance of your file. For example, applying a drop shadow to several objects that are grouped looks different from applying a drop shadow to those very same objects if they aren't grouped. You may even find that using groups and layers is necessary to create the art you need.

Speaking of the appearance of an object, you'll spend a considerable amount of time with the Appearance panel in this chapter. The Appearance panel is arguably the most important panel in Illustrator, and you can apply the concepts you learn in this chapter to just about every other feature in Illustrator.

The artwork featured throughout this chapter comes from Diane Labombarbe (iStockphoto; username: diane555).

Selecting and Targeting

As you begin to learn about appearances in Illustrator, it's important to understand what targets are. In Chapter 2, "Selecting and Editing Artwork," you learned that you can select an object. However, when you apply an attribute to an object, such as a fill or a stroke, that attribute is applied to what Illustrator calls the target.

For the most part, *selecting* is an action that is used to define a set of criteria that will be used for performing transformations. As you learned in Chapter 2, transformations consist of moving, scaling, rotating, skewing, and mirroring objects. You select objects because you want to move them from one side of your document to another, because you want to delete them, and so on.

Targeting, however, is an action that is used to define a set of criteria specifically to apply an attribute such as a stroke, a fill, a transparency setting, or a live effect.

If you look at the Tools panel, though, you'll find a Selection tool, but you won't find a Targeting tool. Why? That's because for the most part, Illustrator targets things for you automatically using something called *smart targeting*. When you select a path with the Selection tool, Illustrator automatically targets that path so you can apply attributes to it. When you're working with a single object, selecting and targeting are pretty much the same. However, when you start working with multiple objects, groups, and layers, it's possible to have one item selected while something else is targeted. You'll see clear examples of this later in this chapter when we discuss groups in Illustrator.

Understanding Appearances

As we discussed in Chapter 3, "Technical Drawing," a vector path can have certain attributes applied that define the appearance of that path. When you print a file, you aren't seeing the vector path; you're seeing the appearance that was specified for that path. An example of an attribute might be a particular fill or stroke. As you'll learn later in this chapter, attributes can also be things such as drop shadows or 3D effects. In addition, you will learn that appearances are applied to something called a *target*. See the sidebar, "Selecting and Targeting," for more information.

When you specify attributes, they appear listed in the Appearance panel. We know this sounds like a late-night infomercial, but if you keep only one Illustrator panel open on your screen while you're working, make it the Appearance panel. In fact, the Appearance panel is probably the most important panel in Illustrator—ever. To open the Appearance panel, choose Window > Appearance.

Like X-ray vision, the Appearance panel enables you to look at your files and see how they were built or created. This panel also gives you access to every attribute of an object. You can also specify appearance attributes directly from the Appearance panel. But before we get ahead of ourselves, let's start with the basics.

Understanding Attributes and Stacking Order

When a path is selected, the Appearance panel displays a thumbnail icon and the word *Path*, which is the target. The panel also lists—from the bottom up—the target's opacity, its fill, and its stroke. To the left of each attribute are visibility icons (**Figure 5.1**). Clicking an attribute in the Appearance panel enables you to modify it, and clicking an attribute name that is underlined in blue opens the panel that controls all the settings for that attribute. For example, click anywhere to the right of the word *Stroke* to change its color or weight (**Figure 5.2**); click the word *Stroke*, and the Stroke panel appears, where you can specify cap, join, and dash settings (**Figure 5.3**).

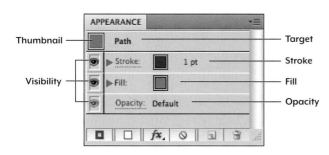

Figure 5.1 *The Appearance panel displays the attributes for the targeted item.*

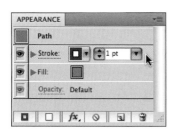

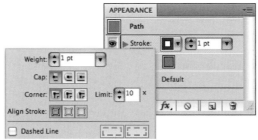

Figure 5.2 *Clicking to the right of an attribute gives you the ability to modify its settings.*

Figure 5.3 *If an attribute has a blue underline, clicking the attribute displays its respective panel or dialog box.*

The order in which the listed items appear in the Appearance panel isn't arbitrary. From the bottom up, these attributes control the overall appearance of the object. To better illustrate this important concept, let's first understand a core aspect of how vector objects are drawn in a document.

Objects are drawn in a hierarchy, determined by the order in which you create your art. For example, if you draw one shape and then draw a second shape, the second shape appears higher in the document's hierarchy than the first object. The easiest way to see this is to create two overlapping objects (**Figure 5.4**). In Illustrator, this hierarchy is called the *stacking order*. You can change an object's place in the stacking order by selecting it and choosing an item from the Object > Arrange menu (**Figure 5.5**).

Figure 5.4 *Modifying the stacking order allows you to overlap artwork in a variety of ways.*

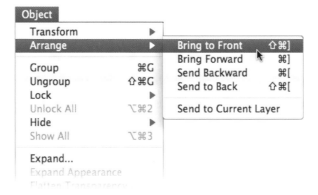

Figure 5.5 *Choosing Object > Arrange > Bring to Front moves a selected object to the top of the stacking order.*

What most people don't realize is that a single object also has a stacking order. By default, Illustrator defines an overall Opacity value for an object and then paints the fill and the stroke in that specific order. Why? One reason could be that strokes are painted along the centerline of a path. That means if the weight of a path is set to 20 pt, the weight is distributed so that 10 pts appear on both sides of the path (**Figure 5.6**). If Illustrator painted the fill after the stroke, the 10 pts of the stroke width that falls on the inside of the path would be covered or hidden by the fill (**Figure 5.7**).

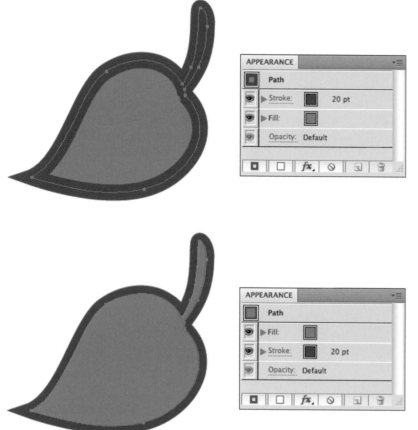

Figure 5.6 *By default, the weight of a stroke is distributed along the centerline of the path.*

Figure 5.7 *By painting the stroke first and the fill second, the inner portion of the stroke becomes hidden by the fill.*

What's great about the Appearance panel is that not only can you use it to change the appearance of an attribute, but you can also use it to see the order that those attributes are applied in. Even better, you can change the stacking order. For example, dragging the Stroke attribute in the Appearance panel so that it appears listed beneath the Fill attribute instructs Illustrator to paint the Stroke attribute before it paints the fill (thus hiding half the weight of the stroke, as in Figure 5.7).

This ability to change the stacking order of attributes in an object's painting order may not seem that exciting or useful right now, but it becomes quite important when we talk about groups and layers later in the chapter.

Targeting Attributes

Upon closer inspection of the Appearance panel, you'll notice disclosure triangles to the immediate left of the Stroke and Fill attributes. Clicking these disclosure triangles reveals an Opacity setting that lets you control the opacity of an object's stroke and fill independently (**Figure 5.8**). In fact, a single path contains three Opacity settings by default: one for its stroke, one for its fill, and one for the overall object. When you apply an Opacity value to a single attribute, you're targeting that specific attribute. And in case you were wondering, yes, it's certainly possible to apply a 50% Opacity value to an object's fill and also apply a 50% Opacity value to an overall object (resulting in a 25% opacity, if you think about it; see **Figure 5.9**).

Figure 5.8 *Although the fill of this object has an Opacity setting of 50%, the stroke appears at 100% opacity.*

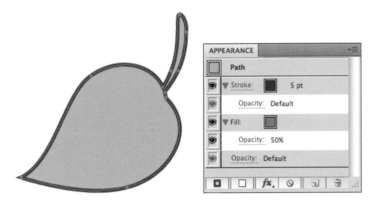

Figure 5.9 *Be aware of the accumulative effect of applying Opacity values to an overall object as well as to its attributes.*

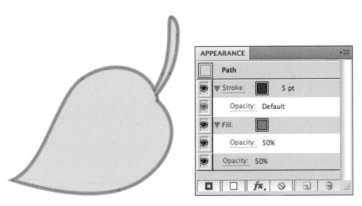

Since it can be confusing at times, it's important to realize that when you click an attribute in the Appearance panel, the attribute becomes highlighted to indicate that it is targeted. If you want to target the overall path or object, click the target that is listed at the top of the Appearance panel, near the thumbnail (**Figure 5.10**). Alternatively, you can click in the empty area that appears beneath all the attributes listed in the Appearance panel.

Figure 5.10 *Clicking the target is a quick way to target the entire object, not just one of its attributes.*

Applying Multiple Attributes

Objects that have a single fill and a single stroke are referred to as having a *basic appearance*. However, vector objects aren't limited to just one fill and one stroke. In fact, a single object can contain as many fills or strokes that your creative mind craves. An object with more than just one fill or stroke is referred to as having a *complex appearance*.

To add an attribute to an object, click the Add New Stroke or Add New Fill button at the bottom of the Appearance panel (**Figure 5.11**). You can also target any existing attribute and click the Duplicate Selected Item button. Once you've added an attribute, you can change its place in the stacking order by dragging it above or beneath other attributes in the Appearance panel. You can also remove targeted attributes by clicking the Delete Selected Item button.

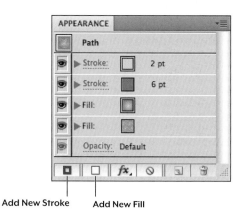

Add New Stroke   Add New Fill

Figure 5.11 *There's no limit to how many fills or strokes you can add to an object in Illustrator.*

TIP To reduce a selected object to a single fill and a single stroke with those attributes set to None, click the Clear Appearance button at the bottom of the Appearance panel.

You may be wondering what good two fills or two strokes do in an object, because one always covers the one beneath it. Earlier, we discussed the ability to target a specific attribute so that you can apply settings to each individually. By applying different attributes to two different fills and by applying an overprint or an Opacity setting to the top fill, you can create some interesting effects (**Figure 5.12**).

Figure 5.12 *Combining two fills in a single object lets you create interesting effects, such as a pattern fill with an overlapping transparent gradient fill.*

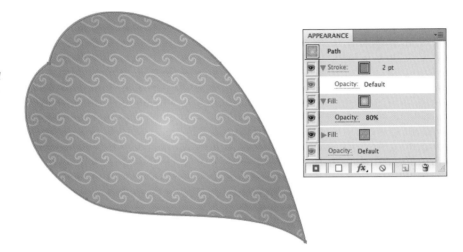

NOTE Even if you don't use the Appearance panel to add multiple Fill or Stroke attributes to an object, you may work with someone else's file that does contain a complex appearance. As such, it's always important to use the Appearance panel when working in any document.

Likewise, you can add numerous strokes, each with different widths, colors, and dash patterns, resulting in useful borders and effects (**Figure 5.13**). Although you can certainly use more traditional methods to simulate these effects by overlapping multiple objects on top of each other, adding multiple attributes to a single path means you have just one path to work with and edit (as opposed to multiple paths). Considering the Illustrator limitation of being able to edit only a single control handle of a single path at any one time, seemingly simple edits to multiple paths could prove extremely difficult and require much time and effort. Another benefit, as you'll learn about in Chapter 9, "Drawing with Efficiency," is the ability to turn complex appearances into graphic styles.

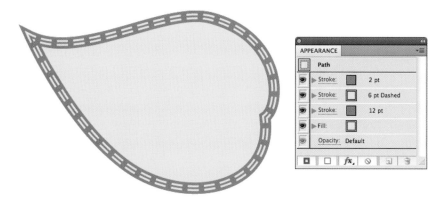

Figure 5.13 *Using overlapping multiple strokes on a single object is one way to simulate stitching patterns.*

New Art Has Basic Appearance

Ordinarily, Illustrator styles a newly drawn object based on the last object that was selected. For example, if you click an object with a black stroke and a yellow fill, the next object you draw will have a black stroke and a yellow fill. However, if you select an object with a complex appearance and then create a new shape, the default behavior is that Illustrator will not style the new object with the complex appearance. Instead, Illustrator uses the basic appearance of the previously selected object (Illustrator uses the topmost Fill and Stroke attributes and does away with any that appear beneath them in the appearance's stacking order).

In the Appearance panel menu, you can deselect the New Art Has Basic Appearance setting (**Figure 5.14**), which instructs Illustrator to draw new shapes using the full complex appearance of any previously selected object. If you ever want to reduce an object to its topmost fill and stroke while removing all additional attributes that appear underneath, you can choose Reduce to Basic Appearance from the same panel menu.

Figure 5.14 *Selected by default, the New Art Has Basic Appearance setting forces newly drawn objects to always have basic appearances.*

Expanding Appearances

NOTE Although some people don't trust Illustrator and expand all appearances before sending final files off to print, we don't condone such behavior. There is no risk in printing files with appearances—they print just fine. Additionally, expanding your appearances limits your options if you have to make a last-minute edit or if your printer has to adjust your file.

You'll notice that you can't target a specific fill or stroke of an object from the artboard—the only place to access this functionality is through the Appearance panel. This makes the Appearance panel infinitely important, but it may make you wonder how an object with a complex appearance will print. After all, how does the printer or export format know how to draw these multiple attributes on a single path?

The answer is that Illustrator breaks these complex appearances down into multiple overlapping paths, and each path contains a basic appearance. This process, called *expanding*, doesn't happen on your artboard—it happens in the print stream or the export process.

Sometimes you may want to manually expand your appearances to access the multiple attributes as individual objects on the artboard. To do so, choose Object > Expand Appearance. Remember that once you've expanded an appearance, you are dealing with a group of multiple objects, not a single object anymore (even fills and strokes are separated into individual objects). Each of the individual objects has a basic appearance, and you have no way to return to the original complex appearance.

Enhancing Appearances with Live Effects

Illustrator refers to effects as *live effects*. There are several reasons for this. First—and most important—any effect you apply from the Effect menu is added as an attribute in the Appearance panel. Second, all effects can be edited at any time, even after the file has been closed and reopened at another date. Finally, when an object's path is edited, any effects that are applied to that object are updated as well. Because these effects are nondestructive, they are considered "live" and are always editable.

The way that Illustrator accomplishes this behavior is by keeping the underlying vector object intact, while changing just the appearance of the object by adding the effect. Think of those 3D glasses you used to get at the movie theater. Without the glasses, the movie is nothing special, but once you don the glasses, the movie appears to be 3D. You can think of the Appearance panel as a pair of 3D glasses in this sense—once you add an effect, the object changes in appearance, but the original untouched vector paths remain beneath the hood (**Figure 5.15**).

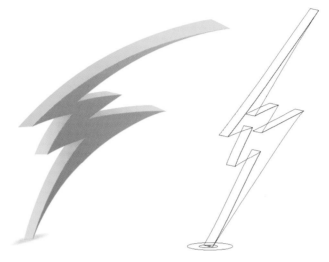

Figure 5.15 *After a Warp effect has been applied, a vector shape appears distorted (left). When viewed in Outline mode, you can see the underlying vector shape still exists, unscathed (right).*

You can choose from many live effects in Illustrator, including those that are vector-based (such as Scribble) and those that are raster-based (such as Gaussian Blur). For the purposes of understanding how these effects work and how they interact with the Appearance panel, we'll discuss what is arguably the most commonly used live effect—Drop Shadow—in this chapter. The remainder of the live effects are covered in detail in Chapter 7, "Working with Live Effects."

TIP Just as adding a second fill or stroke categorizes an object as having a complex appearance, adding a live effect to an object also produces an object with a complex appearance.

Applying a Live Effect

You can apply a live effect, such as a drop shadow, to a target in two ways: choose Effect > Stylize > Drop Shadow or click the Add New Effect button at the bottom of the Appearance panel and choose Stylize > Drop Shadow (**Figure 5.16**, on the next page). The Drop Shadow dialog box appears, where you can specify the exact settings for the drop shadow including the blending mode, opacity, offset (the distance between the object and its shadow), and blur amount (the softness of the shadow). Additionally, you can choose a color or darkness value for your drop shadow (**Figure 5.17**, also on the next page). Note that the dialog box has a Preview option, which, when selected, lets you see your shadow update as you make changes to the settings. Once you're happy with the appearance of your drop shadow, click OK to apply it.

Figure 5.16 *You can apply live effects directly from the Appearance panel.*

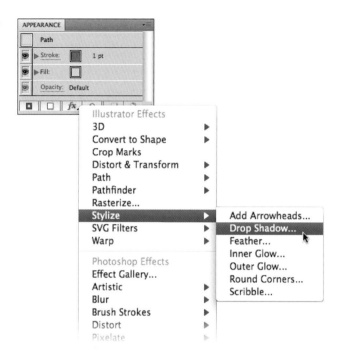

Figure 5.17 *The Drop Shadow live effect gives you the ability to control all the specifics of creating a soft drop shadow.*

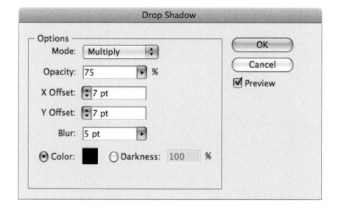

TIP To choose a spot color for your drop shadow, you must first define the desired color as a swatch (covered in Chapter 6, "Coloring Artwork"). Click the color swatch in the Drop Shadow dialog box, and then click the Color Swatches button, where you'll find your custom color in the list of swatches.

Now, let's take a look at the Appearance panel. Note that the path is listed as the target, and then examine the attributes in the object itself. Reading from the bottom up (the order in which the attributes are drawn), you have the default opacity, the Drop Shadow effect you've just applied, the fill, and finally the stroke of the object (**Figure 5.18**). The drop shadow appears beneath the fill and the stroke of the object because it wouldn't be much of a drop shadow if it were painted above the fill and stroke, would it?

Figure 5.18 *By default, the Drop Shadow effect is added underneath the Fill and Stroke attributes in the stacking order.*

The truth is, you can use the Appearance panel to control exactly how and where your drop shadow—or any live effect—is painted. You can target the Fill or Stroke attribute in the Appearance panel and *then* add the drop shadow. In this way, you can add a live effect to just the fill or just the stroke of an object. If your object contains multiple fills or strokes, you can apply live effects to each of them individually (**Figure 5.19**). Even though you've already applied a live effect to an object, you can drag the effect within the Appearance panel to change its place in the stacking order or to apply it to a specific fill or stroke (**Figure 5.20**, on the next page).

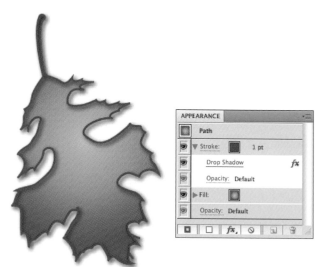

Figure 5.19 *You can apply live effects to fills or strokes of objects individually. Here, the drop shadow is applied just to the stroke of an object.*

Figure 5.20 *When dragging an effect within the Appearance panel, black arrows indicate when you're about to apply the effect to a specific fill or stroke.*

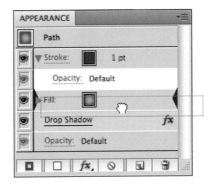

Editing a Live Effect

One of the important benefits of live effects is that you can edit them at any time. Clicking the blue underlined name of an effect that is listed in the Appearance panel opens the dialog box for that effect, where you can view the current settings and change them at will (**Figure 5.21**). This may be confusing initially, because you'd think that in order to change an effect, you'd return to where you first applied the effect (that is, the Effect menu). Doing so actually adds a *second* effect to the selected object (**Figure 5.22**). Illustrator allows you to apply an effect to an object as many times as you'd like, and in Chapter 7, you will explore when that might be beneficial. The important thing to remember is that when you want to *add* a new effect to an object, you do so by using the Effect menu or by clicking the Add New Effect button. To *edit* an effect that already exists, click its name in the Appearance panel.

Figure 5.21 *To edit an existing effect, click its name in the Appearance panel.*

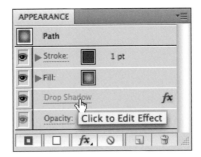

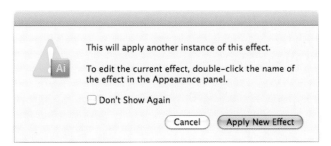

Figure 5.22 *If you try to edit an existing effect by choosing the item from the Effect menu, Illustrator informs you that you must edit existing effects through the Appearance panel.*

Loading Attributes with the Eyedropper Tool

You can use the Eyedropper tool in Illustrator to load the attributes of existing objects quickly. This can be useful in two ways. First, if you already have an object selected when you click another object with the Eyedropper tool, your selected object changes to match the object you clicked. Second, you can click once with the Eyedropper tool to sample the attributes of an object, and you can then Option-click (Alt-click) to apply those attributes to other objects in your file without actually having to select them.

You can configure the Eyedropper tool to sample just the basic appearance of an object (the topmost fill and stroke) or complete complex appearances. To control what the Eyedropper tool can sample, double-click the tool in the Tools panel.

Shift-click with the Eyedropper tool to sample colors from the pixels of raster images (or even the visual appearance of vector objects). In this way, the Eyedropper tool works much like the one in Photoshop.

Working with Groups

As we mentioned at the beginning of this chapter, creating groups is a way to organize the elements in a file. Most importantly, groups allow you to easily select or work with several objects that may belong to a single design element. You can also nest groups, meaning you can have groups within other groups. For example, you might have a logo that consists of an icon and a type treatment that has been converted to outlines. You can group the objects that make up the icon, and you can put the items that make up the type treatment into a separate group. You can then create an overall larger group that contains the other groups within it (**Figure 5.23**, on the next page).

Figure 5.23 *An example of a nested group structure.*

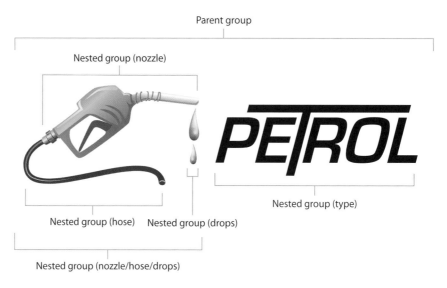

When you think of groups in this way, it's simply a matter of labeling certain objects that belong together. But in reality, a group is more than just a concept—a group is actually an entity itself. A group exists, just as an object does, only we don't see it. Illustrator refers to a group as a *container*—something that contains the objects within it. This introduces two important concepts: The container itself can have attributes applied to it, and the container can affect the way the grouped objects interact with each other and other art elements in your file.

Adding a Soft Drop Shadow to a Group

Let's take a look at a simple example using the Drop Shadow effect you just learned about in the previous section:

1. Start with a set of several overlapping shapes, and create an exact copy of that set of shapes.

2. Select one set of shapes, and choose Object > Group to create a group that contains the set of objects.

   At this point, you're looking at two design elements, each identical in appearance, but one is a group while the other is just several individual objects (**Figure 5.24**).

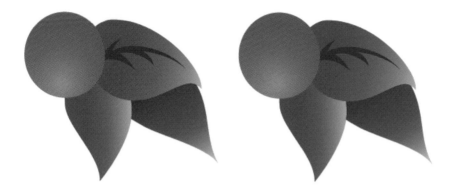

Figure 5.24 *The design elements shown here are identical except for one fact: The elements on the right have been grouped.*

3. Using the Selection tool, select the set of individual objects, and look at the Appearance panel.

    The target for your selection is listed as *Path* with *Mixed Appearances* (because each shape is filled with a different color).

4. Select the grouped objects, and again, take a look at the Appearance panel. The target is now listed as *Group*.

    This is actually the smart targeting in Illustrator at work—by selecting the group, Illustrator didn't target the individual paths within the group; instead, the group becomes the target. When the group is targeted, the Appearance panel displays the word *contents*, which are the paths that are found in the group (**Figure 5.25**).

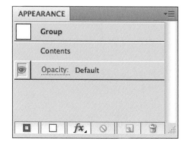

Figure 5.25 *When you select a group, Illustrator automatically targets the group. The elements within the group are referred to as the* contents, *which are listed in the Appearance panel.*

Earlier in the chapter, you learned that appearances aren't applied to a selection; rather, they are applied to the target. Keeping that in mind, let's apply the Drop Shadow effect to these two sets of objects. Select each set of objects, and apply the Drop Shadow effect. You'll notice that when the drop shadow is applied to the set of individual objects, each object appears with its own shadow. However, the grouped objects appear with a single unified drop shadow—as if all the objects were really one single shape (**Figure 5.26**). This happens because the group was the target, so the drop shadow was added to the group, not to the paths. You can clearly see evidence of this by using the Direct Selection tool to select just one of the shapes within the group and then copying and pasting that shape into a new document. You'll notice that in the new document the shape doesn't have a drop shadow at all.

Figure 5.26 *Applying a drop shadow to individual objects (left) is different from the same drop shadow applied to a group of objects (right).*

Let's take this concept, that a group is a container, one step further. Say you have a group of objects and you apply a drop shadow. As you've already learned, the drop shadow is applied to the group. But what happens to the drop shadow if you then choose Object > Ungroup? By ungrouping the objects, you're deleting the container. And it was the container that had the Drop Shadow effect applied to it, not the objects themselves. So if you ungroup the objects, the drop shadow simply disappears.

Adding a Stroke to a Group

To strengthen your understanding of how groups work in Illustrator, let's explore another example using a group of objects. You already know that a group can have attributes applied to it, as evidenced by the drop shadow you applied earlier. You also know you can apply multiple attributes to objects. Using this knowledge, you can add a stroke to a group:

1. With the Selection tool, select the group, and take note that the group is the target in the Appearance panel.

2. Click the Add New Stroke button in the Appearance panel to add a stroke to the group, and just to make it easier to see, change the stroke weight to 4 pt.

   The stroke is applied across all paths within the group (**Figure 5.27**).

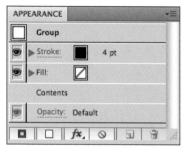

Figure 5.27 *When applied at the group level, a stroke appears across all the paths.*

It's interesting to note that *all* the objects in the group exhibit the appearance of the stroke, even objects that appear beneath other objects in the stacking order. A close examination of the stacking order in the Appearance panel reveals why: the contents of the group are drawn *before* the stroke is painted. At the group level, all objects are considered as they are combined (as you saw with the drop shadow example), so the stroke is applied equally to all paths. Dragging the stroke to appear *beneath* the contents in the Appearance panel stacking order will result in a stroke that appears only around the perimeter of the group (**Figure 5.28**).

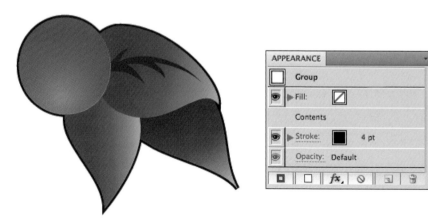

Figure 5.28 *By adjusting the stacking order of the group, the stroke appears only along the perimeter of the group.*

You can clearly see how groups can have attributes applied to them and how they can control how grouped objects interact with each other. In this context, you begin to see that grouping objects is more than just making files easier to manage. Creating groups can have a significant impact on the appearance of your art. Likewise, simply ungrouping art can alter the appearance of your file completely.

TIP The current target is also displayed on the far left side of the Control panel.

The obvious questions you should be asking are "How do I know when I'm applying an attribute to an object versus a group?" and "How can I tell whether ungrouping something will alter the appearance of my file?" The answers lie in the all-important Appearance panel, which tells you what is targeted and what attributes and effects are applied (**Figure 5.29**).

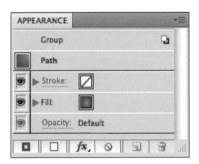

Figure 5.29 *When you select a single path within a group, the Appearance panel tells you that the path is in a group that has a Stroke or Fill attribute applied to it.*

Type as a Group

Type is a special kind of object in Illustrator—it's actually a group. The Type object is the container, and the actual text characters are like the objects inside a group. You can see this by looking at—that's right—the Appearance panel. Select a point text object with the Selection tool, and the Appearance panel shows *Type* as the target. Switch to the Type tool and select the text, and the Appearance panel shows *Characters* as the target.

When you select a Type object with a selection tool, the smart targeting in Illustrator automatically targets the Type container. You can see *Characters* listed in the Appearance panel, and double-clicking the Characters listing automatically switches to the Type tool and highlights the text on your artboard (**Figure 5.30**). The target is now Characters, and you can see the Fill and Stroke attributes.

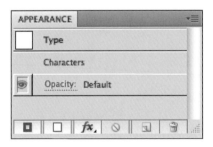

Figure 5.30 *When a Type object is selected, the Appearance panel shows it as the container and the characters within it.*

Using Isolation Mode

Sometimes you'll want to draw a new object and add it to an existing group. For example, say you have several elements in a group that has a drop shadow applied to it and you'd like to add another design element to that same group and have it take on the shadow as well. If you were to ungroup the existing elements, draw the new shape, and then reselect all the objects and create a new group, you would lose the appearance of the drop shadow (this would actually happen as soon as you ungrouped the elements). So, what you really want is a way to add elements to an existing group—without destroying the group. Thankfully, such a method exists in Illustrator, and it's called *isolation mode*.

NOTE Isolation mode is especially useful when you're using Live Paint groups, which are covered in detail in Chapter 4, "Creative Drawing."

Using the example just discussed, you would use the following method to add a new element to an existing group:

1. Using the Selection tool, double-click any object in the group. This activates isolation mode, and it isolates the group. A gray bar appears across the top of the document window, and all other artwork in the file becomes dim, indicating that the group is now isolated (**Figure 5.31**).

Figure 5.31 *When in isolation mode, a gray bar appears across the top of the document window, and all other artwork on the artboard is dimmed. Any new artwork created is drawn directly into the isolated group.*

2. Draw a new element. Any new shapes or objects that are created now become part of the group.

3. Press the Esc key to exit isolation mode. Alternatively, you can double-click any blank area on the artboard, or you can click any empty area in the gray bar at the top of the document window to exit isolation mode as well (**Figure 5.32**).

Figure 5.32 *Icons in the gray bar (referred to as* breadcrumbs) *help identify where the isolation is in the document's object hierarchy. Clicking the arrow moves you up the hierarchy one step at a time.*

In reality, the usefulness of isolation mode extends far beyond working with groups. Adobe has extended the functionality of isolation mode so it works with individual paths as well. In fact, the whole point of isolation mode is to allow for a way to make quick edits in complex documents. If you have nested groups, each double-click isolates another level of the object hierarchy—even down to individual paths. In addition, when artwork is isolated, it temporarily pops to the front of the stacking order (until you exit isolation mode, when it returns to its place). This makes it easy to perform quick edits to just about any part of a complex illustration without having to constantly lock and unlock other objects that might get in the way. Isolation mode is also useful when working with masks, which we'll cover in Chapter 9.

Working with Layers

Layers are nearly identical to groups in concept, but they offer more flexibility and functionality. Whereas groups are used to combine design elements in a file, layers also allow you to organize and combine elements within a file. Just as groups can be nested within each other, so can layers. And just as groups are containers that hold contents within them, layers are containers as well. In addition, layers, just like groups, can also have attributes applied to them. As you explore the power of layers in this section, all of these concepts will come to light.

The Significance of Layers

Don't be fooled into thinking that layers are just for making files neat and organized. Quite the contrary—a file that takes advantage of using layers can benefit from many other features as well:

- **Layer clipping masks.** Illustrator has the ability to make the topmost object in a layer a mask for all items within that layer.

- **PDF layers.** Illustrator can export PDF files with layers intact, allowing users in Adobe Acrobat or Adobe Reader to interactively turn on and off those layers. Additionally, InDesign CS4 and CS5 have has the capability to control the visibility of PDF layers.

- **Photoshop export.** When exporting an Illustrator file to a PSD file, you can choose to have layers preserved, thus making your file easier to edit when you bring it into Photoshop.

- **Flash Catalyst support.** Illustrator layers are preserved when you open native Illustrator files in Flash Catalyst, making it easier to quickly create components and define interactions.

- **Transparency.** Sometimes artwork with transparency can result in files that look less than perfect when printed on a high-resolution press—if the file is built in a certain way. Using layers can significantly reduce the number of issues you might encounter when using transparency features.

- **Animation.** When creating art for frame-based animations, such as those used in GIF and SWF (Flash) animations, Illustrator layers serve as frames. Layers are also integral when you are creating art that will be animated in programs such as Flash Professional and After Effects.

- **Cascading Style Sheets (CSS).** Illustrator layers can be exported as CSS layers when you're creating web layouts and Scalable Vector Graphics files, allowing for greater flexibility and better support for browser standards.

- **Scalable Vector Graphics (SVG).** Illustrator layers serve as basic building blocks when you're creating files that are going to be saved as SVG. Providing structure for SVG files can help make it easier to animate and edit the SVG files in a web or wireless environment.

- **Variables.** The XML-based variables feature in Illustrator relies on the organization of layers in your document. Object visibility and naming conventions are all done through the Layers panel.

There are plenty of other good reasons to use layers in Illustrator, and you're sure to find yourself using layers more and more.

Using the Layers Panel

You'll start learning to use layers by taking a look at the Layers panel and learning some of its simple functions. Then you'll put together everything you've learned in this chapter to take full advantage of the power found in the Layers panel.

By default, all Illustrator documents are created with a single existing layer, called Layer 1. The buttons across the bottom of the panel are used to activate clipping masks (which Chapter 9 will cover in detail), create new layers and new sublayers, and delete layers. To the left of each layer are two boxes: The box on the far left controls layer visibility, and the other box enables locking (**Figure 5.33**). The Layers panel menu contains duplicates of these functions, as well as some other functions that we'll cover when we talk about animation in Chapter 11, "Web Design."

Figure 5.33 *All files are created with a blank layer in the Layers panel.*

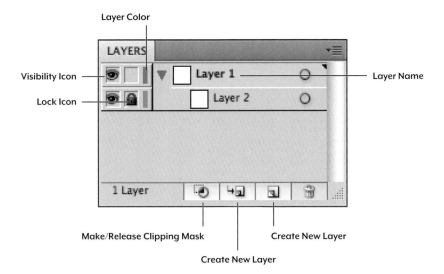

Double-clicking a layer enables you to specify several settings for that layer (**Figure 5.34**).

- **Name.** Every layer can have its own distinct name. Layer names are important when you're creating SVG files, and they generally make files easier to work with. Naming layers is especially important when you're designing templates. A file littered with layers named Layer 1, Layer 2, Layer 3, and so on, can make editing a challenging task.

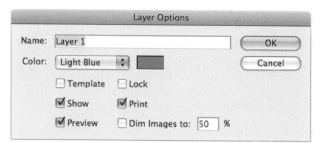

Figure 5.34 *The Layer Options dialog box allows you to specify settings for each layer—most notably, the name of the layer.*

- **Color.** This setting is a bit deceiving because it doesn't add a fill color to the layer but instead defines the selection color used for the layer. When you select an object in Illustrator, the path of that object is highlighted so that you see what is selected. By assigning different colors to each layer, you can tell what objects belong to which layer by selecting the object and observing the highlight color. Setting a layer color to black or really light colors generally isn't a good idea because you won't be able to differentiate a selection from a regular path. A layer's color also appears along the left side of the layer name in the Layers panel.

- **Template.** This setting is used specifically when you want to manually trace placed images. Setting a layer as a template automatically locks the layer, disables printing of that layer, and sets the "Dim Images to" setting to 50 percent. Although this makes it easier to see and draw over placed images, the new Live Trace feature makes this option less important.

- **Show.** This setting controls layer visibility (whether the art on a layer is shown or hidden) and performs the same function as clicking the visibility icon in the Layers panel.

- **Preview.** This setting controls the preview setting for the chosen layer. By default, Preview mode in Illustrator is turned on, but deselecting this option displays the layer in Outline mode.

- **Lock.** This setting controls layer locking and performs the same function as clicking the lock/unlock icon in the Layers panel. Locking a layer effectively prevents you from selecting any object on that layer.

- **Print.** By default, all layers in a file will print. However, Illustrator allows you to deselect this option to create a nonprinting layer. This can be useful when you want to add instructions to a template file or to explain how a file should be folded or printed, but you don't want those instructions to print. Layers that have the Print option deselected appear in italic in the Layers panel.

TIP Option-click (Alt-click) the visibility icon of a layer to hide all other layers with one click. Option-click (Alt-click) once more to show all layers again. The same shortcut applies to the lock icon as well. To change layer visibility for multiple layers, you can click and drag across several layers.

- **Dim Images to.** This option lets you define an Opacity setting for how placed images appear on your screen. By making placed images dim, you can make it easier to manually trace them. This feature is often used in tandem with the Template function.

Configuring the Layers Panel

The Layers panel in Illustrator displays more than just layers—it also displays all the objects in your file. Many people are confused and think that all elements displayed in the Layers panel are layers. (It's called the Layers panel, so can you really blame them?) It's actually pretty easy to determine what is a layer and what is an object—layers appear with a shaded gray background, and objects appear with a white background (**Figure 5.35**). This functionality was added way back in Illustrator 9, and it allows a user to locate any object from the Layers panel.

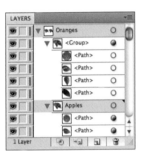

Figure 5.35 *In the Layers panel, objects have white backgrounds, and layers have gray backgrounds.*

If you find that the level of detail offered by the Layers panel is beyond the needs of your simple design tasks, you can set the behavior of the Layers panel to match the functionality that existed prior to Illustrator 9. Choose Panel Options from the Layers panel menu, and select the Show Layers Only check box (**Figure 5.36**). This hides all objects from the Layers panel. Additionally, you can turn off layer thumbnails (which will significantly enhance performance). For documents that have lots of layers (such as maps, for example), you might also choose the Small option for Row Size. One caveat to these options is that they are document-specific, which means you need to change these settings for each document.

Figure 5.36 *The Show Layers Only option keeps the Layers panel from displaying objects.*

Understanding Object Hierarchy

When a layer contains artwork, a disclosure triangle appears just to the left of the layer. Clicking this triangle reveals the contents of the layer within the Layers panel (**Figure 5.37**). Every object that appears in an Illustrator document appears listed in the Layers panel. As you learned earlier in this chapter, the order in which items appear has significance—it indicates the stacking order, or object hierarchy, of the file. Objects that appear at the bottom of the Layers panel are drawn first, and therefore they appear at the bottom of the object stacking order.

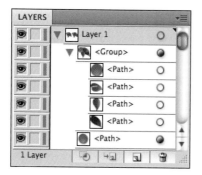

Figure 5.37 *Clicking a disclosure triangle reveals the raw power of the Layers panel—the ability to view the entire object hierarchy of a file.*

You can drag items listed in the Layers panel to adjust where they sit in the stacking order. Dragging an object from the bottom of the Layers panel to the top of the panel places that object at the top of the stacking order. It's important to note that each layer and each group also maintain their own stacking orders. The Layers panel basically represents the stacking order of the entire file.

You can create nested layers by dragging one layer into another layer. You can do the same with groups, which makes it easy to organize your artwork even after the art is created. In fact, this method of dragging items within the Layers panel makes it possible to move objects from one group and place them into another group (**Figure 5.38**, on the next page). As you learned earlier in this chapter, groups can have attributes applied to them; this becomes significant because when you're moving an object into a group that has an attribute applied to it, that object takes on the attributes of the group. The reverse applies as well, so simply moving an object from one layer to another or into or out of a group can change the appearance of the art in your file.

NOTE In the Layers panel, layers and sublayers appear with shaded backgrounds, and objects appear with white backgrounds.

Figure 5.38 *When you're dragging layers in the Layers panel, black arrows on the left and right indicate that you're moving a layer into another layer rather than above or below it.*

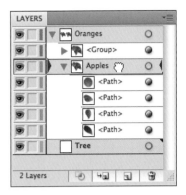

Using Layers and Appearances

When an object is selected, a small colored square appears in the far-right end of the Layers panel. Small squares indicate that an object is selected, and larger squares indicate that all objects on a layer are selected (layers with small squares indicate that only *some* elements on that layer are selected). You can move an object from one layer to another simply by dragging the square into the desired layer. Holding the Option (Alt) key while dragging the square moves a copy of the object into the desired layer.

If you take another look at the Layers panel, you'll notice that to the right of every item listed is a small circle, called the *target indicator* (**Figure 5.39**). If you remember, we spoke earlier about how the target controls where attributes are applied. If you take the same examples we used earlier—the ones of identical design elements of which one is grouped and one is not—you can clearly see how targeting works.

Figure 5.39 *The little circles that appear on the right side of each layer are target indicators.*

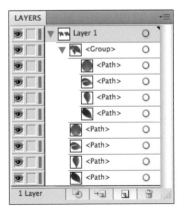

In the Layers panel, ungrouped design elements appear listed as separate paths, whereas the grouped design element appears as objects nested inside a group (**Figure 5.40**). When you select the first design element, a double circle appears on each of the individual paths, indicating that those paths are targeted (**Figure 5.41**). Now select the grouped design element, and you'll see that although the objects are *selected*, the group is *targeted* (**Figure 5.42**).

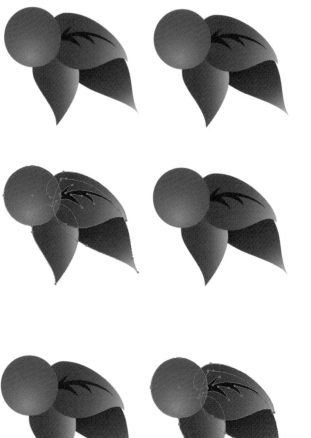

Figure 5.40 *A quick look at the Layers panel reveals the hierarchy of the file. Layer 1 contains four path objects and a group. The group contains four path objects.*

Figure 5.41 *Selecting the path objects also targets the four individual paths. The large squares to the right indicate the objects are selected, and the small square to the right of the layer indicates that some objects on the layer, but not all of them, are selected.*

Figure 5.42 *When selecting the group, the smart targeting feature targets the group, not the objects. Notice the double circle target indicator appears only on the group, not the objects.*

Now add a drop shadow to each of the design elements. A quick glance at the Layers panel now shows that some of the target indicators are shaded or filled, whereas some of the target indicators are hollow (**Figure 5.43**). Hollow circles indicate that the item listed has a basic appearance, whereas filled circles indicate that a complex appearance exists on that object. Just by looking at the Layers panel, you can tell that the second design element has some kind of effect applied to the group. This is your first indication that ungrouping such a group will result in a change in appearance—without having to even select it first.

Figure 5.43 *Shaded target indicators show where complex appearances exist.*

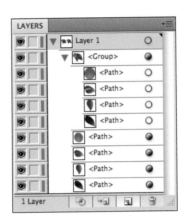

TIP Dragging a filled target circle from one layer or object to another effectively copies the complex appearance and applies it to the object to which you are dragging it.

You can manually target groups or layers by clicking the target indicator for that object. For example, just as you learned how to apply a stroke to a group earlier in this chapter, you can click the target circle of a layer and then add a new stroke to that layer. By moving the Stroke attribute beneath the contents of the layer in the Appearance panel, all objects that appear on that layer will have a stroke at the perimeter. When you move a shape into such a layer, the object automatically appears to have a stroked appearance, and likewise, when you move an object out of the layer, that stroked appearance disappears.

The important concept to remember is that taking a quick look at the Layers panel and scanning for filled target circles helps you find complex appearances in the file. In this way, you won't accidentally change a file's appearance just by grouping or ungrouping objects. The Appearance panel is also useful in helping you understand how files are built because it displays how complex appearances were added to the file.

Putting It All Together

The importance of the Appearance panel is obvious. Without it, you have no way to edit multiple attributes applied to an object, you have no way to edit attributes that are applied to groups or layers, and you have no way to edit the properties of a live effect.

The importance of the Layers panel is equally apparent. Without it, you have no way to understand the hierarchy of a file, and you have no warning as to when a simple action such as grouping or ungrouping will change a file's appearance.

But it's deeper than that. The Appearance panel is like the Matrix—you can look at it and see the underlying makeup of any Illustrator file. By using the Layers and Appearance panels together, you can quickly and efficiently reverse-engineer any file you receive (**Figure 5.44**). If you're a production artist who needs to know every detail about a file or if you're trying to troubleshoot a particular file, these two panels will be your best friends.

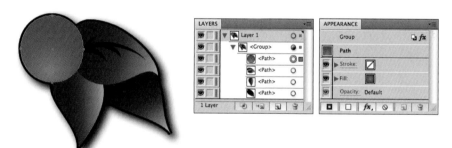

Figure 5.44 *Don't trust everything you see on the artboard. By using both the Appearance panel and the Layers panel, you will be able to see exactly how any art was created and, most importantly, how to edit it quickly.*

Throughout the chapters of this book, you'll see how features such as clipping and opacity masks, envelope distortions, and placed images are all easily identified in the Layers panel. You'll also learn the importance of using layers when you're creating content you're planning to animate in Flash Professional, Flash Catalyst, or with the SWF export feature in Illustrator.

Coloring Artwork

6

At one time, Illustrator (back in version 1.1) was black and white only. Then, Illustrator 88 introduced color features. Of course, back then, few designers could even afford to buy a color monitor. Technology eventually caught up, and color plays a huge role in a graphic designer's life today. We now take for granted the ability to add color and manipulate it, view it accurately on a monitor, and give life to artwork with it, but the challenges of working with color are still present.

In this chapter, you'll learn about creating color in Illustrator and applying it to your artwork, as well as a variety of ways to edit or modify colors. Illustrator features a collection of powerful inspirational tools that you can use to develop color harmonies and custom color palettes; you'll explore them in this chapter. Finally, you'll discover how to trust the color that appears on your computer screen and learn to use various settings to simulate different color-viewing environments.

The artwork featured throughout this chapter comes from Kemie Guaida Ortega (iStockphoto; username: kemie).

Creating and Using Color in Illustrator

Whether you are working with graphics that are to be printed (which use a combination of cyan, magenta, yellow, and black, also known as the *CMYK color model*) or those that are to be displayed on computer screens, televisions, or monitors (which use red, green, and blue, otherwise known as the *RGB color model*), you will always be specifying color as a combination of primary colors. When working in Illustrator, you'll find that, likewise, you define colors by mixing values of CMYK or RGB.

Of course, you can define and apply colors in plenty of ways. Some ways are more efficient than others, and some offer specific benefits. More so, some color features in Illustrator apply specifically to certain kinds of workflows and may even be irrelevant to some users. For example, using spot colors (solid, colored inks) serves no real purpose in the world of web design, while web-safe colors don't interest print designers in the least. But no matter what you're using your colors for, you'll find that, for the most part, you'll be creating and applying them via the Color panel and the Swatches panel (both available via the Window menu).

Using the Color Panel

The Color panel contains sliders that allow you to mix primary colors to create just about any custom color and apply it to your artwork. In fact, some graphics programs (such as FreeHand, for example) refer to this kind of panel as the Mixer. Think of it as a fine artist's palette that contains the primary colors. By mixing these colors, you can achieve any of your color needs. The Color panel doesn't *store* colors, so you can't use it as a repository for frequently used colors (that function is relegated to the Swatches panel, which we'll talk about shortly). However, any time you select an object, the Color panel will display the color values of that object. So, you can use it either to apply color or to modify an existing color (**Figure 6.1**).

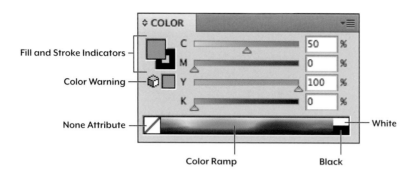

Figure 6.1 *By adjusting the sliders in the Color panel, you can mix any color you need.*

You can use the Color panel to specify colors using any of five sets of sliders: Grayscale, RGB (Red, Green, Blue), HSB (Hue, Saturation, Brightness), CMYK (Cyan, Magenta, Yellow, Black), and Web Safe RGB (216 colors that won't dither on a VGA monitor). To switch between these, either choose one manually from the Color panel menu or Shift-click the color ramp that appears toward the bottom of the Color panel.

The Color panel features fill and stroke indicators in the upper-left corner (similar to those found in the Tools panel). Clicking the fill indicator allows you to specify a color for the Fill attribute of a selection, and clicking the stroke indicator does the same for the Stroke attribute. To save time, pressing the X key on your keyboard toggles between the two attributes (Shift-X will swap the fill and stroke colors).

Although the Color panel doesn't store colors, you'll find that the color ramp at the bottom of the panel contains one-click shortcuts to the None, Black, and White attributes. The keyboard shortcut for the None attribute is the slash (/). The Color panel also displays a color warning in the shape of a small 3D cube beneath the fill and stroke indicators when the chosen color is not a web-safe color. Clicking the cube snaps your current color to the closest web-safe color match. For more information on web-safe colors, refer to Chapter 11, "Web Design."

Using the Swatches Panel

The Swatches panel stores a collection of predefined colors, making it easy to apply specific colors to your document quickly. Think of the Swatches panel as a box of crayons. You just choose the color you need and use it. In fact, the

Swatches panel stores more than just solid colors; it also stores the two other types of fills that Illustrator supports: gradients and patterns. If the Swatches panel seems a bit cluttered with all these types of swatches, you can click the Show Swatch Kinds icon at the bottom of the panel to limit the display to a specific swatch type (**Figure 6.2**).

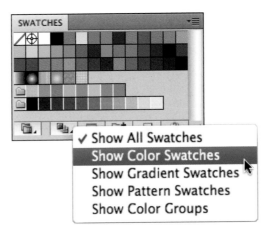

Figure 6.2 *You can set the Swatches panel to display all kinds of swatches or just solid colors.*

You can create a new color swatch in Illustrator in several ways:

- Click the New Swatch icon in the Swatches panel.

- Choose New Swatch from the Swatches panel menu.

- Choose Create New Swatch from the Color panel menu.

- Drag a color from the fill and stroke indicators in the Color panel or the Tools panel to the Swatches panel.

- Drag a color from the Color Guide panel (the Color Guide panel is covered in detail later in this chapter).

Double-clicking a swatch opens the Swatch Options dialog box and lets you edit the swatch (**Figure 6.3**). By default, swatches are named by their color values; however, you can name your swatches as you like. You can also specify a color mode and a color type for your swatch (refer to the "Hitting the Color Swatch Trifecta" section for explanations of these types).

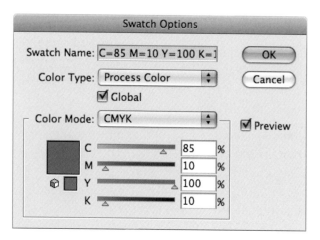

Figure 6.3 *The Swatch Options dialog box lets you quickly edit your swatch settings.*

For files that already contain artwork, you can automatically create swatches from the artwork. With no objects selected, choose Add Used Colors from the Swatches panel menu. If you want to add colors from a specific area in your document, select the objects desired and choose Add Selected Color from the Swatches panel menu. All new colors that are added will appear as global process colors, which are described in the next section.

You can also customize the view of your Swatches panel. By default, the swatches appear as little squares called *thumbnails*. But if you prefer, you can also have your swatches display in List view, which displays a little square beside the name of the swatch (**Figure 6.4**). You can choose from a variety of thumbnail and list sizes by selecting an option from the Swatches panel menu.

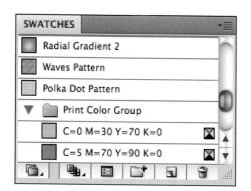

Figure 6.4 *In List view, swatches appear listed by name.*

Hitting the Color Swatch Trifecta

It would be simple if Illustrator offered only one type of solid color swatch, but, alas, it actually offers three: process color, global process color, and spot color swatches. Each serves a specific purpose, and it's important to understand when each should be used.

Process colors. A *process color* is defined by a mixture of primary values. For color print work that is separated and printed using a four-color process (CMYK), for output to a color printer, or for web design and video work, you want to define your swatches as process color swatches. Creating process color swatches allows you to easily apply set colors to art that you create in your document, but updating colors on existing objects is difficult. As you'll see shortly, you'll often want to look into using global process colors instead.

Global process colors. A *global process color* is the same as a process color with one main difference: The swatch is global in that if you ever update the swatch, all objects in the document that have that swatch applied update as well. Most production artists request that designers use global swatches because they are easier to manage in an entire document. To create a global process color swatch, select the Global option in the New Swatch dialog box or Swatch Options dialog box. In the Swatches panel, global process colors display with a small white triangle in their lower-right corners (**Figure 6.5**).

Figure 6.5 *It's easy to identify a swatch by its appearance. Solid squares are process colors, squares with white corners are global process colors, and squares with white corners and dots are spot colors.*

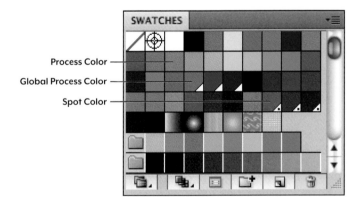

Spot colors. A *spot color* is a named color that appears on a custom plate during the color separation process. Instead of a printer breaking a color into cyan, magenta, yellow, or black, a spot color is a specific custom color ink that the printer creates for your print job. You might have a variety of reasons for using a spot color in a document:

- **Specific color.** Not every color can be reproduced using CMYK, which in reality has a small gamut of color choices. A custom color can be a bright fluorescent color, a color with a metallic sheen, or even one that involves specialized inks, such as the magnetic inks used on bank checks.

- **Consistent color.** Because process colors consist of a mixture of other colors, they can shift and appear differently, even on the same print job. When you're dealing with a company's corporate colors, you want to make sure color is consistent across all print jobs.

- **Solid color.** Process colors are formed by mixing inks in various percentages. Not only does this require perfect registration on a printing press (where all plates hit the same place on each sheet of paper), but the process can also reveal odd patterns in reproduction in some cases (called *moiré patterns*). Spot color inks don't exhibit these issues and present a solid, clean appearance.

- **Cheaper color.** When you are performing a process color job, you're printing with four different color inks. But if you are creating a business card with black text and a red logo, it's cheaper to print using black ink and a single red spot color instead. Sometimes working with two or three spot colors gives your design the color it needs while keeping the printing costs down.

- **Something other than a "color."** Print designs can be extremely creative, using processes such as foil stamping, die cutting, spot varnishing, or embossing. Even though these special effects don't print in ink, they still need to be specified to a printer. Spot colors allow you to easily define areas of color that will ultimately be regions of a gloss varnish effect, a die stamp, and so on.

You can define your own custom color (by choosing the Spot Color option in the Color Type pop-up menu), or you can choose a spot color from an existing library. Pantone libraries are the most common examples; they were created to help printers and designers standardize on colors by using a numbering system. To apply a color from a Pantone library, see "Working with Libraries" later in this chapter.

Process and Global Process Swatches

At first glance, it may seem difficult to understand what the difference is between a process color and a global process color swatch. But once you understand what each has to offer, it's easy to figure out when you should use each type of color swatch.

A process color swatch is simply a way to "memorize" the values for a particular color. The swatch contains the color breakdown (the individual values of each primary color), saving you from having to reapply multiple values to each object that you want to color in your document. To use it, you can select an object and then click a swatch to apply the chosen color to the object.

A global process swatch does the same thing but adds two main benefits in the way of productivity and creativity. First, when you select an object and then you choose a global process color swatch, an invisible "link" is created between the object and the swatch. This means if you ever modify the swatch (that is, edit its values), any objects in your document that you've already colored with that swatch will update as well. Second, global process colors show up in the Color panel with a tint slider, making it easy to specify different shades of your color.

So when defining your swatches, be sure to select the Global check box in order to get the benefits of working with global process color swatches, including the ability to specify tint values.

Working with Groups of Color

As a designer, you may find it easier to organize your swatches into groups (**Figure 6.6**). In this way, you can find the colors you need quickly. More important, however, organizing colors into groups makes it easy to establish relationships between colors, which can be helpful when recoloring artwork using the Live Color feature (covered later in this chapter) or when using the Shape Builder tool or the Live Paint Bucket tool.

Figure 6.6 *Grouping swatches makes it easy to organize colors.*

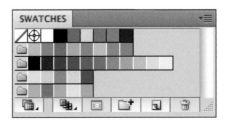

You can create a new group of swatches in several ways:

- With nothing selected, click the New Color Group icon at the bottom of the Swatches panel to create an empty color group. Drag existing swatches from the Swatches panel directly into or out of the group.

- Select multiple swatches in the Swatches panel using the Shift or Command (Ctrl) key, and then click the New Color Group icon at the bottom of the Swatches panel. The New Color Group dialog box appears so you can name your group. Click OK to create the group.

- Select multiple swatches in the Color Guide panel using the Shift or Command (Ctrl) key, and click the Save Color Group to Swatch Panel icon at the bottom of the Color Guide panel.

- With artwork selected on the artboard, click the New Color Group icon at the bottom of the Swatches panel. You can automatically convert all process colors to global process colors, as well as include specific swatches for tints of colors (**Figure 6.7**).

Figure 6.7 *With a single click, you can easily create a new group of swatches from colors that appear in a selection.*

You can edit any single swatch within a group simply by double-clicking it. However, if you want to edit a group (and all the colors within it), you can either double-click the group's folder icon that appears in the Swatches panel or select the group and click the Edit Color Group icon at the bottom of the Swatches panel. It's best to edit color groups when no artwork is selected, or any changes you make will be applied to your selection.

NOTE Swatch groups can contain only color swatches (process, global process, and spot) and not gradients or patterns.

You edit groups in the Edit Colors dialog box (**Figure 6.8**, on the next page). Saved color groups appear listed along the right side of the dialog box (you can click the disclosure triangles to reveal the individual colors within them). Clicking a color group maps the colors within the group onto the color wheel, and clicking a specific color within the group highlights that color on the wheel. You can make adjustments to your colors on the wheel

Figure 6.8 *You can use the Edit Colors dialog box to adjust colors within groups. Existing color groups appear on the right side of the dialog box.*

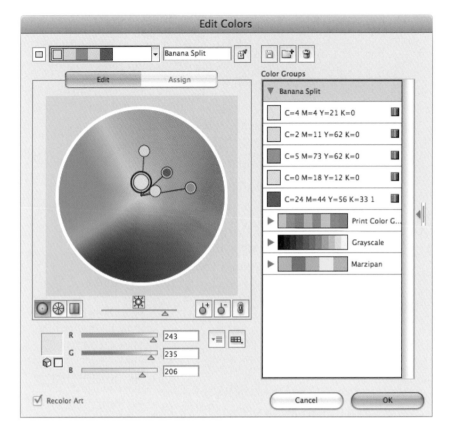

(refer to "Modifying Color" later in this chapter for detailed information on how to do this), and then you can save your changes or create entirely new color groups using the icons at the top right of the Edit Colors dialog box (**Figure 6.9**). Click OK to exit the Edit Colors dialog box and return to your document.

Figure 6.9 *You can modify, create, and delete groups easily within the Edit Colors dialog box.*

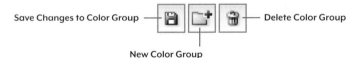

Working with Libraries

Illustrator files can contain all kinds of attributes including colors, gradients, patterns, symbols, brushes, and graphic styles. You can save each of these attributes as libraries so that you can share them between Illustrator documents.

Illustrator makes the process of managing libraries easy by incorporating some features directly into the panels. At the bottom of the Swatches panel, click the Swatch Libraries Menu icon to see a list of libraries you can use (**Figure 6.10**). Choosing a swatch library opens a new panel containing those swatches. Applying any colors from a custom swatch library automatically adds those colors to the document's Swatches panel.

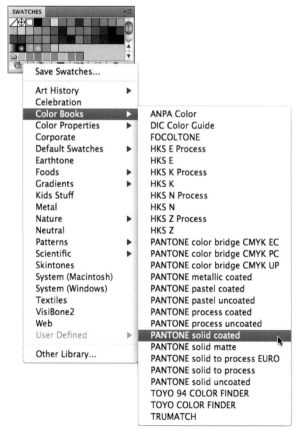

Figure 6.10 *You can load swatch libraries right from the Swatches panel. Libraries appear in hierarchical format according to how they're organized within the Adobe Illustrator CS5/Presets/en_US/ Swatches folder.*

NOTE Commercial color libraries such as Pantone, Toyo, and Trumatch appear listed in the Color Books submenu. You can get newer Pantone GOE libraries from www.pantone.com/goefree and Pantone Plus libraries at www.pantone.com/plus.

You can create your own custom library files by adding swatches to the Swatches panel and deleting any swatches you don't want (choosing Select All Unused from the Swatches panel menu can help in that process). Then choose Save Swatch Library as AI, and name your library. Once saved, you can access your custom library by clicking the Swatch Libraries Menu icon (it will appear at the bottom of the list in a subfolder named User Defined). If you want to use your swatch library in Photoshop or InDesign (versions CS2 or higher) or Fireworks (version CS4 or higher), choose Save Swatch Library as ASE instead (**Figure 6.11**). ASE (Adobe Swatch Exchange) supports solid-color swatches, not gradients or patterns.

Figure 6.11 *You can open an Adobe Swatch Exchange file with Illustrator, Photoshop, Fireworks, or InDesign.*

If you want a custom library to always appear on your screen each time you launch Illustrator, open the library and choose Persistent from that library's panel menu (**Figure 6.12**).

Figure 6.12 *Making a custom library persistent ensures it is always available on your screen.*

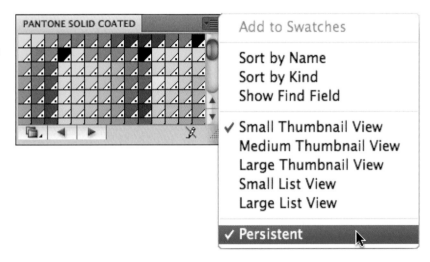

Finding Your Pantone Number

When you load a Pantone color library, you'll find that the library contains hundreds if not thousands of colors. So, how do you find just the number of the color you need? From the library's panel menu, choose Show Find Field. You can then type your Pantone number in the field to jump directly to that color (**Figure 6.13**).

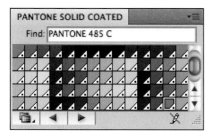

Figure 6.13 *Once you choose Show Find Field from a Pantone color library's menu, you can type a number to quickly find the color.*

But you may also find that, at times, it seems impossible to type your number. For example, if you try entering **485** for Pantone 485, you'll find that instead Illustrator takes you directly to Pantone 1485. To get Pantone 485, you will have to type a space before the numbers 485. Why? That's a great question. I'm glad you asked.

Teri Pettit, an engineer on the Illustrator team at Adobe, offers the following explanation:

"What the search command does is first look for a swatch starting with the characters you type. For example, if you type **lo**, it will first look for colors starting with *lo*, such as Loden Green. But if it finds none, it will then look for the first swatch name containing *lo* and will match Yellow.

"Characters are concatenated into the search string if they occur within the double-click time. Otherwise, it starts over with a new string.

"Since the Pantone libraries are not sorted in numerical order but semialphabetically, if you are searching for something like 613, it will find the substring match in Pantone 2613 before it will find the one in Pantone 613. By typing ' **613**' (there's a space before the 6), you prevent a match in 2613, and so on."

Adding Color with Fills and Strokes

As you know, vector shapes are composed of anchor points, which control how the paths that connect them are drawn. The *fill* of a vector object is the appearance of the area that is enclosed by its path. If the shape isn't a closed path, the fill is defined by the existing path and is closed with a straight line connecting the start and end points (**Figure 6.14**, on the next page). The *stroke* of an object is the appearance of the vector path itself. Fills and strokes can have a variety of appearances, and vector objects can also contain multiple fills and strokes—something you learned in Chapter 5, "Organizing Your Drawing." All vector objects must have both a fill and a stroke color assigned, although that attribute can be set to None. Fills or strokes colored with None appear invisible and have no appearance. There's also one additional attribute called Registration, which is basically the exact opposite of None. Registration is a color that appears on every plate when a file is color separated (see Chapter 13, "Prepress and Printing," for details on color separations).

Figure 6.14 *Open paths can have a fill applied, and Illustrator stops the fill by creating a boundary (no physical path is created).*

Applying Fills

There are three types of fills: solid colors, gradients, and patterns. Each of these fill types can be stored in the Swatches panel. The Swatches panel lets you view these attributes as thumbnails or as a named list, and you can apply these attributes to a selected object simply by clicking the swatches. Alternatively, you can apply fill colors directly via the Control panel and the Appearance panel.

The most common and simple form of a fill is a solid color, which applies a single flat color to the appearance of the fill of a vector shape. For example, a rectangle can have a solid blue fill, a solid yellow fill, or any color of your choosing. Gradients and patterns are more complex fills, so let's take a closer look at each of them.

NOTE Although they share a similar name, gradient fills and gradient mesh are two very different things. For details on the Gradient Mesh feature in Illustrator, refer to Chapter 4, "Creative Drawing."

Gradient Fills

Whereas a solid color fill consists of just one color, a *gradient* fill consists of solid colors that blend into each other. A gradient can contain as few as one color and as many as—well, let's just say we stopped counting at 300. *Linear* gradients start with a color on one end that gradually blends into a color on the other end (for example, from left to right). *Radial* gradients start with a color at the center and gradually blend into another color, radiating outward.

The Gradient panel (Window > Gradient) gives you complete control over the use and appearance of any gradient (**Figure 6.15**):

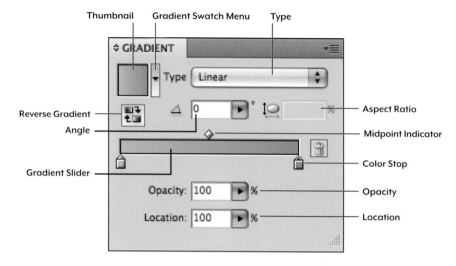

Figure 6.15 *Gradients can be defined and modified in the Gradient panel.*

- **Thumbnail.** The thumbnail shows a preview of the current gradient. You can drag the thumbnail directly onto an existing object on your artboard to fill that object with the gradient, or you can drag the thumbnail into the Swatches panel to create a gradient swatch.

- **Gradient Swatch menu.** Instead of digging in the Swatches panel for a specific gradient, you can open the Gradient Swatch menu to display all gradient swatches in a pop-up menu. You can also click the disk icon that appears in this menu to define gradient swatches.

- **Type.** As described earlier, a gradient can be either linear or radial. Radial gradients can be distorted to create an oval shape (see "Aspect ratio" that follows).

- **Reverse Gradient.** Clicking the Reverse Gradient button reverses the order of all the color stops in a gradient (see "Gradient slider" that follows for information on color stops).

- **Angle.** This sets the direction of the gradient (only for linear gradients).

- **Aspect ratio.** This sets the difference between the width and height of the gradient circle (only for radial gradients).

- **Gradient slider.** The focal point of the Gradient panel, the gradient slider is composed of three elements: a *slider* that displays a preview of the gradient, *color stops* that define the colors (and their positions) that appear in the gradient, and midpoint indicators that define the point at which two colors meet (or blend) at exactly 50 percent of each color. Color stops are small boxes that appear beneath the slider, while midpoint indicators are diamonds that appear above the slider. Every gradient must contain at least two color stops (midpoint indicators are automatically added between every two color stops).

- **Opacity.** The Opacity value determines the transparency setting for a selected color stop.

- **Location.** The Location value represents the precise position of a selected midpoint on the gradient slider.

To create a gradient, drag colors from the Color, Color Guide, or Swatches panel directly onto the gradient slider. Dragging a color directly on top of an existing color stop changes the color of that color stop. Dragging a color onto the slider itself creates a new color stop (you can also click anywhere beneath the slider to add a new color stop). To remove a color stop from a gradient, you can either select it and click the trash can icon in the Gradient panel or simply drag it off the gradient slider. You can also double-click a color stop to change its color and opacity (**Figure 6.16**). To swap colors between color stops, drag one color stop over another one while holding the Option (Alt) key. Drag midpoint indicators to the left or right to adjust how quickly one color blends into the other.

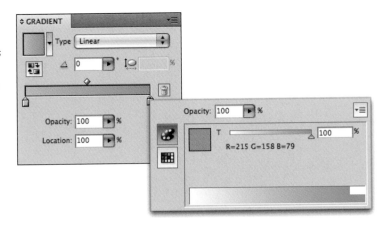

Figure 6.16 *Double-clicking a color stop lets you define its color. The two icons that appear on the left in the pop-up panel let you choose colors via the Color panel and the Swatches panel.*

Admittedly, the practice of applying a gradient to an object on the artboard and then trying to adjust that gradient in the Gradient panel makes for a somewhat disconnected creative experience. It would be far better if you could edit a gradient's settings directly on the object itself—which is exactly why the Gradient tool (G) allows you to do just that—edit gradients in context, right on the artboard.

To modify a gradient, start by selecting an object and filling it with a gradient of your choice (or simply select an object that already has a gradient fill applied to it). Then, select the Gradient tool, and click and drag to define the position of the first color stop of the gradient. The point where you release the mouse button defines the position of the last color stop of the gradient (**Figure 6.17**).

Figure 6.17 *The Gradient tool makes it easy to apply gradients at an angle.*

What makes the Gradient tool so powerful is that you can begin or end a gradient anywhere, even outside the boundaries of the object you have selected (**Figure 6.18**). Additionally, you can select multiple objects and apply a single gradient across all of them using the Gradient tool (**Figure 6.19**, on the next page).

Figure 6.18 *A gradient fills the distance from where you first clicked to where you release the mouse button, even if those locations are beyond the boundaries of your selection.*

Figure 6.19 *The Gradient tool enables you to apply a single gradient across multiple objects.*

But even more exciting about editing gradients with the Gradient tool is how you can adjust all of a gradient's attributes directly on the artboard. When you select an object that is filled with a gradient and you switch to the Gradient tool, Illustrator displays a *fill path* that shows the start and end points of the gradient (**Figure 6.20**). When you move your pointer over the fill path, it expands to reveal an entire functional gradient slider, or widget. (Adobe refers to this as the *Gradient Annotator*, and you can control its appearance by choosing View > Hide/Show Gradient Annotator.)

Figure 6.20 *Selected objects filled with gradients display a fill path when the Gradient tool is active.*

Start Point (Origin)

Fill Path

End Point

The settings and the experience of interacting with the gradient widget are different for linear and radial gradients, so we'll explore each individually:

- **Linear gradients.** As with the Gradient panel, you can use the gradient widget to modify the position of color stops and midpoint indicators (**Figure 6.21**). Drag color stops off the gradient slider to delete them, add new color stops by clicking underneath the slider, and double-click a color stop to change its color and opacity (**Figure 6.22**). Clicking and dragging the circle icon (the start point) allows you to reposition the origin of the gradient. As you do so, a dashed line appears indicating the center of the object, because a linear gradient always runs through the center of an object (**Figure 6.23**). Click and drag the diamond icon at the edge of the fill path (the end point) to adjust the length of the gradient's fill path. If you position your pointer just outside the diamond icon, you'll see a rotation pointer appear, which you can then click and drag to adjust the gradient angle (**Figure 6.24**).

Figure 6.21 *The linear gradient widget lets you modify the position of color stops directly on the artboard.*

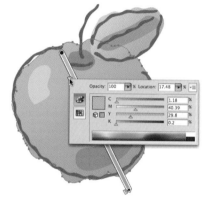

Figure 6.22 *Double-clicking a color stop gives you the ability to change its color instantly.*

Figure 6.23 *Linear gradients always run through the center of an object, as indicated by a dashed line.*

Figure 6.24 *You can easily rotate a gradient visually instead of trying to enter a value numerically in the Gradient panel.*

- **Radial gradients.** As with the Gradient panel, you can use the gradient widget to modify the position of color stops and midpoint indicators (**Figure 6.25**). Drag color stops off the gradient slider to delete them, add new color stops by clicking underneath the slider, and double-click a color stop to change its color and opacity. Clicking and dragging the circle icon (the start point) allows you to reposition the origin of the gradient. Click and drag the diamond icon at the edge of the fill path (the end point) to adjust the radius of the gradient. If you position your pointer just outside the diamond icon, you'll see a rotation pointer appear, which you can then click and drag to adjust the gradient angle. You may ask what good rotating a radial gradient will do, because rotating a circular object doesn't have any visible effect. Good question. The answer is that radial gradients can easily become elliptical (oval) gradients. Clicking and dragging the solid dot that appears along the circumference of the gradient (indicated by a dashed line) lets you adjust the aspect ratio value of the gradient (**Figure 6.26**).

Figure 6.25 *When using the radial gradient widget, the dashed line visually describes the circumference (basically, the end point) of the gradient.*

Figure 6.26 *Applying an aspect ratio results in an elliptical gradient.*

Pattern Fills

A *pattern* fill uses a repeating art element to fill the boundaries of a path or object. To define a pattern, create just about any kind of art on your artboard (including embedded raster images and text objects), and drag it into your

Swatches panel, or choose Edit > Define Pattern. You can apply pattern fills to objects the same way you apply solid color fills—by targeting the fill or stroke of a selection and choosing a pattern swatch from the Swatches panel. When objects are filled with patterns, you can choose to transform the patterns with the objects, or you can have Illustrator rotate just the objects but not the pattern fill.

The Art of Pattern Making

In reality, an entire book could be written on creating patterns, which is an art form in and of itself. The Illustrator Help files actually contain some great information on working with patterns. Creating perfect, repeating patterns that tile seamlessly can take a bit of advance planning, as well as trial and error.

When you drag artwork into the Swatches panel to create a pattern swatch, Illustrator uses the bounding area of the artwork that you selected as the boundary of the repeat area. In many cases, however, this default bounding box does not create a seamless pattern. To create a seamless pattern, you might have to position objects well inside the repeat area or even have artwork extend beyond the repeat area. To define a repeat area for a pattern, draw a no-fill, no-stroke rectangle at the bottom of the stacking order. Even if there are objects that extend outside the rectangle, Illustrator will use that rectangle to define the repeat area (**Figure 6.27**).

Repeat Area

Figure 6.27 *Using a rectangle as the bottommost shape in your pattern art defines a repeat area (left), thus helping create a seamless pattern tile, as in this example from illustrator Von Glitschka.*

Sometimes the best way to learn is to reverse-engineer existing artwork. To get a better feel for how repeats are designed, take a look at some of the patterns that come with Illustrator. Choose Open Swatch Library > Patterns from the Swatches panel menu to view some of these patterns. To access the art that was used to define any pattern swatch, simply drag a swatch from the Swatches panel onto the artboard. For an inspirational book on creating and using patterns, check out Von Glitschka's *Drip Dot Swirl* (How, 2009).

Applying Strokes

A *stroke* is the appearance of the vector path itself. You can specify a stroke color by choosing one from the Stroke pop-up menu in the Control or Appearance panel or by targeting the stroke using the fill/stroke indicator and then choosing a color from either the Color or Swatches panel. You can also choose from several different settings to control the appearance of a stroke, all of which are available in the Stroke panel:

- **Weight.** The thickness of a stroke is referred to as the *stroke weight*, and it is traditionally specified in points (pts). Specifying a stroke weight of less than .25 pt might be problematic for most printing presses. In Illustrator CS5, you can adjust the weight of a stroke at any point along a path, which we'll discuss shortly.

- **Miter limit.** A stroke's *miter limit* specifies the appearance of corners that have very acute angles. If you find that the corner of a stroke appears clipped, you can increase the miter limit to correct the appearance (**Figure 6.28**).

Figure 6.28 *The object on the left has an 18-pt stroke applied with a miter limit of 2, whereas the object on the right has an 18-pt stroke applied with a miter limit of 10.*

- **Cap.** The cap setting is an attribute that affects the appearance of the start and end points of a stroke. Obviously, this setting applies to open paths only (although it can be applied to dashes as well, as you will soon see). You can choose between a Butt, Round, or Projecting cap (**Figure 6.29**).

- **Join.** A join attribute determines the appearance of a stroke as it passes through an anchor point. Miter, Round, and Bevel are the different options you can choose from (**Figure 6.30**).

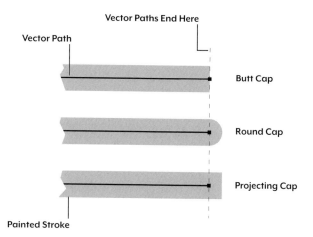

Vector Paths End Here

Vector Path

Butt Cap

Round Cap

Projecting Cap

Painted Stroke

Figure 6.29 *The cap setting defines how the start and end of a stroke appear. From the top, Butt, Round, and Projecting caps can also add to the length of a stroke.*

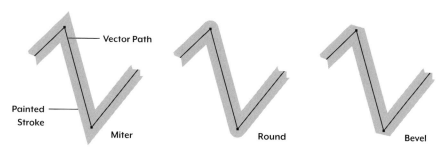

Vector Path

Painted Stroke

Miter

Round

Bevel

Figure 6.30 *The join setting defines the appearance of connecting straight anchor points. From left to right are examples of stroked paths with Miter, Round, and Bevel joins.*

Aligning Strokes

By default, Illustrator paints a stroke on the center of a path. For example, if you specify a 10-pt stroke for an object, the result is 5 pts appearing on the outside of the path and 5 pts appearing on the inside of the path. In the Stroke panel, you can specify whether you want the entire stroke painted on the inside or outside of the vector path (**Figure 6.31**). This setting is available only for closed paths.

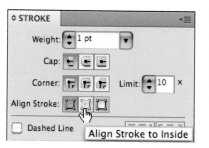

Figure 6.31 *Use the Align Stroke options in the Stroke panel to specify whether a stroke should be painted on the center, inside, or outside of the path.*

Using Dashed Strokes

Strokes don't have to be solid lines. They can have a broken appearance resulting in dashed lines. Rather than just choosing a preset dashed line, Illustrator gives you the ability to specify exactly how the dashes should appear along a stroked path.

When specifying the appearance of a dash, you can specify the length of the dash and the length of the gap—the space that appears after the dash. The Stroke panel contains three sets of dash and gap settings. If you specify a dash without specifying a gap, Illustrator creates a gap equal to the size of the dash. For most standard dashed strokes, you will use only the first dash and gap setting. However, you can use all three to create a sequence of dashes and gaps (**Figure 6.32**). When you specify the Round cap option for the stroke, a dash value of 0 results in a perfect circle, allowing you to create dotted lines.

Figure 6.32 *The ability to set custom dashes for a stroke lets you create a plethora of dashed strokes that you can use for a variety of tasks.*

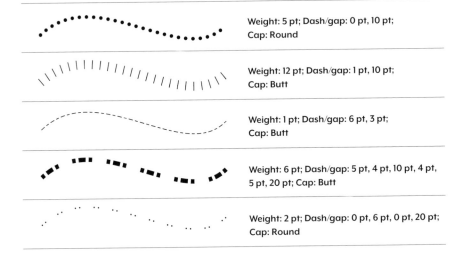

Weight: 5 pt; Dash/gap: 0 pt, 10 pt; Cap: Round

Weight: 12 pt; Dash/gap: 1 pt, 10 pt; Cap: Butt

Weight: 1 pt; Dash/gap: 6 pt, 3 pt; Cap: Butt

Weight: 6 pt; Dash/gap: 5 pt, 4 pt, 10 pt, 4 pt, 5 pt, 20 pt; Cap: Butt

Weight: 2 pt; Dash/gap: 0 pt, 6 pt, 0 pt, 20 pt; Cap: Round

Because dashes and gaps have specific values, you may end up with shapes where dashes and gaps do not align exactly to the corners of your path. This can often give your artwork an uneven appearance. In the Stroke panel, you can choose between two dash alignment options: Preserves Exact Dash and Gap Lengths and Aligns Dashes to Corners and Path Ends, Adjusting

Lengths to Fit (**Figure 6.33**). You can toggle between these two settings to make sure your dashes look just right along the paths of your artwork. Keep in mind that these settings can also ensure that dashes align beautifully on paths without corners—you'll find that dashes also align perfectly on round and non-uniform paths (**Figure 6.34**).

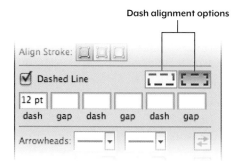

Figure 6.33 *The dash alignment options give you control over the appearance of dashed strokes.*

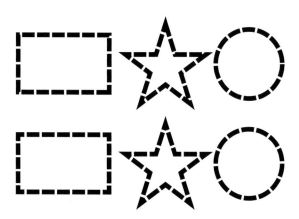

Figure 6.34 *The Preserve Exact Dash (top) and Aligns Dashes to Corners and Path Ends (bottom) settings work on paths of all shapes and sizes.*

Adding Arrowheads

Specifying dashes and gaps is just one way to adjust the appearance of a stroke. Another way is to add ornaments to the start and end of a stroke, which is often used to add arrowheads—perfect for creating diagrams or callouts. Using the Arrowheads pop-up menus in the Stroke panel, you can choose what type of ornament you want to apply at the start and end of your path (**Figure 6.35** on the following page).

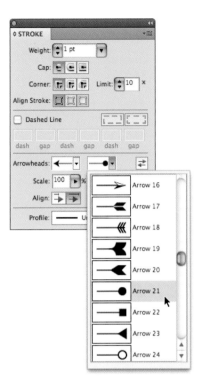

Illustrator uses the stroke width of your path to determine the size of the arrowhead, but you can adjust the size to perfection by using the Scale setting beneath each arrowhead pop-up menu (click the lock icon to keep both the start and end arrowheads the same size).

It's not always easy to determine which side of a path is the start and which is the end, so you can use the handy Swap Start and End Arrowheads button to quickly reverse the arrowheads. In addition, you can specify exactly how Illustrator places the arrowhead art at the end of the path, making it easy to align your artwork perfectly (**Figure 6.36**).

Figure 6.36 *Illustrator gives you two options for aligning arrowheads.*

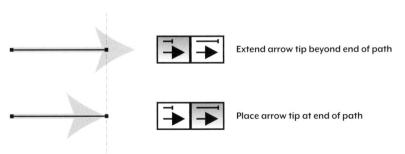

Extend arrow tip beyond end of path

Place arrow tip at end of path

The arrowheads always match the orientation of the path, so if you adjust the path after you've added the effect, the arrowheads update accordingly.

NOTE Arrowheads can be applied both to open and closed paths. Using arrowheads is a great way to quickly figure out the direction of a path.

Define Your Own Customized Arrowheads

If the 39 different arrowhead designs that come with Illustrator don't fit your needs, you can define your own. To do so, follow these directions:

Mac OS X

1. Open the Applications > Adobe Illustrator CS5 folder.

2. Control-click (right-click) the Adobe Illustrator CS5 application icon and choose Show Package Contents.

3. Open the Arrowheads.ai file that is located in the Required > Resources > en_US folder.

4. Follow the instructions that are outlined in the Arrowheads.ai file.

5. Save and close the file. Quit and relaunch Illustrator. Your custom arrowheads will now be available in any Illustrator document.

Windows

1. Open the Program Files (x86) > Adobe > Adobe Illustrator CS5 > Support Files folder.

2. Open the Arrowheads.ai file.

3. Follow the instructions that are outlined in the Arrowheads.ai file.

4. Save and close the file. Quit and relaunch Illustrator. Your custom arrowheads will now be available in any Illustrator document.

NOTE If you open a legacy file that has the older Arrowheads effect applied, Illustrator will display the Add Arrowhead effect for that object in the Appearance panel; the Add Arrowhead effect will also show up in the Effect > Stylize submenu. To convert these legacy effects to the new stroke settings, you must delete the Add Arrowhead effect using the Appearance panel and then apply the arrowhead from the Stroke panel.

Creating Variable-Width Strokes

In the Stroke panel, you have the ability to specify the weight—the thickness—of a stroke as it appears along a path. By default, this weight is applied uniformly along the entire path. However in Illustrator CS5, you can vary the weight of a stroke at different points along a path with absolute precision using the new Width tool.

Before using the Width tool, it's important to get a solid understanding of how variable-width strokes work. Each shape that you draw in Illustrator is made up of anchor points and paths that connect those anchor points. When you apply a stroke attribute to a path, you can think of the stroke as being applied on top of the paths and anchor points—like another layer above it.

In Illustrator CS5, a stroke attribute can have its own set of points, called *width points*, which define the weight of a stroke at a specific position. The exact weight of a stroke at a width point, and the way the stroke weight is distributed on either side of the path, are defined by *width handles* that extend out from each width point (**Figure 6.37**).

Figure 6.37 *Width points and handles determine the thickness of a stroke as it appears along the path.*

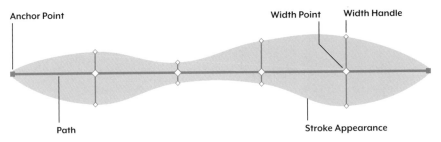

NOTE When a stroke has variable widths, the value that is displayed in the Weight field in the Stroke, Appearance, or Control panels represents the weight of the stroke at its thickest point. An asterisk (*) also appears in the Appearance panel, indicating the targeted stroke has variable widths applied to it.

Using the Width tool

Once you've applied a stroke to a path, you can use the Width tool (**Figure 6.38**) to adjust the thickness of the stroke at any point along the path. You can do this whether or not your object is selected on the artboard. With the Width tool selected, you can make the following adjustments to the thickness of a stroke:

Figure 6.38 *The Width tool can be used to create variable-width strokes.*

- Hover over any point along a path to view the thickness of a stroke at that point of the path (**Figure 6.39**). Note that this will work only if Smart Guides is turned on, with the Measurement Labels option selected in the Smart Guides Preferences panel.

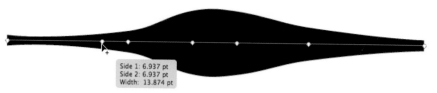

Figure 6.39 *With the help of Smart Guides, you can quickly find the exact stroke width at any point along a path.*

• Click and drag at any point along the path to pull out width handles (**Figure 6.40**). A width point will automatically be defined at that location on the path.

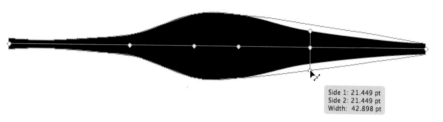

Figure 6.40 *Illustrator creates smooth transitions between width points.*

• Click and drag any width handle to adjust an existing width point.

• Option-drag (Alt-drag) any width handle to adjust the stroke width along just one side of the path.

• Select a width point (or Shift-click to select multiple points) and press the Delete key to remove one or several points.

• Double-click to bring up the Width Point Edit dialog box (**Figure 6.41**). You can then apply specific numerical values to the width handles that appear on either side of the path, or you can specify a total width value. Choosing the Adjust Adjoining Width Points option will also proportionately adjust the widths of neighboring width points, and clicking Delete will remove the selected width point from the stroke.

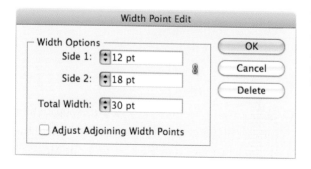

Figure 6.41 *The Width Point Edit dialog box gives you the ability to define precise values for individual width handles.*

- Drag a selected width point to move it along a path.

- Press and hold the Shift key while dragging to adjust the position of all of the width points proportionately along a path.

- Option-drag a width point to make a copy of it.

The Width tool does have a trick up its sleeve. You'll notice that it isn't called the Stroke Width tool, and that's because it isn't limited to only adjusting the thickness of strokes. The Width tool can also be used to adjust the thickness of the appearance of Art and Pattern brushes. For more information on these brush types, see Chapter 4, "Creative Drawing."

Using Variable Width Profiles

Because width points are applied on top of the path itself, Illustrator has the ability to easily save the location and settings of these points, and apply them to other paths. Stroke width details are stored as *variable width profiles*, which are displayed at the top of the screen in the Control panel, and at the very bottom portion of the Stroke panel.

To save a width profile, select a path with a variable-width stroke, open the Variable Width Profile pop-up menu in either the Control panel or the Stroke panel, and then click the Add to Profiles button (**Figure 6.42**).

Figure 6.42 *Variable width profiles are saved in the application, so you can access saved profiles from within any other document.*

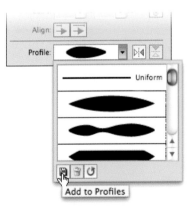

To apply a width profile to any stroked path, or to any path with an Art or Pattern brush applied to it, simply select the path and choose a variable width profile from the pop-up menu. Profiles capture the position and proportions of the width points and handles, and the profile will be applied proportionately to the new path as well.

From the Stroke panel, you can also choose to flip a variable width profile along or across your path.

One of the most powerful aspects of variable width profiles is that they can be applied easily with a single click, making it possible to instantly add expressive detail to your artwork.

Getting Inspired with Color

When you're working on creative projects, sometimes you are told which colors to use by the client directly (in the case of established corporate colors), a creative director, or maybe even a fashion designer in Paris. Other times, you are totally free to dream up any color you'd like to use. Although freedom is nice, it also offers challenges. How do you choose from so many colors? How do you ensure that the colors you have chosen work well with each other? How can you quickly generate numerous color variations to play with and choose from?

Traditionally, designers could garner such inspiration by perusing magazines or annuals or just by going for a walk and observing the outside world. Illustrator offers its own set of inspirational tools to help you choose the perfect colors for the task at hand through the Color Guide panel and something called Adobe Kuler (see the "Tapping Into a Community Around Color with Kuler" section).

Using the Color Guide Panel

Accessible via the Window menu, the Color Guide panel looks rather simple at first glance. However, it's a robust (and fun!) tool to use when you want to generate variations of colors as you work on your design (**Figure 6.43**, on the next page). As you are about to find out, the Color Guide panel offers color suggestions that fit your exacting needs.

Figure 6.43 *The Color Guide panel offers color suggestions.*

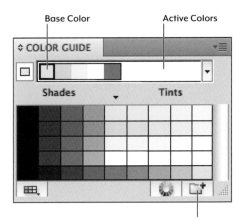

To use the Color Guide panel, start by choosing a color harmony rule from the pop-up menu at the top of the panel. Don't worry if you aren't familiar with any of the harmony rules or their names. It really doesn't matter, because each one is just a different method for how colors are generated and how they relate to each other (refer to the sidebar "Color Harmonies"). There's no such thing as a right or wrong harmony rule—if you aren't happy with the colors you're seeing, just switch to a different rule.

Once you've selected a rule, click any swatch color in the Swatches panel, or mix a color using the Color panel. Alternatively, you can select an object and click the Set Base Color to the Current Color icon in the Color Guide panel. Instantly, the Color Guide panel will generate variations of color for you. If you like any colors you see, you can drag them right to your Swatches panel or even to an object on your artboard. Alternatively, you can select several colors and click the Save Color Group to Swatch Panel icon at the bottom of the Color Guide panel.

By default, the Color Guide panel offers tint/shade variations of your colors. However, you can view warm/cool or vivid/muted variations instead, if you prefer. To do so, choose the desired option from the Color Guide panel menu (**Figure 6.44**). And for specific control over how variations are created, choose Color Guide Options from the Color Guide panel menu. This in turn opens the Variation Options dialog box (we know, it should be named

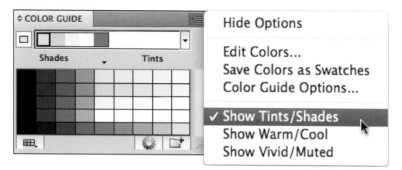

Figure 6.44 *The Color Guide panel offers three methods for generating color variations.*

the Color Guide Options dialog box, right?). The Steps setting determines how many variations of color the Color Guide panel displays in each direction of your color (**Figure 6.45**). For example, if you have the Tints/Shades option selected, a value of four steps will generate four tints and four shades for a total of eight variations of your color (**Figure 6.46**). You can specify as few as three steps and as many as twenty. In addition, you can adjust the Variation slider to control how much of a difference there is between each color that is generated.

Figure 6.45 *You can adjust the number of steps and the amount of difference between generated variations of color.*

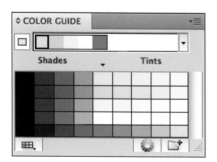

Figure 6.46 *The Color Guide panel displays the active colors down the center, with darker and lighter variations to the left and right, respectively.*

Color Harmonies

A *color harmony* (also referred to as a *color rule*) is a specific relationship between colors. For example, the Complementary color harmony defines two colors that appear exactly opposite each other on the color wheel. Illustrator features 23 different color harmonies that you can choose from, each containing between two and six colors (**Figure 6.47**).

When choosing color harmonies, try not to focus too much on their names. Instead, use this page as a visual reference to better understand what each one represents on the color wheel. There's no such thing as a "good" or a "bad" harmony—choose the one that best fits the needs for a particular job or task. Better yet, experiment with a few of them until you find what you want.

You can choose color harmonies from the Color Guide panel, from the Edit Colors dialog box, and from the Recolor Artwork dialog box.

Complementary

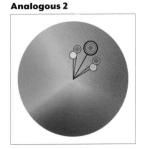

Analogous

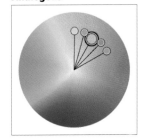

Analogous 2

Triad 2

Triad 3

Compound 2

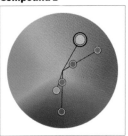

High Contrast 1

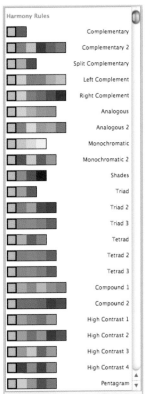

Figure 6.47 *Illustrator features 23 different color harmonies, or specific defined relationships of colors.*

GETTING INSPIRED WITH COLOR

Complementary 2

Split Complementary

Left Complement

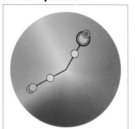

Right Complement

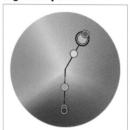

Monochromatic

Monochromatic 2

Shades

Triad

Tetrad

Tetrad 2

Tetrad 3

Compound 1

High Contrast 2

High Contrast 3

High Contrast 4

Pentagram

Limiting the Color Guide Panel

When expressing your creativity with color in Illustrator, the last thing you probably want to hear is how to impose limits. But on the contrary, carefully limiting the Color Guide panel can reap huge rewards. By default, the Color Guide panel offers suggestions of colors from a huge spectrum of color. But sometimes you're forced to work within specific guidelines, or you need to work within a certain range of color. For example, a web designer may want to see only those color suggestions that are web-safe colors. A package designer working in a spot color workflow may want the Color Guide panel to offer suggestions from a Pantone library. Or a fashion designer may be limited to using only those colors available for a specific season or year.

The good news is that not only is custom-fitting the Color Guide panel to your exact needs possible but it's also incredibly easy to do. Let's take the example of a web designer who wants to work within the web-safe color library. At the bottom-left corner of the Color Guide panel is an icon that allows you to limit the color group to colors that appear within a specific library **Figure 6.48**). Click the icon, and choose the Web library. You'll notice that

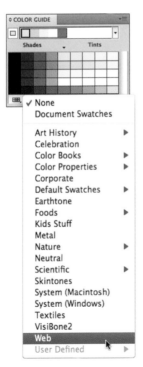

Figure 6.48 *You can limit the Color Guide panel to any custom library—even those you create on your own.*

the name of the chosen library now appears at the bottom of the Color Guide panel, indicating that the colors being suggested in the panel come from that library (**Figure 6.49**). Now, as you choose colors, the Color Guide panel can offer only those color suggestions that are web-safe colors.

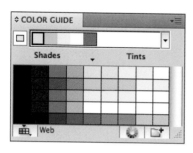

Figure 6.49 *A quick look at the Color Guide panel reveals the library of colors to which it is limited.*

Use the same method to limit the Color Guide panel to a Pantone swatch library, and the Color Guide panel will be able to list only variations of color that are in the chosen Pantone library (**Figure 6.50**). This can be helpful if you're working on a design that will be printed as a one- or two-color job. To release the limit, click the icon, and choose None from the top of the list.

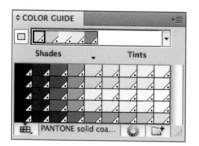

Figure 6.50 *Limiting the Color Guide panel to a Pantone library makes it easier to choose the right spot color for the job.*

Tapping Into a Community Around Color with Kuler

As you know, color is subjective. What looks great to one designer may look awful to another. Likewise, some people might be really good at working with color, while others may be severely color-challenged. What would be wonderful for everyone would be some set of tools that designers could use to quickly generate palettes of color that look great while, at the same time, offer some way for designers to share their skills with others. The good news is that Adobe set out to deliver just that by creating a community of users who share a rather cool set of color tools, called *Kuler* (pronounced "cooler").

Using the Kuler Website

To access the Kuler website, visit http://kuler.adobe.com (**Figure 6.51**). Adobe actually refers to Kuler as a *rich Internet application* (RIA), and you need to have Flash Player 9 or newer to use it (the site will redirect you if you need to download a newer version of Flash Player). Although you can use parts of Kuler without logging in, you'll get the full functionality by entering your Adobe ID. An Adobe ID is free and allows you to post to the Adobe user-to-user forums, access free content from the Adobe Design Center, and purchase items through the online Adobe Store. If you've recently registered any Adobe software, you probably already have an Adobe ID. If not, you can click the Register link at the top right of the Kuler website.

Figure 6.51 *Free to all, Adobe Kuler can also generate themes of colors from photographs that you can upload or import directly from Flickr.*

What's cool about Kuler is that, as part of the online community, you can view color themes that others have created, and you can even rate them. Themes are tagged with metadata, allowing you to easily search for colors (such as *winter* or *chocolate*). In fact, color themes are actually published as RSS feeds, allowing designers to search based on things like the most popular or the highest rated themes.

Using the Kuler Panel in Illustrator

Although the Kuler website is nice and all, you still have to leave your design environment and use your web browser to find your colors. That's why Adobe took the next step and brought Kuler directly into Illustrator (it's also in Photoshop, InDesign, Flash, and Fireworks). Choose Window > Extensions > Kuler to open the Kuler panel (**Figure 6.52**), which gives you access to the themes within the online Kuler community.

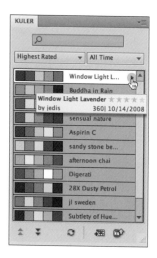

Figure 6.52 *With the Kuler panel, you can browse color themes directly from within Illustrator for instant color inspiration.*

Click the pop-up menus at the top of the Kuler panel to display specific RSS feeds, such as highest rated, most popular, and so on. You can also specify a time constraint (such as list all newest themes within the past 7 days). Enter any keyword in the Search field to find Kuler themes that fit your exact needs. If you find a theme you like, then select it, and click the Add Selected Theme to Swatches icon at the bottom of the panel. Illustrator automatically adds the selected theme to your Swatches panel as a color group. Alternatively, you can click the triangle to the far right of any theme to open it in Kuler directly (Illustrator launches your default web browser to do so).

The Kuler panel is also a two-way street, meaning that if you develop some colors you like while using Illustrator, you can create a group in your Swatches panel (of 3 to 5 colors), and then click the Upload from Swatch Panel to Kuler Community button in the Kuler panel. Illustrator transfers your colors to the Kuler website, where you can then add metadata tags and publish your theme.

Modifying Color

When you're faced with making changes to the color in your existing artwork, you may find that it is extremely time-consuming to do so. But the Live Color feature set in Illustrator makes it easy to modify the colors in your document in a plethora of ways.

In reality, there isn't a tool, function, or button in Illustrator that's called Live Color (it's more of a marketing term). Just about all the color editing you do will involve the Recolor Artwork dialog box. We'll cover this dialog box in detail, but before we get started, it helps to think of Live Color as an engine in Illustrator—a powerful engine that allows you to take control over modifying colors throughout your document. This is especially true when you consider that this color engine is capable of modifying colors that may be contained within symbols, gradients, gradient mesh objects—anything with the exception of placed images.

Recoloring Artwork

The crown jewel of the Live Color feature set in Illustrator is the Recolor Artwork dialog box. With a few clicks, you can easily perform a number of tasks. Some examples are as follows:

- Swap colors that exist in your artwork.
- Adjust saturation, brightness, temperature, and luminosity values in your selected artwork.
- Generate color studies and variations of your artwork.
- Convert colored artwork to grayscale.
- Convert grayscale art to color.
- Convert process colors to spot colors, and vice versa.
- Intelligently reduce the number of colors used in your selected artwork.

As you dive into the Recolor Artwork feature in Illustrator, you should keep three important tips in mind:

- Recolor Artwork works only on selected art. This allows you to specifically target the art you want to modify and can be especially important in documents that contain multiple artboards, where you might want to modify the colors on one artboard but not another. At the same time, this means that locked objects aren't touched by the Recolor Artwork dialog box at all, so you'll want to make sure you have your artwork selected as needed before you proceed.

- As you'll learn, the Recolor Artwork feature is somewhat partial to colors that live inside groups. Although you can access individual swatch colors from within the Recolor Artwork dialog box, it is far easier to work with colors in groups. With this in mind, you might consider creating groups of the colors that you plan on using before you open the Recolor Artwork dialog box.

- The Recolor Artwork dialog box is somewhat daunting. It contains many buttons and settings, and sometimes a seemingly small setting or icon can have a huge impact on the work you're doing. That being said, there's nothing to fear. Many of the functions in the Recolor Artwork dialog box perform the same type of edits, but just in different ways. In all likelihood, you'll find a part of the Recolor Artwork dialog box that you will use far more often than the rest of it. So if you don't end up memorizing what every little button does, don't worry.

OK, now that the ground rules are in place, let's begin. Start by selecting your artwork on the artboard, and then click the Recolor Artwork icon in the Control panel (**Figure 6.53**). Alternatively, you can choose Edit > Edit Colors > Recolor Artwork. The Recolor Artwork dialog box appears, and you'll immediately notice two tabs near the top of the dialog box: Edit and Assign (**Figure 6.54**). For the most part, the Edit tab is used to modify the colors that exist in your file (such as, change a color's hue), while the Assign tab is used to apply completely new colors to your artwork (for example, to reduce the number of colors used in a file). Let's take a closer look at what these two functions do.

Figure 6.53 *The Recolor Artwork icon appears in the Control panel whenever art is selected.*

Figure 6.54 *The Recolor Artwork dialog box features two tabs: Edit and Assign.*

Using the Edit Tab

At the center of the Edit tab in the Recolor Artwork dialog box is a color wheel. Each color in your selected artwork (or group, if you're editing a color group) appears mapped to the color wheel as a small circle (**Figure 6.55**).

Figure 6.55 *Each color used in the selected artwork appears mapped on the color wheel. One circle, larger than the rest, represents the base color.*

The relationships between all the mapped colors are indicated by lines that all connect to each other through the center of the color wheel. Solid connector lines indicate that the colors are locked to each other, meaning that adjusting one color will adjust all others (while maintaining their relationship). Dashed connector lines indicate that the colors are independent, meaning they can be moved individually without affecting the others (**Figure 6.56**). You can toggle between locked and unlocked colors by clicking the Link/Unlink Harmony Colors icon. To add colors to your existing color group, click the color wheel anywhere with the Add Color tool. To remove a color, click its circle with the Remove Color tool.

The color wheel is based on the HSB color model, which is more easily understood as a wheel, compared to other models such as CMYK or RGB (**Figure 6.57**). In the HSB color model, the H value represents *hue,* or the actual color itself; the S value represents *saturation,* or the amount of color; and the B value represents *brightness,* or the lightness/darkness of the color (also referred to as the *value* of the color). You can adjust the mapped circles on the color wheel in Live Color for various results.

- Moving a circle in a clockwise or counterclockwise direction, around the center of the color wheel, adjusts the hue of that color.

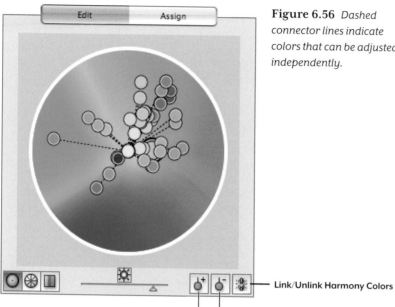

Figure 6.56 *Dashed connector lines indicate colors that can be adjusted independently.*

Link/Unlink Harmony Colors

Add Color Tool   Remove Color Tool

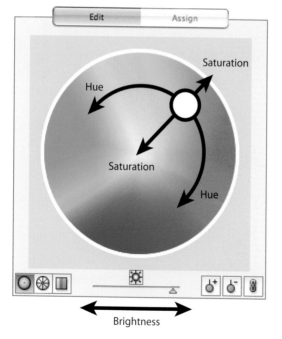

Figure 6.57 *The HSB color model is displayed as 360 degrees of color.*

Saturation

Hue

Saturation

Hue

Brightness

- Moving a circle toward or away from the center of the color wheel adjusts the saturation of that color.

- Dragging the slider that appears directly underneath the color wheel adjusts the brightness of the entire wheel.

- Control-click (right-click) a color circle, and choose Select Shade to edit the saturation and brightness values of that color without changing its hue.

- Double-click a color circle to open the Color Picker.

By default, Illustrator displays a smooth color wheel, but you may prefer a segmented color wheel, showing clear distinctions of hue and saturation. Alternatively, you can view your selected colors as vertical color bars (**Figure 6.58**). These options are accessible via the three icons that appear to the lower left of the color wheel.

TIP Clicking the little sun icon that appears above the brightness slider swaps the brightness and saturation settings, allowing you to use the slider to control saturation and the color circles to adjust brightness.

Figure 6.58 *The Edit tab shown with a segmented color wheel (left) and vertical color bars (right).*

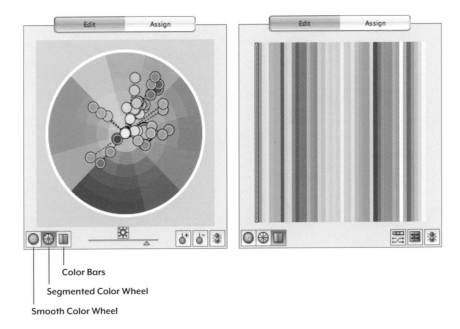

Color Bars

Segmented Color Wheel

Smooth Color Wheel

Although you can certainly have lots of fun dragging color circles all over the color wheel, it doesn't make for the precise kinds of adjustments you may be used to doing in Illustrator. To achieve a higher level of precision, you'll want to edit colors numerically. Click a color circle to select it, and then use the sliders and values that appear beneath the color wheel. These sliders are identical to those in the Color panel. You can switch between the RGB, HSB,

CMYK, web-safe RGB, Tint (for global process and spot colors), and Lab sliders. In addition, you can also choose a setting called Global Adjust that lets you edit all colors using the Saturation, Brightness, Temperature, and Luminosity sliders (**Figure 6.59**).

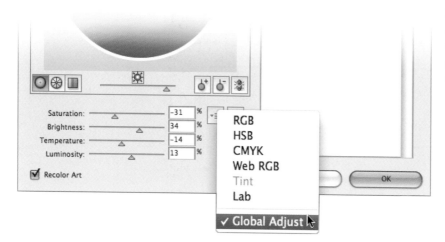

Figure 6.59 *The Global Adjust sliders let you modify colors similarly to how you might adjust colors in Photoshop.*

As with the Color Guide panel, you can also limit the Recolor Artwork dialog box to a specific library of colors (**Figure 6.60**). This extremely powerful feature makes it possible to remap entire artwork or entire groups of color to a specific library of color...instantly. When you've completed editing your colors to your liking, click OK to return to your artboard.

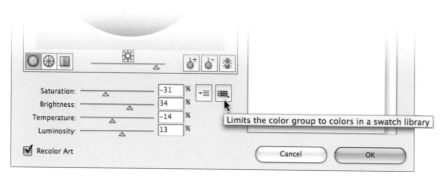

Figure 6.60 *Just as in the Color Guide panel, you can limit the colors that the Recolor Artwork feature can work with.*

As you experiment with the colors on the color wheel, you may find that you'd like to undo the last adjustment you made. Unfortunately, there is no undo function in the Recolor Artwork dialog box. This is a huge oversight, and it can be extremely frustrating to have to cancel the dialog box and start over again. Of some consolation is an icon at the top of the Recolor Artwork dialog box called "Get colors from selected art" (**Figure 6.61**). Clicking this icon resamples the selected artwork and remaps all the colors as they were when you first opened the Recolor Artwork dialog box.

Figure 6.61 *Click the "Get colors from selected art" icon to load all colors from the selected art in your document as the active colors and map them onto the color wheel. In the context of assigning colors, this acts much like a "reset" or "start over" button.*

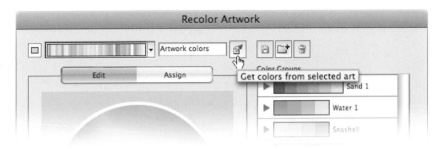

Understanding the Recolor Art Check Box

People often mistake the Recolor Art check box that appears at the lower-left corner of the Recolor Artwork dialog box as a preview option. But that isn't the case at all. The Recolor Art check box does exactly what its name represents—it recolors any artwork you have selected (it's dim if you launch the Recolor Artwork dialog box without any art selected). So, why is this setting useful? Well, it's useful because you can turn it off. For example, you may want to start tweaking the color of an illustration only to realize that you want to leave the color as it was before you started editing it. But at the same time, you like the color variations you created and want to save those colors as a new color group. By deselecting the Recolor Art box, the selected artwork remains untouched on your artboard, but you can still access and work with those colors in the Recolor Artwork dialog box.

NOTE The quickest way to recolor your artwork is to select any of the color groups listed on the far right side of the Recolor Artwork dialog box. This is why it makes sense to define color groups in the Swatches panel before you open the Recolor Artwork dialog box, if your workflow allows it.

Using the Assign Tab

The main part of the Assign tab is the list of current (or old) and new colors (**Figure 6.62**). Colors that exist within your selected artwork appear as wide bars along the left side, while the colors you are using to recolor your artwork appear in shorter bars along the right side. Each bar sits in a color row, and if you follow the direction of the arrow, you're indicating that the color appearing in the wide bar becomes the color that appears in the short bar. In fact, the arrow controls the recoloring behavior, and clicking the arrow in a color row toggles the recoloring on and off for that color row (**Figure 6.63**). For example, you'll notice that, by default, Illustrator preserves black and white colors in your artwork (meaning they aren't recolored), so those colors will appear listed in color rows with the arrows turned off.

Figure 6.62 *The Assign tab seems a bit complex at first glance, but it will quickly become your friend. The main section in the middle lists all the colors from the selected artwork on the left (wide bars) and all the colors they are being remapped to on the right (narrow bars).*

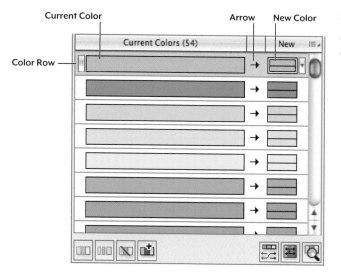

Figure 6.63 *Color rows help you easily recolor your artwork.*

By default, when you first open the Recolor Artwork dialog box to the Assign tab, Illustrator has no idea what you want to do with your colors. As such, Illustrator simply remaps each color to itself. This is why each color row features the same color in the Current and New columns.

Deconstructing a Color Row

A color row that appears in the Assign tab of the Recolor Artwork dialog box is really a lot like a mathematical formula, describing how recoloring will occur (**Figure 6.64**).

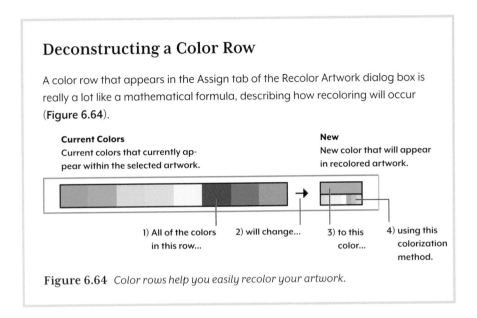

Current Colors
Current colors that currently appear within the selected artwork.

New
New color that will appear in recolored artwork.

1) All of the colors in this row...

2) will change...

3) to this color...

4) using this colorization method.

Figure 6.64 *Color rows help you easily recolor your artwork.*

Clicking the Color Reduction Options icon on the Assign tab of the Recolor Artwork dialog box opens the Recolor Options dialog box (**Figure 6.65**). The presets that appear in the pop-up menu at the top of the dialog box offer quick shortcuts to reducing artwork to one-, two-, or three-color jobs and to limiting the colors to a specific library of color. The Color Harmony preset sets the Colors value to Auto and results in the number of current colors listed in the dialog box to match the number of active colors in the chosen color harmony rule. This lets you easily experiment with different color harmonies, because each time you choose one, the number of current colors will automatically adjust to match the harmony. The others settings in the dialog box are as follows.

Figure 6.65 *The Recolor Options dialog box gives you control over how your artwork is recolored.*

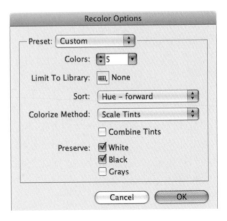

- **Colors.** You can manually set the number of colors to which you want to reduce your artwork.

- **Limit to Library.** You can limit new colors to a specific color library.

- **Sort.** You can choose to sort colors in the Assign tab using any of four different settings, or you can set it to None (where you can manually sort the colors yourself).

- **Colorize Method.** When reducing many colors to a single color, you must instruct Illustrator how to handle different shades of colors. The differences between the five available options (Exact, Preserve Tints, Scale Tints, Tints and Shades, and Hue Shift) are illustrated in detail in the sidebar "Colorization Methods."

- **Preserve.** You can select these options to preserve (leave untouched) artwork that is colored white, black, and/or gray.

To identify where a specific color appears in your artwork, highlight a color row, and then click the magnifying glass icon (**Figure 6.66**) at the lower right of the Assign tab in the Recolor Artwork dialog box. This reduces the opacity of all colors except for the selected color, making it easy to identify where the color is used. Shift-clicking multiple colors or rows will highlight all the selected colors at once.

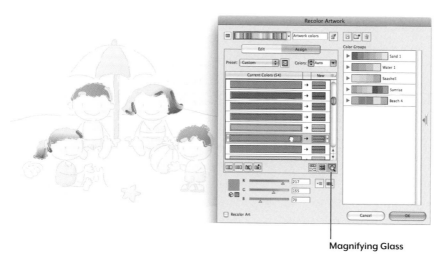

Figure 6.66 *Use the magnifying glass to quickly identify where colors appear in your artwork.*

Magnifying Glass

You can manually reduce colors by dragging the wide color bars from one row to another. Combining two or more colors in a single wide color bar instructs Illustrator to reduce those colors to one new color (**Figure 6.67**). You can double-click a small color bar to access the Color Picker. You can also choose a colorize method by clicking the far-right edge of a small color bar. Deselecting the Apply To All box will allow you to specify different colorize methods for each new color.

Figure 6.67 *You can drag as many colors as you like to a color row to convert all those colors to one new color.*

Icons that appear beneath the color bars allow you to randomly change color order and the saturation and brightness settings, as well as manage color rows. When you've recolored your artwork, click OK to apply the settings and return to the artboard.

Converting Art to Grayscale

Sometimes you might need to convert color artwork to shades of gray. Traditionally, such a task in Illustrator has always been difficult because colors can be present in symbols, patterns, gradients, gradient meshes, and so on. Editing all the colors in these separate places would normally take quite some time, but not with the help of the Live Color engine.

It's important to realize that changing artwork from color into shades of gray isn't necessarily automatic. In other words, you can take different roads to perform such a conversion, and depending on the artwork at hand, you may choose a particular method in order to achieve a desirable result. For example, if you've used Photoshop to convert color images into grayscale, you know you can simply change your color mode from RGB or CMYK to

Colorization Methods

When simply recoloring art, Illustrator takes one color and changes it to another. However, when reducing colors, you're often taking many different colors and asking Illustrator to represent all of those colors using a single color. Choosing a colorization method tells Illustrator how to use a single color to represent all the colors in a selected row. In these examples, a color illustration is reduced to one color (PANTONE Reflex Blue). Various results are achieved as you select different colorization methods (**Figure 6.68**).

Original art

Figure 6.68 *Colorization methods.*

Exact

Exactly replaces each current color with the specified new color.

Preserve Tints

Replaces the darkest current color in the row with the specified new color. Other current colors in the row are replaced with a proportionally lighter tint. For spot or global colors, it applies the current color's tint to the new color. This setting is best used when all the current colors in the row are tints of the same or similar global color. For best results, also select Combine Tints in the Recolor Options dialog box.

Scale Tints (the default option)

Replaces the darkest current color in the row with the specified new color. Other current colors in the row are replaced with a proportionally lighter tint.

Tints and Shades

Replaces the current color with the average lightness and darkness with the specified new color. Current colors that are lighter than the average are replaced with a proportionally lighter tint of the new color. Current colors that are darker than the average are replaced by adding black to the new color.

Hue Shift

Sets the most typical color in the current colors row as a key color and exactly replaces the key color with the new color. The other current colors are replaced by colors that differ from the new color in brightness, saturation, and hue by the same amounts that the current color differs from the key color.

grayscale, but that the result may not look that great. Seasoned users know they can use functions such as the Photoshop Channel Mixer or the Black and White adjustment command to garner more pleasing grayscale conversions. Advanced users could probably rattle off several other methods as well.

In Illustrator, though, we've identified four ways to convert artwork from color into grayscale. These methods all take advantage of the Live Color engine, so they work on any artwork in your Illustrator document with the exception of linked or embedded raster images (see the sidebar "Converting Raster Content to Grayscale" for more information on that).

- **Use the Convert to Grayscale command.** Select your color artwork, and choose Edit > Edit Colors > Convert to Grayscale (**Figure 6.69**). Using this method is obviously the fastest method, but the results aren't always pretty. Different colors may convert to similar shades of gray, and often you'll find that this setting gives low-contrast results.

Figure 6.69 *The Convert to Grayscale function now works on all objects with the exception of placed images.*

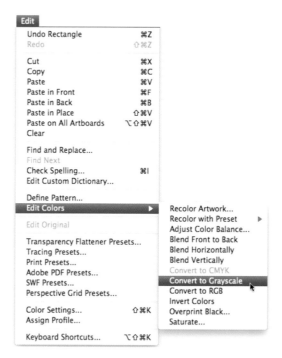

- **Desaturate the art.** Select your artwork, and click the Recolor Artwork button in the Control panel. At the bottom of the dialog box, change the mode of the color adjustment sliders to Global Adjust. Drag the

Saturation slider all the way to the far left (the setting should read -100). This method requires an extra click or two, but by desaturating the color in this way, your result will have more contrast.

- **Use Adjust Color Balance.** Select your artwork, and choose Edit > Edit Colors > Adjust Color Balance. In the Adjust Colors dialog box, choose Grayscale from the Color Mode pop-up menu, and select the Convert box. Adjust the Black slider until you get the desired result. This method is rather straightforward and gives you the freedom to adjust the density of the black values (**Figure 6.70**).

Figure 6.70 *The Adjust Color Balance function is great for making color adjustments, as well as making black and white adjustments.*

- **Recolor the art using a grayscale color group.** When you create a new print document, you'll notice that the Swatches panel already contains a color group labeled Gray, which contains 10 shades of gray. Select your artwork, and click the Recolor Artwork button in the Control panel. In the Recolor Artwork dialog box, click the Gray color group. This forces Illustrator to remap your existing colors to those colors of the selected group (**Figure 6.71**). Use the Assign tab in the Recolor Artwork dialog box to move colors around to control exactly the shade of gray to which each color will remap. For an even greater level of control, you can create your own grayscale color group with values you specify. This method requires more interaction than the previous ones but yields the most control over the conversion.

Figure 6.71 *By recoloring your artwork with a gray-scale color group, you have complete control over the color conversion.*

Converting Raster Content to Grayscale

Although Illustrator gives you plenty of options for converting color artwork to grayscale, what do you do when you also need to convert rasterized content—such as placed images—to grayscale?

If possible, you should convert your raster content to grayscale using Photoshop, which excels in editing bitmapped artwork. Don't fool yourself into thinking that Illustrator can do it all. For best results, use the Black and White adjustment feature in Photoshop. You can use the Edit Original feature in Illustrator (in the Links panel) to quickly open your image in Photoshop, make the change and save your file, and then return to Illustrator where the image will update itself. For detailed information on the Edit Original work-flow, refer to Chapter 10, "Working with Images."

If you absolutely must convert pixels from color to grayscale directly in Illustrator, select the image, and choose Object > Rasterize. From the Color Model pop-up menu, choose Grayscale. Make sure you specify an appropriate resolution, and click OK. As an alternative, you can choose Effect > Rasterize to apply the conversion in a reversible way.

Performing One-Click Color Fixes

Although the Recolor Artwork dialog box is certainly powerful, sometimes you might need to make a quick adjustment. If you select some artwork, you'll find a collection of functions available in the Edit > Edit Colors menu. These settings have been available in Illustrator for many versions now, but prior to CS4 they were limited in that they worked only on certain basic vector objects (excluding gradients, patterns, symbols, gradient meshes, and so on). The functions you'll find here now use the Live Color engine and will work on everything with the exception of linked raster images. The functions (listed in the order in which they appear) are as follows: Adjust Color Balance, Blend Front to Back, Blend Horizontally, Blend Vertically, Convert to CMYK, Convert to Grayscale, Convert to RGB, Invert Colors, Overprint Black, and Saturate.

Viewing Color on the Screen

There was a time when we were all trained never to trust the color we saw on our computer screens. The myth has always been that although color management exists, it doesn't work. Some users even try to turn off color management (not something we suggest, even if it were possible, which it isn't). The reality is that these days the color we see on our screens is generally better than it has been in the past. Color management settings that were once inconsistent (even among Adobe applications) are now in sync with each other. The result is a more reliable viewing experience.

This section of the chapter in no way, shape, or form attempts to explain how color management works. Likewise, it doesn't explain how to ensure that your ink-jet printer output and your computer screen look the same. The topic of color management really requires an entire book of its own. In fact, if you really want to learn everything there is to know about color management, you should check out *Real World Color Management, Second Edition,* by Bruce Fraser, Chris Murphy, and Fred Bunting (Peachpit Press, 2005). For the scope of this book, you'll learn where to access your color management settings and how you can use some of the color management features in Illustrator to simulate your artwork as it might appear on specific devices.

Controlling Color Management Settings

You can access the color management settings by choosing Edit > Color Settings. This opens the Color Settings dialog box, and if you installed Illustrator as part of Creative Suite, an icon and a message at the top of the dialog box will indicate whether your settings are in sync with other CS components (**Figure 6.72**).

Figure 6.72 *The Color Settings dialog box informs you whether your color settings are in sync with other Creative Suite components.*

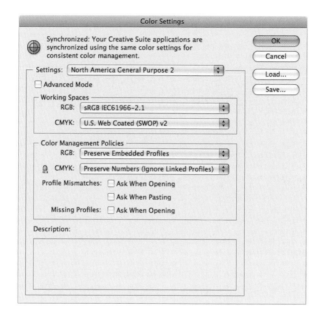

NOTE Selecting the Advanced Mode option in the Color Settings dialog box populates the Settings color with many additional color management settings.

Out of the box, Adobe has set all CS applications to use the North America General Purpose 2 color setting. This is actually a generic "middle of the road" setting, meant to be used by those who are cross-media designers, meaning those who often work with both RGB and CMYK documents. However, if you work specifically in the print field or if you primarily work with video or the web, you might be better off using North America Prepress 2 or North America Web/Internet. If you aren't sure, leave it set to the default setting.

Proofing Colors

One of the most powerful functions of color management is the ability to simulate the viewing of your artwork on other devices. If you have the profile for another device, Illustrator can show you what your file will look like when it's displayed (or printed) on that device. Don't worry about hunting down device profiles either—your system already contains many useful ones. Let's take a closer look.

Choose View > Proof Setup > Customize to open the Proof Setup dialog box. From the Device to Simulate pop-up menu, choose a profile. For example, you might use the Uncoated FOGRA29 profile to simulate what your art might look like when printed in a newspaper (**Figure 6.73**). Select the Preview check box to see your artwork change in appearance as you select different profiles.

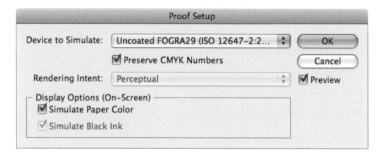

Figure 6.73 *The Proof Setup dialog box gives you the ability to specify what kind of device you want to simulate when proofing your artwork on your screen.*

When your document is CMYK and you're choosing a CMYK profile, no color conversion occurs, and you can choose the Preserve CMYK Numbers option. Likewise, when viewing an RGB document and choosing an RGB profile, you can choose Preserve RGB Numbers. The option is obviously not available when proofing with a device profile that uses a different color model than the document (in such cases, a color conversion must take place, and there's no way to preserve the numbers).

When proofing artwork on devices with smaller color gamuts, you must also choose a rendering intent. The most commonly used method, Relative Colorimetric, moves out-of-gamut colors to the closest possible color that will print on the device. It also adjusts other colors so that colors appear to be accurate. The Absolute Colorimetric setting adjusts only out-of-gamut colors and may result in *posterization*, where many shades of similar colors are used. The Perceptual method shifts colors so they appear correct relative to each other, but it may not represent colors as being the most accurate match to the original values. The Saturation method enhances colors and makes them more vibrant and most suitable for business presentations where bright colors are more important than accurate colors.

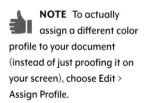

NOTE To actually assign a different color profile to your document (instead of just proofing it on your screen), choose Edit > Assign Profile.

For an accurate onscreen representation of your artwork, you can choose to simulate paper color (avoiding the problem of viewing too bright of a white screen) and black ink (if you find the preview of black is too rich). Once you've specified your proof settings, you can quickly preview your artwork on your screen by choosing the View > Proof Colors setting.

Previewing Contrast for Color Blindness

Although it's certainly helpful to be able to proof colors onscreen as they might appear when output on different devices, it is also extremely helpful for designers to be able to visualize how other people may view their art and designs. For example, 7 percent of Americans are color blind (that's more than 10.5 million people). When creating artwork that will be used as public signage, how can a designer be sure that the art will be clearly visible to all—even those who don't see with the same range of color as they do?

In the View > Proof Setup menu, you can choose to display the art on your screen as though it were being viewed by a color-blind person (**Figure 6.74**). Illustrator can simulate two types of color blindness, Protanopia and Deuteranopia (both variations of red-green color blindness). By ensuring a high enough level of contrast in your design, a larger audience will be able to understand and benefit from your art.

Figure 6.74 *Illustrator can simulate art as if it were being viewed by someone who is color-blind.*

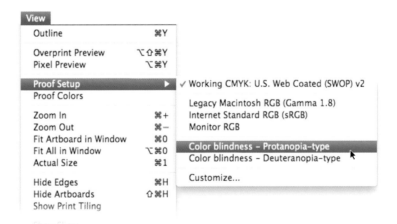

Understanding Book Color

Although consistent color management settings will help ensure that your colors look the same in different software (Photoshop, Illustrator, InDesign, Acrobat, and so on), you may still experience colors that don't match up correctly. This is usually something that happens when spot colors appear in your file, but the good news is that it's easy to fix.

The problem is that, by default, Photoshop displays spot colors using LAB values (which are bright, vibrant, and match their printed color better). The default setting for Illustrator and InDesign is to use CMYK values instead, which often results in muted colors, especially when compared to Photoshop. The thing is, both Illustrator and InDesign support the ability to use LAB values when displaying spot colors, so it's simply a matter of turning the feature on. Before you do that, however, you need to understand something called *Book Color.*

Book Color is a setting that first appeared in Adobe CS2 components. You may notice that when double-clicking a spot color swatch to view its settings, you'll see that the color mode for the swatch is set to Book Color (**Figure 6.75**).

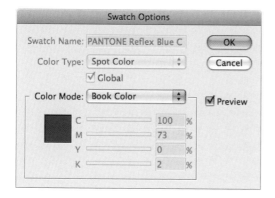

Figure 6.75 *A Pantone color swatch shows up in Illustrator as a Book Color.*

One of the reasons why designers use spot colors is simply because some colors aren't reproducible in CMYK. Bright blues, purples, greens, and oranges are perfect examples. Pantone delivers an entire Microsoft Excel spreadsheet to Adobe that lists each Pantone color, along with their LAB color equivalents. Obviously, the LAB color values match closer to the real color. However, many designers specify Pantone colors, even though they will be printing their file on a press in a four-color process. Pantone also delivers a Solid to Process library that specifies the CMYK values of Pantone colors. Obviously, the latter is far less accurate and results in color shifts.

Since you now know that Photoshop uses LAB values to display spot colors on your screen and that Illustrator and InDesign use CMYK values for the same, you can begin to understand why spot colors viewed in Photoshop look different.

So, what does all this have to do with Book Color? Ordinarily, you can define a color swatch in Illustrator using CMYK values or LAB values, but not both. But a Book Color is special and *can* contain both CMYK and LAB information within it. By definition, a Book Color swatch contains both the CMYK and LAB values specified by Pantone. The question is, how does Illustrator determine when to preview the colors using the LAB values instead of the CMYK ones?

The answer is an odd one, only because of the name of the feature you need to use: Overprint Preview. If you choose View > Overprint Preview in Illustrator (or in InDesign or Acrobat, for that matter), the LAB values generate the onscreen preview. The regular preview settings use the CMYK values. In this way, you can preview the more vibrant LAB values on your screen, but if you ever decide later in your workflow to convert your Pantone color to CMYK, you'll get the exact CMYK values you expect (otherwise you'll get a LAB-to-CMYK version).

Likewise, if you'd like more accurate colors when printing composite proofs from Illustrator, select the Simulate Overprint check box in the Print dialog box.

Working with Live Effects

7

So far, we've only scratched the surface with the kinds of effects Illustrator has to offer. Soft drop shadows (which we discussed in Chapter 5, "Organizing Your Drawing") are certainly cool, but they are only a small sampling of live effects in Illustrator, which include 3D effects, warp distortions, and a wide range of pixel-based Photoshop effects.

As you read this chapter, remember that you can apply live effects to fills and strokes individually, as well as to objects, groups, and layers. You apply all live effects via the Effect menu or the Appearance panel, and once applied, they appear listed in the Appearance panel and can be edited or deleted at any time. Additionally, you can apply multiple live effects to a single target.

It's also important to realize you can apply live effects to type without needing to convert to outlines. As you make changes to the text, the applied effect updates.

The artwork featured throughout this chapter comes from Che McPherson (iStockphoto; username: chemc).

Combining Features and Effects

New features aren't added haphazardly in Illustrator. Rather, each new feature is carefully thought out in regard to how it might interact with existing features in Illustrator. One of the most powerful things you can do with live effects in Illustrator is apply several of them to a single object or, even better, use effects in combination with other features, such as transparency and blends (**Figure 7.1**).

Figure 7.1 *You don't have to be a high roller to see the benefits of combining features in Illustrator. This example uses the 3D effect with artwork mapping, transparency, and blends.*

When using Illustrator, you should always be asking yourself "what if" questions. For example, you know that you can apply transparency to objects in Illustrator, so what if you applied transparency to a 3D effect? Would you be able to see through the 3D object? Experimenting in Illustrator is a great way to discover new techniques and creative ideas. The worst that can happen is you get something that doesn't look that great; the Undo function serves nicely at this point.

Throughout this chapter, we ask "what if" questions and explore the ways that live effects integrate with other Illustrator features. These questions are answered with advice on how to get the most out of Illustrator. More importantly, the "what if" scenarios will open your eyes to the power of the Illustrator live effects.

Deconstructing the Effect Menu

NOTE The effects are listed in this chapter in the order in which they appear in the Effect menu. The 3D effect is covered in its entirety in a chapter available online, at www.peachpit.com/rwillcs5.

The Effect menu is basically split into four main sections. The section at the very top contains two settings: Apply Last Effect and Last Effect. The former allows you to duplicate the last effect you applied, including all its settings; the latter opens the dialog box for the last effect you applied so you can choose different settings. The next section of the Effect menu is something called Document Raster Effects Resolution, which we'll get to in a moment. The remaining two sections are Illustrator Effects and Photoshop Effects;

each section contains a collection of effects in those two categories. For the most part, Illustrator effects are Illustrator-specific features, whereas Photoshop effects are a collection of filters taken from Photoshop.

Is It Vector, or Is It Raster?

You already know that a live effect is simply an appearance that is added to an object, meaning the underlying vector object exists in your document in its original state. As you change the underlying object, the appearance updates to reflect that change. If you want to lock in an appearance, you need to choose Object > Expand Appearance to alter the actual vector paths, at which point the effect is no longer live and can't be edited.

Some effects, such as Drop Shadow, are raster-based. Even though this effect appears grouped in the Illustrator Effects section (**Figure 7.2**), when the appearance is expanded, the drop shadow becomes a raster image. The same applies when you print a file, because all effects are expanded when they are sent to the printer (your file remains in an unexpanded state, how-ever, allowing further editing).

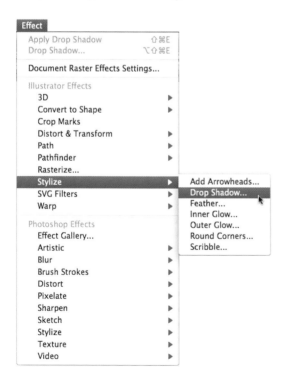

Figure 7.2 *Many of the Stylize effects, including Drop Shadow, produce raster-based results, even though they are listed in the Illustrator Effects section of the Effect menu.*

TIP   Refer to Chapter 13, "Prepress and Printing," for more information on what happens when you print Illustrator files.

The following features appear in the Illustrator Effects section of the Effect menu; these produce raster images when output or expanded:

- 3D Extrude & Bevel and 3D Revolve, when raster images or gradients are present in mapped artwork

- Rasterize

- Stylize > Drop Shadow

- Stylize > Feather

- Stylize > Inner Glow

- Stylize > Outer Glow

Massaging Pixels in Illustrator

NOTE   When you choose to save a file as EPS, all effects are expanded, and any raster-based effects are rasterized. This means Illustrator EPS files can contain raster content and can't be scaled infinitely when placed in other applications. See Chapter 12, "Saving and Exporting Files," for information.

If it is true that some effects in Illustrator produce a rasterized result, who determines the resolution of those rasters? When you work in Photoshop, you can't even create a new file without first defining its resolution. But with Illustrator, which is vector-based, you don't think much about resolution. So the question is, what determines the resolution of these raster-based effects? To find the answer, choose Effect > Document Raster Effects Settings.

The Document Raster Effects Settings dialog box is where you can specify the resolution for raster-based effects. In fact, the dialog box offers all the necessary settings for determining how raster-based effects eventually print (**Figure 7.3**).

The Document Raster Effects Settings dialog box gives you seven options:

- **Color Model.** Depending on the document's Color Model setting to which your file is set, you'll see either CMYK, Grayscale, and Bitmap or RGB, Grayscale, and Bitmap listed here. This is because a document cannot contain both CMYK and RGB elements. This setting can be extremely useful, because it allows you to change the color model of an object (even an image) as a live effect, which can always be edited. For example, you can turn a colored object into grayscale as an effect.

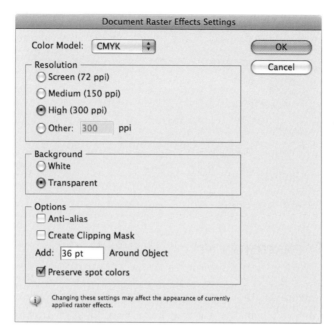

Figure 7.3 *When using live effects, choosing the right settings in the Document Raster Effects Settings dialog box is key to achieving the best results from your files.*

- **Resolution.** This setting determines the resolution at which raster-based effects (both the Illustrator effects mentioned earlier and the Photoshop effects) are rendered. You can also specify this resolution setting in the Raster Effects pop-up menu (under Advanced) when you create a document using a new document profile. The default resolution setting in Illustrator is 300 ppi for print documents and 72 ppi for web, mobile, and video documents. The Resolution setting has a direct bearing on the performance of Illustrator, and just as in Photoshop, working at higher resolutions means more number crunching for your computer and more time for you to stare at your screen watching the progress bars slowly creep along. This is an extremely important setting and should not be overlooked.

- **Background.** You can choose whether the resulting raster has a transparent background or a white background. If your effect overlaps other objects, you probably want to use the Transparent setting (**Figure 7.4,** on the next page), although remember that the file still needs to be flattened (see Chapter 13, "Prepress and Printing," for more information on transparency flattening).

Figure 7.4 *In this example, the artwork on the left used the White setting for Background, whereas the artwork on the right used the Transparent setting.*

- **Anti-alias.** You can define whether the raster image is antialiased. *Antialiasing* slightly blurs color boundaries to avoid the appearance of jagged edges. For more information on antialiasing, refer to Chapter 11, "Web Design."

- **Create Clipping Mask.** This setting creates a clipping mask around the area of a shape so you can have it blend into a background (raster images are always rectangular and may block out objects that appear behind them). This setting won't work well for objects that have Drop Shadow, Feather, and Glow effects applied, because clipping masks have hard edges. You don't need this setting if you specify the Transparent option for the background.

- **Add:** *x* **Around Object.** This is a very important setting. When certain effects, such as Feather or Gaussian Blur, are applied, the resulting raster image has a soft edge. To ensure that this soft edge fades into the background correctly, you must make the bounding box of the raster image larger than the actual object. If you don't, the fade stops abruptly, and you see a visible line where it ends. By default, Illustrator adds 36 points (.5 inch) of space around an object, but if you have a large blur setting, you may need to increase this amount (**Figure 7.5**).

Figure 7.5 *On the left is a circle with a 60-pixel Gaussian Blur effect applied. With the default of Add: .5 Space Around Object, the blur is visibly clipped. On the right, that same blur appears correctly with the Add: 1.5 Around Object setting.*

- **Preserve spot colors.** If your artwork contains spot colors and you want to prevent those from being converted to process colors, this setting instructs Illustrator to preserve those spot colors, employing over-printing where necessary. Refer to Chapter 13 for more information on overprinting.

Any live effects you apply in your document will use the settings in the Document Raster Effects Settings dialog box, and you can't have different settings for different effects. Well, you can, sort of—just not in any way that Adobe intended, though. All live effects update when you make a change in the Document Raster Effects Settings dialog box, but once you expand a live effect, that object no longer updates when you change the settings. So if you need to use different settings for different objects, then apply an effect to one object, use the Object > Expand Appearance function to expand the effect, lock in the document raster effects settings for that effect, and finally apply a different setting to another object. Of course, once you expand an effect, you have no way to go back and perform edits on it.

Convert to Shape: Changing for the Better

The Convert to Shape effect takes the fill of your targeted selection and con-verts it to a rectangle, a rounded rectangle, or an ellipse. When you first see this effect, you might scratch your head thoughtfully and ask yourself, "Well, if I had wanted a rectangle, wouldn't I have drawn the shape that way in the first place?" This is a good question if your object has only one fill, but if you've added multiple fills, you can apply the Convert to Shape effect on just one of them to get a single shape with fills that have different shapes. This effect is particularly useful for text objects and for groups and layers as well.

Applying the Convert to Shape Effect

To apply the Convert to Shape effect, target the fill of an object, group, or layer, and choose Effect > Convert to Shape > Rectangle. Although you can choose between the Rectangle, Rounded Rectangle, and Ellipse options, it doesn't matter which one you choose because the ensuing Shape Options dialog box allows you to easily switch between the three options via a pop-up menu at the top of the dialog box (**Figure 7.6**).

Figure 7.6 *It doesn't make a difference which shape you choose from the Convert to Shape submenu, because you get a chance to change your mind in the Shape Options dialog box.*

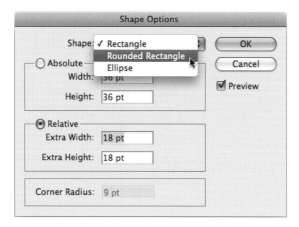

The Shape Options dialog box gives you two options for specifying the size of the targeted fill:

- **Absolute.** The Absolute setting allows you to define a specific width and height for the fill shape, which can be completely different from the size of the object's actual path.

- **Relative.** The Relative setting allows you to define a specific amount that is added to the object's actual size. For example, if the object's actual path is 4 x 4 inches and you use a relative setting with the Extra Width and Extra Height settings set to .5 inch, the shape effect produces a shape that is 4.5 x 4.5 inches. The Relative setting is useful when you want to create a shape that changes when the original object changes (see the next section).

When you choose the Rounded Rectangle setting from the Shape pop-up menu, you can also specify a corner radius for the fill shape.

What If...You Apply the Convert to Shape Effect to Text?

A practical use for the Convert to Shape effect is to create a background for an object that dynamically adjusts itself as you change the object. A good example is when you want to create a button that has text inside it. Using the Convert to Shape effect, you can have Illustrator automatically resize the button as you change the text within it. Here are the steps required to create this dynamic shape:

1. Choose the Type tool, and click a blank area on the artboard to create a Point Type object.

2. Using your keyboard, type **Dynamic**.

3. Set your text to 12-point Myriad Roman.

4. Switch to the Selection tool, and select the Type object.

5. Open the Appearance panel, and from the panel menu, choose Add New Fill.

6. In the Appearance panel, drag the fill you just created so it appears listed beneath the characters in your Type object (**Figure 7.7**).

Figure 7.7 *Move the fill you created so it appears below the characters in the Type object.*

7. With the new fill highlighted in the Appearance panel, choose a color from either the Control panel, the Color panel, or the Swatches panel.

   At this stage, you won't see the color change in your text, because the fill you are coloring appears beneath the characters in the Type object.

8. With the colored fill still highlighted in the Appearance panel, choose Effect > Convert to Shape > Rounded Rectangle.

9. In the Shape Options dialog box that appears, choose the Relative options, and specify 4 pt for Extra Width and 2 pt for Extra Height.

10. For the Corner Radius, specify a value of 2 pt, and click OK to apply the effect (**Figure 7.8**, on the next page).

Figure 7.8 *The second fill you created now acts like a background for the text.*

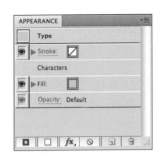

11. Switch to the Type tool, and edit the text.

You will notice that as you change the text, the colored background expands or contracts as necessary to match the text.

TIP For a tutorial on creating more complex autoresizing buttons, visit http://bit.ly/9q4HRy.

As always, a little bit of experimenting not only gets you more comfortable with these kinds of effects but also helps you think of ways you can get your work done faster and more efficiently (which is a good thing).

Crop Marks: Cut Here, Please

When preparing custom art for a printer, you often need to indicate where the printer should trim the paper. Especially when you're printing several items on a single large sheet (sometimes referred to as *ganging up*), a printer needs to know how and where to cut the sheet of paper. Traditionally, designers create *crop marks*, a series of lines just outside the boundary of the artwork that indicate where the paper should be trimmed (**Figure 7.9**).

NOTE The lines that the Crop Marks effect creates are .3 pt in weight and are colored with the Registration swatch so that the marks appear on each plate when the file is color separated.

Instead of drawing these lines manually, you can use the Crop Marks effect to have Illustrator draw them automatically. To apply the effect, select an object or a group, and choose Effect > Crop Marks. Illustrator automatically adds trim marks around the boundary of the artwork. Since Crop Marks is a live effect, as you move or update your artwork, the trim marks update accordingly.

In a real-world workflow (that's what this book is all about, isn't it?), applying the Crop Marks effect to your actual artwork probably makes little sense, for a variety of reasons. Often, the trim area doesn't end exactly where the artwork does. For example, artwork may be centered on a larger sheet of paper, with white space intended to be around it. Alternatively, if artwork needs to print to the edge of the paper, you need to specify bleed, or extend the artwork beyond the boundary of the trim marks.

Figure 7.9 *Crop marks indicate where a printer should trim the sheet of paper after it has been printed.*

The solution is to draw a rectangle and apply the Crop Marks effect to the rectangle, not to your actual artwork. In this way, you can still make changes or adjustments to your artwork without moving the trim marks. In addition, as with any other effect, you can choose Object > Expand Appearance to convert the crop marks to editable artwork as needed.

NOTE If you don't want to apply trim marks as a live effect, you can also choose Object > Create Trim Marks to add them to your artwork.

Distort & Transform: Transforming Your Design

Throughout your design process, you are constantly making changes to your artwork. Sometimes you need to alter paths by distorting them, and other times you need to transform them using functions such as Scale or Rotate. Illustrator features a variety of these functions as live effects, which makes it easy to perform tweaks or changes to these settings as necessary.

Distortion Effects

Illustrator features six different distortion effects, each providing a different type of look and feel. Distortion effects in particular are useful when applied to strokes or fills individually, and this is especially true when you're building complex appearances that contain multiple fills and strokes. You can find each of the effects listed here by first choosing Effect > Distort & Transform and then choosing one of the distortion effects:

- **Free Distort.** The Free Distort effect displays your art with a rectangular bounding box. You can drag any of the four corners to stretch or apply a distortion (**Figure 7.10**). This is useful if you want to add perspective to make art appear as if it has a vanishing point, although the 3D Rotate effect offers similar functionality in that regard.

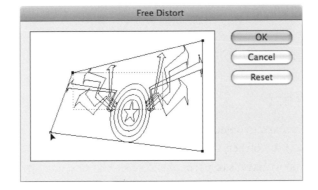

Figure 7.10 *The Free Distort effect lets you stretch artwork to apply perspective or distortion.*

- **Pucker & Bloat.** The Pucker & Bloat effect offers a slider that applies distortion to your objects by spiking paths. When you're looking for a really funky shape, this distortion effect probably fits the bill.

- **Roughen.** The Roughen effect allows you to take straight paths and make them appear as if they just experienced an earthquake (**Figure 7.11**). The Roughen dialog box offers the ability to adjust size and detail; you can also specify whether you want the result to have smooth (rounded) or corner (straight) path segments.

Figure 7.11 *You can use the Roughen effect to create torn paper effects or simply to apply an uneven look to vector art.*

- **Tweak.** At first, the Tweak effect appears to be similar to the Pucker & Bloat distortion, but the Tweak effect adjusts control points in addition to anchor points on paths. The result is a path that is far less predictable.

- **Twist.** The Twist effect allows you to twist art from its center using a specified angle.

- **Zig Zag.** The Zig Zag effect is similar to the Roughen effect, but it creates methodical zigzag patterns on selected objects.

Illustrator also has other distortion tools and effects. The Warp effect, covered later in this chapter, provides a way to stretch art using predefined warp styles. We covered other distortion features such as envelopes and the Liquify set of tools in Chapter 2, "Selecting and Editing Artwork."

Transform Effect

If you want to rotate or scale an object on your artboard, using the Transform effect is overkill. Rather, the Transform effect is useful when you want to apply transformations to parts of an object. For example, you might scale two different fills within the same object so they are different sizes. To do so, apply the Transform effect by choosing Effect > Distort & Transform > Transform.

The Transform Effect dialog box is actually identical to the one that appears when you use the Transform Each function (which we covered in Chapter 2). However, the Transform Effect dialog box has one huge addition—the ability to specify copies (**Figure 7.12**).

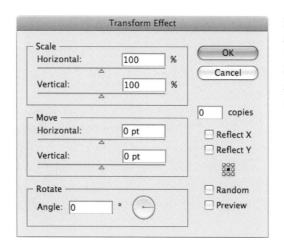

Figure 7.12 *The Transform Effect dialog box mimics the Transform Each dialog box, but it includes the ability to set the number of copies you want transformed.*

Transforming Objects with Effects

Because we're on the topic of transformations, we'll discuss a few concepts you should be aware of when performing standard transformations on the artboard—specifically when scaling or rotating objects that have live effects applied to them.

By default, when you scale an object on the artboard, Illustrator does not scale the values that you may have specified for any live effects applied to that object. For example, if you specify a 30-pixel Gaussian Blur effect and then scale that object 200 percent, the Gaussian Blur is still set to 30 pixels.

If you're using one of the Illustrator live effects, you can choose to scale an object's live effect attributes. To do so, select the Scale Strokes & Effects setting, which you can find in the General panel of Preferences or by double-clicking the Scale tool in the Tools panel.

It's also important to realize that the values of certain effects have limits. For example, you can't set a Gaussian Blur to anything greater than 250 pixels. Even if you have Scale Strokes & Effects selected, you can scale your artwork only up to the limit, at which point Illustrator just uses the maximum value it allows. If you need to scale objects to extremely large sizes (for creating signs or banners, for instance), you first have to expand the effect and then scale it as you would any object.

Finally, the values that are specified in the dialog boxes of live effects are relative to the rulers of your document. In many cases, modifying your object may cause unexpected results. For example, say you apply a drop shadow to an object and specify an offset that sets the shadow down and to the right. If you rotate the object 180 degrees on your artboard (effectively turning it upside down), the drop shadow still displays at the lower right of the object. To get the correct appearance, you need to edit the drop shadow effect and set the offset so that the drop shadow now falls up and to the left, or even better, you can convert your artwork to a symbol before applying the transformation. Alternatively, you can expand the effect before you perform the rotation. This issue requires special attention from printers, who often compose files or create work and turn layouts for their presses. Drop shadows in InDesign suffer from the same symptoms.

Paths: Drawing Outside the Lines

At some point, editing vector paths is something that just about every Illustrator user has to come to terms with. However, sometimes performing these edits makes sense as a live effect, which allows the paths to be updated easily. Specifically, three path functions—Offset Path, Outline Object, and Outline Stroke—are available as live effects. You can find all these effects by choosing Effect > Path and then selecting the required function.

For the most part, these effects are useful when you apply them to Type objects. The Outline Object effect is particularly useful for using text in a way that normally requires the text to be outlined into vector paths. In addition, the Offset Path effect can be helpful when you're trying to create type effects in tandem with the Pathfinder effects, as described in the next section.

TIP You can use the Outline Object effect to help add strokes to images. Refer to Chapter 10, "Working with Images," for details.

Pathfinder: Creating Complex Shapes

The Pathfinder effects are identical to those in the Pathfinder panel (covered in Chapter 2), only here they are applied as live effects. Before you question the reason for making these available as live effects, remember that you can apply live effects to groups and layers. Applying these effects to type objects may also prove useful.

The following Pathfinder commands are available as live effects: Add (Unite), Intersect, Exclude, Subtract (Minus Front), Minus Back, Divide, Trim, Merge, Crop, Outline, Hard Mix, Soft Mix, and Trap. Refer to Chapter 2 for details on most of these functions.

NOTE The Hard Mix, Soft Mix, and Trap commands, which combine the appearance of overlapping colors, are available only as live effects. They are not available through the Pathfinder panel.

To apply any of the Pathfinder effects, make a selection, choose Effect > Pathfinder, and select the Pathfinder function you need.

What If...You Combine Offset Path and Pathfinder Effects on a Group?

A design may sometimes call for artwork to be outlined with a single line that encompasses all the objects. The Offset Path function is perfect for this, but the effect outlines each object that appears in the group, resulting in a mess of paths that overlap each other. If you were to expand the appearance of the overlapping paths, you might use the Pathfinder Unite or Add function to create a single unified shape, but if you do, any change to the group will mean you'll have to repeat the steps all over again. This is where a Pathfinder live effect can be really helpful.

Follow these steps to learn how you can apply both the Offset Path and Path-finder effects to a group:

1.   Choose the Selection tool, and select any group of objects.

2.   From the Appearance panel, choose Add New Stroke.

3.   With the new stroke highlighted in the Appearance panel, choose Effect > Path > Offset Path.

4.   In the Offset Path dialog box that appears, specify a value (this example uses 4 pt), and click OK to apply the effect (**Figure 7.13**).

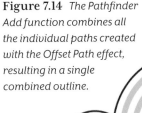

Figure 7.13 *Adding an Offset Path effect to the new stroke you created adds an outline around the artwork.*

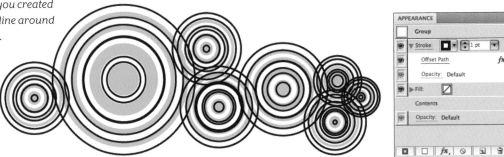

5.   With the new stroke still highlighted in the Appearance panel, choose Effect > Pathfinder > Add. The effect is applied immediately (**Figure 7.14**).

Figure 7.14 *The Pathfinder Add function combines all the individual paths created with the Offset Path effect, resulting in a single combined outline.*

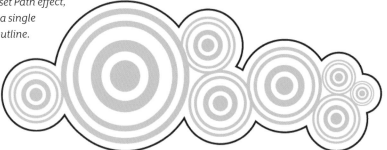

6.   With the Selection tool, double-click any object in the group to isolate it. Notice that as you move objects around in the group, the outline updates accordingly.

Rasterize: Creating Vectors That Act Like Pixels

Illustrator has a Rasterize command in the Object menu that gives you the ability to rasterize any object in Illustrator. The Rasterize effect in the Effect menu gives you the same functionality—but as a live effect. When you think about it, the result of applying this effect is a bit of an oxymoron: The object is a vector, yet it appears and acts like a raster image.

To apply the Rasterize effect, select an object, and choose Effect > Rasterize. The options that appear in the Rasterize dialog box are similar to those in the Document Raster Effects Settings dialog box, and you can even choose to have the Rasterize dialog box pick up the resolution settings from that dialog box by selecting the Use Document Raster Effects Resolution radio button (**Figure 7.15**).

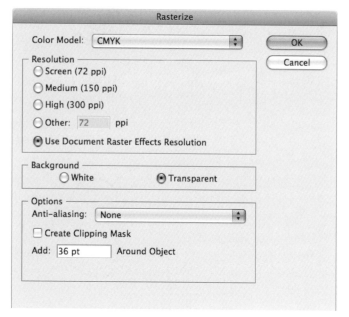

Figure 7.15 *To ensure a consistent overall appearance, you might want to have the Rasterize effect in the Rasterize dialog box share the same resolution setting as in the Document Raster Effects Settings dialog box.*

You might want to use the Rasterize effect for several reasons. For example, you might want to disable antialiasing on small text so that it appears easier to read when displayed on a website (you can find more information on this in Chapter 11). In addition, you can use the Rasterize effect to change the color model of selected artwork (see the following section).

TIP You might also apply a Rasterize effect to very complex artwork (or art that contains many pattern-filled objects) to enable the file to print quickly when proofing. When you're ready to send the file off to print, remove the Rasterize effect.

What If...You Apply the Rasterize Effect to a Raster Image?

It doesn't take a whole lot to realize that the Rasterize effect can turn vector elements into raster elements, but have you ever thought about the possibility of applying the Rasterize effect to a placed raster image in Illustrator? Not only is it possible, but it's also extremely useful. Besides the obvious ability to temporarily downsample high-resolution files to a lower resolution for faster processing, the Rasterize effect has the ability to change color modes. That means you can place a full-color photo into a layout but use the Rasterize effect to change the image to grayscale. Of course, since it's a live effect, you can always switch it back to color at any time.

In addition, you can use this method of converting images to grayscale for when you want to convert an entire file to grayscale—including both raster and vector objects. In such a case, you may find it easier to apply the Rasterize effect at the layer level, where all items on a layer can be converted to grayscale.

Stylize: Now You're Stylin'!

NOTE The Drop Shadow live effect is covered in Chapter 5.

The group of Stylize live effects gets a bit more visibility than other effects for one main reason: the celebrity factor. Among the different effects you'll find in the Stylize submenu is the rock star of all live effects, the Drop Shadow. Although there's nothing that special about the Drop Shadow effect per se, it seems designers these days are trying to find untold ways to add drop shadows to their artwork. We don't discriminate between different live effects (we're an equal-opportunity educator), and the reality is, plenty of other useful effects appear in the Stylize submenu, including Feather, Inner and Outer Glow, Round Corners, and the sleeper live effect of the year—Scribble.

The Feather Effect

TIP Try using a Feather on an object you're using as an opacity mask; this allows you to create a mask with soft edges.

Vector paths are known for their clean, crisp edges, but at times, you want a softer edge to your objects. That's where the Feather effect can help. Choose Effect > Stylize > Feather, and specify an amount to determine how soft of an edge you want your shape to have (**Figure 7.16**). You can even apply a Feather effect directly to a placed photograph.

Figure 7.16 *If you thought soft edges were for pixel-based programs only, think again. The Feather live effect can add that perfect touch to vector art.*

The Inner Glow and Outer Glow Effects

As a variation to the Drop Shadow effect, Illustrator also offers Inner Glow and Outer Glow effects. You can find both of these effects in the Effect > Stylize submenu.

The Inner Glow effect adds a soft glow to the inside area of an object. From the Inner Glow dialog box, you can choose the Center option that starts the glow from the center of the object and extends it toward the edges, or you can choose the Edge option that begins the glow in the opposite direction—from the edge toward the center of the shape (**Figure 7.17**). The Outer Glow effect adds a soft glow to the outside edges of an object.

TIP Glow effects can sometimes appear too soft for your needs. To beef up a glow effect, try applying two or three glow effects to the same object.

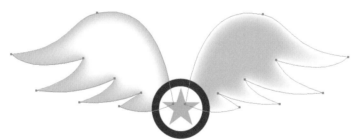

Figure 7.17 *Depending on the desired effect, you can specify an Inner Glow effect to start from the center (left wing) or the edge (right wing).*

The Round Corners Effect

The Rounded Rectangle tool is so year 2000. Welcome to today's fast-paced world where you can add rounded corners to any object, no matter how many corners the object has (**Figure 7.18** on the following page). When you select an object and choose Effect > Stylize > Round Corners, you can use the Preview check box to experiment with different Radius settings until you get just the look you need. Of course, you can always change the Radius setting because it's a live effect.

Figure 7.18 *The usefulness of the Round Corners effect becomes apparent when you apply it to objects with many corners.*

! TIP For an interesting effect, try applying the Round Corners effect to type.

Unfortunately, you can't specify which corners of your object will get rounded—the Round Corners effect rounds all corners. If you want only some corners to be rounded in your object, you need to apply the Round Corners effect and then expand the effect so that you can manually adjust each corner as necessary.

The Scribble Effect

! TIP The Scribble effect looks simple at first glance, but refer to "What If... You Apply the Scribble Effect to Multiple Fills?" later in this chapter to see how powerful the effect can be.

If there's one thing you can count on with vector graphics, it's clean, sharp edges. However, sometimes a design calls for something a little bit less technical and more natural. The Scribble effect in Illustrator is perfect for this task. And, as you will see, the power of the Scribble effect lies in its ability to randomize individual attributes, giving the effect a truly natural and hand-drawn appearance. One of the nicest aspects of the Scribble effect is its ability to draw outside the lines. In fact, what the Scribble effect really does is convert your object into one long stroke (**Figure 7.19**).

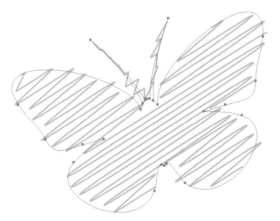

Figure 7.19 *The Scribble Effect gives the object's fill the appearance of a single continuous stroke.*

To apply the Scribble effect, select an object, and choose Effect > Stylize > Scribble to open the Scribble Options dialog box. The dialog box contains five main settings that control the overall appearance of the Scribble effect. Some of the settings also have a Variation slider, allowing the scribble appearance to vary throughout your object.

As you will quickly find out, making even small adjustments to the Scribble effect settings can have a large impact on the appearance of the object. Using a combination of different settings, you can also achieve a variety of different styles for your scribble. Adobe added a pop-up menu at the top of the dialog box that contains different presets (**Figure 7.20**). Switch between the different presets to see the ways you might use the Scribble effect. Unfortunately, you cannot define your own presets. However, you can always save your Scribble setting as a graphic style once you've applied it to an object.

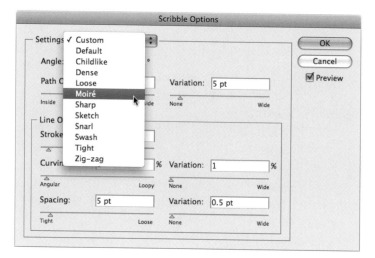

Figure 7.20 *The variety of presets helps you quickly learn the different types of styles you can achieve with the Scribble effect.*

Although it may seem a bit daunting at first, the different settings in the Scribble Options dialog box are rather straightforward:

- **Angle.** The Angle setting defines which direction the stroke will travel. Click and drag the dial to adjust the setting, or enter a value manually in the field.

- **Path Overlap.** The Path Overlap setting defines how far the stroke overlaps the edge of the object's path. You can also set this to a negative value, which effectively defines how close the stroke can come to the edge of an object's path. You can also set a variation, which allows the Path Overlap setting to randomly change throughout the object within the value you define (**Figure 7.21** on the following page).

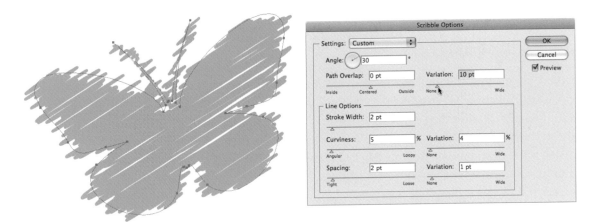

Figure 7.21 *Adding a variation to the Path Overlap setting allows the Scribble effect to draw outside the lines using a natural technique.*

- **Stroke Width.** The Stroke Width setting defines the thickness of the stroke that Illustrator uses to create your Scribble effect. Unfortunately, this setting does not have a variation slider.

- **Curviness.** The Curviness setting defines how much a stroke loops when it changes direction. A very small number produces more of a straight zigzag effect with pointy ends, while a larger number produces loose changes in direction with loopy ends (**Figure 7.22**). You can also define a Variation value so that this setting appears differently throughout the object.

Figure 7.22 *Smaller Curviness settings create sharp lines (left), while higher values create a more freestyle appearance (right).*

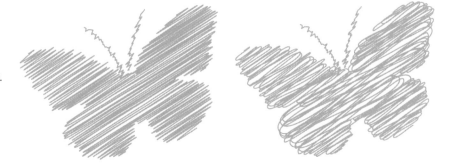

- **Spacing.** The Spacing setting defines how dense the strokes appear. This setting has a Variation slider, which allows the Scribble effect to vary the spacing throughout the object.

What If...You Apply the Scribble Effect to Multiple Fills?

Adding a Scribble effect to an object can certainly give it a hand-drawn look and feel, but sometimes you need something more than just strokes traveling in the same direction. Combining multiple fills—each with a different Scribble effect setting—can produce crosshatching effects that produce wonderful patterns, textures, and edges. Here's how it is done:

1. Select any path.

2. With the object selected, open the Appearance panel, and target the fill by clicking it.

3. Click the Add New Effect button on the Appearance panel, and then choose Stylize > Scribble to open the Scribble Options dialog box.

4. Choose Default from the Setting pop-up menu, and make the following adjustments: set Path Overlap to 0 pt, and set the variation to 5 pt. For Line Options, change Stroke Width to .5 pt, set both the Curviness and Variation settings to 0, and specify .5 pt for the Spacing attribute with a 1 pt variation. Click OK to apply the effect (**Figure 7.23**).

Figure 7.23 *Applying the Scribble effect to the butterfly gives it an interesting appearance.*

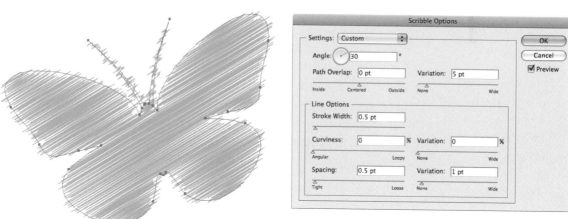

5. With the fill still highlighted, click the Duplicate Selected Item button in the Appearance panel to create a second fill with the same attributes as the first.

6. Double-click one of the Scribble effects listed in the Appearance panel (it doesn't matter which one) to edit the effect.

7. Change the Angle setting to 130 degrees, and click OK to apply the edit (**Figure 7.24**).

Figure 7.24 *Adding a second fill with another Scribble effect gives the shape a lattice-like appearance. Notice the crosshatch effects around the edges of the shape as well.*

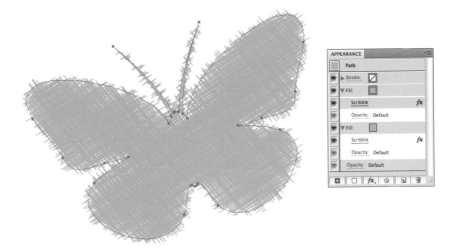

SVG Filters: Applying Technical Effects

Scalable Vector Graphics (SVG) is a vector-based file format that can be used for displaying graphics on the web and on handheld devices. We discuss SVG graphics in detail in both Chapter 11 and Chapter 12, but you can apply certain effects to graphics that are saved in the SVG format. These effects, called *SVG filter effects*, are really XML-based instructions that are applied when the SVG graphic is rendered in a web browser or viewer. As a result, these effects are useful only when applied to graphics that will eventually be saved as SVG.

NOTE For information on how to create your own SVG filter effects (and download existing code), visit www.w3.org/TR/SVG/filters.html.

Illustrator ships with a collection of 18 SVG filter effects, although if you know how to code them yourself, you can also write your own. To apply an SVG filter effect, select an object, and choose Effect > SVG Filters > Apply SVG Filter. Once the Apply SVG Filter dialog box is open, you can click a filter from the list and click OK. Alternatively, you can highlight a filter and click the Edit SVG Filter button to modify the selected filter effect, or you can click the New SVG Filter button to create a new SVG filter effect from scratch. Additionally, you can delete selected filters by clicking the trash can icon in the Apply SVG Filter dialog box.

Illustrator can also import SVG filters. To do so, choose Effect > SVG Filters > Import SVG Filter. In the dialog box, open an SVG file with a filter effect in it; when you do, Illustrator will import that filter into your current file.

NOTE SVG effects should be the last effects applied in the stacking order when multiple effects are being specified; otherwise, the SVG effect will end up being rasterized.

Warp: Choosing Your Distortion

The Warp effect is one of several distortion functions in the Illustrator arsenal. You can use Warp to apply any of 15 different preset distortions to any object, group, or layer.

To apply a Warp effect, make a selection, and choose Effect > Warp > Arc. Even though all 15 warp styles are listed in the submenu, you don't have to worry about choosing the right one just yet—the Warp Options dialog box lets you choose from any of the preset warp styles.

When the Warp Options dialog box appears, select the Preview check box so you can preview your warp on your artboard as you adjust the settings. Click the Style pop-up menu to choose from the list of warp styles: Arc, Arc Lower, Arc Upper, Arch, Bulge, Shell Lower, Shell Upper, Flag, Wave, Fish, Rise, Fisheye, Inflate, Squeeze, and Twist. Little icons appear to the left of each warp style to help you visualize what each one does, although trial and error probably works better (**Figure 7.25**).

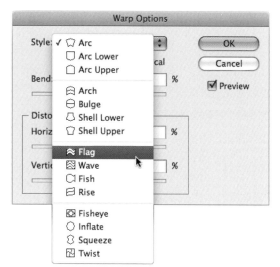

Figure 7.25 *The little icons that appear to the left of each Warp effect help you understand what each option does.*

NOTE Refer to Chapter 2 for detailed information on the other distortion features in Illustrator, as well as a sidebar comparing the Envelope distortion features to the Warp effect.

Once you've chosen a warp style, you can specify whether the warp is applied horizontally or vertically, and you can adjust how slight or extreme the warp is applied by adjusting the Bend slider. Also, you can use the Horizontal and Vertical sliders to apply additional distortion to your selection.

Warp effects are particularly useful when applied at the group or layer level, where you might often add or remove elements from the group. For example, you might apply a Warp effect to a logo to show movement or excitement. If you applied the Warp effect at the group level, adding new art to the group will automatically cause the new art to take on the same Warp effect.

Applying Photoshop Effects

The effects we have discussed to this point are considered Illustrator effects, and for the most part, they are vector in nature and make adjustments to vector paths (with the obvious exception of the Rasterize effect and most of the Stylize effects).

However, Illustrator also has the ability to apply a variety of purely pixel-based effects to any object, group, or layer. These effects are grouped in the Photoshop Effects section of the Effect menu. The same rules as to how effects are applied through the Effect menu and edited via the Appearance panel apply to these effects as well.

In truth, the Photoshop effects in the bottom portion of the Effect menu are really Photoshop filters. You can copy Photoshop filters and plug-ins into the Illustrator Plug-ins folder (found in the same folder in which the Illustrator application file appears), and they appear listed in the Effect menu as well.

At first, it may seem unnatural to find that you can apply a Gaussian Blur or Unsharp Mask effect in Illustrator, but you'll quickly find that you can achieve wonderful designs and cool effects by employing Photoshop filters such as Crystallize and Mezzotint. Some of the graphic style libraries that ship with Illustrator employ a variety of these effects, and by reverse-engineering them, you can learn how to use them.

A Gallery of Effects

Going through each Photoshop effect listed in the Effect menu is beyond the scope of this book, but one feature that really makes it easy to experiment with a wide range of Photoshop effects is the Effects Gallery. If you're familiar with the Photoshop Filter Gallery feature, you'll find that the Effects Gallery is the same. Once you've targeted an object, group, or layer, choose Effect > Effects Gallery, which opens the Filter Gallery dialog box. The dialog box is split into three main sections: a preview on the left, a list of the different effects you can apply in the center, and the parameters for the selected effect on the right (**Figure 7.26**).

To preview different effects, click an effect in the center area (expand the folders to see the individual effects), and adjust the settings at the upper right of the dialog box. Once you've found the effect you like, click the OK button to apply it.

Figure 7.26 *You can spend hours going through the effects in the Filter Gallery dialog box.*

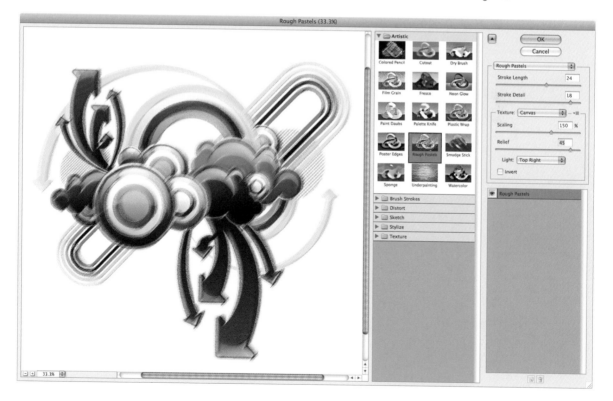

8

Working with Typography

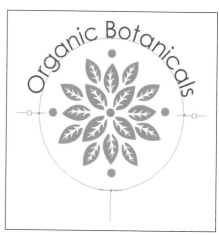

Though a picture speaks 1,000 words, you still need to type words every once in a while. Illustrator has very powerful typography features, which we'll cover in detail later in this chapter. Illustrator is a top-notch illustration tool, but it is also capable of setting professional-level type—its typography features are on par with those found in the award-winning InDesign. And although InDesign shines when it comes to setting pages and pages of type, Illustrator is the program of choice for creative uses of type. Graphical applications, such as putting type on a path, putting it around a circle, putting it inside a shape, and wrapping it around an object, are all quick and easy tasks in Illustrator.

In this chapter, in addition to the creative uses of type, we'll explore some important technologies, such as Unicode compliance, as well as some of the newer typography features found in Illustrator. Toward the end of the chapter, we'll discuss a very important side effect of all this new technology— backward compatibility with previous versions of Illustrator.

Working with Text Objects

NOTE Illustrator can also create another other kind of type—path type, which is explained later in this chapter.

For now, it's sufficient for you to learn about the two kinds of type objects that Illustrator can create: point text and area text. Naturally, each has its own benefits. *Point text* gets its name from the fact that it is anchored, so to speak, by a single point you create when you first click with the Type tool. Point text is fine if you want to enter just a few words or so. The problems are that the type doesn't wrap automatically and that many typographic controls are not available to you. *Area text* is contained by a text frame or shape and behaves more like the text you create in a page layout program like InDesign. This is the kind of text object you'll want to use for longer chunks of type.

Working with Point Type

The simplest form of text in Illustrator is point type, which you can create by choosing the Type tool and clicking any blank area on your artboard. Once you've defined a point at which to start typing, you can enter text on the artboard. Point type doesn't have defined boundaries, so text never wraps automatically, although you can press Return (Enter) to manually type on a new line. When you use point type, the paragraph alignment settings (left, right, and center) refer to the single point that you created when you first clicked with the Type tool (**Figure 8.1**).

Figure 8.1 *Point type aligns differently depending on the paragraph alignment options you set for the text.*

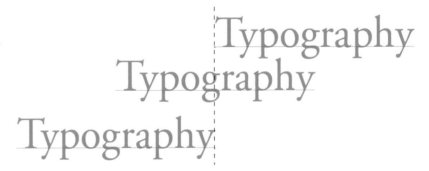

Although point type is easy to create, many of the powerful text features that Illustrator has, including the Adobe Every-line Composer, text threading, and the ability to set text in columns, are not available. However, if you want to place text in numerous areas of an illustration (such as callouts, maps, graphs, and so on), point type is the way to go.

Working with Area Type

As with most page-layout applications, you can also place text within a frame, although with Illustrator, any vector object can serve as a text frame. Area type is text that is enclosed within the confines of a vector shape (**Figure 8.2**). To create an Area Type object, you can either use the Area Type tool to click an existing vector shape or use the Type tool to click inside any closed vector shape (**Figure 8.3**). Alternatively, you can click and drag a blank area of the artboard with the Type tool to create an Area Type object.

At Design Responsibly, we teach technique. We teach why and when you would use a particular application. We teach best practices. Sure, features are nice, but learning how to apply them to real world design projects and customized workflows is key.

"Give a man a fish and you've fed·him for a day. Teach a man to fish and you've fed him for a lifetime." That's what we value at Design Responsibly. Rather than just a brain dump of feature upon feature, out training truly teaches designers and printers how to think about a project before starting, or how to best attack any

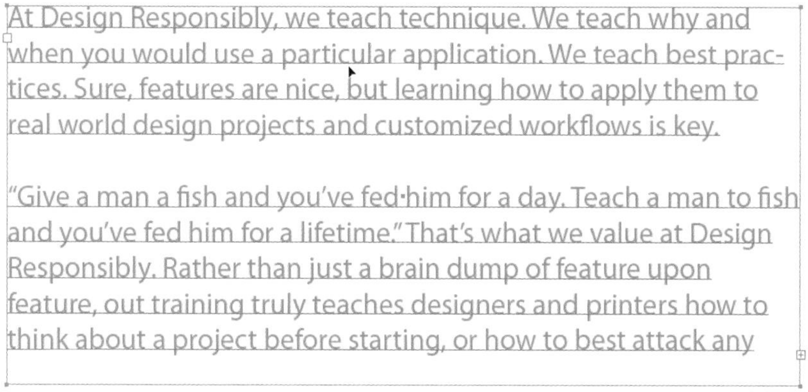

Figure 8.2 *Area type is enclosed within a frame, as here, or a vector shape.*

Figure 8.3 *As you drag the Type tool over an object that can become a text frame, Illustrator displays the tool icon in parentheses.*

Multiple Area Type objects can be linked to have a single story flow across them called a *thread of text*. Text flows from line to line automatically within an Area Type object, and more advanced paragraph settings such as columns, composition, hyphenation, and indents are available. We'll cover text threading and the advanced text features that are available later in the chapter.

Area type might take an extra click or two to create, but for uniform layouts and longer runs of copy, you'll want to use it.

Converting Text to Editable Vectors

In Chapter 3, "Technical Drawing," you learned about the primary shape tools in Illustrator. The characters in both Point Type and Area Type objects are vector shapes too, but they can't be edited as regular vector shapes can because you can't access their anchor points or direction handles. In essence, text is a special kind of vector object. Fonts have specific information built into them, called *hinting*, which modifies character shapes slightly based on the size in which text is printed. For example, a lowercase *e* character has a small hole in the middle, and at really small point sizes, that hole might appear to close up or fill in when printed. Font hinting adjusts the size of that hole to be slightly larger at smaller point sizes.

You can select any text object and choose Type > Create Outlines to convert text into regular, editable vector shapes. Doing so allows you to perform edits on the actual shapes of the characters (for example, extending an ascender or removing the dot from an *i*) but results in the loss of any font hinting (**Figure 8.4**).

Figure 8.4 *Converting text to outlines (right) gives you unlimited freedom to edit the vector paths (left).*

Where possible, it's always best to leave text in an editable state and avoid converting it to vector outlines. In this way, you'll be able to make edits easily, and you'll preserve font information. However, sometimes it's a good idea to convert text to outlines, such as when you've created artwork that will be distributed or used in many different places (logos are good examples). In this way, you don't need to worry about passing font files around (which has legal ramifications anyway—something we'll discuss in Chapter 12, "Saving and Exporting Files.")

Why Text Looks "Fatter" When Converted to Outlines

You might notice that when you convert text to editable vector outlines, the appearance of that text is bolder than text that is not outlined. There are two main reasons behind this (both technical in nature):

- The loss of hinting makes certain features potentially inconsistent. For example, letter strokes that you expect to be the same width might turn out to be different widths depending on how they fall on the grid of the output device. Slight differences can get magnified unexpectedly, such as rounded letters going below the baseline. This happens because the information that makes the outlines round consistently to the pixel grid has been lost.

- The change in the fill algorithm combines with the lack of hinting to make the letters look fatter. Font rasterizing uses a fill algorithm that turns on a pixel only when the center of the pixel is within the glyph outline (center-scan). Graphics rasterizing uses a fill algorithm that turns on a pixel when any part of the pixel is within the graphic outline (overscan). Given that the outline is no longer being rounded to pixel boundaries at key points, the rendering will generally be at least 1 pixel thicker and occasionally 2 pixels thicker.

Of course, how much difference this makes depends on the size and style of the type and especially on the resolution of the output device. At 2,400 dots per inch (dpi) with typical text sizes, the effect is pretty subtle. At 600 dpi with 6-point text, the effect is quite obvious.

Special thanks to Thomas Phinney for providing this information.

Getting Global Text Support with Unicode

When you use your keyboard to type words on your computer, each character you type is stored on your computer by a number. Every font also has a number assigned to each of its characters. This method of mapping characters to numbers is called *character encoding*. The idea is that when you type an *a*, your computer matches up its code with the code in the selected font, and an *a* shows up on your screen. Simple, right?

The problem is that not every computer uses the same encoding system. For example, Mac and Windows use different character encodings. Operating systems in different languages and countries around the world also use a variety of encodings. Conflicts also exist in that one system may encode a certain character with a number, whereas another system may have a completely

NOTE Besides Unicode support, Illustrator also has fantastic support for Asian languages and type features such as Mojikumi, Kinsoku, and composite fonts. To activate these extended features in the English-language version of Illustrator, turn on Show Asian Options in the Type panel of Preferences.

different character encoded for that same number. Because there are so many different ways of encoding characters, you can run into a situation where you create a file on one computer, and simply opening that same file on a different computer results in words not appearing correctly. If you've ever typed something on Windows and transferred it to a Mac and noticed that certain characters appear as question marks, appear as weird boxes, or disappear completely, you can now understand why that happened.

NOTE For more about the Unicode standard, see www.unicode.org.

In 1991, a standard was formed called Unicode, which, as its name implies, is a single encoding that can be used to describe every single character, in any language, on any computer platform. The text engine that was introduced in Illustrator CS uses Unicode, and if you use Unicode-compliant fonts to create your documents, you can pass your documents across the world and have them display correctly on any computer.

Understanding the Way of the Font

Have you heard about the latest reality show? Ten designers have to create a logo, but first they have to get their fonts to work on their computers. Seriously, though, we'd think that in a day and age where we can put people on the moon and do just about anything wirelessly, we would have figured out the whole font thing by now. As you will soon learn, different font formats are available, and each offers different capabilities. In addition, Illustrator is specifically sensitive to corrupted fonts, and although a bad font may work in other applications, it can cause problems in Illustrator. Several font management utilities are available, including Suitcase, Font Reserve, FontExplorer, and Font Agent, and each of these has components to help you identify and repair problematic fonts.

TIP If you find that Illustrator is crashing frequently, the cause might be a corrupted font. By turning off all fonts and activating them one by one, you can help troubleshoot these issues and locate a problematic font.

More importantly, different font formats are available. As a designer, you may be familiar with PostScript Type 1 fonts, TrueType fonts, or Multiple Master fonts. Adobe reduced support for Multiple Master fonts with the release of Illustrator CS, and although those fonts might still work in Illustrator today, there's no way to take advantage of the extended technology that they were meant to bring. TrueType fonts aren't used as much in print workflows because when they were first introduced, they weren't as reliable as PostScript Type 1 fonts (although nowadays, those problems no longer exist). Because of this, PostScript Type 1 fonts have always been perceived as being higher-quality fonts.

Another font type, called OpenType, has introduced a new era in working with fonts, bringing extended functionality and even higher quality to the desktop.

What's Your Type?

We once had a bumper sticker that declared, "Whoever dies with the most fonts wins." There's nothing a designer loves more than a unique font that no one else has. At the same time, with so many fonts out there, you want to make sure you're using high-quality fonts. These days, fonts come in several formats:

- **PostScript Type 1.** Originally developed by Adobe, PostScript Type 1 fonts consist of a printer or outline font, a screen or bitmap font, and usually a font metrics file (an .afm file). Type 1 fonts have been considered the high-quality standard over the years, although OpenType is changing that.

- **TrueType.** Originally developed by Apple and Microsoft, the intent of TrueType was to overtake the Type 1 font standard. A TrueType font consists of a single file. TrueType fonts have traditionally been prevalent on Windows computers.

- **Multiple Master.** Originally developed by Adobe, Multiple Master fonts were intended to give the designer creative freedom to scale fonts to custom widths and weights. They are actually a flavor of Type 1 fonts. Some Multiple Master fonts also allow designers to scale serifs as well. Adobe has since dropped development and support for this format.

- **OpenType.** Originally developed by Adobe and Microsoft, the intent of OpenType is to create a universal font format that includes the benefits of Type 1 and TrueType font technologies. In fact, an OpenType font can contain either Type 1 or TrueType outlines. An OpenType font is Unicode compliant, is cross-platform, and consists of a single font file.

Introducing OpenType

Although PostScript Type 1 fonts are great, they have some issues and limitations that make them difficult to use. For one, Type 1 fonts are not Unicode compliant. Second, Type 1 fonts are platform dependent, which means that if you have the Mac version of a font, you can use that font only on a Mac. You need to purchase a Windows version of a Type 1 font to use it on a Windows computer. Additionally, a Type 1 font consists of two files: a screen font and a printer font, both of which you must have to correctly print a file. If you forget to send either of these files to a printer, the file won't print. Finally,

NOTE At one time, Adobe offered certain fonts in "expert" collections; these were created because the type designer wanted to create additional glyphs and characters but ran out of space. Creating an expert version of the font gave the designer another 256 glyphs to work with.

a Type 1 font is limited to 256 glyphs per font. A *glyph* is a specific graphical representation of a character. For a given character, there may be a default glyph and then alternates. For example, a *ligature* is a glyph that represents multiple characters. Although the English language doesn't usually require that many glyphs, some languages, such as Chinese, Japanese, and Korean, are severely affected by this limitation.

OpenType fonts address all these limitations and offer extended functionality. OpenType fonts are Unicode compliant, are platform independent (you can use the same font file on both Windows and Mac), and consist of a single font file (both printer and screen fonts are embedded into a single file). In addition, OpenType can contain more than 65,000 glyphs in a single font. With the 256-glyph limit gone, type designers can create fonts with extended character sets that include real small caps, fractions, swash characters, and anything else they dream up.

NOTE OpenType fonts work with applications that don't support OpenType, but those applications see only the first 256 glyphs in that font.

The good news is that you already have OpenType fonts! Illustrator (whether you bought it separately or as part of the Adobe Creative Suite family) automatically installs more than 100 OpenType fonts on your computer. You can quickly identify OpenType fonts in two ways: a green *O* icon appears to the left of their font names when you're scrolling through the font menu (**Figure 8.5**), and they end in the letters *Std* (standard) or *Pro*. OpenType Pro fonts contain extended character sets.

Figure 8.5 *The WYSIWYG font menu in Illustrator not only displays a preview of the font but also displays icons to identify the font type—this is especially helpful when you have multiple versions of a font.*

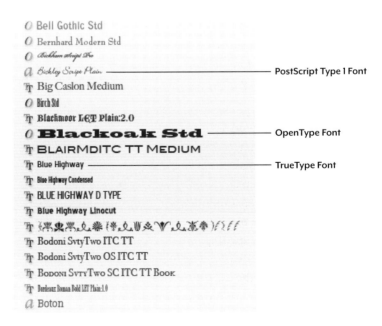

OpenType + Illustrator = Intelligent Fonts

Although the technological benefits of OpenType fonts are nice, they are just half the story. From a design perspective, OpenType fonts also offer superior typographical functionality through something called *automatic glyph replacement*.

To best describe what automatic glyph replacement is, we'll use ligatures as an example. A *ligature* is a special combination of characters that don't ordinarily look that great when they appear together. For example, common ligatures include *fi* and *fl* where the lowercase *f* collides with or overlaps the following *i* or *l* character. So, type designers create a new glyph, called a *ligature*, that somehow connects the two letters and makes them aesthetically pleasing (**Figure 8.6**).

Figure 8.6 *An f and an i character as they appear together in a word (left) and appearing combined as a ligature in the same word (right).*

The way ligatures are traditionally applied, a designer locates two characters that appear together, and if the font has a ligature for that character pair, the designer manually deletes the two characters and replaces them with the ligature character. Besides the extra time it takes to make this switch, this method has two issues. First, a spell checker will find errors when ligatures are used, because the spelling checker sees a ligature and not two separate letters. Second, if you change the font of your text to a typeface that doesn't have a ligature, you end up with a garbage character where the ligature was.

Automatic glyph replacement happens when Illustrator automatically inserts a ligature for you, as you type, when you're using an OpenType font. Illustrator watches as you enter text, and if it finds a ligature in the font you are using for the characters you type, it automatically swaps the individual characters for the ligature. But that isn't even the cool part. Even though the ligature appears on your screen and prints, Illustrator still sees it as two separate characters (you can even place your cursor between the two characters). That means if you run the spelling checker, you won't get a spelling error, and you won't run into issues if you change fonts. If the font you switch to doesn't have a ligature, the individual characters are displayed.

What's astounding is that if you take into account that each OpenType font can contain up to 65,000 glyphs, you'll realize that this functionality goes way beyond simple ligatures. Many OpenType fonts can also automatically replace fractions, ordinals, swash characters, real small caps, discretionary ligatures, contextual alternates, and more. Of course, the beauty of this functionality is that it happens automatically, so you don't have to even search through a font to find these special characters.

Using the OpenType Panel

Although automatic glyph replacement is nice, giving a computer program total control over how your text appears is something that should exist only in the movies. In real life, a designer has complete control over a project. Choose Window > Type > OpenType to open the OpenType panel where you can specify exactly where and how Illustrator replaces glyphs. When you select text that is styled with an OpenType font, you can use the eight icons at the bottom of the panel to turn on and off the automatic glyph replacement for each kind of feature (**Figure 8.7**). If icons appear dimmed, the font you have selected doesn't contain those kinds of glyphs.

Figure 8.7 *With text selected, clicking the different icons in the OpenType panel gives you instant feedback about the different glyphs available in a particular OpenType font.*

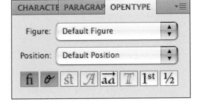

OpenType sets perfect fractions because each typeface can contain all 10 numbers at normal, numerator, and denominator sizes.

NOTE OpenType features can also be set within paragraph and character styles, which are covered later in this chapter.

The nice aspect of using the OpenType panel is that you can experiment with different type treatments simply by toggling a few of the panel icons. You can still use Type 1 and TrueType fonts with Illustrator, of course, and you can even mix them within the same document, but the OpenType panel works with OpenType fonts only.

Finding Glyphs and Fonts

If you are trying to find a specific glyph in a font, it is usually a tiresome game of trying to find the right keystroke combination. If you've ever run your fingers across the keyboard, typing every key just to find where the square box is in the Zapf Dingbats typeface (it's the lowercase *n*, by the way), you know what we mean.

The reality is, because a font can have up to 65,000 glyphs, it can be almost impossible to find the glyph you need. More to the point, how do you even know what glyphs are in a font to begin with? The answer is that you use the Glyphs panel.

You can see a graphic representation of all the glyphs in any font installed on your computer by opening the Glyphs panel (choose Type > Glyphs).

You can resize the Glyphs panel by dragging from the lower-right corner. By clicking the two icons at the bottom-right side of the panel, you can make the previews bigger and smaller. You can choose any font (even non-OpenType ones) from the pop-up menu at the bottom of the panel, and you can use the pop-up menu at the top of the panel to show only specific kinds of characters in a chosen font. If your cursor is in a text object on your artboard, double-clicking any icon in the Glyphs panel places that glyph in your text. If an icon contains a small black arrow in its lower-right corner, that indicates alternative glyphs for that character (**Figure 8.8**).

Figure 8.8 *OpenType fonts can contain a variety of glyphs for each character, including small caps, old style, numerator, and denominator versions.*

Using the Find Font Dialog Box

Knowing what fonts are used in your document is important when you're sending files out for others to use, especially printers. Sometimes it might be necessary to switch fonts, either when you want to replace a Type 1 font with an OpenType version or when you are missing fonts and want to substitute them for ones you have installed on your computer.

Choose Type > Find Font to open the Find Font dialog box where you can see a list of all fonts used in an open document. An icon at the far right of each listing identifies the type of font. Fonts in this list don't appear in alphabetical order. Rather, they appear according to where they appear first in the document's object stacking order.

The bottom portion of the dialog box allows you to replace fonts with those that already exist in the document or with those that are installed on your computer (**Figure 8.9**). You can also use the check boxes to filter the kinds of fonts you want to see listed. If your system contains many fonts, deselecting some of the options that appear at the bottom of the dialog box will limit the results you see in the Find Font dialog box, making it easier to make font choices and changes.

Figure 8.9 *The Find Font dialog box is great for replacing fonts, but it's even better for quickly seeing all the fonts used in a document.*

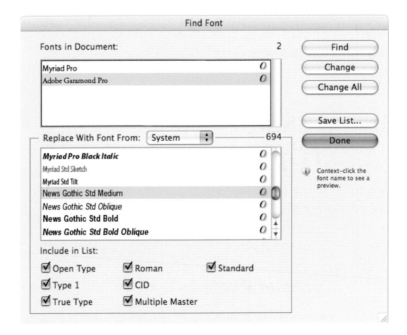

Earlier in the chapter, in the "What's Your Type?" sidebar, we defined PostScript Type 1, Multiple Master, and OpenType, Type 1, and TrueType fonts. Here's a description of the remaining options found in the Find Font dialog box:

- **Roman.** *Roman* doesn't mean "not italic," as in the face. *Roman* here instead refers to the language or character set. Fonts that use alphanumeric characters are roman fonts.

- **CID.** CID fonts are basically the opposite of roman fonts. CID is short for *Character IDentifier.* CID fonts were developed for Asian markets and languages such as Chinese, Japanese, and Korean (what Adobe often refers to as *CJK*). CID fonts are usually several fonts "sewn" together because many Asian fonts contain far more than 256 glyphs (the limit with PostScript Type 1 fonts). OpenType fonts and something called *composite fonts* (available only when using Asian fonts in Illustrator) have replaced much of the need for CID fonts these days.

- **Multiple Master.** Multiple Master fonts are a special flavor of Type 1 PostScript and were originally developed to allow designers to interactively scale fonts on horizontal and vertical axes. This would give a great amount of control to designers to customize a font as needed, but the need for this kind of control never really materialized. The features available in OpenType fonts are far more important to designers. Adobe has not made Multiple Master fonts for some time now.

- **Standard.** Standard fonts are fonts that are installed and used by the operating system.

Specifying Character and Paragraph Options

Just about all the text settings you would expect to find in a page layout program are present in Illustrator. You can find these settings in the Control panel when you select the Type tool or in the Character and Paragraph panels, both of which you can open by choosing the Window > Type menu.

Using the Character Panel

The Character panel allows you to specify the font family and font style (italic, bold, and so on) as well as the settings for type size and leading (pronounced *ledding,* which controls the vertical distance from one baseline to the next). You can also specify *kerning*, which is the amount of space that appears between text characters (see the sidebar "Optical Kerning"), and *tracking*, which is the amount of space that appears between characters over a range of text (entire words, paragraphs, and so on).

Horizontal and vertical scaling can make type appear narrower or wider, although most designers avoid these settings because they can distort text. Use the condensed or extended versions of fonts instead, if they are available. You can apply the Baseline Shift setting to individual characters and use it to adjust where the selected text sits relative to the baseline of the type object. The Character Rotation setting allows you to rotate individual characters within a text string, although you should be aware that you'll most likely need to perform manual kerning when you use this setting. You can specify whether you want selected text underlined or crossed out (the strikethrough feature), and you can also choose from the Language pop-up menu to tell Illustrator what language the selected text is (**Figure 8.10**). This is helpful for hyphenation and spelling dictionaries.

Figure 8.10 *When creating multilingual documents, choosing a language for text tells Illustrator which spelling and hyphenation dictionaries to use.*

Optical Kerning

Getting just the right kerning is critical when you're working with logos and headlines; it can often mean the difference between text that is easy to read and text that is difficult to understand. Kerning is usually set in a typeface automatically and described in a metrics file that identifies the amount of space each letter has. Some font designers also include kerning pairs, which are letters that have natural white space between them when set side by side (the letters *V* and *A* are the most commonly used example of this).

Illustrator has a setting in the Kerning field of the Character panel called Optical, which performs kerning automatically. Rather than using metrics tables to define the space between letters, Illustrator looks at the actual glyph shapes and kerns the characters as they appear to the eye (**Figure 8.11**). Using optical kerning has two immediate benefits.

mustard

mustard

Figure 8.11 *The word on the top is set to Auto kerning and is using metrics to determine kerning. Notice the open space between the m and the u and how the u almost touches the base of the s. The word on the bottom is set to Optical kerning. Notice how the letters appear evenly spaced.*

First, you can apply optical kerning to any text in your file—even body copy or the 4-point legal text that appears at the bottom of an advertisement. Although designers spend time kerning logos and headlines, it's too time-consuming to kern all the text in your file. With optical kerning, you can kern all the text in your document with a single click. You can even specify optical kerning in a character or paragraph style.

Second, kerning applied by hand is good only for the typeface you've chosen. Once you change your text to use a different typeface, you need to redo the kerning. When using optical kerning, Illustrator automatically makes adjustments because it is always using the visual appearance of the text to do the kerning.

Of course, you can always override or make additional adjustments to optically kerned text. Once you've specified optical kerning to text, you can kern that text as you would normally. Generally, for well-designed fonts, metrics kerning is superior to optical. But optical kerning is very useful for poorly made fonts (almost every shareware font, for instance). It's also handy for specific pairs that the type designer might have missed.

In one case, optical kerning can work against you, and that's when you're using the underscore character to create fields when you're designing forms. With optical kerning turned on, the underscore characters won't touch each other; the result is what appears to be a dashed line. However, you can select the underscore characters and change the kerning to the Auto setting to get the appearance of a solid line (**Figure 8.12**).

Account:_____

Account:_ _ _ _ _ _ _ _ _ _ _ _ _

Figure 8.12 *The top line is set to Auto kerning, and the underscore characters appear as one line. The bottom line is set to Optical kerning, and the underscores appear as a dashed line.*

Using the Paragraph Panel

The Paragraph panel allows you to choose among seven different ways to align your text. You can also specify left, right, and first-line indents and add space before or after paragraphs. There's also a check box to enable/disable hyphenation for the selected paragraph(s).

Through the Paragraph panel menu, you can also choose to use the Adobe Single-line Composer or the Adobe Every-line Composer to determine how line breaks are specified in a paragraph of text (see the "Adobe Single-Line Composer vs. Adobe Every-Line Composer" sidebar).

Setting Tabs

To create tab settings in Illustrator, select a Path Type or Area Type object, and choose Window > Type > Tabs. Clicking the magnet icon at the far right of the panel aligns the panel with your selected text. Choose between one of the four kinds of tabs (left, center, right, and decimal), and click the ruler to add a tab (**Figure 8.13**). As you drag a tab on the ruler, a vertical line appears onscreen to help you visualize where the tab stop will be. You can add multiple tabs on a single line (if you can find a page big enough), and to delete a tab, you simply drag it off the ruler. Clicking a tab selects it, and you can specify an exact coordinate for it if you don't have a steady hand. Additionally, you can specify any character as a *leader*; doing so fills up the space between tabs with the specified character.

Figure 8.13 *Setting tabs in previous versions of Illustrator was never fun. Now, it's easy to align tabs perfectly.*

Units Ordered 16,319
Units Sold 2,472

Adobe Single-Line Composer vs. Adobe Every-Line Composer

When good designers talk about setting a nice paragraph of text, they refer to the *color of the type*. In this case, they aren't referring to black, blue, or yellow. Rather, they are talking about how readable the text is, which is heavily influenced by the spacing that appears between letters and words and by how text is broken from line to line. It is especially common to see *rivers* in justified text, which are areas of white space that seem to connect from line to line so that your eyes see them when you are looking at the paragraph.

Using a technology that first appeared in InDesign, Illustrator offers two "engines" that you can use to compose a paragraph of text. The Adobe Single-line Composer looks at each line as it flows text into an Area Type object. Based on hyphenation and justification settings, as well as on font and point size, the Single-line Composer determines how many words can fit on each line. It does so by looking at the first line, flowing the text, then moving on to the next line, and so on. Once a line of text has been set, it's as if Illustrator isn't even aware of its existence. Sometimes, the result is a line that doesn't fit right. As a designer, you might look at such a line and manually break it differently by adding a forced line break somewhere in the paragraph in an attempt to create better spacing.

In contrast, the Adobe Every-line Composer looks at the entire paragraph as it flows text into an Area Type object. As it composes type, Illustrator analyzes the previous lines and sees whether it can get better spacing, fewer hyphens, and so on. The result is a paragraph of text (shown on the right in **Figure 8.14**) that has superior color and that requires less manual work from the designer.

New versions of design software are released in what seems to be a constant stream, making it difficult (to say the least) to keep up to date. Many designers are also considering moving to Adobe's InDesign and Creative Suite platform. Additionally, with everyone making the jump to Mac OS X or Apple's new MacTel systems (and some to Windows even), many designers (and printers) are faced with making major hardware and software upgrades all at once. What is compatible? Are there issues with backwards compatibilty? What's the best way to roll out new technology in a design environment that continues to demand quick turnarounds, constant changes, and most importantly, reliable and cost-effective printing? At Design Responsibly, we can help both designers and printers sort out the unknowns, plan a course of action, and execute on it. Our experience and forward-looking eye towards technology and trends assures a solution that fits today, and that is expandable for future growth.

New versions of design software are released in what seems to be a constant stream, making it difficult (to say the least) to keep up to date. Many designers are also considering moving to Adobe's InDesign and Creative Suite platform. Additionally, with everyone making the jump to Mac OS X or Apple's new MacTel systems (and some to Windows even), many designers (and printers) are faced with making major hardware and software upgrades all at once. What is compatible? Are there issues with backwards compatibilty? What's the best way to roll out new technology in a design environment that continues to demand quick turnarounds, constant changes, and most importantly, reliable and cost-effective printing? At Design Responsibly, we can help both designers and printers sort out the unknowns, plan a course of action, and execute on it. Our experience and forward-looking eye towards technology and trends assures a solution that fits today, and that is expandable for future growth.

Figure 8.14 *The paragraph on the left was set using the Single-line Composer. The paragraph on the right, which has fewer spacing problems and a more even look, was set using the Every-line Composer.*

Keep in mind that with the Every-line Composer, adding a manual line break might result in text reflowing above your cursor, not just after it. This happens because Illustrator is relentless in trying to set the perfect paragraph of text; by making a forced line break, you've changed the layout of the paragraph. If you are manually breaking lines in a paragraph of text, you should consider using the Adobe Single-line Composer.

Defining Text Styles

NOTE Some people who use page layout programs refer to paragraph styles as *text style sheets*.

Sure, there are lots of text settings, and having to constantly choose between them can make design work boring and time-consuming. Have no fear, though, because paragraph and characters styles can get you back to having fun designing in no time. As with page layout applications, you can define a style that stores paragraph- and character-based settings that you can apply to selected text with the click of a button. In Chapter 9, "Drawing with Efficiency," you'll learn how to create graphic styles, which are similar in concept.

TIP If a style appears with a plus sign after its name, the selected text contains an *override*, or a setting that doesn't match the style. Pressing the Option (Alt) button while clicking the style name clears the override.

To define a paragraph or character style, you can use one of two methods. The first is what some call the "show me" way, where you style text on your artboard in the usual way. Once you have your text styled the way you want, you select the text and click the New Style button in either the Paragraph Styles or Characters Styles panel. This way is more visual and allows you to experiment with ideas before committing to creating a particular style. The second way is the "flying blind" method, where you create a new style and then double-click the style name in the panel to define the settings for that style (**Figure 8.15**). This way is useful when you already have a pretty good idea of what settings you want to define in the style.

Figure 8.15 *When flying blind, you can quickly specify font style settings in the Paragraph Style Options dialog box.*

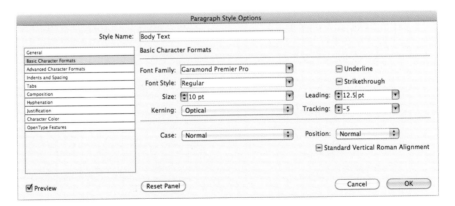

Everything we've discussed in this chapter with regard to styling text can be stored as an attribute in a paragraph or character style. Once a style is defined, you can apply the style to selected text just by clicking the style name in the Character Styles or Paragraph Styles panel. To modify a style, double-click its name, and when you've made changes, any text that has that style applied in your document is updated with the changes.

Working with Area Type

Earlier in this chapter, you learned the differences between point type and area type (or point text and area text). Because area type has more structure than point type, you will find that area type has many features that you would expect to find in a page layout application. For example, an Area Type object can contain multiple columns of text within a single frame and can flow text from one frame to another, which is called *text threading*.

Creating and Editing Text Threads

Text that flows across multiple type objects is called a *text thread*. In previous versions of Illustrator, this was called *linking text boxes* and was difficult to work with. Taking a note from its sister application InDesign, Illustrator makes it possible to easily manage text threads.

An Area Type object always displays two boxes on its path, one located at the upper left of the object, called the *in port*, and one located at the lower right, referred to as the *out port* (**Figure 8.16**). Text flows into an Area Type object through the in port and exits the object via the out port. The ports themselves are also used to control text threads.

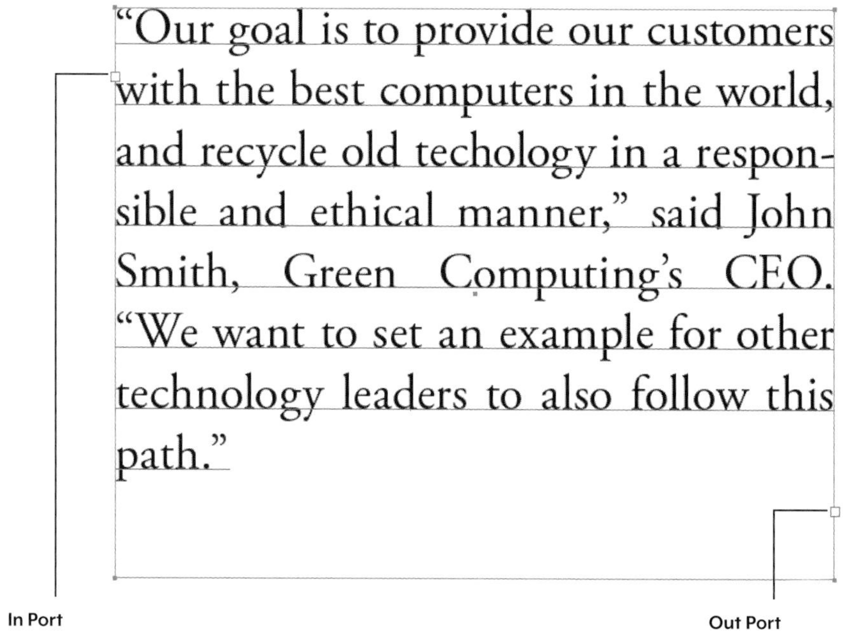

"Our goal is to provide our customers with the best computers in the world, and recycle old techology in a responsible and ethical manner," said John Smith, Green Computing's CEO. "We want to set an example for other technology leaders to also follow this path."

In Port

Out Port

Figure 8.16 *Every Area Type object in Illustrator has an in port and an out port.*

To create a new text thread, you must first have an existing text object to work with.

1. Use the Type tool to drag out an Area Type object or click any closed vector path with the Type tool to convert the shape to an Area Type object.

2. Switch to the Selection tool, and select the Area Type object.

    With the object selected, you'll see the in and out ports, which will both be empty (colored white). An empty in port indicates the beginning of the story, and an empty out port indicates the end of a story.

3. Using the Selection tool, click the Area Type object's out port, and you'll notice your cursor changes to the place text icon.

4. At this point, you can either click an existing closed vector path or click and drag an empty area on the artboard to create a second Area Type object. The two objects are now linked together.

    You can see that the objects are linked because the out port of the first object and the in port of the second object are filled with a blue arrow. A line connects the two ports so that you can easily identify the direction of a thread when the Area Type objects are selected (**Figure 8.17**). To turn this preview off, choose View > Hide Text Threads.

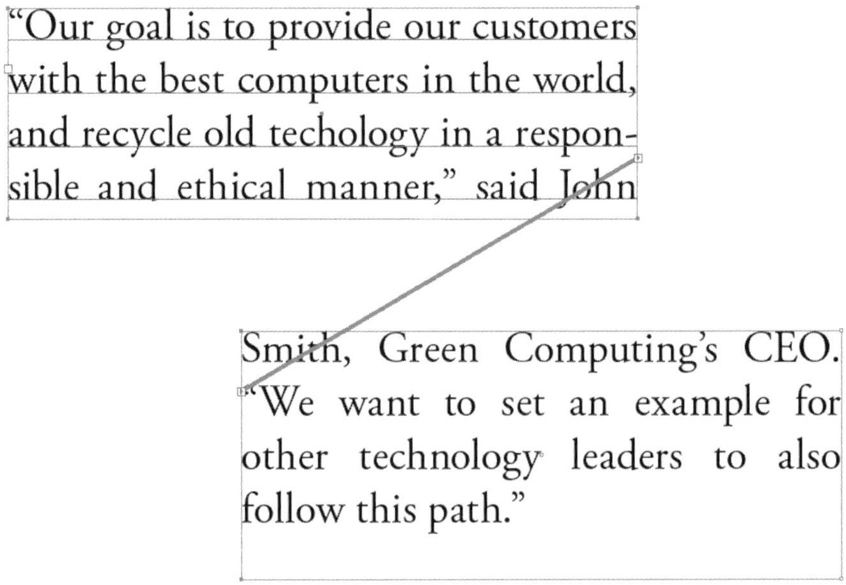

Figure 8.17 *A blue arrow and a connecting line help identify the direction of a text thread.*

"Our goal is to provide our customers with the best computers in the world, and recycle old techology in a responsible and ethical manner," said John

Smith, Green Computing's CEO. "We want to set an example for other technology leaders to also follow this path."

You can add as many objects to a text thread as you'd like. To remove an object from a text thread, select it and press the Delete key. Illustrator automatically updates the thread in the remaining objects for you. To add a new Area Type object in the middle of an existing thread, you can always click the out port (even though it has a blue arrow in it) and drag out a new text object, which will be inserted into the thread.

Because Area Type objects are enclosed areas, a finite amount of text can fit within them. *Overset text* is what happens when you have an Area Type object that has more text than it can handle and doesn't have another text object to link to. An object's out port displays a red plus sign to indicate where overset text exists (**Figure 8.18**). When working with objects that contain overset text, you can either edit the text so that there are fewer words, enlarge the Area Type object to allow for more text, or create a thread and link the object with other text objects.

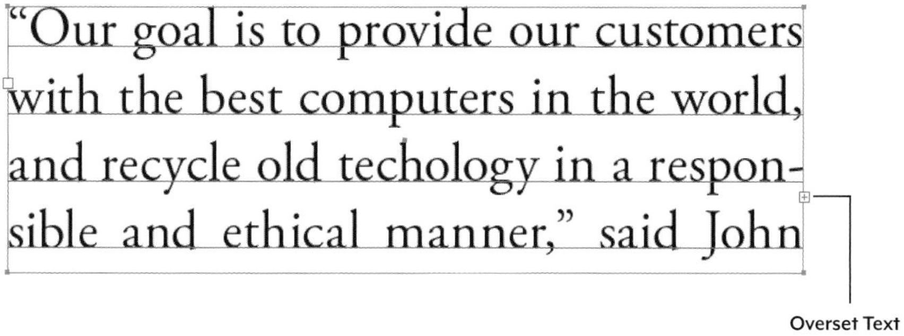

TIP You can also extend a text thread from the beginning of a story by clicking the empty in port and then drawing a new Area Type object.

"Our goal is to provide our customers with the best computers in the world, and recycle old techology in a responsible and ethical manner," said John

Overset Text

Figure 8.18 *A production artist never wants to see one of these. The plus sign in the out port indicates that there is overset text, and it could mean text reflow has occurred.*

Transforming Type

When you have the bounding box option turned on (View > Show Bounding Box), you can use the Selection tool to resize text objects, but there's a difference between transforming Point Type and Area Type objects in this way. When you are working with a Point Type object, the bounding box that appears around the text gives the illusion of an Area Type object (without in and out ports). When you use the Selection tool to scale the Point Type object by dragging any of the eight handles, the text scales in size as well. If you hold the Shift key while scaling, the text will scale in proportion.

In contrast, when you select an Area Type object with the Selection tool, you can click and drag any of the eight handles to resize the text frame, but the text that resides inside the Area Type object will not be scaled. Of course, you can always use the Scale tool or the Free Transform tool to apply the transform to the text as well.

Setting Area Type Options

One of the benefits of working with area type is that you can easily define the area in which the text will be contained. You can also specify many different settings as to how text will fill this defined area, which you can access by selecting an Area Type object and choosing Type > Area Type Options.

In the Area Type Options dialog box, you can adjust the overall width and height of the Area Type object, as well as specify both rows and columns. The *Gutter value* determines the amount of space that appears between each row or column. The *Inset Spacing setting* determines the amount of space that appears between the border of the actual Area Type object and where the text begins. You can think of it like margins that are specific to this Area Type object. You can also choose from a variety of settings to determine where the first baseline is calculated. By specifying a text flow, you can also control whether text flows from column to column or from row to row. Click the Preview button so that you can preview the changes you make before you apply them.

Achieving Perfect Alignment

As designers, we are extremely particular about the appearance of the art we create. Setting type can present a designer with a variety of challenges because each character of each font is different. Even though a column of text is set to be justified, that doesn't mean that, from a visual perspective, it will appear so. Punctuation and special characters can present optical illusions and make text appear as though it is set incorrectly, even though mathematically it is set correctly. Because of these issues, a designer might struggle to align text so that punctuation marks sit just outside the actual margin of text to ensure a clear line that the human eye can follow.

However, this sort of struggling is no longer necessary because Illustrator has two features that take care of these optical issues. With an Area Type object selected, you can choose Type > Optical Margin Alignment to have Illustrator make sure that margins on both sides of an Area Type object are visually straight from a design perspective (not a mathematical one). Additionally, you can select an Area Type object and choose Window > Type > Paragraph to open the Paragraph panel. Then, choose Roman Hanging Punctuation from the Paragraph panel menu to force all punctuation marks such as commas, periods, and quote marks to appear outside the margin of the text at the beginning and end of a line (**Figure 8.19**).

> "Our goal is to provide our customers with the best computers in the world, and recycle old techology in a responsible and ethical manner," said John Smith, Green Computing's CEO. "We want to set an example for other technology leaders to also follow this path."

Figure 8.19 *The Roman Hanging Punctuation setting makes creating great-looking text almost too easy.*

Putting Type on a Path

Having text follow along a path is nothing new to Illustrator users. However, if you've used Illustrator before, you'll find that since Illustrator CS, type on a path is implemented quite differently than in previous versions—to the point where it might even seem like a new feature.

To make it easier to learn how to use this feature, you will start by creating type on an open path. After you've done this, you will understand how to perform the same function on a closed path (a closed path is continuous).

1. Using your tool of choice, create an open path, or select an open path that already exists on your artboard.

2. Choose the Type tool, and move your cursor so that it touches the path and changes to the Type on a Path tool icon, with a line through the icon.

3. Click the path to create a Type on a Path object.

   This action removes any strokes from the path, but apply them to the path again later if you want. At this point, you'll see the blinking text insertion cursor, and you can enter or copy text onto the path.

4. Now switch to the Selection tool, and select the path with the text on it (you can click either the path or the text).

NOTE Everything you're learning about type on a path here can be applied to InDesign as well, because the functionality is similar to Illustrator.

As you look at the selection, you'll notice a line with a small white box on the left, a line at the center, and a small white box and a line on the far right (**Figure 8.20**).

Figure 8.20 *A Path Type object is similar to an Area Type object in many ways.*

The small boxes should look familiar to you—they are in and out ports. The ports are there because Illustrator treats type on a path like area type. The two vertical lines that appear on either end define the boundary, or the start and end points, of the text. The line in the center determines the center point between the start and end points and allows you to specify which side of the path the text sits on.

You can use the in and out ports to thread text across multiple Path Type objects, and you can even create a thread of text that includes both Path Type and Area Type objects (très cool). By dragging the start and end points, you can define the area of the path that can contain text. For example, you can have a long path but have text appear on just a small portion of that path (**Figure 8.21**). If you think about it, adjusting the start and end points on a Path Type object is akin to adjusting the width of an Area Type object. You can also drag the middle line to either side of the path to flip the text.

Figure 8.21 *By moving the position of the start and end points, you can control the portion of the path that can contain text.*

Working with Path Type with Closed Paths

Now that you understand how path type works, you're ready to learn how to work with path type on a closed path. When you convert a path to a Path Type object, the point at which you click the path becomes the start point. On an open path, you can easily see the start and end points because they are on opposite sides of the path. However, when you are working with a closed path, the point you click becomes the start point *and* the end point.

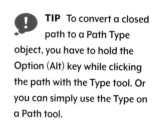

If, for example, you want to place text on a circle, click the top of the circle to create the start point and the end point; if you center your text, it actually aligns to the bottom of the path (**Figure 8.22**). To get text to align to the top center of a circle, either click at the bottom of the circle when you're creating the Path Type object or adjust the start and end points so that the center of the text rests at the top of the circle (**Figure 8.23**).

Figure 8.22 *At first placing text on a circle seems nonintuitive—clicking at the top of a circle centers your text at the bottom of the circle.*

Figure 8.23 *Changing the position of the start and end points can make it easier to center text at the top curve of a circle.*

Setting Path Text Options

Positioning text on a path—especially a curved path—can be difficult because the spacing can look irregular. However, you can adjust the spacing and other settings by selecting the Path Type object and choosing Type > Type on a Path > Type on a Path Options. The following settings are available in the Type on a Path Options dialog box:

- **Effect.** The Effect setting controls the orientation of the text relative to the path. Prior to Illustrator CS, all Type on a Path objects used the Rainbow setting, which rotated each character to be tangent to the path. Illustrator now allows you to also choose from Skew, 3D Ribbon, Stair Step, and Gravity (**Figure 8.24**).

Figure 8.24 *Listed here are the five effect settings you can use with path type.*

- **Align to Path.** The Align to Path setting determines which part of the text lines up with the path. You can choose from Baseline (the default), Ascender, Descender, and Center (**Figure 8.25**).

Figure 8.25 *Listed here are the four align settings you can use with path type.*

- **Spacing.** You can use the Spacing setting to help get consistent spacing between characters on curved paths (the setting doesn't do much on straight paths). Where paths make sharp curves, the spacing between characters could appear at odd angles or with inconsistent spacing. Specifying a higher spacing value brings characters closer to each other and corrects the spacing issues.

- **Flip.** The Flip setting allows you to control the side of the path on which the text appears.

If you want to apply an appearance to the path itself on a Path Type object, click just the path with the Direct Selection tool (it might be easier to do this while you are in the Outline view mode). You can then apply attributes to the path as you would normally. To offset text from the path itself, use the Baseline Shift setting; however, if you're working with wavy or curved paths, using one of the Align to Path settings offers better results because it takes advantage of the Spacing setting.

Wrapping Text Around Objects

Graphic layouts sometimes call for text wrapping around the perimeter of other objects. Because the wrap is an attribute of the object, not the text, you'll find the Text Wrap option listed in the Object menu. You can specify text wraps for individual objects or for groups. Similar to what you learned about groups in Chapter 5, "Organizing Your Drawing," applying a text wrap to an entire group allows you to specify one text wrap setting for the entire group. Choosing several objects and then applying a text wrap simply applies an individual text wrap to each selected object. Once you've made a selection, choose Object > Text Wrap > Make.

TIP Older versions of Illustrator required that you apply a text wrap by selecting both the text and the object. Doing this in Illustrator now creates a wrap around both the text and the object, so make sure you have just the object selected.

Unlike layout applications such as InDesign, the text wrap functionality in Illustrator doesn't allow you to edit the text wrap in the form of a path. You can specify only the offset value, which you can access by selecting the object with the wrap and choosing Object > Text Wrap > Text Wrap Options.

A text wrap's boundary is defined by the object's appearance, not its vector path. If you have live effects applied to an object, a text wrap that is applied to that object will follow the appearance.

Once a text wrap has been applied to an object, any area text that appears below it in the stacking order will wrap around the object (**Figure 8.26**). Point type is not affected at all by text wraps. To remove a text wrap, select an object that has an existing text wrap already applied, and choose Object > Text Wrap > Release.

Figure 8.26 *Illustrator offers a simple text wrap feature. For more sophisticated text wraps, InDesign is a good alternative.*

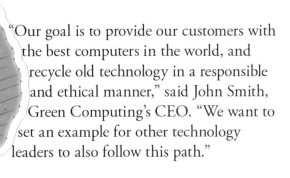

"Our goal is to provide our customers with the best computers in the world, and recycle old technology in a responsible and ethical manner," said John Smith, Green Computing's CEO. "We want to set an example for other technology leaders to also follow this path."

Editing Text

There's a saying that goes "The written word is forever." Obviously, that saying was meant to be applied *after* the client had already reviewed the job. As a designer, making text edits is a part of life. Illustrator has several features that make an author's alterations (AAs) a bit easier to digest, including a powerful find-and-replace function and a spectacular spelling checker.

Using Find and Replace

The find-and-replace feature can be helpful when you're making specific edits across large amounts of text. Choose Edit > Find and Replace to search across all text within a single Illustrator document. The arrows at the end of both the Find and Replace With fields allow you to specify special characters, including tab characters, and nonbreaking hyphens (**Figure 8.27**).

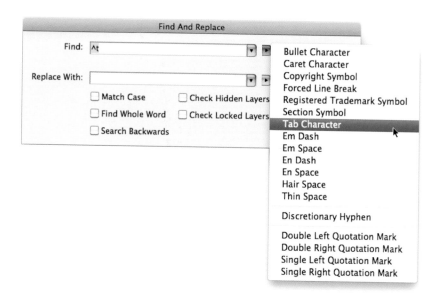

Figure 8.27 *You don't have to remember special codes to find special characters. Illustrator provides you with a list of common characters for search-and-replace functions.*

Displaying Invisible Characters

When performing text edits, it can be helpful to identify where nonvisible characters appear. You can make spaces, tabs, soft and hard returns, and end-of-story markers visible by choosing Type > Show Hidden Characters. When visible, these characters display in blue icons.

Checking Spelling

We're sure that you've never sent a job off for printing or uploaded a web page with a typo in it. But just in case, it never hurts to learn how to check your spelling, especially since the spelling checker in Illustrator is quite the linguist—it speaks many languages.

You can specify what language a selected string of text is by choosing from the pop-up menu that appears at the bottom of the Character panel. You can also specify the language within a character or a paragraph style sheet. When the spelling checker encounters text that is specified as Spanish, it uses its Spanish dictionary to check the spelling, and it does the same for any other language that you've specified.

To run the spelling checker, choose Edit > Check Spelling, and click the Start button. Illustrator starts suggesting corrections for misspelled words; you

can also choose to ignore them or add a word to the dictionary in
Illustrator (**Figure 8.28**).

Figure 8.28 *The spelling checker in Illustrator can prove to be helpful, even for documents that contain a small amount of text.*

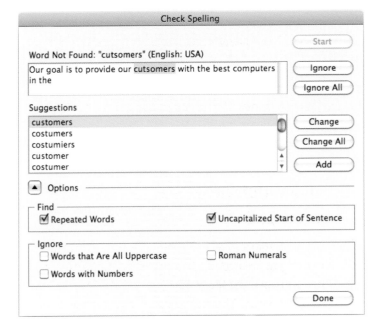

Working with Legacy Text and Backward Compatibility

After reading this chapter, you'll probably agree it's obvious that the text features that appear in the next-generation text engine in Illustrator are powerful tools that bring a professional level of typography into the hands of users such as yourself. Beyond that, the advanced technology that enables Unicode and OpenType support and features such as optical kerning means you can rely on consistent type today and in the future.

All this functionality comes at a price, though, when you consider backward compatibility with versions of Illustrator that use the older text engine. At the end of the day, the text engine that appeared in Illustrator CS wasn't just an enhancement—it was a new feature.

When you have a particular feature in a new version—say symbols in Illustrator 10—you can use this feature in that version, but you can't export that file to an older version and expect to edit it, right? For example, you can't create a symbol in Illustrator 10, save the file as an Illustrator 8 file, open it in Illustrator 8, and expect to edit the symbol. This is because the symbol feature doesn't exist in version 8. The visual appearance is correct, but the art isn't editable as a symbol anymore.

Because of the huge advancement in technology of the text engine introduced in Illustrator CS, text isn't compatible with versions of Illustrator before Illustrator CS. You can think of this as a line drawn in the sand, with all Illustrator CS versions on one side and all older versions (Adobe calls these *legacy* versions) on the other.

Opening Legacy Illustrator Files in Illustrator CS5

Let's take a common design scenario. You launch Illustrator CS5 and open a file that contains text that was created in a legacy version of Illustrator (say Illustrator 10). When you open the file, you're presented with a warning dialog box that states the following: "This file contains text that was created in a previous version of Illustrator. This legacy text must be updated before you can edit it." The dialog box presents you with three options:

- **Update.** Clicking the Update button converts all the legacy text in your file so it is compatible with the new text engine. This process may result in some of your text reflowing and displaying different line breaks and kerning. However, sometimes no reflow occurs at all. Because this happens as you open the file, you won't see the reflow or kerning changes happen if they do, so if text placement is critical, you should avoid clicking this button (you'll see how you can update the text manually later). The only time it makes sense to click Update is when you know you will be changing or deleting the text anyway.

- **Cancel.** In essence, clicking Cancel is like saying, "I always wanted to be a welder anyway." Cancel simply closes the file, and Illustrator forgets this little incident ever happened.

- **OK.** If you click OK, the file opens, and none of the legacy text is affected at all—the file opens just as it did in Illustrator 10. The catch is, you can't edit the legacy text, which appears in the document much like a placed file—in a box with an *x* through it. You can print the file perfectly and make edits to other art in the file, but Illustrator treats the text as a *foreign object*, which cannot be edited. However, you can convert individual legacy text objects to the new text engine as you need to, as you will soon learn.

Basically, if you are opening a file and you know you will be changing or deleting the text, clicking Update is the best way to go because you don't care whether the text reflows. If, however, you just want to open a file so that you can print it, or if text placement is important (which it usually is), clicking the OK button is the smart choice.

Updating Legacy Text in an Open Document

If you choose to open a legacy Illustrator file by clicking OK, the file opens, but each text object is not editable until you convert it to the new text engine (**Figure 8.29**). You can do so on an object-by-object basis by selecting the Type tool and clicking a legacy text object, at which time Illustrator presents you with another dialog box that offers three options (**Figure 8.30**):

- **Copy Text Object.** Clicking the Copy Text Object button converts the legacy type to the new text engine, and therefore the text is editable. Some reflow may occur in the conversion, but Illustrator creates a copy of the legacy text on a locked and dimmed layer beneath the new converted text. If the new text does actually reflow, you can see the difference between the new text and old text, which is on the layer beneath it. You can then adjust the new text to perfectly match the legacy text.

- **Cancel.** Clicking Cancel leaves the legacy text as a foreign object—it can be printed but not edited.

- **Update.** Clicking Update converts the text to the new text engine so that you can edit it. However, a copy of the legacy text is not created, so if the text does reflow, you might not be able to tell.

Figure 8.29 *A legacy text object is not editable, and it appears much like an image does.*

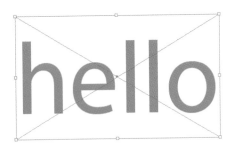

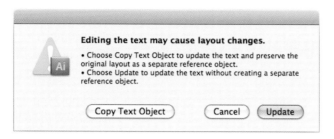

Editing the text may cause layout changes.

• Choose Copy Text Object to update the text and preserve the original layout as a separate reference object.
• Choose Update to update the text without creating a separate reference object.

(Copy Text Object)   (Cancel)   (Update)

Figure 8.30 *Trying to edit legacy text with the Type tool results in another dialog box.*

For converting tag lines, logotype, and other sensitive type treatments, clicking the Copy Text Object button is obviously the best. However, if you have a lot of text objects to convert, it can take a long time to ensure that all the text matches the legacy document (although depending on the task, you might not have a choice). The Update option can be useful if you want to make an edit to just a few lines of text and the reflow there won't make a difference anyway.

You may find that when you're updating text, no significant reflow occurs. If, after updating several text objects, you decide to convert all the legacy text at once, you can choose Type > Legacy Text > Update All Legacy Text. Additionally, you can select several legacy text objects on your artboard and choose Type > Legacy Text > Update Selected Legacy Text. Both of these options perform the same function as clicking the Update button, but they apply to multiple legacy text objects at once.

If you do click the Copy Text Object button so that you can see whether there is text reflow, remember that the copy of the legacy text that was created will still print. Once you have matched the new text to the legacy text, you must delete the legacy text copy either by removing it manually from the Layers panel or by choosing Type > Legacy Text > Delete Copies.

In addition, a Type on a Path text engine was added in Illustrator CS4. If you want to edit type on a path that was created in Illustrator CS, CS2, or CS3, you need to choose Type > Type on a Path > Update Legacy Type on a Path. If you click Update when opening legacy files with type on a path, that type will automatically be updated to the newer text engine. If you didn't click Update upon opening the legacy file, you can, of course, choose the Update Legacy Type on a Path command at any point prior to your editing.

TIP When opening files that were created in previous versions of Illustrator (what Illustrator refers to as *legacy files*), you might have to adjust text objects. To prevent you from accidentally overwriting your original files, Illustrator tacks on "converted" to your file name when it opens legacy files. You can disable this behavior in the General panel of Preferences, although we don't suggest it.

Saving Illustrator CS5 Files to Illustrator Legacy Versions

NOTE Type on a path created in Illustrator CS4 or CS5 with the new type on a path text engine and saved in Illustrator CS, CS2, or CS3 may cause the appearance and positioning of the text to not be preserved, because the type will be rendered with the engines for those particular older versions.

It's said that sticking your hand into a thorn bush isn't painful because the thorns are shaped facing in toward the center of the bush. It's pulling your hand out of the thorn bush that causes the wounds. With Illustrator, moving text from legacy versions to the CS versions is a straightforward transition. However, trying to move text from CS versions of Illustrator so that it is compatible with legacy versions can be painful.

Based on a preference in your Document Setup dialog box, either the text is broken up into individual Point Type objects (the default setting) or the text is converted to outlines. You can change this setting by choosing File > Document Setup and in the Type Options area choosing Preserve Text Editability or Preserve Text Appearance in the Export pop-up menu. In Chapter 12, "Saving and Exporting Files," you will learn how to create files that are compatible with legacy versions of Illustrator.

Basically, you can't do much to avoid this issue. Some scripts (such as Rick Johnson's excellent Concat Text script, which you can find at http://rj-graffix.com/software/scripts.html) allow you to select broken up text and combine it into a single string of editable text. Although these scripts will help, they certainly aren't a solution. If you're creating a file that must have editable text that you can use in a legacy version of Illustrator, you might consider creating your file in Illustrator CS5 but saving it in Illustrator 10 format and adding the text using version 10.

Drawing with Efficiency

9

Take a moment to think about the true strength of what a computer offers a designer. Is it fancy drawing tools? Is it cool special effects? Is it the speed at which you can create art? Maybe. But that's all on the surface. In truth, you may find that a designer can draw something with a pencil and paper in half the time it would take to draw it using a computer. To designers, the real benefit of using a computer is that once they have created a design on a computer, they can edit it at will. When you're working with a deadline, it's far easier to make a small edit to a file than to have to redraw the whole design from scratch.

As you build files with Illustrator, you'll find you can accomplish a particular task in any of several ways. Your job is to find the most efficient way to create the art you need, which doesn't necessarily always mean the fastest way. You might be able to create two identical Illustrator files: in one, the file is huge, takes a long time to print, and is difficult to edit or update; the other is created using different features or techniques and results in a leaner, cleaner, and more editable file.

You already know about groups, layers, and live effects—all of which you can use to build more efficient objects. In this chapter, you'll learn to take advantage of other features such as symbols, graphic styles, and masks. In addition, you'll learn some automation techniques that can mean the difference between being home in time for dinner with the family and pulling another all-nighter at the office when that deadline looms.

The artwork featured throughout this chapter comes from Jennifer Borton (iStockphoto; username: bortonia).

Saving Space and Time with Symbols

Sometimes, a project calls for a range of repeating design elements. For example, when creating a map of a park, you might use icons to indicate restrooms or picnic areas. And when designing an item of clothing, you might draw the same button in several places. Illustrator has a feature called *symbols* that was created specifically to manage repeating graphics in a document.

You can think of a symbol as a master art item, which is defined once per Illustrator document. Once you've created a symbol, you can place multiple *instances* of it within a document. Each instance is simply an *alias*, or a placeholder, that points to the original defined symbol. Using symbols in a document offers several benefits. First, if you edit or modify a symbol, all instances of that symbol are automatically updated as well. Second, because Illustrator stores only a single copy of a symbol per document, you can take advantage of smaller file sizes. Smaller file sizes translate to faster open and save times, faster print times, and faster server transfer times.

Designers who create certain kinds of web graphics can also take advantage of using symbols. In Chapter 11, "Web Design," we'll discuss how you can use symbols to generate smaller file sizes when creating SWF and FXG files.

Working with Symbols and Instances

Defining a symbol is quick and easy. Select any artwork on your artboard, and drag it to the Symbols panel. Even faster, select your artwork, and press the F8 key. The Symbol Options dialog box appears, giving you the opportunity to name the symbol and to specify several important settings (**Figure 9.1**).

Figure 9.1 *The Symbol Options dialog box gives you the ability to name your symbol as you create it, making it easier to reference later.*

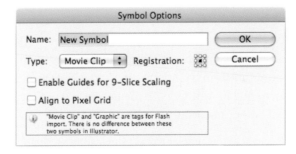

The Symbol Options dialog box contains the following settings:

- **Type.** Illustrator gives you the ability to classify a symbol as either a graphic or a movie clip. If you are eventually going to bring your artwork from Illustrator into Flash Professional, you can select the symbol type now and save yourself a few steps later. However, the type of symbol that you choose has absolutely no effect inside of Illustrator. If you aren't going to be bringing the artwork into Flash Professional, you can ignore the Type setting.

- **Flash Registration.** The Flash Registration setting lets you define an origin point for the symbol. This origin point is used when you apply transformations, and can also help you position artwork correctly when updating the symbol. This setting is similar to what you learned in Chapter 2, "Selecting and Editing Artwork," with the Transform panel.

- **Enable Guides for 9-Slice Scaling.** Scaling artwork horizontally or vertically can often distort the image. With 9-slice scaling, however, you can indicate which parts of your artwork should scale when you stretch it (**Figure 9.2**). Using 9-slice scaling is a two-step process: first, turn the option on here in the Symbol Options dialog box; second, once the symbol is created, double-click it to edit it in isolation mode and position the guides appropriately (**Figure 9.3**).

NOTE The majority of symbols used in a Flash project are movie clips, which contain their own timelines.

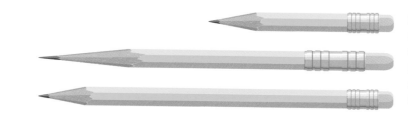

Figure 9.2 *The original artwork (top), the artwork stretched horizontally (middle), and the artwork stretched horizontally with 9-slice scaling (bottom).*

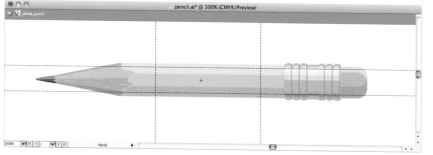

Figure 9.3 *The four guides create nine areas, or slices, each scaling according to different rules. The center slice scales both vertically and horizontally; the middle left and right slices scale vertically; the middle top and bottom slices scale horizontally; and the corner slices don't scale at all.*

- **Align to Pixel Grid.** Selecting the Align to Pixel Grid check box will force the artwork within each symbol instance to snap to the pixel grid. More information on antialiasing and pixel grid alignment can be found in Chapter 11, "Web Design."

Unlike with brushes, which are limited in the kinds of artwork they can contain, you can use any kind of artwork to define a symbol—with the exception of place-linked images (for more information on linked images, see Chapter 10, "Working with Images"). Embedded images, objects with live effects applied, and even editable text can be stored inside a symbol in Illustrator. Once you've defined a symbol, your artwork is stored in the Symbols panel, and a symbol instance is placed on your artboard in its stead. Like brushes, symbols belong to the Illustrator document and travel with it, meaning anyone who opens your document will always see the symbols listed in the Symbols panel. Copying an instance from one document to another automatically copies the symbol as well.

TIP Although you can't include linked images in a symbol, you can include embedded images. Because you can use symbols many times in a document with no adverse effect on file size, it makes sense to think about creating symbols from an embedded image if you need to use them often in a file.

You can drag additional instances from the Symbols panel to your artboard, or you can select a symbol in the panel and click the Place Symbol Instance button to add an instance to the center of your screen (**Figure 9.4**). Once it's on the artboard, you'll notice that a symbol instance doesn't give you access to the actual artwork because it is simply a placeholder (**Figure 9.5**, on the next page). However, you can use any of the transformation tools and functions in Illustrator with symbol instances. For example, you can scale or rotate a symbol instance as necessary. Additionally, you can specify transparency features and even apply live effects to symbol instances. You can place as many symbol instances in a document as you desire, and you can scale or transform each instance differently.

Figure 9.4 *You can use the Place Symbol Instance button to place symbols in the center of your screen.*

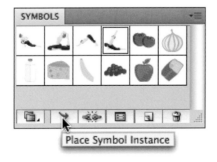

Figure 9.5 *Even though a symbol may consist of many individual objects, it is treated as a single object on the artboard.*

At any time, you can select a symbol instance on the artboard and click the Break Link button in the Control panel. Alternatively, you can click the Break Link to Symbol button in the Symbols panel. This action *expands* the symbol instance on the artboard, allowing you to access and edit the individual components (**Figure 9.6**). However, the artwork is no longer an instance, and it loses any connection with the symbol that is defined in the Symbols panel. The symbol itself remains untouched, and any other instances that exist on your artboard still reference the original symbol.

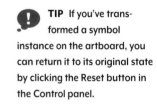

TIP If you've transformed a symbol instance on the artboard, you can return it to its original state by clicking the Reset button in the Control panel.

Figure 9.6 *Once you break the link between the symbol and a particular instance of it, you can edit the artwork freely, although the art no longer has any association with the symbol.*

Replacing Symbols

NOTE In Illustrator CS5, symbols can also contain their own layers.

If you think about it, a symbol instance is just a container that references real artwork that resides in the Symbols panel. With this fundamental understanding, it should be possible to take a symbol instance that references one symbol and change it so it references a different symbol that you've defined. In Illustrator, the ability to switch an instance to point to a different symbol is called *replacing symbols*.

To replace a symbol instance, select it on the artboard, and then choose another symbol from the Replace Instance with Symbol pop-up menu in the Control panel. Alternatively, you can select the symbol instance on the artboard and click the symbol in the Symbols panel that you want to replace it with. With both the symbol instance on your artboard and the new symbol in the Symbols panel selected, choose Replace Symbol from the Symbols panel menu. The selected symbol instance updates accordingly. When replacing symbol instances, any transformations or effects you've applied to any individual instances will remain intact.

Modifying Symbols and Instances

Before you modify a symbol, it's important to understand a key concept: editing a symbol causes any instances of that symbol that appear in your document to update. The easiest way to edit a symbol is to simply double-click it, which isolates the symbol (just as with isolation mode, as you learned in Chapter 5, "Organizing Your Drawing"). Alternatively, you can double-click any symbol icon in the Symbols panel. You'll experience a different behavior depending on whether you double-click a symbol instance on the artboard or a symbol in the Symbols panel. Let's take a look at the difference:

- **Double-clicking a symbol instance on the artboard.** When you double-click a symbol instance on the artboard, Illustrator dims all other artwork in your file, and you can edit your symbol in the context of your entire document (**Figure 9.7**).

- **Double-clicking a symbol in the Symbols panel.** When you double-click a symbol in the Symbols panel, Illustrator hides all other artwork in your file and displays just the symbol artwork, in the middle of your document window (**Figure 9.8**).

When a symbol is redefined, all instances on the artboard that reference the symbol are updated to reflect the change. Any attributes or transformations that were applied to the instances are preserved.

Figure 9.7 *Double-clicking a symbol instance on the artboard tells Illustrator you want to edit your symbol art in the context of the other art on your page. As you edit your symbol, you'll see the other art in the background.*

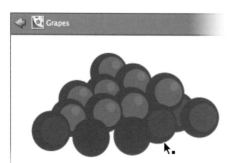

Figure 9.8 *Double-clicking a symbol in the Symbols panel tells Illustrator you want to edit the symbol without anything else getting in the way. All other art disappears, allowing you to focus just on the symbol artwork.*

Using Symbols in Different Ways

NOTE You can nest symbols, meaning you can place one symbol inside another. To edit nested symbols, keep double-clicking each symbol to drill down further within the symbol.

When you take a moment to think about your project before you start working on it, you might be able to determine whether using symbols will benefit you. Here are several ways symbols can help build better files:

• Although Illustrator doesn't use master pages, symbols can act like miniature "master art elements" in a file. For example, when creating several different ideas for a packaging concept, use symbols as the base for each design (that is, ingredients, nutrition information, weight, and so on). Updating a symbol then instantly updates all the designs in the file at once.

• Create symbol libraries to store commonly used logos and icons. (You learned how to create custom libraries in Chapter 6, "Coloring Artwork.")

• Create symbol libraries to store collections of fashion elements, such as buttons, zippers, or labels, or to store other specific art elements, such as architectural elements or cartography symbols.

• Using symbols is required in order to map artwork onto the surfaces of 3D objects.

• Symbols can help you conserve file size when creating SWF and FXG Web graphics. More detail can be found in Chapter 11, "Web Design."

Of course, you can use symbols in Illustrator in plenty of other ways. The next section deals with some special tools created specifically for working with symbols: the Symbolism tools.

Having Fun with the Symbolism Tools

So, you've been reading along and totally get the benefits of using symbols where possible to create more efficient files. Say, for example, you are going to create an illustration of a plate of sumptuous salad (true, an oxymoron). You create some symbols of toppings, including onions, cheese, croutons, and maybe some pepper and a lemon wedge (**Figure 9.9**). One by one, you drag out symbol instances and scale and rotate each topping to achieve a more natural look (**Figure 9.10**). As you drag out yet another symbol instance, you think, "There's got to be a better way to do this!" The good news is, there is. The great news is, the better way is extremely fun!

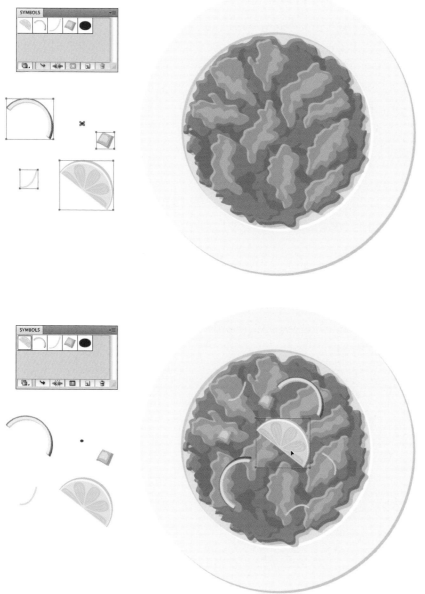

Figure 9.9 *With all your salad toppings defined as symbols, you're ready to start garnishing.*

Figure 9.10 *Dragging and positioning individual symbol instances can be tedious.*

In the Tools panel, you'll find the Symbol Sprayer tool. Hidden beneath it, you'll find seven more tools; together, these tools are referred to as the Symbolism tools (**Figure 9.11**, on the next page). The reason for the name is that these tools all work using symbols—and not by any coincidence, the tools all begin with the letter *s*. (See? Adobe actually *does* pay attention to detail.)

Figure 9.11 *The Symbolism tools all appear grouped in the Tools panel with the Symbol Sprayer tool.*

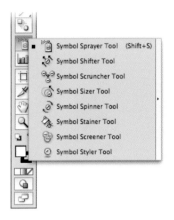

Creating a Symbol Set

The Symbol Sprayer tool lets you easily add multiple symbol instances to a document. Select the Symbol Sprayer tool from the Tools panel, and then click any symbol in the Symbols panel. Because the Symbol Sprayer tool works only with symbols, it's important to first select a symbol to work with—otherwise the Symbol Sprayer won't work. Click and drag on the artboard, and you'll begin to see the Symbol Sprayer adding symbols to your page (**Figure 9.12**). When you release the mouse button, a single outline appears around the perimeter of the symbols. What you have created is a *symbol set*, which is a collection of symbol instances (**Figure 9.13**). If you switch to the Selection tool, you'll find you can't select the individual symbol instances, but you can move the entire symbol set as a whole.

Figure 9.12 *As you click and drag with the Symbol Sprayer tool, instances appear to flow onto your artboard.*

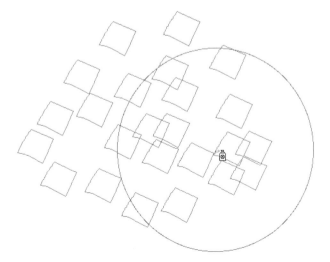

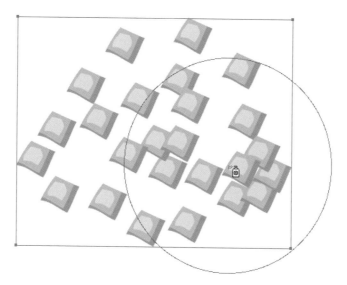

Figure 9.13 *Once you release the mouse button, the symbol instances appear united in a single symbol set.*

Although it may seem silly that you can't select individual instances within a symbol set, that notion quickly changes when you realize that the Symbol Sprayer tool is interactive. Select the symbol set, and switch back to the Symbol Sprayer tool. If you click and drag, the Symbol Sprayer tool adds more symbol instances to the set. If you press the Option (Alt) key while dragging, you remove symbols from the set. In addition, the Symbol Sprayer tool has support for pressure-sensitive tablets, so the harder you press, the faster the instances appear.

It's certainly fun to spray symbols all over your document, but you can also control the individual symbols that appear inside a symbol set. To do this, you need to employ the other Symbolism tools.

TIP You can add different symbols to the same symbol set. Once you've created a symbol set using one symbol, choose another symbol from the Symbols panel, and add more symbols to your symbol set. You can add as many different kinds of symbols as you want to a symbol set.

Using the Specialized Symbolism Tools

Once you've created a symbol set with the Symbol Sprayer tool, you can switch to any of the other Symbolism tools to adjust the symbols within the set. It's important to realize that symbol sets are intended to create a natural collection of symbol instances. You'll find that you can't position symbol instances precisely with the Symbolism tools. On the contrary, the Symbolism tools are meant to offer Illustrator users a more free-flowing style, and it almost feels as if you are suggesting a particular movement or behavior to symbol instances rather than performing a definitive action on them. As you try each of these tools, you'll get a better feel for how they function and for how you might be able to use them for your projects.

For each of these tools, you'll notice that a circle appears, which indicates the diameter of the tool's area of influence (**Figure 9.14**). You can make this area larger or smaller by pressing the bracket keys ([ ]) on your keyboard (similar to the Photoshop keyboard shortcut for changing brush size).

Figure 9.14 *You can resize the circle area, which indicates the tool's area of influence, to be bigger or smaller.*

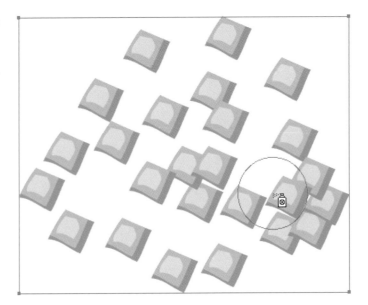

- **Symbol Shifter tool.** The Symbol Shifter tool moves symbol instances around. Clicking and dragging this tool pushes symbols in the direction of your pointer. If you hold the Shift key while dragging, Illustrator brings the symbol instances from the back of the symbol set's stacking order to the front.

- **Symbol Scruncher tool.** The Symbol Scruncher tool moves symbol instances closer together, making the appearance more dense. Clicking and dragging with the Symbol Scruncher tool causes instances to become attracted to your pointer and to slowly gravitate toward it. If you hold the Option (Alt) key while dragging, the reverse effect applies, and instances move farther away from your pointer.

TIP Although the Symbolism tools aren't meant to work on just one symbol instance at a time, you can make your area of influence small enough that you can affect a much smaller area or even individual symbols.

- **Symbol Sizer tool.** The Symbol Sizer tool scales symbol instances within a symbol set. Clicking and dragging with the Symbol Sizer tool causes instances to become larger. If you hold the Option (Alt) key while dragging, the reverse effect applies, and instances become smaller (**Figure 9.15**).

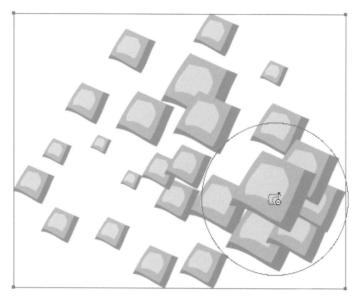

Figure 9.15 *The Symbol Sizer tool allows you to interactively scale the symbol instances within a symbol set.*

- **Symbol Spinner tool.** The Symbol Spinner tool rotates symbol instances. Clicking and dragging with the Symbol Spinner tool causes instances to rotate toward the direction of your pointer. As you drag, arrows appear that indicate the direction in which the instances will rotate (**Figure 9.16**). Instances that appear closer to the center of the area of influence rotate at a lesser rate than objects toward the edges of the area of influence.

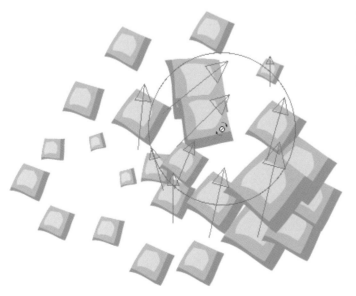

Figure 9.16 *When dragging with the Symbol Spinner tool, arrows appear, helping you get an idea of how the instances will rotate.*

- **Symbol Stainer tool.** The Symbol Stainer tool applies color tints to symbol instances (**Figure 9.17**). To use the Symbol Stainer tool, you must first select a fill color from either the Control, Swatches, or Color panel. Once a color is selected, clicking and dragging with the Symbol Stainer tool gradually tints the symbol instances. If you hold the Option (Alt) key while dragging, the reverse effect applies, and the instances will gradually return to their original colors.

Figure 9.17 *Here in the finished salad, the Symbol Stainer tool was used to create the various shades of color in the cheese toppings.*

- **Symbol Screener tool.** The Symbol Screener tool applies opacity to symbol instances. Clicking and dragging with the Symbol Screener tool causes instances to become transparent. If you hold the Option (Alt) key while dragging, the reverse effect applies, and instances become more opaque.

- **Symbol Styler tool.** The Symbol Styler tool applies graphic styles to symbol instances. To use the Symbol Styler tool, you must first select an existing named graphic style from the Graphic Styles panel. Once you've selected a style, click and drag with the Symbol Styler tool to gradually add appearances from the style to the symbol instances. If you hold the Option (Alt) key while dragging, the reverse effect applies, and the instances gradually return to their original appearances. Note that using this particular tool can result in extremely slow performance, especially with complex symbols.

Switching Symbolism Tools

When using the Symbolism tools, you'll often find yourself jumping from one Symbolism tool to another. You can either tear off all the Symbolism tools to access them more easily, or you can use a special context-sensitive menu. If you're on a Mac, with any of the Symbolism tools selected, press Control-Option, and click. If you're on Windows, press Alt, and right-click to access a circular context menu that contains all the Symbolism tools (**Figure 9.18**). Move your pointer over the tool you want, and release the keys to switch to the Symbolism tool you have chosen.

Figure 9.18 *The Symbolism context menu in Windows makes it easy to switch between the tools.*

TIP If you add multiple symbols to a single symbol set, using any of the Symbolism tools affects only the symbol that is currently selected in the Symbols panel. If no symbols are selected in the Symbols panel, the tools applies to all the symbols.

Double-click any of the Symbolism tools to see the options for the entire Symbolism toolset (**Figure 9.19**). The Intensity setting controls how quickly the Symbolism tools work, and choosing Pressure for the Intensity setting if you have a pressure-sensitive tablet makes it easier to control the flow of symbols and the edits you make to them.

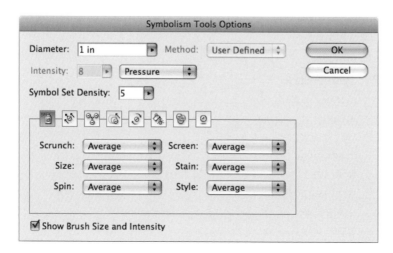

Figure 9.19 *In one dialog box, you can set the behavior and view options for all the Symbolism tools.*

Expanding a Symbol Set

Although the Symbol Sprayer works only with symbol sets, the remaining Symbolism tools work on individual symbol instances. You can reduce a symbol set to a group of individual symbol instances by selecting the symbol set and choosing Object > Expand. You can also select several symbol instances and use a Symbolism tool to adjust them all at once. Still, you'll find that most times, you'll be using the regular Scale and Rotate tools to adjust individual symbol instances, and you'll be using the Symbolism tools for when you're working with symbol sets.

Scatter Brush vs. Symbol Sprayer

You may be wondering why there's a Symbol Sprayer tool in Illustrator, since you know that in Chapter 4, "Creative Drawing," we discussed the Scatter brush that allows you to distribute graphics along a path.

Although the concept of creating multiple copies of art is common between the two features, the differences end there. A Scatter brush is limited by what can be defined as a brush, whereas you have far fewer limitations when you are defining symbols. Additionally, using a Scatter brush to add many shapes to a file increases file size and adds complexity to the file. The Symbol Sprayer tool can spray hundreds of symbols onto a page without you having to worry about files getting too big.

Of course, you can adjust symbol sets that are created with the Symbol Sprayer tool using a range of Symbolism tools. This allows you to tweak a design until you're happy with the results. In contrast, when using a Scatter brush, you've already specified the settings of the brush before you've created the path. However, a Scatter brush can follow a specific path, whereas the Symbol Sprayer tool is harder to control if you need art placed at specific intervals.

Looking Behind the Mask

When we refer to masks, we're not talking about the kind you wear during Mardi Gras. *Masking* in Illustrator is a way to define parts of your artwork as being hidden from view. Rather than having to delete unwanted parts of your art, you can use a vector shape to define an area that acts like a window: Anything that appears within the borders of the shape is visible, and anything that falls outside its boundaries is not visible. The main benefit derived from using masks is that you aren't deleting anything from your file, and once a mask is created, it's possible to change the mask or the artwork behind it, as well as reposition the mask to show or hide different parts of your artwork.

When you use masks in a file and are required to make changes, you'll never have to re-create art that you've already deleted. Instead, everything you create is always in the file, and you simply choose what is or isn't visible. Additionally, a mask allows you to instantly clip parts of an image or an object. By using a mask, you can do with one click what might take tens of clicks if you use pathfinder functions to chop up and delete parts of objects. Of course, you can't remove parts of some kinds of objects at all, such as placed images, in which case masking is required anyway.

You can create three kinds of masks in Illustrator, each with its own benefits. A *clipping mask* allows you to specify a certain vector shape as a mask for other individual or grouped objects. A *layer clipping mask* allows you to specify a certain vector shape as a mask for all the objects within the same layer. An *opacity mask* allows you to use the luminance value of any object to create a mask for other individual or grouped objects. As you will see, this last type of mask—one of the most well-hidden features of Illustrator—is also the most powerful.

CAUTION Because Illustrator creates a group when creating a clipping mask, all artwork is brought into the topmost layer. If you want to preserve the layer structure within masked artwork, you might want to look at "Organizing Masking with Layer Clipping Masks," later in this chapter.

Creating Clipping Masks

A common use of clipping masks is showing only a portion of a placed image. For example, page layout applications such as InDesign allow you to place images into a frame. By resizing the frame and positioning the image within the frame, you can "crop" an image so that only a portion is visible. Being that Illustrator allows you to place images directly on the artboard (without requiring a frame), you must use a mask to achieve the effect of cropping an image in Illustrator.

Clipping masks are used on all kinds of art in Illustrator—not just placed images. For example, you might create an interesting background design (made of multiple elements) in Illustrator and want to have this background appear within a specific shape or area.

TIP When working with images, Illustrator provides a quick way to create a mask. Select the image, and then click the Mask button in the Control panel.

In reality, a clipping mask can consist of any vector object, including editable text. To create a clipping mask, you first move the object that will become the mask to the top of the object stacking order (**Figure 9.20**, on the next page). Then, you select *both* the path that will be the mask and the art you want to appear inside the mask (which will become the contents of the mask). Choose Object > Clipping Mask > Make (or press Command-7 [Ctrl-7]), and only the art that falls within the boundaries of the mask object remains visible (**Figure 9.21**).

Figure 9.20 *Placing the text at the top of the stacking order is the first step in using the text as a mask.*

Figure 9.21 *Once the mask is created, the artwork is visible only through the text. A soft drop shadow was then added to the text for effect.*

When you click a mask to select it, just the mask itself becomes selected, and you can move it around your artboard, just like any object. But at times, you may want to reposition the art within the mask, or you may want to edit either the mask itself or the artwork within the mask. You can take several routes to do these tasks.

When you first create a mask, Illustrator automatically assumes you want to edit the mask, so the Edit Clipping Path option is active. However, once the mask is already created and you've deselected it, the behavior is different in the following ways:

- Although you don't see it happen, when you create a clipping mask, Illustrator automatically creates a group. Double-clicking with the Selection tool isolates this group, giving you access to the mask (moving it won't move the masked artwork along with it) and to the actual masked artwork as well. This method isn't as easy to do when you're using live editable text as a mask only because double-clicking a text object automatically switches you to the Type tool. But the method works wonderfully for any other type of mask object. If your masked artwork contains nested groups, you can continually double-click to isolate groups and artwork in the hierarchy. Once you're done editing the contents of your mask, press Esc to exit isolation.

- When a clipping mask is selected, the Control panel displays two icons on the left side of your screen. Clicking the Edit Clipping Path button enables you to edit the mask, without touching the contents within the mask. Clicking the Edit Contents button enables you to edit the image, without touching the mask (**Figure 9.22**).

NOTE When using the Selection tool, masked artwork can be selected only if your cursor is positioned inside the mask shape. You can use the Lasso tool to select anchor points that are hidden by the mask, or you can toggle to Outline mode.

TIP Of course, you can always use the Direct Selection tool to select and edit a mask or its contents individually.

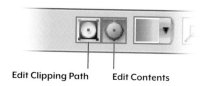

Edit Clipping Path   Edit Contents

Figure 9.22 *Clicking Edit Contents in the Control panel makes it easy to edit or adjust the art that appears within the mask.*

Organizing Masking with Layer Clipping Masks

A layer clipping mask is similar to a clipping mask, with one main difference: Instead of using a shape to mask other selected objects or group of objects, it uses one shape to mask an entire layer. In reality, layer clipping masks are far easier to control and work with because you aren't constantly selecting and deselecting objects to define what is or what isn't in a particular mask. Instead, you use the Layers panel, which you use to organize your artwork anyway, to create these kinds of masks. In fact, when creating a clipping mask, you don't need to have any art selected on your artboard at all, because the mask is an attribute of the layer.

NOTE A clipping mask uses the vector path as the boundary for the mask, even if the object has an appearance applied to it. If you want the appearance to become the mask, you'll need an opacity mask, covered later in this chapter.

To create a layer clipping mask, place the vector object that will be your mask at the top of the layer's stacking order. Click the layer name in the Layers panel once, which selects the layer (you don't want to target the layer; just highlight it in the panel). Then, click the Make/Release Clipping Mask button at the bottom of the Layers panel (**Figure 9.23**). The topmost object in your layer now becomes a mask for all objects in that layer. The mask appears listed in the Layers panel with an underline, giving you a visual indication of its behavior (**Figure 9.24**).

Make/Release Clipping Mask

Figure 9.23 *To create a layer clipping mask, select the layer first, and then define the mask.*

Figure 9.24 *If you see something listed in the Layers panel with an underline, you know that object is a clipping mask.*

With layer clipping masks, you can easily drag items into a masked layer to have them affected by the mask, and vice versa. To release a layer clipping mask, select the layer, and click the Make/Release Clipping Mask button.

NOTE Because of an apparent bug, releasing a layer clipping mask from the Layers panel also releases all layer clipping masks and clipping masks within any sublayers, forcing you to reapply the masks. Let's hope Adobe fixes this issue in the future.

Working with layer masks has an added benefit. As we mentioned earlier, when you create a regular clipping mask, Illustrator automatically creates a group that contains the mask and art within it. In Chapter 5, you also learned that a group in Illustrator is like a container that stores all objects within it. Because of this behavior, objects that reside within a group must always live within the same layer. That means if you have artwork that appears across several layers and you choose to mask that artwork with a clipping mask, you will lose all your layers. That's because in order to create the group with the mask, Illustrator has to bring all the artwork to the topmost layer. When using layer masks, however, you can organize nested layers to easily mask the artwork you want, while preserving your entire layer structure in your file.

Seeing Through Objects with Opacity Masks

When you're creating clipping and layer clipping masks, the vector path of the mask is what defines the boundary of what is visible and what is not. Additionally, anything that falls inside the mask area is completely visible, and anything that falls outside that area is completely hidden. Opacity masks bring a whole new level of functionality to Illustrator because in addition to using the vector path itself as the mask, the visual appearance of the mask defines what is shown and what is hidden.

If you've used Photoshop before, you're familiar with something called an *alpha channel.* In reality, an alpha channel in Photoshop is just like a mask, where the color black represents areas of the image that are visible and the color white represents areas of the image that are hidden. However, you can also specify a color of gray that translates to part of an image that's partially visible. In fact, alpha channels support up to 256 levels of gray, which translate to up to 256 levels of visibility in such a mask. Because of this functionality, users can specify masks with soft edges and fades when they use Photoshop. Each pixel of the mask can represent a different opacity value. Opacity masks in Illustrator can take advantage of that same functionality.

When you use an object as an opacity mask, the vector path is not the only thing that determines what it shown and what is hidden—the visual makeup of the object determines the mask as well. Opacity masks support 256 levels of gray, meaning you can create a soft-edged mask in Illustrator. In the next section, you'll see how this works by using a gradient as an opacity mask.

Creating an Opacity Mask

For this exercise, imagine you want to create some artwork that fades from 100-percent color to none. Once the artwork is created, draw a rectangle that covers the entire art, and set its fill to a regular default black-to-white linear gradient. You now have the original artwork and a rectangle (which will become the mask) stacked on top of each other, with the gradient visible on top (**Figure 9.25**). If you were to create a regular clipping mask now, the *path* of the gradient-filled rectangle would define the mask. But by using an opacity mask, the gradient (or more specifically, the *appearance*) defines the mask.

Figure 9.25 *On the left is the original artwork. On the right is the same artwork with the gradient-filled rectangle placed above it.*

Use the Selection tool to select both the artwork and the rectangle, and open your Transparency panel (Window > Transparency). You will see a thumbnail of your selection in the Transparency panel (**Figure 9.26**). If you don't see the thumbnail, choose Show Thumbnails from the Transparency panel menu. Finally, choose Make Opacity Mask from the Transparency panel menu (**Figure 9.27**). The result is a mask that uses the values of the gradient to define which parts of the object are visible below it—resulting in artwork that effectively fades to transparent (**Figure 9.28**).

Figure 9.26 *A thumbnail of your selected art is visible in the Transparency panel.*

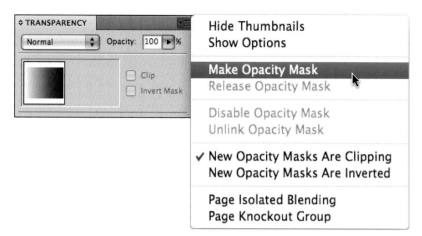

Figure 9.27 *The Make Opacity Mask feature, one of the most powerful commands in Illustrator, is hidden (masked, if you will) in the Transparency panel menu.*

Figure 9.28 *Once the opacity mask is applied, the artwork fades to transparent.*

Editing an Opacity Mask

Once you've created the opacity mask, you can use the thumbnails in the Transparency panel to work with both the mask and the artwork beneath it. Instead of one thumbnail as you saw before, there are now two thumbnails: The one on the left is the artwork, and the one on the right is the mask. To edit the artwork, click the left thumbnail. If you look at your Appearance panel, you'll notice that the object you have selected is a normal path that has a solid fill attributed to it. The name of the path displays with a dashed underline in both the Appearance panel and the Layers panel, indicating that it has an opacity mask applied (**Figure 9.29**). At this point, the mask is not editable, and it can't even be selected.

> **TIP** Opacity masks can be applied to objects, groups, or even entire layers.

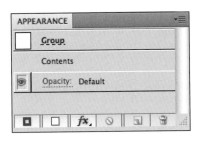

Figure 9.29 *A target with a dashed underline quickly identifies an object that has an opacity mask applied to it.*

> **TIP** Shift-click the mask icon to temporarily disable the opacity mask. Option-click (Alt-click) to display just the contents of the mask.

Clicking the right thumbnail selects the mask, allowing you to edit its attributes (**Figure 9.30**). Take a look at the Layers panel; doing so reveals something very interesting. Instead of displaying all the layers and objects in your file, when you click the mask thumbnail, the Layers panel switches to display just the opacity mask (**Figure 9.31**). The title bar of your document also indicates you are editing the opacity mask and not the art. These visual indications help you easily identify when you are editing art and when you are editing an opacity mask. To return to artwork-editing mode, simply click the left thumbnail icon again.

Figure 9.30 *Clicking a thumbnail in the Transparency panel tells Illustrator what you want to edit. A black outline around the thumbnail indicates which one is selected.*

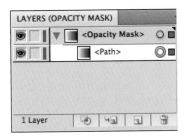

Figure 9.31 *The Layers panel offers a visual cue to indicate when you are editing an opacity mask.*

> **TIP** Clicking the Invert Mask button reverses a mask, and rather than having the color black appear as transparent, black represents areas that are opaque. The Transparency panel menu also has an option to set all new masks to be created so that they are inverted.

When you are editing either the artwork or the opacity mask, using the Selection tool to move items will result in both the artwork and the mask moving together. The reason for this is that, by default, a mask and its artwork are linked with each other, indicated in the Transparency panel by a link icon that appears between the two thumbnail icons (**Figure 9.32**). Clicking the link icon allows you to move the mask and artwork independently of each other, and clicking between the thumbnails toggles the link behavior.

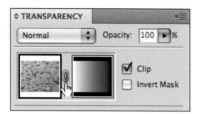

Figure 9.32 *Clicking the link icon between the thumbnails allows you to move the art and the mask independently.*

Clipping Masks and Opacity Masks

When do you use an opacity mask instead of a clipping mask? One certainly doesn't replace the other, because each mask has specific benefits. A clipping mask uses the actual path of the vector object to define the clipping area. This means a clipping mask always has a hard vector edge. In contrast, an opacity mask uses the actual appearance of a shape as the mask, meaning you can create masks with soft edges or different levels of opacity. Additionally, opacity masks are controlled via the Transparency panel, making it easier to choose when you want to work with the mask or the artwork behind the mask. Of course, using an opacity mask means you're using transparency in your file, which requires flattening. When you're creating files for certain workflows that become complicated when you use transparency effects, using a clipping mask is beneficial. For more information about transparency and flattening, see Chapter 13, "Prepress and Printing."

Taking Opacity Masks to the Next Level

Because opacity masks are "hidden" deep within the Transparency panel, they don't get much publicity. However, they are really one of the most sophisticated features you'll find; they offer a wide range of functionality. If you truly understand that opacity masks are just levels of gray that determine visibility, you can use these to achieve effects that you once thought were possible only in Photoshop. Take photographs, for example. By using a vector object with a Feather live effect applied to it, you can create a soft-edged vignette for a placed photograph right in Illustrator. Additionally, you can use placed images themselves as opacity masks. Think about scanning interesting textures and using them to mask vector artwork.

Using Drawing Modes

When drawing in Illustrator, you're used to adding some artwork to a page and then placing that artwork in the correct spot. For example, if you have some artwork that will eventually be partially hidden inside of a mask, you might first create the full artwork, and then create a mask to get the final desired result. Alternatively, you might add some artwork to a document and then move it behind other objects in the stacking order.

New to Illustrator CS5 are drawing modes, which allow you to be proactive in creating your artwork. Using one of three drawing modes, Draw Normal, Draw Behind, and Draw Inside (**Figure 9.33**), you can tell Illustrator where your artwork will ultimately end up, so that artwork appears in its correct place as you draw it.

Figure 9.33 *The controls for the drawing modes can be found at the bottom of the Tools panel. Depending on what state your Tools panel is in (one column or two column), the icons will appear slightly different.*

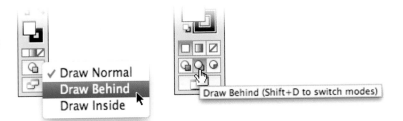

Draw Normal and Draw Behind

The default drawing behavior in Illustrator is called Draw Normal. When you're drawing artwork, new art is added to the top of the object stacking order (within the currently selected layer).

If you'd like to draw some art that will ultimately be sent to the back of the stacking order, you can click on the Draw Behind icon in the Tools panel. Perhaps more easily, you can press Shift-D to toggle from Draw Normal mode to Draw Behind mode. When Draw Behind mode is active, all artwork that you draw will appear *beneath* other artwork within the currently selected layer.

Unfortunately, other than the tiny icon at the bottom of the Tools panel, there's no visual indication in the Illustrator user interface that lets you know you're in Draw Behind mode. This can potentially cause confusion if you activate Draw Behind, walk away from your desk for a moment, and then return to Illustrator.

Using the Draw Inside Mode

Previously in this chapter, we learned about various masking techniques, including the clipping mask. The usual workflow involves creating some artwork or placing an image, drawing a vector shape, and then using both elements to define a mask. However, with the new Draw Inside mode, you can first choose a vector object, and then have any new or placed art appear directly inside of that shape. In other words, you can define the mask first, and then place art into the mask afterwards.

To use the Draw Inside mode, you must first select an object that can become a clipping mask. Paths, compound paths, and text objects are valid, but groups, compound shapes, and images are not. With a valid object selected, you can click the Draw Inside icon at the bottom of the Tools panel, or you can press Shift-D repeatedly until the Draw Inside mode is active. It's easy to identify when you're in Draw Inside mode as the selected artwork appears with a dotted border around its perimeter (**Figure 9.34**).

Figure 9.34 *A visible border appears around selected artwork, indicating Draw Inside mode.*

As you draw artwork, it will automatically appear masked (**Figure 9.35**). Perhaps more significantly, while in Draw Inside mode, you can perform functions such as Place or Paste to have objects or even images placed within the mask as well.

Figure 9.35 *As you draw art, it appears within the boundaries of the mask.*

To exit Draw Inside mode, you can either click the Draw Normal icon in the Tools panel or double-click an area outside the dashed borders.

Using Graphic Styles

You probably already have a sense of how powerful appearances and live effects are. However, if you have several objects in your file to which you need to apply the same appearance, it can be inefficient to do this manually, all through the Appearance panel. Additionally, if you ever needed to update the appearance you applied, you would need to do so for each object individually. Graphic styles can help.

A *graphic style* is a saved set of attributes, much like a swatch. When you apply a style to an object, that object takes on the attributes that are defined in the style. At any time, you can redefine the attributes of a particular style, and when you do, any objects in your file that already have that style applied are updated as well. The best part about graphic styles is how easy they are to use. And you'll never guess which panel plays an integral part in creating graphic styles—that's right, the Appearance panel.

Defining a Graphic Style

As we mentioned, a graphic style is a saved set of attributes. You know that the Appearance panel lists all attributes, so you already understand the first step in creating a graphic style—specifying the attributes you want defined in the style. Once you've specified stroke and fill settings and added live effects to an object, click the New Graphic Style button in the Graphic Styles panel (**Figure 9.36**). Alternatively, you can drag the target thumbnail from the Appearance panel and drop it on the Graphic Styles panel. Double-click a style in the Graphic Styles panel to give it a name (which is always helpful). If you Option-click (Alt-click) the New Graphic Style button, you can define a new style and give it a unique name in a single step.

Figure 9.36 *Once you've specified your attributes in the Appearance panel, you can use the Graphic Styles panel to create a new graphic style.*

Notice that when you apply a graphic style to an object in your file, the Appearance panel identifies the target and the style that is applied. This makes it easy to quickly see which style is applied to an object (**Figure 9.37**).

Figure 9.37 *When a graphic style is applied, the Appearance panel helps you easily identify the target and the applied style.*

Editing a Graphic Style

Editing a graphic style is an exercise that involves both the Appearance panel and the Graphic Styles panel, so it makes sense to position them side by side. You don't need to have an object selected in order to modify an existing graphic style, but if you do have an object selected, you'll be able to preview the changes you're making to the style.

In the Graphic Styles panel, click the style you want to edit. The Appearance panel lists all the attributes for the selected style. You can modify the style by adding attributes, by deleting existing ones, or by changing the paint order by dragging attributes in the Appearance panel. Once you're happy with the modifications, choose Redefine Graphic Style from the Appearance panel menu to update the style (**Figure 9.38**).

Figure 9.38 *Once you've modified the attributes, you can update the style, which updates all other objects that have the style applied.*

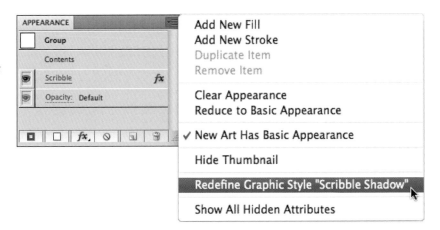

Any objects in your file that have that particular style applied then immediately update to reflect the modifications. Alternatively, you can Option-drag (Alt-drag) the target thumbnail on top of the existing style in the Graphic Styles panel.

Adding a Graphic Style to an Object

Normally, when you apply a graphic style to an object (or a group or a layer, for that matter), the attributes specified in the graphic style replace the current attributes applied to the target. However, you can also add the attributes from a graphic style to a target. For example, if a graphic style contains just a drop shadow effect, adding this graphic style would simply add the drop shadow without removing any other effects that might have already been applied to the object. To add a graphic style without replacing the current attributes, press the Option (Alt) key while applying the style.

For some inspiration on how to implement graphic styles, Adobe has added some additional content with this specific functionality in mind. Choose Window > Graphic Style Libraries, and explore the Additive for Blob Brush and Additive libraries.

Using Automation with Illustrator

With today's "need it now" mentality, we've been thrust into an era in which deadlines and delivery dates are shorter than ever—at the same time, we're being asked to perform twice as much work. If you take a moment to read just about any press release and marketing document produced by companies in the high-tech industry, you'll find promises of faster performance and higher productivity with each new software release.

The good news is that Illustrator supports several techniques for streamlining workflow through automation—in essence, you can have Illustrator do all the hard work for you while you take a few moments to grab some lunch (but who takes lunch anymore?).

Although *automation* may sound like a scary technical word, it doesn't have to be. Illustrator supports automation via two methods:

- **Actions.** This feature allows you to record specific steps that you can then reproduce by simply clicking a button. For example, an action may contain the steps necessary to select all text objects in an open document and rasterize them at a specific resolution. Actions are simple to record and don't require any code-writing knowledge. However, not every feature in Illustrator is actionable, so there's a limit to what an action can do.

- **Scripting.** Scripting is essentially a programmatic way to interact with an application. Instead of clicking with a mouse or pressing a few keys on your keyboard to control Illustrator, you use a script—a set of commands instructing Illustrator what to do. Because these commands can contain math and logic, a script can create artwork based on variables. For example, a script might draw a graph in which numbers greater than a certain amount appear in black and numbers less than that appear in red. Most Illustrator functionality is available through scripting (significantly more so than with actions), but to write a script, you need to know a scripting language. Illustrator supports AppleScript (Mac), VBScript (Windows), and JavaScript (cross-platform). The good news is that you don't need to know how to write scripts in order to use them (that is, you can have someone write a script for you).

Recording and Playing Actions

Recording an action is very simple and straightforward in Illustrator; playing back an action is even easier. To access the list of preset actions via the Actions panel, choose Window > Actions. The 22 actions in Illustrator are grouped within the Default Actions set. In addition, you can also create your own sets and actions.

To create a new set and an action within it, follow these steps:

1.   Choose Window > Actions to open the Actions panel (**Figure 9.39**).

2.   Click the Create New Set button at the bottom of the Actions panel. Give your set a unique name, and click OK.

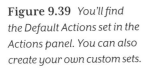

Figure 9.39 *You'll find the Default Actions set in the Actions panel. You can also create your own custom sets.*

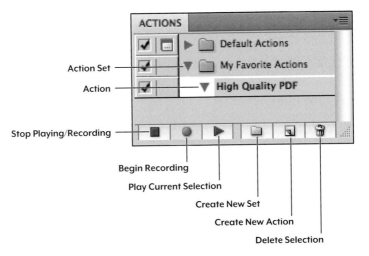

3.   Click the Create New Action button at the bottom of the Actions panel. When you do, Illustrator prompts you to name the action you're about to record. Choose the set you just created, and if you'd like, choose a function key so that later you can perform the action using a keystroke. When you're done, click OK.

At this point, you'll notice that the red recording icon at the bottom of the Actions panel is highlighted, indicating that recording has begun.

4. Perform the steps you want to record in Illustrator.

    You can see each step being added as a line item to your action as you perform it. If a step doesn't appear in your action, it is probably because the function you performed is not actionable.

5. Once you have completed the steps for your action, click the Stop Recording button. At this point, the action is complete.

6. To play back your action—or any other one—highlight it in the Actions panel, and click the Play Current Selection button. If you assigned a keystroke to your action, you can play it back by pressing the correct key combination on your keyboard.

Once you've recorded an action, you can also modify individual steps by double-clicking them, or you can delete those steps by dragging them to the trash can icon. Highlight a specific item by clicking it in the Actions panel, and choose any of the Insert commands in the Actions panel menu to add specific menu commands, stops, or paths to your action as well. You can also save and load entire sets of actions from the Actions panel menu.

> **TIP** To apply actions with a single click, you can activate Button mode in the Actions panel. Choose Button Mode from the Actions panel menu.

Scripting in Illustrator

You can script in Illustrator using AppleScript, Visual Basic Scripting Edition (VBScript), or JavaScript. Actually, Illustrator uses a language called ExtendScript, which is an Adobe flavor of JavaScript. You can find resources for this language, such as scripting dictionaries and sample scripts, in the Adobe Illustrator CS5/Scripting folder.

In general, ExtendScript is used to drive functionality within Illustrator. For example, you might use an ExtendScript script to reverse the direction of a selected vector path. In contrast, AppleScript or VBScript can drive functionality that uses different applications. For example, an AppleScript script might pull data from an external file or from the web, use that data to generate a graphic, and then export that graphic in a specified format and email it.

Each sample script included with Illustrator contains either separate PDF files describing how the script works or comments embedded directly in the script. You can open and view a script using a script editor or any text-editing applications, such as BBEdit, TextEdit, or TextPad.

Working with Images 10

There's no velvet rope barring entry to the Illustrator exclusive vector graphics club. Pixels are always welcome inside. In fact, you've already learned how certain live effects use pixels to produce their appearance. In Illustrator, vectors and pixels peacefully coexist, and you can benefit by combining both vectors and pixels (such as adding a soft drop shadow to text). You shouldn't feel you have to choose only one graphic type or the other.

Although Illustrator does have the ability to support pixels in some ways (as you'll see throughout this chapter), it in no way replaces the need for applications such as Photoshop. Quite the contrary; in this chapter, you'll see how you can bring pixel-based images from Photoshop into Illustrator documents. You will also learn how both Photoshop and Illustrator can work together by enabling you to share editable content between them. You can then focus on producing the kinds of graphics you need by relying on the strengths of each of these powerful applications.

So, turn up the music and feel the pulsing beat of vectors dancing with pixels, because this chapter will also cover the Illustrator ability to assimilate pixels and convert them into vector paths using a feature called Live Trace.

Placing Raster-Based Files

When creating designs and layouts in Illustrator, at times you will need to incorporate raster-based content, such as photographs. Naturally, these images are neither created nor edited in Illustrator—raster-based applications such as Photoshop take care of doing that. However, you can *place* raster-based content into your Illustrator file. In fact, Illustrator works very much like a page layout application in this way.

When you place an image, Illustrator can incorporate that image in the file in two ways. In the first technique, Illustrator places a preview of the image on your artboard, but the image file itself is not incorporated into the Illustrator file. The image file exists as an external reference, separate from the Illustrator file. This technique is referred to as *place-linking* because the image file is linked to the Illustrator document. If you were to misplace the linked file, Illustrator would not be able to print the image.

In the second technique, Illustrator places the actual image file in the Illustrator document and incorporates the image into the Illustrator file. This is referred to as *place-embedding*, where the image becomes part of the Illustrator file.

You can choose which technique you want to use when you physically place the file. For a detailed explanation of the numerous benefits and caveats of using each technique, refer to the sidebar "Place-Linked Files and Place-Embedded Files."

Placing an Image

You can place a raster file into an Illustrator document using one of three methods. You can either place a file, open it directly, or drag it right onto your artboard. Each method has its own benefits; your task is to determine which one you will use.

Method One: Placing a File

When you already have a file open and you need to place an image into your document, this method offers the most options and is one of the most commonly used ways to place a file:

1. From an open document, choose File > Place, and navigate to a raster file on your hard drive or server.

2. In the Place dialog box are three check boxes (**Figure 10.1**). Select one of the following options:

    •   Select the Link check box to place-link the file (deselecting the Link check box place-embeds the file).

    •   Select the Template check box to have the image automatically placed on a template layer.

    •   Select the Replace check box to have the image replace one that is already selected on the artboard.

3. Click the Place button to place the file into your document.

TIP See "Using Template Layers to Manually Trace" later in this chapter for more information on creating a template layer.

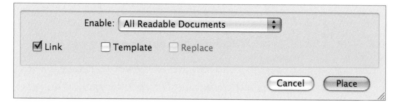

Figure 10.1 *When placing a file, you can control whether an image is place-linked by selecting the Link check box in the Place dialog box.*

Method Two: Opening a File

Choose File > Open, choose a raster file on your hard drive or server, and then click the Open button. Illustrator creates a new letter-sized document and places the image in the center of it. When you're opening a raster file in this way, the image is always place-embedded in your Illustrator document. The document takes on the color mode of the image.

Method Three: Dragging a File

From Adobe Bridge, from the Finder on Mac OS, or from any Windows Explorer window, drag a raster file right onto your Illustrator artboard. You can also select multiple files and place them all at once (**Figure 10.2**). Using this method, Illustrator place-links the files. To place-embed images while dragging them into your document, hold the Shift key while dragging the images.

Figure 10.2 *When you're dragging several images at once from Bridge, an icon indicates the placement of multiple files into your Illustrator document.*

Place-Linked Files and Place-Embedded Files

When placing an image into Illustrator, you can choose to have the image linked to your document or embedded within it. Each method has its own benefits, and which you choose depends on your needs and your workflow.

When you place-link an image, a preview of the image appears in your layout, but the actual image exists in a completely separate file. At all times, Illustrator needs to know where this file is. Otherwise, Illustrator won't be able to print the file correctly. In fact, if you were to save your Illustrator file and send it off to someone else (such as a service provider, for example), you would have to send the external linked image along with the file. If you have several linked images in your document, you have to keep track of many files. In contrast, a place-embedded file exists in your Illustrator document, and therefore, the original external image that you placed is no longer required. When you send the document to another user, the image travels along with the single Illustrator file.

Images—especially high-resolution ones—feature hefty file sizes. When you choose to embed a placed image, the file size of the image is added to the size of your Illustrator file. For example, if your Illustrator file is 1 MB in size and you place-embed a 30 MB image into your document, the size of your Illustrator document grows to 31 MB. When you place-link an image, however, the file is never added to your document, so the Illustrator file stays at 1 MB.

Although managing multiple files and file size is an issue that will affect your decision to link or embed image files, one of the main reasons you will choose to link a file rather than embed it is so you can easily update the image when necessary. When you place-link a file, the image you see in your layout is a preview of the file that really exists elsewhere. When you make an adjustment to the original image (say, in Photoshop), the preview in your layout updates to reflect those changes. Illustrator even has a feature called Edit Original that assists in this process of updating linked images (see "Managing Placed Images" later in this chapter). However, if you place-embed an image, you can no longer update that image easily.

Placing Native Photoshop Files (PSD)

In addition to universal image formats like TIFF and EPS, Illustrator also allows you to place Photoshop files (PSD).

Generally, placing a native Photoshop file isn't any different from placing any other file. Illustrator enjoys a wonderful relationship with Photoshop, however, and you can take advantage of extended functionality when placing Photoshop files.

If the PSD file you are placing contains Photoshop layer comps, Illustrator presents you with the Photoshop Import Options dialog box, where you can choose which layer comp will be visible in the file from the Layer Comp pop-up menu (**Figure 10.3**). Select the Show Preview check box to see what the layer comp looks like before you place the file. You can also choose whether Illustrator or Photoshop controls how layer visibility is updated by choosing from the When Updating Link pop-up menu. The Photoshop Import Options dialog box offers additional options, which are covered later in this chapter in the "Working with Photoshop" section.

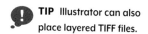

TIP Illustrator can also place layered TIFF files.

NOTE The Layer Comps feature in Photoshop allows you to create named sets of visible layers. For more information on the Layer Comps feature, refer to Photoshop Help or *Real World Adobe Photoshop CS4* by David Blatner and Conrad Chavez (Peachpit Press).

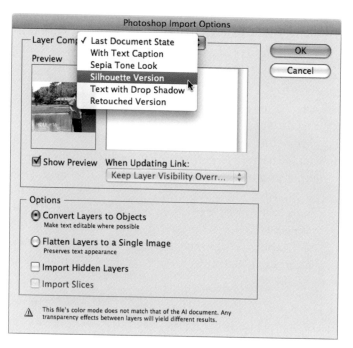

Figure 10.3 *The Photoshop Import Options dialog box lets you control the appearance of your Photoshop file before you place it into your document.*

NOTE For a detailed description of the different file formats and their benefits and roles in a design workflow, refer to Chapter 12, "Saving and Exporting Files."

Unfortunately, once you place an image into an Illustrator document, you don't have any way to access the Photoshop Import Options dialog box to change to a different layer comp. To work around this apparent oversight, you can use the Relink function, which effectively places the file again and opens the dialog box (see "Managing Placed Images" for information on relinking files).

Working with Placed Images

Once you've placed an image into an Illustrator document, the image acts like a single rectangular shape that can be transformed (moved, scaled, rotated, sheared, and reflected). You can apply opacity and blending mode values from the Transparency panel, and you can also apply many different live effects to a placed image, including Feather and Drop Shadow.

Sometimes a design calls for showing only a portion of a placed image. Programs such as Photoshop (which can crop images) and page layout applications such as InDesign (which use picture frames) are able to display only portions of an image. Illustrator, however, has no such tool or functionality. To have only a portion of an image display on your artboard, you have to create a mask (**Figure 10.4**). (See Chapter 9, "Drawing with Efficiency," for more information on creating masks.)

Figure 10.4 *Using a clipping mask, you can display just a portion of a placed image.*

You can also apply color to certain kinds of placed images. Illustrator lets you apply either a solid process or a spot color to a 1-bit TIFF image or to any image that uses the grayscale color model. Simply select the image on the artboard, and choose a fill color as you would for any vector object.

Using Template Layers to Manually Trace

Sometimes you may want to place an image into Illustrator—not as a design *element* but rather as a design *guide*. For example, you might sketch an idea for a design on paper and then scan that sketch into your computer. Then, you would place that scan into your Illustrator document as a guide for drawing final shapes with the Illustrator vector tools. Alternatively, you may place a map into Illustrator so that you can create your own customized directions to an event.

In these cases, you may not actually want to trace the scan exactly as it appears (using the Live Trace feature in Illustrator, covered later in this chapter, might be a better choice for such a task), but rather, you may just want the image to act as a reference. To prevent the image from getting in the way of your design, you might want to adjust the opacity of the image (**Figure 10.5**). Additionally, you may want to lock the image so that you don't move it accidentally.

NOTE Template layers are not to be confused with Illustrator templates, which are actual Illustrator files that contain elements already inside them. Illustrator templates are covered in Chapter 1, "Creating and Managing Documents."

 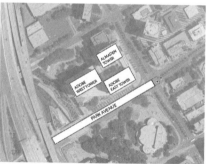

Figure 10.5 *Drawing on top of an image at full strength may be difficult (left). Placing an image on a dimmed template layer allows you to trace over the image with ease (right).*

Rather than going through the process of adjusting and locking images, Illustrator has a way to manage this process in a more dignified manner—using a template layer. Once a template layer has been created, the image on that layer automatically becomes locked, and the opacity level of the image is set to 50%. You can select the Template option at the bottom of the Place dialog box when placing an image to have the image automatically appear on a template layer, or you can double-click any layer and select the Template option in the Layer Options dialog box (**Figure 10.6**, on the next page).

Figure 10.6 *The Template option appears in the Layer Options dialog box and applies to a single layer.*

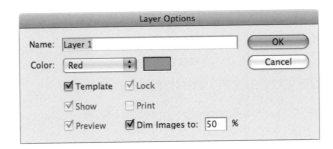

Adding Keylines to Placed Images

Often, when you place a photograph in an Illustrator document, you want to create a *keyline*, or an outline around the photo. It's important to understand that a placed image is not a vector object and, hence, can't have a fill or stroke. So, you'll need to create another vector object to contain your stroke. Rather than create this new shape on your own, there are two methods you can use: have Illustrator automatically create a mask for the image or use an effect to convert the bounds of the object into a vector object.

To add a keyline using a mask, follow these steps:

1. Choose File > Place, and pick an image to place into your Illustrator document. You can either link or embed the image. Once you've chosen the image, click the Place button.

2. The image is selected (or if your image already exists in your document, select it), so you'll see the Mask button in the Control panel. Click it. This creates a mask at the exact bounds of the image.

3. Press the D key for Default. This gives the mask a black 1-point stroke. Feel free to adjust the stroke per your design needs (who uses a 1-point stroke anyway?).

An additional benefit to this method of using a mask is that you now have the elements in place to simulate a "frame and image" paradigm like InDesign uses. Once you've created your mask, you can decide to "crop" your image by double-clicking the photo. This will put you into isolation mode. Now click the frame edge and resize at will. When you're done, double-click outside the image to exit isolation mode and continue working. This method works wonderfully when you're using the Selection tool (black arrow) and have the Bounding Box option selected (in the View menu).

To add a keyline using a live effect, follow these steps:

1. Choose File > Place, and pick an image to place in your Illustrator document. You can either link or embed the image. Once you're chosen the image, click the Place button.

2. With the image selected, open the Appearance panel, and click Add New Stroke. You won't see the stroke appear just yet, but don't worry, it will show up in the next step.

3. With the stroke highlighted in the Appearance panel, choose Effect > Path > Outline Object. The stroke will appear around the boundary of the photograph.

To make the live effect easier to apply in the future, define a graphic style. For details on graphic styles, refer to Chapter 9.

Managing Placed Images

Whether the images you place in a file are linked or embedded, it's important to be able to track where those images came from and to access additional information about the images. To manage all the placed images in your document, choose Window > Links to open the Links panel.

By default, the Links panel lists all the images in your document. However, from the Links panel menu, you can specify that the Links panel should display only missing, modified, or embedded images (**Figure 10.7**). In addition, you can choose to have the Links panel list images sorted by name (file name), kind (file type), or status (up-to-date or modified).

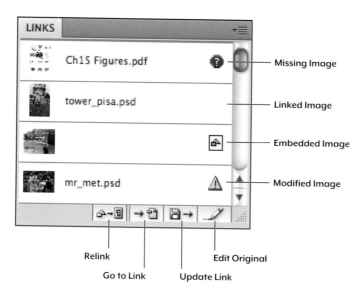

Figure 10.7 *Icons in the Layers panel indicate additional information about the images that are placed in your document. No icon indicates a place-linked file.*

Double-clicking any file listed in the Links panel opens a Link Information dialog box, offering additional information about the image. Besides listing the file size of the image, the Link Information dialog box also gives you the location of the image (the file path) and detailed scaling and rotation information (**Figure 10.8**, on the next page).

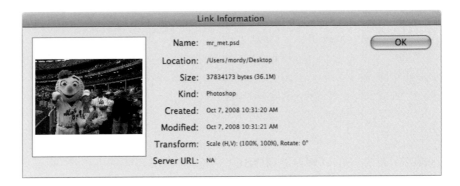

Along the bottom of the Links panel are four buttons (Figure 10.7, on the previous page) that allow you to perform certain functions with the images in your document. To use these functions, first highlight an image in the Links panel, and then click the desired button:

- **Relink.** The Relink button allows you to replace one image with a different one. When you click the Relink button, the Place dialog box appears, allowing you to choose another file, which replaces the selected image. You can use Relink either to swap high-resolution files for low-resolution ones or to replace FPO (For Position Only) placeholder images with final copies. Additionally, you can use the Relink function and choose to replace your file with the same image (replacing it with itself), which allows you to access different Place settings or to replace an embedded image that was updated.

- **Go to Link.** The Go to Link button adjusts the view setting of your document window so that the highlighted image in the Links panel is centered on your screen. In addition, the image becomes selected. This makes it easy to quickly find an image, and it is especially useful in documents that contain many placed images.

- **Update Link.** The Update Link button allows you to update place-linked images when Illustrator detects that external files have been modified outside of Illustrator. Images that have been modified appear with a yellow warning icon in the Links panel. The Update Link button is dim when an embedded image is chosen.

- **Edit Original.** You can click the Edit Original button when you want to modify a place-linked image in the image's creator application. When you highlight an image in the Links panel and click Edit Original,

NOTE Refer to the Appendix, "Application Preferences," for information on the Update Links setting in the File Handling & Clipboard panel in Preferences that controls whether Illustrator updates modified files automatically or manually.

Illustrator launches the application that was used to create the file (or that is set to open files of that type on your system) and then opens the file for you. Once you perform any necessary edits on the file, simply save and close it and return to Illustrator, where the image updates accordingly. The Edit Original button is dim when you highlight an embedded image.

Additional Links Panel Functionality

In addition to the functions in the Links panel that we've already discussed, you can take advantage of several important settings in the Links panel menu (**Figure 10.9**).

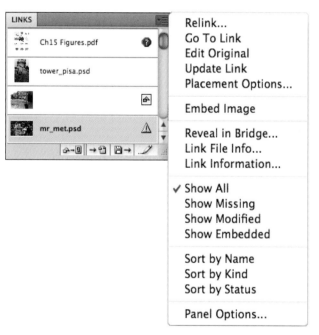

Figure 10.9 *The Links panel menu grants you access to additional features for working with placed images.*

Here are a few of the options:

*   **Placement Options.** When you relink or replace a file, you can use the Placement Options setting to define how an image appears once it has been placed into your document. By default, Illustrator preserves any transforms you've applied to the image that you're replacing, but

you can also choose from four other settings. A helpful illustration in the Placement Options dialog box explains what each setting does (**Figure 10.10**).

Figure 10.10 *Each setting in the Placement Options dialog box offers an illustration and a description for what it does.*

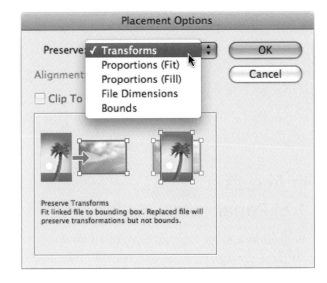

- **Embed Image.** If you have a place-linked image in your document, you can select the image in the Links panel and choose the Embed Image option from the Links panel menu to embed that image in your file.

- **Link File Info.** Images and files can contain metadata (refer to Chapter 1, "Creating and Managing Documents," for more information), and at times, you may need to view the metadata of images you've placed into your document. For example, you may want to know whether you have the rights to reproduce the image or whom you need to credit for using an image. The Link File Info option in the Links panel menu allows you to view the placed image's metadata (you won't be able to edit it, however).

- **Panel Options.** Always trying to accommodate, Illustrator lets you customize the Links panel by choosing Panel Options from the Links panel menu. You can choose to display images in a thumbnail size, or if you prefer, you can eliminate thumbnails altogether (**Figure 10.11**), which is useful when you have many placed images in your document. Additionally, you can choose the Show DCS Transparency Interactions option

NOTE Illustrator supports linked DCS 2.0 files that interact with transparency.

to have Illustrator alert you when placed Desktop Color Separations (DCS) 1.0 files interact with transparency in your document. This setting results in slower performance, though.

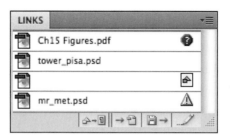

Figure 10.11 *With thumbnails turned off, the Links panel can display more items in less space—perfect for documents with lots of placed images.*

Getting Faster Access to Image Settings with the Control Panel

Although the Links panel offers a single location from which to track information about your placed images, you can also use the Control panel to quickly access certain settings and features that pertain to a selected image. The Control panel displays the file name, the color mode, and the resolution of a selected image. In addition, for linked images, the Control panel offers options to embed or edit the file via the Edit Original feature, which was discussed earlier in the chapter. You can also click the image's file name in the Control panel to access additional features in the Links panel (**Figure 10.12**).

TIP When you select an image on your artboard, a Mask button appears in the Control panel, making it easy to quickly apply a mask and crop the image. Refer to Chapter 9 for more information on using masks.

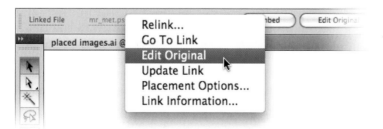

Figure 10.12 *Clicking the file name of a linked image in the Control panel offers a shortcut to several often-used functions.*

Using the Document Info Panel

The Links panel isn't the only place where you'll find information about place-linked and place-embedded images. You can choose Window > Document Info to open the Document Info panel that offers information on a lot more than just images. In fact, the Document Info panel can prove quite useful for providing document information on a variety of attributes and settings (**Figure 10.13**).

By default, the Document Info panel shows information about only those objects that are selected on the artboard. To find out information about all the objects in a file, deselect the Selection Only option in the Document Info panel menu.

To find out information about certain aspects of an Illustrator document, choose from one of these settings in the Document Info panel menu:

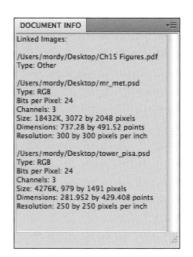

Figure 10.13 *The Document Info panel provides detailed information on just about anything you could ask for about your file, including linked images.*

- **Document.** The Document setting displays the color mode for your document, along with a listing of other important document settings such as text editability and color profile.

- **Objects.** This setting displays the total number of objects in your file, broken down by object type. This setting offers a quick way to find out how many linked or embedded images you have in your document, how many objects are colored with spot colors, or how many transparent objects there are.

- **Graphic Styles.** To see a list of all the graphic styles that are used in your document, as well as to how many objects each style is applied, choose this setting.

- **Brushes.** The Brushes option lists all the brushes used in your document.

- **Spot Color Objects.** This setting lists the spot colors used in your document.

- **Pattern Objects.** The Pattern Objects option lists all the patterns used in your document. This is especially helpful because it includes patterns that are used inside complex appearances and Pattern brushes.

- **Gradient Objects.** This setting lists all the gradients that are used in your document.

- **Fonts.** The Fonts option lists all the fonts used in your document.

- **Linked Images.** The Linked Images option lists all the linked images that appear in your document, along with information about each image.

- **Embedded Images.** The Embedded Images setting lists all the embedded images that appear in your document, along with information about each image.

- **Font Details.** The Font Details option lists information about the fonts used in your document. This is helpful when you want to quickly find out whether you are using OpenType, TrueType, or PostScript fonts in your document.

You can save all the information listed in the Document Info panel by choosing Save from the Document Info panel menu. A text file is created that contains the information for all the items just outlined.

Converting Rasters to Vectors Using Live Trace

Certain Illustrator features, such as Pathfinder, are incredibly useful and, as a result, are used many times a day. Features such as 3D are also extremely cool, but they aren't used as often. Every once in a while, a feature comes along in Illustrator that is cool and fun to use but that is also practical enough that you use it on a regular basis. Live Trace is such a feature.

The concept is simple enough: Take a raster-based image, and convert it into a vector-based image. You would want to do this to get around the limitations of a raster-based file. For example, if you want to scale artwork up in size or if you want to edit the artwork easily and use spot colors, you want to work with a vector-based file.

Separate applications (such as Adobe Streamline) and Illustrator plug-ins (such as Free Soft's Silhouette) have the ability to convert raster content into vectors, but Live Trace is a step far above and beyond what those tools are capable of doing. One of the main reasons for this is because of how Live Trace works.

Live Trace uses a two-step process when converting rasters to vectors. In the first step, Live Trace *conditions* the raster image for optimal tracing. This means Illustrator makes adjustments to the raster image, such as adjusting contrast or blurring jagged edges. In the second step, Live Trace draws vector paths, creating highly accurate vector art (**Figure 10.14**, on the next pages). Although the tracing is theoretically done at that point, Illustrator retains a link to the original raster image so you can adjust the tracing settings. As you update the different raster conditioning and vector tracing settings, you can preview the results immediately. This makes it easy to get just the right tracing result that suits your needs best.

Figure 10.14 *The Live Trace feature in Illustrator starts with the original raster image (top row), conditions the image (middle row), and then converts it to clean vectors (bottom row).*

ORIGINAL SCAN

ORIGINAL SCAN ENLARGED 300%

CONDITIONED IMAGE

CONDITIONED IMAGE ENLARGED 300%

TRACED RESULT

TRACED RESULT ENLARGED 300%

ORIGINAL SCAN

ORIGINAL SCAN ENLARGED 300%

CONDITIONED IMAGE

CONDITIONED IMAGE ENLARGED 300%

TRACED RESULT

TRACED RESULT ENLARGED 300%

(continues)

ORIGINAL SCAN

ORIGINAL SCAN ENLARGED 300%

CONDITIONED IMAGE

CONDITIONED IMAGE ENLARGED 300%

TRACED RESULT

TRACED RESULT ENLARGED 300%

Tracing an Image

Tracing an image is simple. Select any raster image in your Illustrator document, and click the Live Trace button in the Control panel. Alternatively, you can choose Object > Live Trace > Make. This action traces the image using the Illustrator default trace preset. Illustrator comes with 14 tracing presets, each optimized for different kinds of images and desired result. Once the image is traced, it maintains a live link to the raster image, and you can customize the tracing settings. For example, once the image is traced, the Control panel changes to reflect different settings, including a Preset pop-up menu (**Figure 10.15**). Choose from any of the different Illustrator presets to see a different traced result on your screen.

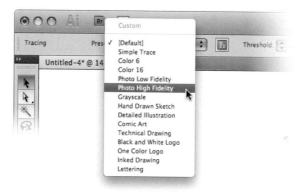

Figure 10.15 *The Preset pop-up menu in the Control panel lets you quickly experiment with different tracing presets.*

If you know which tracing preset you want to use before you trace your image, you can select it directly by clicking the upside-down triangle that appears just to the right side of the Live Trace button and choosing it from the pop-up menu (**Figure 10.16**).

Figure 10.16 *It doesn't look like a pop-up menu, but it is. Clicking the upside-down triangle lets you apply a specific tracing preset when you first choose to trace an image.*

As long as Illustrator maintains a live link to the raster image, you won't be able to edit the actual vector paths that were created during the tracing process. In order to do so, you either have to expand the traced object or convert it to a Live Paint group. We discuss both of these options later, but for now, we'll focus on how to customize the tracing settings so that you can get the best results from the Live Trace feature.

NOTE If you're happy with the traced results, there's no need to expand the object. Illustrator can print the vector paths just fine (it expands the paths in the print stream).

Exploring the Live Trace Preview Options

Once you've traced an image, Illustrator displays the traced result on your artboard so you can see the results. However, Illustrator offers a variety of settings that you can use to control how both the raster image and the traced vector result appear on your artboard.

When a traced image is selected on the artboard, the Control panel updates to contain two icons that, at first glance, look like triangles. Upon closer inspection, you'll notice that one icon features a jagged edge; this icon is used to control how the raster image is previewed. The icon on the right, which has a smooth edge, is used to control how the traced vector result is previewed (**Figure 10.17**).

Figure 10.17 *Once you've traced an image, you can use the two icons in the Control panel to control how the artwork appears on the artboard.*

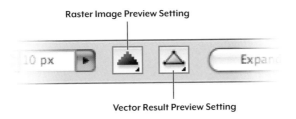

Raster Image Preview Setting

Vector Result Preview Setting

Previewing the Original Raster Image

In the Control panel, the jagged triangle on the left controls how the raster image is viewed. Click the icon once, and choose from one of the following four available settings (**Figure 10.18**):

- **No Image.** This setting completely hides the raster image from the screen (and is the default setting).

- **Original Image.** This setting displays the original raster image in your document, which can be useful when you're comparing the original image to the traced result.

- **Adjusted Image.** This setting displays the raster image as it appears after Live Trace has applied the raster conditioning adjustments. This preview mode is great for seeing how Live Trace works, and it makes it easier to preview any adjustments you make to the raster image settings.

ORIGINAL IMAGE

ADJUSTED IMAGE

TRANSPARENT IMAGE

Figure 10.18 *You can preview the raster image with the Original Image setting (left), the Adjusted Image setting (center), or the Transparent Image setting (right). The No Image option is not shown for obvious reasons.*

ORIGINAL IMAGE

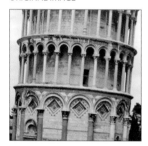

ADJUSTED IMAGE

TRANSPARENT IMAGE

ORIGINAL IMAGE

ADJUSTED IMAGE

TRANSPARENT IMAGE

- **Transparent Image.** This setting displays a dimmed preview of the bitmap image beneath the traced result, letting you see the traced results as compared to the original raster image.

Previewing the Traced Vector Result

In the Control panel, the smooth triangle on the right controls how the traced vector result is viewed. Click the icon once, and choose from one of the following four available settings (**Figure 10.19**, on the next page).

Figure 10.19 *You can preview the vector result with the Tracing Result setting (left), the Outlines setting (center), and the Outlines with Tracing setting (right). The No Tracing Result option is not shown.*

TRACING RESULT

OUTLINES

OUTLINES WITH TRACING

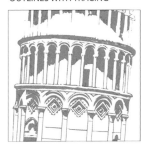

TRACING RESULT

OUTLINES

OUTLINES WITH TRACING

TRACING RESULT

OUTLINES

OUTLINES WITH TRACING

- **No Tracing Result.** This hides traced vector objects from the screen.

- **Tracing Result.** This setting displays the vector result of the tracing (the default).

- **Outlines.** This setting highlights the actual Bézier paths that were created when the image was traced.

- **Outlines with Tracing.** This highlights the Bézier paths as semitransparent, enabling you to compare filled areas of the traced vector result with the original image. The color of the outlines will match the color specified for guides in the Guides & Grid panel in Preferences.

Tweaking to Get the Perfect Trace

What makes the Live Trace feature a joy to use is the ability to make adjustments to the settings while you see the results update on your screen. Aside from the presets you can apply, Illustrator contains a dialog box chock-full of settings you can use to ensure that you get the results you need from the Live Trace feature.

To access these settings, select a Live Trace object, and click the Tracing Options dialog box button in the Control panel. Alternatively, you can choose Object > Live Trace > Tracing Options. Once the Tracing Options dialog box appears on your screen, you'll notice that it's split into several different sections (**Figure 10.20**).

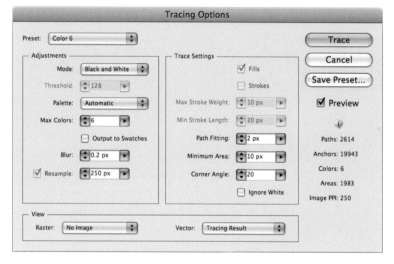

Figure 10.20 *The Tracing Options dialog box offers a smorgasbord of settings to achieve the perfect trace.*

First, a Preview check box appears on the far right of the dialog box, which allows you to see results update as you make changes to the different settings. Next, directly underneath the Preview check box is a list of important details about your traced object. The values for the number of paths, anchor points, colors, distinct closed areas, and image resolution update as you adjust the settings in the dialog box. Keeping an eye on these values helps you make decisions as you edit your trace settings. At the top of the dialog box is a Preset pop-up menu, similar to what you see in the Control panel when you have a Live Trace object selected. Stepping through the different presets in the Tracing Options dialog box allows you to see the settings for each of the presets.

The rest of the Tracing Options dialog box is separated into three sections called Adjustments, Trace Settings, and View. The View section allows you to specify how the traced object appears on your artboard, as discussed in the earlier "Exploring the Live Trace Preview Options" section.

The following "Modifying the Raster Adjustments" and "Adjusting the Vector Trace Settings" sections will help you clearly understand the two-step process that the Live Trace feature performs when converting raster images into vector form.

Modifying the Raster Adjustments

The Adjustments settings on the left side of the Tracing Options dialog box apply to the raster conditioning that occurs before the image is traced:

- **Mode.** Live Trace converts a bitmap image to either 1-bit black and white, 8-bit grayscale, or 8-bit color, which you can choose from the Mode pop-up menu.

- **Threshold.** The Threshold setting determines the boundaries between pixels when using the Black and White trace setting. For example, in a gray bitmap, a high Threshold setting results in more gray pixels becoming black vector objects and thus a heavier appearance. In that same image, a low Threshold setting results in more gray pixels ignored, making for more white-colored objects and an overall lighter or more delicate appearance (**Figure 10.21**). Too low of a Threshold setting may also result in a loss of image detail. The Threshold setting is also available in the Control panel when a Black and White Live Trace object is selected.

- **Palette.** By default, Illustrator uses the selective color reduction method to choose the best colors to fit the image (based on the Max Colors value, also set in this dialog box). However, you can choose specific colors that Illustrator should use when tracing your image. To do so, you must first load a custom swatch library (Window > Swatch Libraries). When a custom swatch library is opened in your document, the Palette pop-up menu displays all the loaded custom libraries (**Figure 10.22** on page 358). Live Trace then uses the colors that appear within the custom swatch library that you choose.

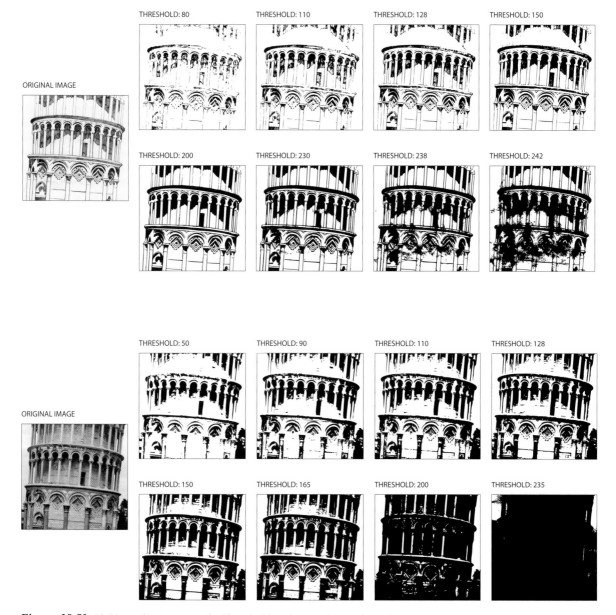

Figure 10.21 *Making adjustments to the Threshold setting can have a large impact on the overall appearance of the traced result. Here are examples of an image with a variety of Threshold settings.*

Figure 10.22 *Loading several custom libraries lets you quickly experiment with a variety of color schemes.*

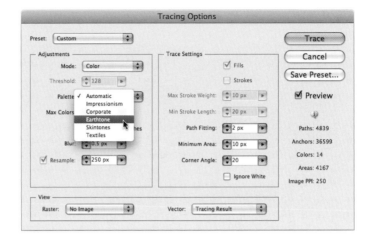

- **Max Colors.** The Max Colors setting determines the maximum number of colors that can be used in the final traced result. This setting is not available for the Black and White Mode setting or when you choose a custom color palette. Live Trace uses the selective color reduction method to reduce the number of colors in the raster image to match this setting during the conditioning process. The Max Colors setting is also available in the Control panel when a Grayscale or Color Live Trace object is selected.

- **Blur.** The Blur setting applies a Gaussian Blur to the image, which helps remove noise from the raster image. This reduces the number of anchor points in the tracing result, especially when you are tracing photographic images.

- **Resample.** The Resample setting lets you change the resolution of the bitmap image to help obtain a better traced result. Resampling a high-resolution image to a lower resolution greatly enhances the speed performance of Live Trace.

Adjusting the Vector Trace Settings

The Trace Settings that are on the right side of the Tracing Options dialog box apply to the actual tracing of the image and determine how the final vector paths are drawn.

- **Fills.** When you have Fills selected, Live Trace creates closed and filled vector paths for all resulting vector objects. Fill tracing produces results that more closely match the original image, including variable-width lines that are common in marker or ink renderings (**Figure 10.23**). Fill tracing also results in more complex vectors because it needs more anchor points.

Figure 10.23 *When you choose the Fills setting, the traced paths appear with thick and thin edges, closely matching the original image.*

- **Strokes.** With the Strokes setting selected, Live Trace creates stroked open paths for all areas that fall within the Max Stroke Weight setting. Areas that exceed this setting result in unfilled areas outlined with a 1-point stroke. Stroke tracing results in paths with fewer anchor points (**Figure 10.24**).

Figure 10.24 *When you choose the Strokes setting, the traced paths appear consistent, which results in a less complex traced image overall.*

- **Max Stroke Weight.** The Max Stroke Weight setting determines the heaviest stroke weight Live Trace can use when tracing the image. This setting is available only when you use the Strokes trace setting.

- **Min Stroke Length.** The Min Stroke Length setting determines the shortest path that Live Trace can use when tracing the image. This setting is available only when you use the Strokes trace setting.

- **Path Fitting.** Path Fitting determines how closely Live Trace follows the shape of the original raster image. A lower Path Fitting setting results in paths that closely match the original raster image yet might also reveal imperfections or irregular paths that aren't smooth. A higher setting produces smoother paths with fewer anchor points but might not match the raster image as closely (**Figure 10.25**).

- **Minimum Area.** The Minimum Area setting sets a threshold for how large a section of the raster image has to be in order to be traced into a vector object. By setting a minimum area, you can have the Live Trace feature trace only those areas of pixels that meet a minimum size. For example, if Minimum Area is set to 9 pixels, Live Trace ignores regions of pixels that are less than 3 by 3 pixels in size.

- **Corner Angle.** The Corner Angle setting defines the sharpness of the angles used in the resulting vector objects. This setting is measured in degrees, not pixels. If you think of 0 degrees as perfectly flat and 180 degrees as a hard corner (rather than a rounded one), anything sharper than the Corner Angle setting (the default is 20) is converted to a corner anchor point rather than a smooth anchor point.

- **Ignore White.** White areas in a trace are filled with the color white by default. This means that if you position your traced artwork over a background, the white areas will block out the background. If you'd like your trace to treat white areas as being filled with the None attribute, you can select the Ignore White setting. In this way, backgrounds will show through the nonblack areas of your traced artwork.

TIP The Minimum Area setting is also available in the Control panel when you have a Live Trace object selected.

TIP Once you've specified your settings in the Tracing Options dialog box, you can click the Save Preset button to define your own tracing presets.

Editing Live Trace Paths

Once you've achieved a trace result that you're satisfied with, you might want to edit the Bézier paths, either to delete portions of the image or to apply your own colors, gradients, or patterns. To edit the vector paths of the traced object, you will need to either expand the trace or convert the traced object to a Live Paint group.

ORIGINAL SCAN ENLARGED 300%

PATH FITTING: 1 pixel

Figure 10.25 *This figure shows examples of a variety of Path Fitting settings for the same image. Notice how the paths get smoother as the number is increased but that the result doesn't match the original sketch as much.*

PATH FITTING: 2 pixels

PATH FITTING: 4 pixels

PATH FITTING: 6 pixels

PATH FITTING: 8 pixels

Expanding a Live Trace Object

With a Live Trace object selected, click the Expand button in the Control panel. Alternatively, you can choose Object > Live Trace > Expand. You can then use the Direct Selection tool to edit anchor points and Bézier paths (**Figure 10.26**). At this point, the traced object is no longer linked to the original raster image, and you can no longer adjust the traced result using any of the Live Trace options.

Figure 10.26 *Once you've expanded a Live Trace object, you can edit the paths as you would with any vector object.*

Converting Traced Images to Live Paint Groups

In Chapter 4, "Creative Drawing," you learned about the Illustrator Live Paint feature, which allows you to apply fill attributes to areas, even if they aren't fully enclosed shapes. If you've traced an image because you want to fill regions of the image with color, converting the Live Trace object to a Live Paint group makes a lot of sense.

With a Live Trace object selected on the artboard, click the Live Paint button that appears in the Control panel. This action expands the traced object and converts all the resulting vector objects into a Live Paint group in a single step. You can then use the Live Paint Bucket tool to fill your art with color without any additional steps (**Figure 10.27**). For more information on Live Paint groups, refer to Chapter 4, "Creative Drawing."

Figure 10.27 *What started out as a pencil sketch quickly turns into final art when you combine the Live Trace and Live Paint features in Illustrator.*

Exploring an Alternative to Trace: Object Mosaic

As you've learned so far, the Live Trace feature in Illustrator offers a creative way to stylize photographic content. Another way to generate stylized artwork using photographic content as a source is a feature called Object Mosaic. The feature takes any embedded rasterized content and converts it to a matrix of vector rectangles that resemble mosaic tiles.

To use the feature, select an embedded image, and choose Object > Create Object Mosaic, which opens the Object Mosaic dialog box (**Figure 10.28**, on the next page). You can specify a new size for the final result, and you can also specify the number of tiles the feature should use. The larger the number of tiles you choose, the more detail you'll get in your result (think smaller mosaic tiles). If you want the tiles to be perfectly square, you can enter a value for either the width or the height for the number of tiles and then click the Use Ratio button. Specifying a value for Tile Spacing will simulate *grout*, or the space that appears between each tile.

Figure 10.28 *The Object Mosaic feature converts raster-based images to tiles of color squares.*

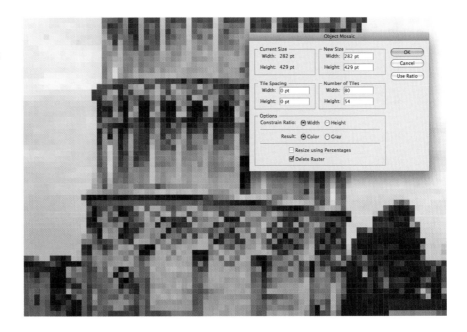

The Constrain Ratio setting allows you determine which value the Use Ratio button uses. You can choose to end up with a color or a grayscale version of your art. Selecting the Resize Using Percentages option lets you specify a new size for your overall result in the form of percentage values instead of absolute values. If you have no need for the original embedded image after you've applied the Object Mosaic function, you can select the Delete Raster option.

Turning Vectors into Rasters

It's easy to see the benefits of converting raster images into vector-based artwork to allow for better scaling and editing. Interestingly enough, Illustrator can also perform the transition in reverse—converting vector-based artwork into rasterized art. Sometimes this is done to achieve a special effect where you might want to see a pixelated image (**Figure 10.29**). Alternatively, you might start with a gradient mesh object that you then rasterize and convert back to vectors using Live Trace to achieve a posterized graphic effect.

Figure 10.29 *Rasterizing text at an extremely low resolution can add an interesting design element to your layout.*

To convert vector artwork to pixels, select the art, and choose Object > Rasterize, which opens the Rasterize dialog box. You'll find you can choose from a variety of settings when rasterizing artwork (**Figure 10.30**).

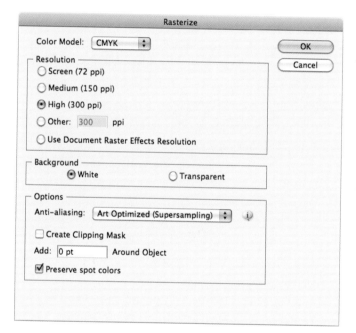

Figure 10.30 *The Rasterize dialog box should look familiar—it's nearly identical to the Rasterize Effect dialog box.*

- **Color Model.** Depending on the document color mode setting to which your file is set, here you'll see CMYK, Grayscale, and Bitmap, or you'll see RGB, Grayscale, and Bitmap. This is because a document cannot contain both CMYK and RGB elements. This setting can be extremely useful because it lets you change the color model of an object (even an image). For example, you can convert colored objects to grayscale.

- **Resolution.** Here in the Rasterize dialog box, the default resolution is set to 300 ppi, which is usually sufficient for print-related artwork. If you want all your artwork in your document to appear consistent, you can also specify that the Resolution setting should match the setting in the Document Raster Effects Settings dialog box.

- **Background.** You can choose whether the resulting raster will have a transparent background or a white background. If your effect overlaps other objects, you probably want to use the transparent setting, although remember that the file still needs to be flattened (see Chapter 13, "Prepress and Printing," for more information on transparency flattening).

- **Anti-aliasing.** You can define whether the raster image will be antialiased. Antialiasing slightly blurs color boundaries to avoid the appearance of jagged edges. For more information on antialiasing, refer to Chapter 11, "Web Design."

- **Create Clipping Mask.** This creates a clipping mask around the area of a shape so that you can have it blend into a background (raster images are always rectangular in shape and may block out objects that appear behind them). This setting won't work very well for objects that have Drop Shadow, Feather, or Glow effects applied, because clipping masks have hard edges. This setting is not necessary if you specify the Transparent option for the Background.

- **Add *X* Around Object.** Depending on the kind of artwork you are rasterizing, you may experience some clipping when the artwork becomes rasterized. This is especially possible when rasterizing objects that have soft edges, such as Feather effects, applied. Specifying extra space around the object results in a larger raster image, but that incorporates all the artwork.

- **Preserve Spot Colors.** If your artwork contains spot colors, selecting this option will preserve the spot colors in the resulting raster image.

Working with Photoshop

Photoshop is the sister application of Illustrator, and throughout this entire book, we have discussed how both Illustrator and Photoshop are different. Yet, at the same time, they have a lot in common. For one, they are both Adobe products, and therefore, they share similar user interfaces and many of the same tools and panels. At a much deeper level, however, they share common technology. For example, both applications use the Adobe Color Engine, an Adobe shared component used for color management. Both Illustrator and Photoshop also use the Adobe Text Engine, which makes it possible for both applications to exchange text easily and share many of the same text features.

At the end of the day, a graphics professional can gain a tremendous amount of power from using both of these applications. Rather than trying to force one of these powerhouse applications to do everything, you can take advantage of the benefits that each application offers and use both to complete your work.

Whether you're starting in Illustrator and then bringing your art into Photoshop for finishing touches, or whether you're starting in Photoshop and then bringing your designs into Illustrator, both applications can work together in many ways. For the remainder of this chapter, we explore how you can use both Illustrator and Photoshop in your workflow.

Going from Illustrator to Photoshop

When you want to bring art from Illustrator into Photoshop, you can open an Illustrator file directly in Photoshop, but doing so results in a single flat image that isn't editable. Instead, consider exporting a Photoshop PSD file from Illustrator; this preserves certain elements in an editable form. Using the Export command in Illustrator results in a Photoshop file that you can edit far more easily when you open it in Photoshop.

To export a Photoshop file from Illustrator, choose File > Export, and choose Photoshop (.psd) for the file format.

When exporting a PSD file, you can choose between CMYK, RGB, and Grayscale color models, and you can specify a resolution for your file. If you choose to export a flat image, all Illustrator layers are flattened into a single nontransparent layer (what Photoshop calls the Background layer). Alternatively, you can choose the Write Layers option, which preserves the Illustrator layering where possible. You can also choose to preserve text and other native elements.

The following is a list of the attributes that can be preserved when Illustrator exports a native Photoshop file; see "The Adobe Photoshop (.psd) Format" in Chapter 12, "Saving and Exporting Files," for additional details:

- **Layers.** Any layers that you've created, and the names of those layers, are preserved when you open the file in Photoshop. By carefully creating a layer structure in Illustrator, you can take advantage of greater editability when the file is opened in Photoshop.

- **Vectors.** If you used the shape modes in the Pathfinder panel to create compound shapes, these objects are converted to Photoshop shape layers, which are editable vectors in Photoshop. If you want a path to be preserved as a vector shape, you must apply a shape mode to it in order to preserve it as a vector in Photoshop. If you have a single shape that you want to preserve as a vector, select the shape and choose Make Compound Shape from the Pathfinder panel menu.

- **Text.** Illustrator preserves text objects (including text antialiasing settings) so that they are editable when the file containing them is opened in Photoshop.

- **Transparency.** If you've applied opacity values or blend modes from the Transparency panel in Illustrator, those values are also preserved when the file is opened in Photoshop.

- **Masks.** If you create clipping masks in your file, those masks are preserved and show up in Photoshop as layer masks. Because masks allow you to work in a nondestructive fashion, you can create files that are more flexible in your workflow.

- **Slices.** If you create web slices in your Illustrator file, those slices appear when the file is opened in Photoshop. Additionally, any optimization settings that you've applied to your slices, including settings that you've applied from the Save for Web dialog box, are preserved and can be edited once the file is opened in Photoshop.

Illustrator does its best to keep elements editable during the export process. However, if you find that certain elements are not being preserved, the cause may be that preserving editability would change the appearance of the artwork. Try rearranging the layers in Illustrator to avoid issues where artwork appearance is dependent upon the interaction of multiple layers.

TIP Often, layers are combined because over-print commands are applied to some objects on those layers. Targeting each layer and checking the Isolate Blending option in the Transparency panel can help keep the layers from merging on export.

> ## Copying and Pasting Between Illustrator and Photoshop
>
> Copying and pasting art between Illustrator and Photoshop works extremely well. You can copy text freely between the two applications, and when you paste art from Illustrator into Photoshop, you can paste the art as a Photoshop smart object that preserves editability in Photoshop. In fact, when you paste art from Illustrator in Photoshop, you are presented with a dialog box asking whether you want the art to be pasted as pixels, a path, a shape layer, or a smart object.

Going from Photoshop to Illustrator

When you open a native Photoshop file in Illustrator or place-embed one into an existing document, Illustrator prompts you with the Photoshop Import Options dialog box, asking how you want the Photoshop file to be placed (refer back to Figure 10.3, on page 337). You can select the Flatten Photoshop Layers to a Single Image option, or you can select the Convert Photoshop Layers to Objects option, in which case Illustrator tries to keep as many of the elements in the Photoshop file editable as possible.

The following are the attributes you can preserve when Illustrator embeds a native Photoshop file using the Convert Photoshop Layers to Objects option in the Photoshop Import Options dialog box:

- **Layers.** Any layers you've created, and the names of those layers, are preserved when you open the file in Illustrator. If you've created groups of layers in Photoshop, those groups show up in Illustrator as sublayers, thus preserving the hierarchy of the file.

- **Vectors.** If you've created vector shape layers in Photoshop, those layers are converted into editable compound shapes when the file is opened in Illustrator.

- **Text.** Text objects that appear in the file are editable when the file is opened in Illustrator.

- **Transparency.** If you've applied opacity values or blend modes from the Layers panel, those values are preserved when you open the file in Illustrator as well. Because Photoshop applies these settings at the layer level, you may find that these transparency settings are applied to the layer that an object is on rather than to the object itself.

- **Masks.** If you create layer masks in your Photoshop file, those masks are preserved and show up in Illustrator as opacity masks. Additionally, the boundaries of the file become a layer-clipping mask, acting almost like crop marks.

- **Slices.** If you create web slices in your Photoshop file, those slices appear when you open the file in Illustrator. Additionally, any optimization settings that you've applied to your slices, including settings that you've applied from the Save for Web dialog box, are preserved and can be edited once the file is opened in Illustrator.

- **Image Maps.** If you've assigned a URL to a web slice, that URL is also preserved when the file is opened in Illustrator.

NOTE Feather and Density settings applied to layer masks in Photoshop are discarded when you choose to preserve layers.

Illustrator does its best to keep elements editable during the embedding process. For example, if you have a text object with a drop shadow that overlaps a background, Illustrator keeps the text editable and also places the drop shadow on a separate layer, allowing you to position the text and the drop shadow without affecting the background beneath it. If you find that certain elements are not being preserved, the cause may be that preserving editability would change the appearance of the artwork. Try rearranging the layers in Photoshop to avoid issues where appearance is dependent upon the interaction of multiple layers.

Web Design

11

There's no question that Illustrator suffers from schizo-phrenia. One moment it's a print-based application with spot colors and crop marks, and the next it's a web-based application with HTML slices and Flash symbols. And that's okay, because as designers living in the 21st century, we all suffer from the same schizophrenia. We are called upon to create art that will be used in many different ways—most notably in print, on the web, and even now on handheld mobile devices such as cell phones. Even if you are living in a print- or web-centric world, others may use and repurpose the art you create. That's where Illustrator excels—in repurposing artwork for a variety of uses.

In this chapter, we focus on web and mobile technologies and how web browsers display graphics. Illustrator, Flash Professional, and Flash Catalyst all work hand in hand, giving designers new options for working between these powerful applications. We'll discuss these features and how you can use your favorite design application—Illustrator—to create quality web graphics with ease.

The artwork featured throughout this chapter comes from Fanelie Rosier
(iStockphoto; username: absolutely_frenchy).

The Role of Illustrator in Web Design

Before we dive into the world of web design, it's important to realize where Illustrator fits in when it comes to creating web graphics. There's certainly more to creating a website than drawing pretty pictures. Software such as Adobe Dreamweaver or Microsoft FrontPage is dedicated to creating and maintaining websites, and in no way does Illustrator replace those applications.

You can use Illustrator to design how a web page looks (by creating a composition), but you wouldn't normally use Illustrator to create an HTML-based web page. Similarly, you wouldn't use Illustrator to manage a multipage website because Illustrator lacks the toolset to do so.

The strength of Illustrator is in designing web interfaces and the navigation bars, buttons, individual web graphics, and general artwork that appear within a web page. You can place elements such as these that you design in Illustrator into Dreamweaver or any other application you use to create your web pages. Alternatively, you can create graphics in Illustrator, which you can then bring into Photoshop, Flash Professional, or Flash Catalyst as well, if your workflow requires it.

Two Approaches to Web Design

Throughout this book, you have been learning how to create vector-based artwork. You've even learned how to use the Illustrator Live Trace feature, which converts pixel-based images into Bézier paths. So, it's with a large spoonful of irony that we inform you how important pixels are in the world of web graphics.

Unlike printed artwork that is produced with imagesetters or digital presses that are capable of resolutions upward of 3000 dots per inch (dpi), artwork that is created for the web is always viewed on a computer screen, usually at 72 pixels per inch (ppi). Features that a print designer might be used to, such as working with high-resolution images, choosing spot colors, or carefully calculating where fold lines or trim lines will be, are of no concern to someone who is designing a website.

However, don't be fooled into thinking that web designers have it easier than print designers. A web designer faces plenty of challenges—issues that never cross the minds of print designers. For example, because people view websites on computer screens, a designer has no way of knowing what size a viewer's screen is. Especially now, when you have Internet kiosks and web-capable cell phones, it is important for web designers to create their art so that it can be displayed on virtually any device.

With that in mind, ultimately two mainstream workflows exist when you think about Illustrator and the web:

- **Pixel-based graphics.** The most common image file formats in use on the web today are raster-based images. Illustrator can generate these formats easily, and you can place these images directly into CSS and HTML layouts. Whether you're creating artwork that will be displayed directly on the web, or whether you're bringing artwork into Photoshop or Dreamweaver, your ultimate goal will be to ensure a seamless translation from the vector-based world in Illustrator to the raster-based image file format you need. The first half of this chapter will primarily deal with creating pixel-based web graphics.

- **Vector-based graphics.** Through the use of extended technologies that have become standard parts of today's most popular web browsers (such as Adobe Flash Player), vector-based graphics play a large role in web design as well. Whether you're looking to export SWF files directly for the web from Illustrator or whether you're going to bring your artwork into Flash Professional or Flash Catalyst for additional interactive work, keeping the structure of your artwork intact is key. The second half of this chapter will deal primarily with creating vector-based web graphics.

Finally, although print and web technologies are different, it's important not to lose sight of your goal as a designer—to communicate a message in an effective manner. The same rules of design that apply to the print world also apply to artwork destined for the web. If you keep this at the forefront of your mind and if you follow the advice and techniques revealed throughout the rest of this chapter, you're sure to create effective and compelling web graphics.

Maximizing Image Quality on the Web

In the business world, there's a saying that goes like this: "We offer excellent service, exceptional quality, and cheap prices—pick any two out of the three." You can apply a similar saying to web graphics; it would sound something like this: "There's color, quality, and file size—pick any two out of the three."

NOTE Although the argument can be made that file size isn't that important anymore because of the growing population of broadband Internet installations, remember that many people still have slower dial-up connections (especially outside the United States). In addition, handheld wireless devices and web-based cell phones are becoming ubiquitous, and those devices have much slower download capabilities.

With web graphics, there's a delicate balance between the way an image looks when viewed on a computer screen and the time it takes to download the image so that the user can view it. No matter how good the image looks, if viewers have to wait too long for a graphic to appear on their screens, their patience runs out, and they click to some other website in the blink of an eye. In general, there is a direct correlation between the detail and number of colors in an image and the size of the file. A file with many colors may have a large file size, but an image with a small file size may not have enough colors or detail to look good. As a designer, your job is to find a happy medium—an image that looks good and is small enough that it downloads quickly. Luckily, you have Illustrator on your side, which has the tools you'll need to get results.

Three issues affect the overall appearance of web graphics: dithering, antialiasing, and compression. We mentioned earlier how computers display different colors. Higher-end graphics cards allow computers to display many millions of colors, whereas lower-end cards restrict the display to a far smaller number of colors. Therefore, the following question arises: "If you create multicolored artwork on a high-end machine (which most designers use), what happens when that graphic is displayed on a low-end machine that can't display all of those colors?" The answer is dithering.

Dithering

Dithering is a process in which a computer simulates a color that it doesn't have by mixing colors it does have. For example, if you have a set of paints, you might have only a few colors, but you can create more colors by mixing the paints. Although the dithering concept is nice in theory, the results are not always great. The problem is that a computer can't mix colors within a single pixel, so the dithering process creates a pattern of different-colored pixels in an effort to appear as another color. Many times, this pattern is visible and can give an odd appearance to a graphic (**Figure 11.1**). In fact, the entire concept of using a web-safe color is to ensure that you'll be using a color that won't dither. As you'll see later in the chapter, Illustrator contains certain settings that can control how dithering is applied to a graphic.

Figure 11.1 *The image on the left has been enlarged to show the effects of dithering. Notice the pattern of pixels that are visible where colors blend into one another. The same artwork on the right, however, exhibits no dithering.*

Antialiasing

The second issue that arises with screen-rendered graphics has to do with the low resolution that a monitor uses—in most cases, 72 ppi. At such a low resolution, the eye actually sees pixels, and curved edges display with jagged edges (often referred to as *jaggies*). To make graphics look better onscreen, computers use a method called *antialiasing* to slightly blur the edges of boundaries between colors. The result is an image that looks smooth instead of jagged (**Figure 11.2**). As you'll see shortly, antialiasing can have a tremendous impact on the final appearance of your web graphics.

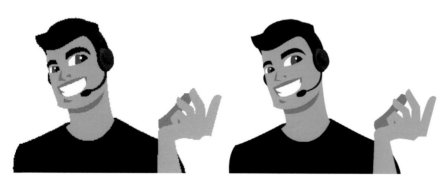

Figure 11.2 *Pictured here are identical designs. The object on the right has antialiasing turned on, resulting in a smoother appearance onscreen.*

Understanding and Using Web-Safe Colors

Most designers have a swatch book by their side—such as a Pantone book—that helps them choose colors to use in a design. And even though color management technologies have been getting better over the years, most people still don't trust the color they see on their computer screens. If you're designing web graphics, though, you don't have much of a choice: The computer screen is the delivery medium for your artwork. Therefore, it's entirely possible that you can choose a nice yellow color on your screen, but when someone views your website on a different computer, that color might appear green or orange. So, what's a designer to do?

With a little bit of information and some simple math, it's possible to narrow the number of colors that you might use to ensure your color looks decent on someone else's computer screen. Although all types of computers and graphics cards exist, the minimum number of colors that all systems support is 256 (also referred to as VGA). However, not all computer systems use the same set of 256 colors. In fact, Windows-based computers use a different system set of colors than Mac-based computers (not surprising). The good news is that of these two mainstream systems, only 40 colors are different, which leaves 216 common colors. This means if a designer were to use one of these 216 colors, referred to as *web-safe colors*, they would be assured that their artwork would display properly on just about any computer.

Illustrator can help you choose from these web-safe colors in several ways. First, you can load a custom library that contains all 216 web-safe colors by choosing Window > Swatch Libraries > Web. Illustrator also features a library called VisiBone2 that displays web-safe colors in a more intuitive way (**Figure 11.3**). Alternatively, you can choose Web Safe RGB from the Color panel menu, which allows you to choose web-safe colors by using the color ramp, by using the RGB sliders, or by directly entering their hexadecimal values. If you are using the regular RGB sliders in the Color panel, Illustrator lets you know when a color is not web safe by displaying a small cube under the color icon. If you click the cube, Illustrator chooses the closest web-safe color for you (**Figure 11.4**).

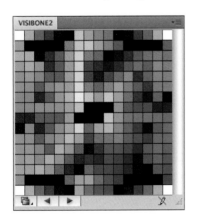

Figure 11.3 *When the panel is resized correctly so that there are white swatches in each of the four corners, the VisiBone2 panel displays the 216 web-safe colors in a way that closely matches a color wheel, making it easier to use when designing.*

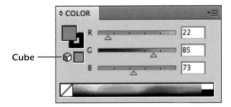

Figure 11.4 *A small cube in the Color panel indicates when a chosen color is not a web-safe color. You can have Illustrator snap to the closest web-safe color by clicking the cube.*

(continued on next page)

Understanding and Using Web-Safe Colors
(continued)

As if that weren't enough, you can also take advantage of the Color Guide panel's ability to work within a specific library of colors. By clicking the icon in the lower-left corner of the Color Guide panel, you can choose to limit the Color Guide panel to suggesting web-safe colors only.

In reality, choosing a web-safe color may not be that important anymore, considering that just about all modern computer systems sold today support a minimum of millions of colors. The chance of your color being dithered and looking really bad is small. If your graphics are being developed for websites geared toward people or services in third-world countries, where hardware isn't as up-to-date, choosing a web-safe color may still be a good idea.

Compression

The last—and possibly the most important—attribute of a web graphic is its file size. Anyone can create great-looking graphics with large, high-resolution images, but a web designer has to deliver the best possible graphics using low-resolution images that download fast.

For the most part, web designers can save files in a variety of file formats, each of which uses compression techniques to help reduce file size. In general, file formats use one of the following two types of compression: lossless and lossy. *Lossless* compression reduces file size without any loss in image quality or image detail. In contrast, *lossy* compression reduces file size by sacrificing image data, resulting in images that have less detail. As with just about anything else in life, there's a compromise involved: The designer needs to make decisions based on which attributes are most important on an image-by-image basis. In the next section, you'll learn about all the different file types Illustrator can use and the compression techniques these file types use.

Creating Perfect Web Graphics

If your goal is to create pixel-based graphics for use on the web, it may seem an odd choice to use a primarily vector-based program like Illustrator. However, you'll find that Illustrator can create pixel-perfect web graphics while allowing you to stay in the easy-to-edit creative environment you're already familiar with. Illustrator CS5 makes creating web graphics even easier with several settings that can help you make your artwork look perfect on virtually any screen.

Antialiasing and the Pixel Grid

High-end print graphics are often rasterized at resolutions that exceed 2400 dots per inch, producing razor-sharp curves and lines in your artwork. As you learned earlier in this chapter, onscreen graphics are rendered at resolutions far lower than that—enough so that the human eye can easily identify the individual pixels in a file. To prevent artwork from displaying with jagged edges onscreen, artwork is antialiased: The edges are slightly blurred, resulting in a smooth appearance. But antialiasing is a double-edged sword, because it can produce side effects that can make artwork look worse instead of better. One such example is that when edges are blurred, contrast and detail are lost. This is especially true for small text, which may even be unreadable when antialiasing is applied.

NOTE When you're in Pixel Preview mode, you can view the pixel grid when your zoom level is at least 600 percent.

On a computer screen, a pixel represents the smallest element that can be drawn. A pixel is either on or off. In other words, you can't have a computer screen draw only half a pixel. In addition, a pixel can display only a single solid color. Knowing this, you'd have to make sure that your artwork would always align itself perfectly to the pixels on the screen. Otherwise, antialiasing would blur the edges of your artwork, resulting in soft or blurry edges. More importantly, this blurring could mean your pixel dimensions will change.

Illustrator solves this problem with a setting called Align to Pixel Grid, which forces your artwork to snap perfectly to the pixel grid, resulting in graphics that look crisp and sharp in a web browser (**Figure 11.5**). You can take advantage of Align to Pixel Grid in the following ways:

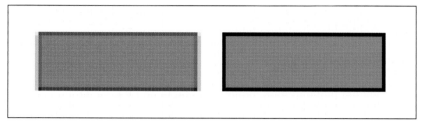

Figure 11.5 *No matter where you position your artwork, Illustrator can always ensure that your graphics look clean and sharp (right) without the adverse effects of antialiasing (left).*

- **The Web New Document Profile.** The Web New Document Profile contains an advanced option called Align New Objects to Pixel Grid (**Figure 11.6**). Whenever you create a new document based on this profile, all of your artwork will automatically snap to the pixel grid—and you don't have to do anything other than create your artwork. As you work, Illustrator ensures that all artwork will translate perfectly to the web.

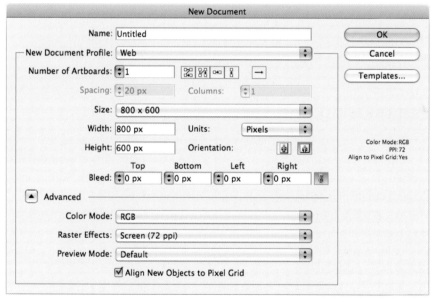

Figure 11.6 *By default, the Web profile turns on the Align New Objects to Pixel Grid setting.*

- **The Transform panel.** If you are working in a document that wasn't created with the Web profile (as listed above), you can have Illustrator snap individual artwork to the pixel grid. To do so, select an object and select the Align to Pixel Grid option in the Transform panel (Window > Transform). If you want all new art to also snap to the pixel grid, choose

Align New Objects to Pixel Grid from the Transform panel menu (**Figure 11.7**).

Figure 11.7 *At any time, you can use the Transform panel to force all new artwork to align to the pixel grid.*

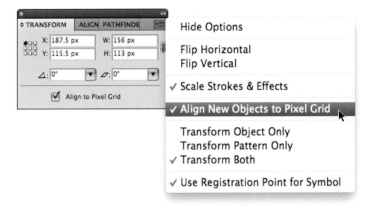

- **Symbols.** When you define a symbol, you have the ability to choose Align to Pixel Grid in the Symbol Options dialog box. This ensures that all symbol instances will align perfectly to the pixel grid.

Antialiasing and Text

While it may be rather straightforward to snap artwork to the pixel grid, it is significantly more difficult to snap text to the pixel grid. This is because text is often set at various sizes, and appears in a variety of typefaces. Some fonts are extremely ornate or have fine serifs—details that are often lost when viewed on a computer screen. In fact, some typefaces are simply unreadable on a computer screen altogether.

Rather than attempt to force all text to use a single method for antialiasing, Illustrator offers several settings that you can apply to type objects. In this way, you can experiment to see which method works best for each type treatment.

To apply different antialiasing settings to text, select the type object and open the Character panel (Window > Type > Character). From the Character panel menu, choose Show Options. Toward the bottom of the panel you can set the antialiasing method to None, Sharp, Crisp, or Strong (**Figure 11.8**).

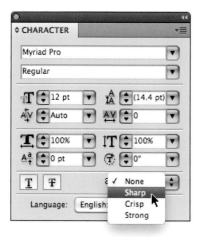

Figure 11.8 *The text antialiasing options in Illustrator match the settings you'll find in Photoshop.*

NOTE Make sure the Type Optimized antialiasing method is selected in the Save for Web & Devices dialog box or when using the Rasterize effect to preserve the text antialiasing settings chosen in the Character panel.

What Is the Resolution of Onscreen Graphics?

Most people think of web graphics as 72 ppi, but the reality is that many of today's modern displays are closer to 120 ppi. The Apple iPhone 4 features a "high-resolution" display, weighing in at 326 ppi. In reality, a web designer can't specify artwork in terms of measurements like inches. If you think about it, a laptop computer with a 15-inch screen might be set to a resolution of 1024 x 768, 1344 x 840, or 1440 x 900. Obviously, the screen itself always stays at 15 inches (it would be quite a trick otherwise), but the pixels just change in size. Web graphics display larger at lower-resolution settings and appear smaller on a user's computer screen as the screen's resolution increases.

For this reason, web designers don't focus on measurements like inches, and they don't care about resolution. Most important to a web designer are pixel dimensions. Ad banners are specified at an amount of pixels in width and an amount of pixels in height (such as 468 x 60). When creating web graphics in Illustrator, your best friend is the Transform panel or the Width and Height settings found in the Control panel, because they offer a precise way to enter exact pixel dimensions.

Slicing Up the Web

The process of preparing graphics for display on the web is called *optimization*. This process entails choosing how artwork is exported from Illustrator, what file formats are being used, and what settings are being used for each file type. One way to optimize web graphics is to use a technique called *web slicing*. In simple terms, web slicing is the process of cutting a large image into several smaller images, which is desirable for various reasons.

First, there's user perception. If you try to load a web page that has a single large image on it, the user sits there impatiently waiting for it to download and appear on the page. But when an image is sliced into smaller parts, each smaller image loads faster, and as a result, it seems like the image itself is loading faster.

Second, you can use different file formats for each image slice, which can save some valuable file size space, resulting in a faster-loading graphic overall. As you'll see in the section "Exporting Pixel-Based Images with Save for Web & Devices," these settings directly impact the final file size of your total image.

Slicing is also helpful if parts of a graphic need to be updated often. Instead of always creating larger images, you can update just part of the image. Swapping out a slice or two can be more efficient than having to work with one large, bulky file all the time.

Finally, because each slice is its own image, you can assign a link (a URL) to it, effectively making it a button. When someone clicks a sliced part of an image, they are linked to another web page. Of course, you can specify other functionality for such a button (or slice) as well.

Any Way You Slice It...

Illustrator offers two ways to create web slices. The more traditional way is to draw them yourself, but Illustrator can also create slices from objects automatically using a feature called *object-based slicing*. Let's explore both methods.

Once your artwork is created, you can choose the Slice tool from the Tools panel and click and drag in your document window. When you do, Illustrator draws rectangular regions—*slices*—and each appears with a number that identifies it (**Figure 11.9**). As you create slices, other dimmed slices might appear automatically in the document. These are called *auto slices*. Slices that you create are called *user slices*. Because the overall image has to be rectangular (for an explanation, see the sidebar "Web Slices = HTML Tables") and all the slices must be rectangles as well, Illustrator creates slices as necessary (**Figure 11.10**). As you continue to create slices, Illustrator updates the auto slices accordingly.

Figure 11.9 *Create slices where it makes sense to do so to allow for interactivity or future editing.*

User Slices ———

Auto Slices ———

Figure 11.10 *As you draw slices with the Slice tool, Illustrator creates other slices to fill out the rest of the document.*

Web Slices = HTML Tables

So, what exactly happens when you create a slice? Illustrator splits a single graphic into multiple images. It creates an HTML table, with each cell of the table containing one of these slices, or pieces of the image. In this way, when you display the web page in a browser, all the sliced-up images appear together, almost like a puzzle. This is an important concept to keep in mind because you can create only rectangular slices.

Another thing to keep in mind is that when an Illustrator document contains multiple artboards, each artboard maintains its own set of slices by default. In essence, this means each artboard results in a separate HTML table.

When you draw a slice with the Slice tool, Illustrator is really drawing a rectangle with no fill and no stroke and making it a slice (**Figure 11.11**). When you want to edit the slice, you can use the Slice Select tool to change the boundaries of the slice.

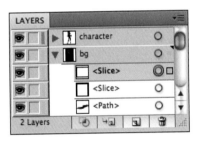

Figure 11.11 *Slices you create with the Slice tool appear listed in the Layers panel. They are special rectangles that have their Fill and Stroke attributes set to None.*

However, Illustrator also has a different kind of slice. Instead of creating graphics and drawing slices over them, you can apply a slice as an attribute to a selection—something Illustrator calls an *object-based slice*. To apply this kind of slice, make a selection, and then choose Object > Slice > Make. Illustrator uses the bounds of your selected artwork as the area for the object-based slice. Using this method, if you make an edit to your graphic, the slice updates automatically along with it.

If you want to hide all the little squares and numbers that indicate slices on your screen, you can do so by choosing View > Hide Slices.

Editing Slice Attributes

You can specify certain attributes for a slice. Remember that a slice is really a cell in an HTML table. So, for example, a slice can have its own background color or URL link. Once a slice has been defined using either of the two methods described earlier, you can select it with the Slice Select tool. To edit the attributes of a slice, select a slice, and choose Object > Slice > Slice Options to specify a URL and alternative (Alt) text, which is used for accessibility (**Figure 11.12**). When you specify text as an object-based slice, you can also set the slice to be an HTML slice (rather than an image slice). In that case, Illustrator exports the text as editable HTML instead of as a graphic.

Figure 11.12 *The Slice Options dialog box gives you the ability to assign specific URLs and additional information for each slice in your document.*

HTML text slices might not show up in a browser exactly as you see them in Illustrator. Although bold or character attributes are preserved, exact fonts and sizing depend on the browser used. The browser ignores other text features, such as kerning and baseline shift.

Once you have created all your slices, you can choose individual file formats and additional settings by using the Save for Web & Devices feature, which we discuss in detail right about…now.

NOTE When exporting files in the Photoshop file format, you can preserve slices defined in Illustrator. Refer to Chapter 12, "Saving and Exporting Files," for more details.

Exporting Pixel-Based Images with Save for Web & Devices

At one time, saving a graphic for use on the web was a difficult task that involved saving an image, opening it in a web browser, and then repeating that process again and again. The Save for Web & Devices feature in Illustrator—which is also found in Photoshop—lets you speed up the process of optimizing and saving web graphics.

Once you're ready to export a final version of your web graphic, choose File > Save for Web & Devices to open the Save for Web & Devices dialog box.

TIP To save time, you can select slices on your artboard and choose File > Save Selected Slices. This allows you to bypass the Save for Web & Devices dialog box altogether when you want to quickly export an image.

The dialog box, which fills up most of your screen, is split into several sections (**Figure 11.13**). Along the far left are several tools you can use within the Save for Web & Devices dialog box. In the center, a preview pane lets you view up to four versions of your art. The upper-right side offers a variety of export formats and their settings, and the lower-right side offers a trio of panels that control color, image size, and layer settings. Along the bottom of the dialog box are zoom controls, color information, and a Preview in Browser button.

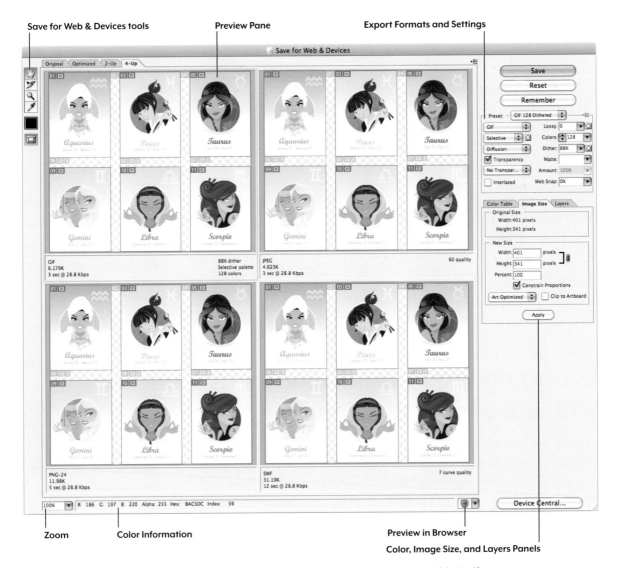

Figure 11.13 *The Save for Web & Devices dialog box is almost an entire application within itself.*

Let's take a closer look at each of the sections of the Save for Web & Devices dialog box:

- **Save for Web & Devices tools.** The Save for Web & Devices dialog box has its own set of tools, which is the first indication that this feature is above and beyond just a simple dialog box. The Hand tool lets you pan the view of your artwork; it is especially useful when you are viewing your art at higher zoom levels. The Slice Select tool enables you to select a particular slice with which to work. The Zoom tool allows you to change the zoom setting of your artwork. The Eyedropper tool allows you to sample color from an image that appears in the preview pane. In addition to the icon that indicates the eyedropper color (you can click it to open the Color Picker), there's a button that toggles slice visibility on and off.

- **Preview pane.** The preview pane is the main feature of the Save for Web & Devices dialog box. By clicking any of the four tabs, you can choose to view your original art (as it appears on the Illustrator artboard), an optimized version of your art (based on the current file settings chosen), and 2-up and 4-up versions of your art. Using the 2-Up and 4-Up tabs, you can easily compare different file settings or how an optimized file looks compared to its original version. Illustrator displays useful information below each preview, including file size and estimated download times, making it easy to find just the right file type for your image (**Figure 11.14**).

Figure 11.14 *Besides being able to preview the results of different file and compression settings, you can also view file size and estimated download times.*

- **Zoom control.** The zoom control allows you to easily choose from a preset zoom level to view your artwork. Alternatively, you can enter any number in the Zoom field.

- **Color information.** As you move your pointer over artwork in the preview pane, the Save for Web & Devices dialog box provides feedback for colors in real time. This is helpful if you want to confirm color information or if you want to sample a specific color from an image.

- **Preview in Browser icon.** The Preview in Browser icon is a huge time-saver. Although you get a beautiful preview of your artwork in the preview pane of the Save for Web & Devices dialog box, it can be useful at times to see what your artwork looks like in an actual web browser. This is especially useful for when you want to preview SWF animations, because those do not preview in the Save for Web & Devices dialog box. Clicking the icon previews the selected artwork in your computer's default web browser. Clicking the arrow opens a list of installed browsers that you can choose from, or you can edit the list of browsers to customize it to your needs.

The two remaining sections feature the group of three panels and the ability to choose from different file types.

Choosing the Right Image File Type

Overall, the main benefit of using the Save for Web & Devices dialog box is the ability to compare the final results of multiple file formats and choose the one that fits best for a particular use. To make the right decision, you have to understand the differences between each of these file formats and what their strengths and weaknesses are. Here we'll discuss the pixel-based GIF, JPEG, PNG, and WBMP formats.

Choosing the GIF File Format

A common image file format used on the web is the Graphics Interchange Format (GIF). The format was developed by the people at CompuServe, one of the pioneers of the Internet and the web, though you hardly hear that name mentioned today (it's amazing how fast things change). Recognizing the need to send graphics files across modem connections (which in those days were quite slow), they developed GIF. This file format can contain a maximum of 256 colors and uses a lossless method of compression. A GIF file tries to save space by looking for large areas of contiguous solid color; this makes the format perfect for logos, backgrounds, text headlines, and the like. However, the 256-color limit and the limited compression for images with a lot of detail make the GIF file format a bad choice for photographic content.

The GIF file format supports other features, including the ability to control the exact number of colors present in the file and the ability to specify transparency for a single color of the file.

When you choose the GIF file format in the Save for Web & Devices dialog box, you have the following settings available:

NOTE GIF files can also contain multiple images or frames for creating an animation, although Illustrator doesn't support the creation of animated GIF files.

- **Color settings.** The Color Table settings enable to you to specify exactly how many colors the GIF will contain. Lower numbers of colors result in smaller file sizes but could also result in lower-quality images. Because a GIF can contain a maximum of 256 colors, you can choose from several color-reduction algorithms, including the Restrictive option that chooses only web-safe colors.

- **Dithering.** The Dither settings control what method of dithering is used when the image calls for a color that isn't available in the reduced set of colors or when the image is displayed on a computer screen that doesn't support enough colors to display the image.

- **Transparency.** The Transparency setting enables to you to define colors that will display as transparent in a browser. For example, if you want to place a logo on a colored background, you can specify the background color of the GIF to be transparent; doing so causes the background color in the browser to show through those transparent areas. The edges where color meets the transparent edge are usually white when displayed in a browser, and specifying a matte color that matches the background ensures that the edges of your art blend seamlessly into the background (**Figure 11.15**).

- **Interlacing.** An interlaced image loads gradually in a web browser, first in a low resolution and then in a higher resolution in a second and third pass. This allows the image to appear in the browser immediately so that viewers can get an idea of what the page will look like, and then after a few seconds, the higher-quality image appears. Turning interlacing off means the image won't display on a web page until the entire image has downloaded.

Figure 11.15 *The image on the left was saved with a matte setting that matched the background on which the art would eventually appear. The image on the right used the default matte setting of white.*

- **Web Snap.** By specifying a value in the Web Snap field, you can have Illustrator ensure that a certain percentage of the colors used in the graphic are actually web-safe colors.

Choosing the JPEG File Format

JPEG (pronounced "jay-peg") stands for Joint Photographic Experts Group, and it was created to allow photographers to share images using a standard file format. JPEG files can contain millions of colors and use a lossy compression method. Digital images usually contain more color information than the human eye can see or detect, and by throwing out some of that extra information, JPEG images can achieve amazing file size savings. For example, a 10 MB photograph can easily be compressed into a JPEG that's less than 1 MB.

Because the JPEG format supports millions of colors (as opposed to only 256 in a GIF), it's the perfect format to use for photographs or images with complex colors and gradient fills. However, JPEG files do not support transparency as GIF files do.

When you choose the JPEG file format in the Save for Web & Devices dialog box, you can choose from the following settings:

- **Compression/Quality.** The Quality settings enable you to specify how much information is thrown out of a file when the file is compressed.

The settings are actually a bit confusing in the way they are presented in the dialog box. You might think that a setting of Maximum would mean the highest compression with a smaller resulting file size, but that's incorrect. To prevent confusion, it's best to think of these settings as quality settings. A setting of Maximum means the best quality of an image, meaning less information is being tossed from the image. The result is a better-looking image that is larger in file size. Alternatively, you can specify numerical values in the Quality field. A setting of 100 is the same as choosing the Maximum setting.

- **Blur.** One of the most noticeable side effects of compression in a JPEG file is artifacts, or stray pixels, that appear in the image. Specifying a blur amount can help cover up those artifacts.

- **Matte.** The Matte setting enables you to specify a color for the edge of the graphic, thus allowing it to blend smoothly into colored backgrounds.

- **Progressive.** The Progressive setting allows a JPEG image to load gradually in a browser, similar to the interlacing setting that is available for GIF images.

Choosing the PNG File Format

The PNG (pronounced "ping") format was developed mainly as an alternative to GIF. Shortly after GIF became popular on the web, the Unisys corporation, which developed the compression algorithm used in GIF, tried to collect royalties on its technology from those who used GIF. To get around the legal issues, an open standard called Portable Network Graphic (PNG) was developed. The PNG format uses lossless compression and can support millions of colors. Instead of allowing you to specify a single color as being transparent, the PNG format also supports 256 levels of transparency, similar to alpha channels in Photoshop.

Older web browsers require a special plug-in to view PNG files, although most newer browsers can display them natively. PNG files also might not be compatible with some handheld devices and cell phones. PNG files come in two varieties: 8-bit and 24-bit. The different optimization settings for PNG-8 are identical to those found for GIF, mentioned previously.

Choosing the WBMP File Format

The Wireless Bitmap (WBMP) is a file format that is optimized for wireless devices that have slow connections and limited display capabilities. These devices are quickly fading away because newer phones are being introduced constantly, and cell phones are the largest-selling consumer electronic devices worldwide. WBMP files are black-and-white images (color isn't supported) and are optimized via a dithering setting.

Specifying Additional Image Settings

In addition to choosing a file format, the Save for Web & Devices dialog box in Illustrator lets you control how colors, image sizes, and layers are treated when saving your files. You can find these settings within the three panels that appear at the lower-right side of the Save for Web & Devices dialog box.

Color Table

The Color Table panel lists all the colors contained within the selected slice. Colors that appear with little diamond icons are web-safe colors (**Figure 11.16**). Using the Eyedropper tool to sample colors, you can click the Maps Selected Colors to Transparent icon beneath the panel to specify a color that will appear as transparent (when saving to file formats that support transparency).

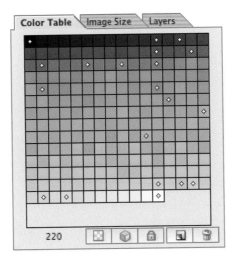

Figure 11.16 *Illustrator indicates web-safe colors in a color table with tiny diamond-shaped icons.*

Image Size

The Image Size panel gives you feedback on the actual size of the selected slice, and it also lets you specify new sizes, although it's always better to make changes to image size on the Illustrator artboard before launching the Save for Web & Devices dialog box. Of importance are the Anti-Alias settings, of which you can choose None, Art Optimized, or Type Optimized, and the Clip to Artboard check box, which allows you to choose whether the exported graphic is clipped to the size of the bounding box of your artwork or to the active artboard.

Layers

If you specified layers in your Illustrator document, you have the option of exporting them as Cascading Style Sheet (CSS) layers by selecting the Export as CSS Layers option in the Layers panel in the Save for Web & Devices dialog box. CSS lets you take advantage of absolute positioning and overlapping objects within a web page. Although the technical aspects of CSS are beyond the scope of this book, it's important to realize that CSS has become a standard, especially when you're generating content that will be displayed on a wide range of devices.

If you choose to export Illustrator layers as CSS layers, you can choose whether each top-level layer in your document should be exported as visible or hidden (**Figure 11.17**). Alternatively, you can specify that certain layers aren't exported at all.

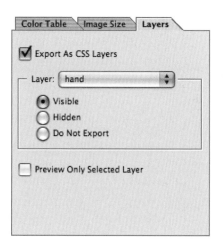

Figure 11.17 *CSS layers that are exported as hidden can be activated via JavaScript on the server using Dynamic HTML.*

Adding Interactivity and Creating Animations

Although it's nice to admire graphics on a web page, nothing is quite like a graphic that invokes action on the viewer's part. It is those images that move with animation or that contain clickable *hotspots* that can take a viewer to additional content that make the web such an exciting medium. Although Illustrator isn't a replacement for an application such as Flash Professional or Dreamweaver, you can still create web graphics that come to life using your favorite vector graphics application.

Creating Image Maps

On the web, a designer's job is far more than just creating a pretty graphic. Rather, a graphic must draw a viewer to action. The action could be as simple as switching to a different page or as significant as generating a sale. In Illustrator, you can assign a URL to an object, which results in an *image map*. An image map is a region or portion of a graphic on which a viewer can click.

To create an image map, follow these steps:

1. Select an object on your artboard, and choose Window > Attributes to open your Attributes panel.

2. Once the panel is open, choose Rectangle or Polygon from the Image Map pop-up menu (**Figure 11.18**). For objects that are rectangular, choose the Rectangle option. For images that fit any other shape, choose the Polygon option.

Figure 11.18 *Older browsers supported only rectangular image maps, but just about all of today's browsers support polygonal image maps.*

3. Once you've chosen an image map type, enter a URL in the field below the pop-up menu. For the best results, enter the complete URL, including the **http://**.

Illustrator keeps track of all the URLs you enter, so if you're applying the same URL to multiple objects in your document, you can choose the correct URL from the URL pop-up (**Figure 11.19**). To test a URL to see whether it is correct, click the Browser button; when you do, Illustrator launches your system's default browser and navigates to the chosen URL.

Figure 11.19 *Once you've entered a URL in the Attributes panel, Illustrator remembers it so you can easily apply it to other objects in your document.*

Animation: Making It Move

There's no question that adding motion to web graphics enhances their appearance and ability to garner attention. Illustrator can build frame-based animations quite easily, although if you're looking for a high-end animation tool, you'd best look elsewhere. The techniques we discuss here are indicative of the simple animations you can create quickly and easily with Illustrator. You might still want to look to Flash Professional, Flash Catalyst, and Adobe After Effects for more complex work.

The key to creating great animations in Illustrator is to use layers carefully. Illustrator doesn't have an animation panel or a timeline. Rather, Illustrator treats each top-level layer in your document as a frame in your animation. As you build your animation with each new layer, keep in mind the advice you've learned, especially with regard to using symbols (**Figure 11.20**, on the next page). Illustrator allows you to create blends between symbols and even create objects with live effects applied. Refer to Chapter 2, "Selecting and Editing Artwork," for detailed information on creating blends.

Once you've created the art for your animation, choose File > Export, and choose the Flash (SWF) file format. When you select the AI Layers to Flash Frames setting, your resulting SWF file plays through each layer sequentially. Setting the animation to loop causes the animation to repeat endlessly (always fun!). Refer to Chapter 12, "Saving and Exporting Files," for information on the settings found in the Flash (SWF) Export dialog box.

NOTE Animation in SVG is not directly supported in Illustrator. To add animation to SVG files, you can add the code by hand once you've exported the SVG from Illustrator, or you can use an SVG animation application, such as Ikivo Animator (www.ikivo.com).

Figure 11.20 *In this illustration, the heart shape was defined as a symbol and then used in a blend with a custom spine. The symbol on the top was then set to 0% opacity, resulting in a blend that makes the heart appear to fade out as it moves toward the top.*

Designing for Flash Professional

By now, you've undoubtedly realized that you can use Illustrator to create interactive SWF files. However, if you're looking to develop truly interactive websites, interfaces, and experiences, you'll soon find that the Illustrator capabilities top out rather quickly. Flash Professional is the application you want to use to create truly interactive and engaging content.

However, many Flash designers and developers use Illustrator to create their artwork and then bring that artwork into Flash, where they add the interactivity. Both Illustrator and Flash Professional are vector-based applications, and many designers are familiar with the design environment and powerful design features found in Illustrator. In addition, it's easy to create mock-ups and PDF files to submit to clients for approval from Illustrator. The challenge, however, is finding a way to bring rich Illustrator content into Flash Professional while keeping features such as artwork, text, gradients, masks, and symbols in an editable state.

The good news is that you can easily move your artwork between the two applications—all while keeping the fidelity of your content. In fact, if you know that your artwork will end up in Flash Professional, you can save valuable time by taking advantage of certain features in Illustrator. Let's take a look at some of these features.

Working with Symbols

In Chapter 9, "Drawing with Efficiency," you learned how to both define and edit symbols. When working with Flash Professional, creating symbols is extremely important because they allow you to easily add interactivity and make global changes, all while keeping files sizes small and manageable.

When you define a new symbol in Illustrator (F8), you're presented with the Symbol Options dialog box (**Figure 11.21**), where you can set the symbol type to Graphic or Movie Clip. In addition, you can set the registration and even define 9-slice scaling.

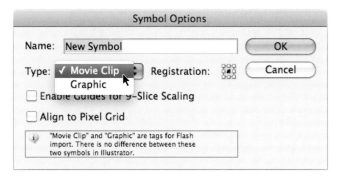

Figure 11.21 *The Symbol Options dialog box gives you the ability to name the symbol and to choose a symbol type.*

In addition, you can name each symbol instance that you place on your artboard. Giving an instance a name lets you reference that instance from within ActionScript code in Flash Professional. When any symbol instance is selected on your artboard, you can give it a name in the field that appears in the Control panel (**Figure 11.22**).

Figure 11.22 *Applying instance names in Illustrator can save plenty of time later in your workflow, after bringing your art into Flash.*

Working with Text

As you learned in Chapter 8, "Working with Typography," Illustrator has sophisticated type controls and features. However, when developing Flash content, text can also be interactive. Rather than waiting to add that interactivity in Flash Professional, you can specify the interactive options right in Illustrator. Choose Window > Type > Flash Text to define text destined for Flash Professional as either static, dynamic, or input text (**Figure 11.23**). Static text doesn't change within the SWF file, while you can change dynamic text using ActionScript. Input text is used when building things such as forms, where a user would be asked to enter custom information.

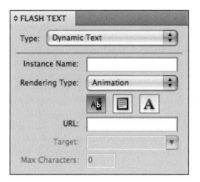

Figure 11.23 *The Flash Text panel gives you control over how text objects in Illustrator will behave when brought into Flash Professional.*

Bringing Your Artwork into Flash Professional

Once you've created your artwork in Illustrator, you need a reliable way to bring your graphics into Flash Professional. In previous versions this was anything *but* easy. However, in the CS5 versions of these components, it's actually quite easy.

To quickly move individual pieces of art, you can simply copy and paste from Illustrator into Flash Professional. Any defined symbols will be retained, as well as text and other settings. However, you may want to bring an entire Illustrator file into Flash Professional, preserving layers and document structure as well. To do so, save your file as a native Illustrator document (.ai), and from Flash Professional, choose File > Import to Stage, then choose the Illustrator file you saved. An import dialog box will appear, listing each object in your file. The import dialog box offers many options, including the ability to choose from multiple artboards, to keep text editable, and to convert objects to movie clip symbols on the fly.

Designing for Flash Catalyst

While Flash Professional is a powerful application, you really have to learn how to write ActionScript code in order to get the most out of it. For many designers, the concept of learning to write computer code is daunting, and leaves them less time to focus on their true talents—which is to be creative.

To help designers create interactive content without having to write code, Adobe created Flash Catalyst. Perhaps one of the greatest things about Flash Catalyst is how much it feels like a design application. And if you create your artwork in Illustrator, you can easily bring that art right into a Flash Catalyst project. If you're going to do so, it's a good idea to take the following items into account:

- **Pay attention to structure.** Layers and groups are maintained when Illustrator artwork is brought into Flash Catalyst. If you're careful about how you organize your layers, how you build your groups, and how you name them, you'll have a much easier time building interactive components once you get your artwork into Flash Catalyst.

- **Use symbols wisely.** Flash Catalyst automatically converts your Illustrator artwork into Flex code. However, complex artwork that contains many paths and objects can result in large chunks of code that need to load over and over again in a web browser. If you create symbols for your complex artwork in Illustrator, that artwork is automatically converted to Flex-optimized graphics when brought into Flash Catalyst. The result is a project that runs optimally in a web browser.

- **Flash Catalyst supports round-trip editing with Illustrator.** Once you've brought your artwork into Flash Catalyst, and you've defined interactive components and even specified transactions, you can bring your artwork back into Illustrator for editing. To do so, while in your Flash Catalyst project select the artwork and choose Modify > Edit in Illustrator CS5.

Once you've created your design in Illustrator, you can simply open your native Illustrator file right in Flash Catalyst. Just launch Flash Catalyst and choose File > New Project from Design File, then choose the Illustrator (.ai) file. In addition, you can copy and paste individual elements from Illustrator directly onto the artboard in Flash Catalyst.

Saving and Exporting Files

12

The task of saving and exporting your Illustrator files is obviously very important. Illustrator is a fantastic utility that can open a wide variety of file types, including EPS and PDF. Additionally, you can use Illustrator to save and export files in just about any format you need, including SWF and FXG. If you aren't familiar with these file types, it's okay, because that's what this entire chapter is about.

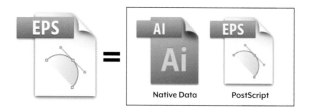

With so many file formats to work with, how do you know which format to use when you're saving or exporting a file? How do you know what each file format supports and what they are each used for? Throughout this chapter, you will learn the strengths and weaknesses of each file format and see examples of when to use or not use each one.

Saving Files from Illustrator

When you save a document from Illustrator using any of the file formats found in the Save or Save As dialog box, you are able to reopen that file and edit it as needed. When you do, all native information, by default, is preserved in the file. For example, if you save a file as an EPS document, you can reopen the EPS file in Illustrator and make edits to the file with no loss of functionality or editability. Adobe calls this *round-tripping*, and working in this way has many benefits.

NOTE The latest version of QuarkXPress available at the time of the printing of this book, version 8, features the ability to place native Illustrator files in addition to EPS files. See the section "Print Workflows" later in this chapter for more information.

If you create a file in Illustrator but you need to place it into a QuarkXPress document, you can create an EPS file. Because an Illustrator EPS file is round-trippable, you can place the EPS file into your QuarkXPress layout, yet you can edit that same EPS file in Illustrator if you need to make changes.

As you will find out, Illustrator accomplishes this by using what engineers call *dual-path* files. This means a single file contains two parts in it: One part contains the EPS data that QuarkXPress needs; the other contains the native Illustrator information that Illustrator needs. As we explore the different formats and their settings, this dual-path concept will become clear.

The Native Illustrator (.ai) Format

By default, when you choose to save a new file, the file format setting is Adobe Illustrator Document (.ai). Whenever you create documents, it's best to save them as native Illustrator files, because they will *always* contain rich and editable information.

NOTE When creating documents that you plan to use as a base for other files, you may choose to save your file as an Illustrator Template (.ait). Details on this format appear in Chapter 1, "Creating and Managing Documents."

Up until Illustrator 8, the native file format for Illustrator was based on PostScript (EPS), but for a variety of reasons, with the release of Illustrator 9, Adobe changed the native file format to be based on the PDF language. In fact, Adobe is quick to tell you that a native Illustrator file can be opened and viewed in Adobe Acrobat or the free Adobe Reader. Adobe also advertises that you can place native Illustrator files directly into InDesign layouts. It makes sense when you think about it, because if the native file format for Illustrator is using the PDF language, then placing it in InDesign is similar to placing a PDF file in InDesign.

In reality, though, the native file format is a special flavor of the PDF language—a flavor that only Illustrator can understand. Certain constructs exist in Illustrator that do not exist in the PDF language, such as live blends, Live

Paint effects, and perspective (these effects are all expanded when printed or translated to regular PDF). You can think of the native file format for Illustrator as a superset of the PDF language. If this is the case, however, how is InDesign or Acrobat able to import and display native Illustrator files? That's where the dual-path concept comes in.

When you save a native file, Illustrator actually saves two files—a native Illustrator file (.ai) and a standard PDF file (**Figure 12.1**). These two files are combined to appear as a single Illustrator file on your computer. When you place the native Illustrator file into InDesign, the application sees the PDF portion and uses that for display and printing. When you reopen the file in Illustrator, the application sees the native Illustrator portion and uses that for editing. In the end, everyone is happy, and you get to work with a single file.

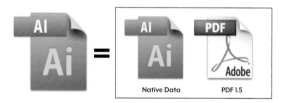

Figure 12.1 *When you save a native Illustrator file, you're really saving two files. The PDF file that is created with the native Illustrator file is PDF 1.5, which preserves transparency.*

To save your file as a native Illustrator file, choose File > Save, and choose Adobe Illustrator (ai) from the format pop-up menu. When you click Save, you are presented with the Illustrator Options dialog box where you can specify settings for how your file should be saved. These are described in the section "Native Illustrator File Format Settings."

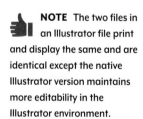

NOTE The two files in an Illustrator file print and display the same and are identical except the native Illustrator version maintains more editability in the Illustrator environment.

Legacy Illustrator Formats

Illustrator CS5 allows you to save your file so that it is compatible with a variety of previous versions of Illustrator. Obviously, the older the version you specify, the less editable your file will be. Specifically, you should be aware of these distinctions:

• Adobe introduced a new text engine in Illustrator CS. If you save your file to any version prior to Illustrator CS, your text is either broken apart or converted to outlines. For more details, see "Saving Illustrator CS5 Files to Illustrator Legacy Versions" in Chapter 8, "Working with Typography."

- Adobe introduced transparency features in Illustrator 9. If you save your file to any version prior to Illustrator 9, transparency flattening will occur, resulting in a document that may be extremely difficult, or even impossible, to edit. For more details, see "Learning the Truth About Transparency" in Chapter 13, "Prepress and Printing."

Your file will print or display correctly when you're saving to older versions because the appearance is always maintained. However, you are limited in what kinds of edits you can make in your file. For this reason, we recommend you *always* save a native CS5 version of your file to keep on your computer or server for editing purposes. If someone else requests a file from you that is compatible with a previous version of Illustrator, send them a *copy* of your file.

Native Illustrator File Format Settings

A variety of settings are available in the Illustrator Options dialog box (**Figure 12.2**), and depending on your needs for each particular workflow, you can adjust these settings.

Figure 12.2 *The Illustrator Options dialog box allows you to specify which version of Illustrator you want your file to be compatible with, among other settings.*

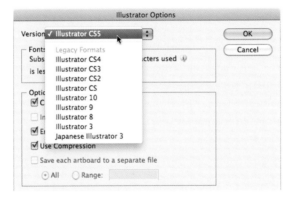

- **Version.** The Version pop-up menu allows you to choose which version of Illustrator you want your file to be compatible with. See the "Legacy Illustrator Formats" section earlier in this chapter for more information.

- **Fonts.** When you're saving a file, any fonts you use are embedded in the PDF portion of the file. This allows other applications to print the file without requiring the fonts. However, you still need the fonts installed if you are going to reopen the file in Illustrator. This setting is disabled when the Create PDF Compatible File option is deselected (see the next description). At the 100% setting, Illustrator embeds only those characters of a font that are necessary to print the text in your document.

Using a setting much lower (such as to 0%) embeds the entire font, resulting in a larger file. Fonts with permission bits turned on cannot be embedded (see the sidebar "Font Embedding and Permissions" later in this chapter).

- **Create PDF Compatible File.** The Create PDF Compatible File option embeds a full standard PDF 1.5 file in your Illustrator document. As just mentioned, this allows applications such as Acrobat or InDesign to read and place native Illustrator files. *Deselecting* this option effectively cuts your file size in half and also reduces how long it takes to save an Illustrator file (**Figure 12.3**). If you use Illustrator for all your work and print directly from Illustrator, you can disable this option to enhance performance and to create smaller file sizes, but be aware that you won't be able to place your file into an InDesign layout. Even if you do deselect this option, you can always reopen the file in Illustrator and resave the file with the option selected.

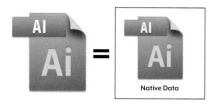

Figure 12.3 *When you have the Create PDF Compatible File option deselected, only the native Illustrator portion is saved with the file, cutting save time and file size in half. The result, however, is a native file that cannot be placed into another application.*

- **Include Linked Files.** When you select the Include Linked Files option, any place-linked files are embedded in your document. Although this means you can send the file to someone without requiring any external links, it also means you can't easily update linked graphics anymore. This option also increases file size because the images are now included in the file.

- **Embed ICC Profiles.** The Embed ICC Profiles option includes any color profiles (including those from placed images) in your document.

- **Use Compression.** The Use Compression option employs compression algorithms to your file to try to reduce file size.

- **Save each Artboard to a Separate File.** If your file contains multiple artboards, you can have Illustrator create individual files for each artboard (or a specified range of artboards). Alternatively, leaving this option deselected will result in all your artboards being combined into a single large artboard when saving to older versions (with guides indicating where the original artboards were).

- • **Transparency.** When you're saving to an Illustrator 8 or Illustrator 3 format, transparency flattening must occur in documents that contain transparency effects. You can choose to discard the transparency effects completely (which preserves path geometry), or you can choose to preserve the appearance of your file. You can also choose from the list of available transparency flattener presets. For more information on which flattener preset to use, refer to Chapter 13.

The Encapsulated PostScript (.eps) Format

When Adobe introduced PostScript to the world, it forever changed the face of design and publishing. Since desktop publishing became a buzzword, the format in which designers and printers exchanged file information was always EPS. To this day, EPS is a reliable, universal format that can be used to reproduce graphics from just about any professional (and even some non-professional) graphics applications.

PostScript doesn't support transparency, so if your file contains any transparency effects, those effects are flattened when the document is saved in EPS format (see Chapter 13). However, you can still reopen and edit the native transparency in Illustrator CS5 because Illustrator also uses a dual path when saving EPS files. An Illustrator CS5 EPS file has two portions in it: a native version for editing in Illustrator and an EPS version that other applications, such as QuarkXPress, use (**Figure 12.4**).

Figure 12.4 *When you save a document as an EPS file, Illustrator also embeds a native version of the file so that you can reopen and edit the file in Illustrator with no loss in editability.*

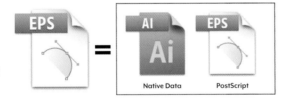

To save your file as an EPS file, choose File > Save, and from the pop-up menu choose Illustrator EPS. When you click Save, you are presented with the EPS Options dialog box where you can specify settings for how your file should be saved, as described later in the section "EPS File Format Settings."

Legacy EPS Formats

As with native files, Illustrator allows you to save your file so that it is compatible with a variety of versions of Illustrator EPS. This setting affects both the native portion and the EPS portion of the file. When you save a file that is compatible with an older version of Illustrator, both the native data and the PostScript are written so they are compatible with that version (**Figure 12.5**). Obviously, the older the version you specify, the less editable your file is. The same rules mentioned for native Illustrator files apply here (with regard to versions that result in loss of text and transparency editability), and it always makes sense to save an Illustrator CS5 EPS for your own needs and deliver older or legacy EPS versions for others, as needed.

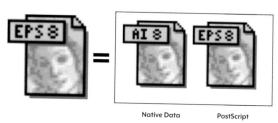

Native Data   PostScript

Figure 12.5 *When you save a file in Illustrator 8 EPS format, the native portion of the file is also saved in Illustrator 8 format, which doesn't support transparency. Even if you reopen the file in Illustrator CS5, any transparency that was in the file is flattened.*

Note that with the inclusion of multiple artboards in Illustrator CS4 and CS5, you now have the additional option of Use Artboards in the Save dialog box. For details, see the sidebar "Saving and Exporting Artboards" later in this chapter.

EPS File Format Settings

A variety of settings are available in the EPS Options dialog box (**Figure 12.6**, on page 409). Depending on your needs for each particular workflow, you can adjust these settings:

- **Version.** The Version pop-up menu allows you to choose which version of Illustrator EPS you want your file to be compatible with. See the preceding section, "Legacy EPS Formats," for more information.

- **Preview.** The Preview setting lets you choose from different options for embedding a preview in your EPS file. Because most programs can't display PostScript on your computer screen, a low-resolution preview is stored along with the file so that programs such as QuarkXPress or Microsoft Word can give you a visual representation of what the file will look like in your layout.

- **Transparency.** If your file contains transparency, your file must be flattened so that it can be saved in PostScript and printed from another application (remember, the version you choose determines whether the native portion of the file, which Illustrator reads when it reopens the file, still contains editable, unflattened data). Although you can choose different transparency flattener presets from the pop-up menu, it almost always makes sense to choose the High Resolution setting, because you'll always want to get the best possible results when printing the EPS file from other applications (see "Choosing File Formats Based on Workflow" later in this chapter).

- **Embed Fonts.** When this option is selected, any fonts used are embedded in the EPS portion of the file. This allows other applications to print the file without requiring the fonts. However, even with the setting selected, you still need the fonts installed if you are going to reopen the file in Illustrator. Fonts with permission bits turned on can't be embedded (see the sidebar "Font Embedding and Permissions" later in this chapter).

- **Include Linked Files.** Selecting the Include Linked Files option embeds any place-linked files in your document. Although this means you can send the file to someone without requiring any external links, it also means you can't easily update linked graphics anymore. This option also increases file size because the images will now be included in the file.

- **Include Document Thumbnails.** Use this option if you want to be able to see a preview of your file in the Open and Place dialog boxes in Illustrator.

- **Include CMYK PostScript in RGB Files.** This setting allows you to maintain RGB colors in your Illustrator file but have the EPS portion of the file converted to CMYK so other applications that don't support RGB can still print the file correctly.

- **Compatible Gradient and Gradient Mesh Printing.** If you experience problems printing EPS files saved from Illustrator on older print devices, try selecting this option.

- **Use Printer's Default Screen.** This instructs the PostScript to use the line screen of the default setting of the printer.

- **Adobe PostScript.** Use this pop-up menu to write the EPS file as PostScript LanguageLevel 2 or LanguageLevel 3. Illustrator uses LanguageLevel 2 as the default setting in order to create a file that is compatible with a wider range of devices, but LanguageLevel 3 offers certain benefits such as smooth shading technology to prevent banding in gradients.

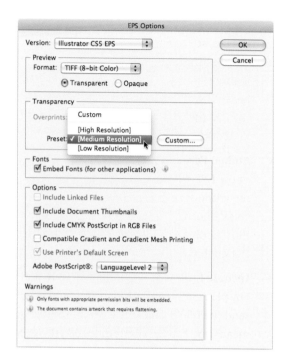

Figure 12.6 *The EPS Options dialog box offers a variety of settings to choose from when you're saving an EPS file, including the flattener preset to use when transparency is present.*

The Portable Document Format (.pdf)

Walk up to just about anyone on the street these days and ask them about Adobe. Most will reply, "Oh, sure, I have Adobe on my computer." What they are probably referring to is the free Adobe Reader file viewer, which enables just about anyone to view and print PDF files. Now that Reader has surpassed a billion downloads worldwide, PDF files are ubiquitous. PDF has become a standard format used not only by designers and printers but also by governments and enterprise corporations.

Over the past few years, PDF has become the format of choice for both printers and designers, replacing EPS and other formats. There are several reasons for this, including the following:

- **Smaller file sizes.** PDF supports a variety of image compression techniques, resulting in smaller file sizes. In addition, users can easily create low-resolution files to send to clients for review and can create high-resolution files to send to printers for high-quality output.

- **A free universal viewer.** Reader is free and available for nearly every computer platform, including handheld devices. This means a designer can deliver a PDF file and be assured that anyone can view the file correctly.

TIP You can instruct clients or users to download the free Reader at http://get.adobe.com/reader/. Reader is available for Mac, Windows, Unix, and a variety of mobile platforms.

- **Ability to embed fonts.** A PDF file is a single, self-contained file that includes all necessary images and fonts. This makes it easier to distribute and reduces the chance of error.

- **Easy to create.** Designers can easily create PDF files from any Adobe application. Additionally, Adobe supplies a utility called PDFMaker, which comes with Acrobat, that enables users to instantly create PDF files from Microsoft Office documents or AutoCAD files. (Note that PDFMaker was dropped for the Mac in Acrobat 9.) A PDF virtual printer also enables a user to create a PDF file simply by printing a file from any application.

- **Security.** PDF files can contain multiple levels of security that can restrict functionality such as printing or editing. This ensures the integrity of a file and gives designers the ability to protect their work.

By default, a PDF saved from Illustrator is also a dual-path file, containing both PDF data and native Illustrator data (**Figure 12.7**). In fact, if you think about it, saving a native Illustrator file and an Adobe PDF file is quite similar. When you save a PDF file from Illustrator, though, you can control a variety of settings in the resulting PDF data of the file.

Figure 12.7 *If you've ever heard that Illustrator creates large PDF files, it's probably because by default Illustrator embeds a native version of the file along with the PDF data, resulting in a PDF file that appears twice as large.*

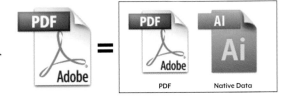

To save your file as a PDF file, choose File > Save, and select Adobe PDF from the pop-up menu. When you click Save, you are presented with the Save Adobe PDF dialog box where you can specify settings for how your file should be saved.

Different Uses of PDF Files

Before we discuss all the different options available when saving a PDF file, it's important to realize that PDF files have many uses. For example, you might create a PDF file to send to a client so that they can approve a design, or you might create a PDF file to send to a printer for final output. Alternatively, you might even create a PDF file to upload to a website so that anyone can view the content. Each of these PDF files serves a different purpose, and therefore each can have very different settings. Just because you create a PDF file doesn't mean you can use it for any and all purposes.

Instead of having to manually specify PDF settings each time you want to create a file for a specific purpose, Illustrator offers to let you create Adobe PDF presets, which capture all the settings a PDF can have. At the top of the Save Adobe PDF dialog box, a pop-up menu lets you choose from some presets that ship with Illustrator (**Figure 12.8**), or you can define your own by clicking the Save Preset button at the bottom left of the dialog box.

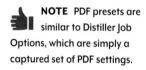

NOTE PDF presets are similar to Distiller Job Options, which are simply a captured set of PDF settings.

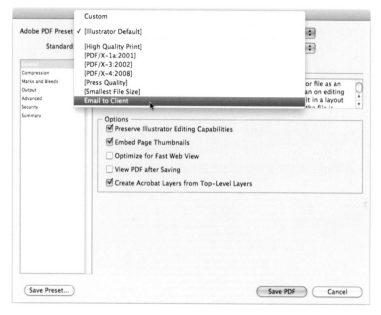

Figure 12.8 *Illustrator ships with several predefined PDF presets. If you're using other Adobe Creative Suite components, any PDF preset you save in Illustrator also becomes available in all the other applications.*

Acrobat Version Compatibility

When PDF was first introduced, it had limited support (spot colors weren't supported until version 1.2), but as each new version of Acrobat has been introduced, Adobe has updated the PDF language specification (called PDFL for short) to include more advanced functions and to feature new capabilities.

Adobe released PDFL version 1.3 when it introduced Acrobat 4.0, which was the first mainstream version of Acrobat and the free Reader. With each new version of Acrobat, Adobe has also revised the PDFL version (Acrobat 5 = PDF 1.4, Acrobat 6 = PDF 1.5, and so on), although trying to remember all of these different numbers can prove quite confusing. An easy way to figure it out is to remember that if you add up the numbers in the PDFL version, it equals the corresponding version of Acrobat (1 + 4 = 5).

In any case, when you save a PDF file from Illustrator, you can specify which version of Acrobat you want your file to be compatible with in the Save Adobe PDF dialog box (**Figure 12.9**). Although saving a file using a newer version compatibility setting offers more options when saving, anyone who wants to view that PDF file needs to use a newer version of Acrobat or Reader to see and print the file correctly.

Figure 12.9 *The Save Adobe PDF dialog box offers a plethora of settings for creating PDF files for a wide variety of purposes. The Compatibility setting determines the version of Acrobat that the resulting PDF file needs to display and print correctly.*

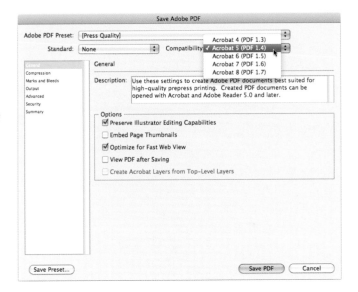

The most important point to remember is that from a print perspective, there's a line in the sand between PDF 1.3, which doesn't support transparency, and all later PDF versions, which do support live transparency (**Table 12.1**). See "Choosing File Formats Based on Workflow" later in this chapter to learn when to use each version.

Table 12.1 *Acrobat Version Compatibility*

Version of Acrobat	PDFL Version	Transparency Support	Main Features Introduced
Acrobat 4	PDF 1.3	No	Smooth shading, digital signatures
Acrobat 5	PDF 1.4	Yes	Transparency, XML tagging, and metadata
Acrobat 6	PDF 1.5	Yes	Layers, JPEG2000 compression
Acrobat 7	PDF 1.6	Yes	Object-level metadata, AES encryption
Acrobat 8	PDF 1.7	Yes	Enhanced 3D support, PDF packages

The PDF/X Standard

Imagine the following scenario: A designer submits a PDF file to a printer for final printing. When the job is complete, the designer is horrified to find that the wrong fonts printed and that the colors weren't anywhere near close to those that appeared on the screen when the designer designed the job. How did this happen? After all, didn't the printer say they accept PDF files? For designers, and especially for printers, this is a scenario that unfortunately happens too often.

This happens because PDF is a "garbage in, garbage out" file format. Whatever you put into it, that's what you can expect to get out of it. If you don't embed your fonts when you create a PDF file, a printer can't print your file unless they also have your fonts. If you embed RGB images when a printer needs CMYK, you will see color shifts in your output (some devices may not print RGB images at all).

With so many other possible things that could go wrong with a PDF file, printers and publishers realized that they needed a way to ensure that a PDF file meets certain requirements before it is submitted for final printing or publication.

One way to do that was by providing designers with a detailed list of the settings they needed to use whenever they created a PDF file. Although this was a nice idea in concept, printers and publishers soon realized that designers use a variety of different programs, and each has different ways of creating PDF files. They also realized this meant that each time a new version of software was introduced, a designer would need to learn new settings.

Instead, an International Organization for Standardization (ISO) standard was created, called *PDF/X*. A PDF/X file is not a new kind of file format but rather a regular PDF file that simply meets a list of predefined criteria. Now, when a designer submits a PDF/X file for final printing, a printer can assume that the file meets the minimum requirements to reproduce it correctly.

By choosing a standard from the Standard pop-up menu in the Save Adobe PDF dialog box, you are embedding an identifier in the PDF file that says, "I am a PDF/X-compliant file." Certain scripts and preflight utilities can read these identifiers and validate PDF/X-compliant files in a prepress or publishing workflow. See the sidebar "Understanding Supported PDF Standards in Illustrator" for an explanation of the different kinds of PDF/X versions.

Understanding Supported PDF Standards in Illustrator

Because PDF files have so many uses and because each workflow is different, many PDF standards exist. The following is an explanation of what each standard is and what each is best used for:

- **PDF/X-1a:2001.** The PDF/X-1a standard was defined to allow for the reliable exchange of files between designers and printers or publishers. The standard, which was first defined in 2001 (which is where it gets its name), is based on PDF 1.3 and therefore doesn't support transparency. When you save a PDF/X-1a file from Illustrator, a transparency flattener preset is used to flatten the transparency in the file. A PDF/X-1a-compliant file must also have all fonts embedded in the file. If your file uses a protected font that cannot be embedded (see the sidebar "Font Embedding and Permissions" later in this chapter), Illustrator can't create a valid PDF/X-1a file. Additionally, PDF/X-1a files are CMYK and spot only (any RGB information is converted to CMYK). For ad submission or for sending final files to a printer for offset printing, PDF/X-1a:2001 is the preferred choice.

- **PDF/X-3:2002.** In recent years, print service providers have been adopting color management technologies to offer better color matching. Rather than converting images to CMYK early in the process, in a color-managed workflow you can have images remain in RGB and tag them with profiles that allow color integrity to be preserved from proof to final print. Because PDF/X-1a doesn't support RGB or embedded color profiles, PDF/X-3:2002 was created to allow for these variables. If you or your printer are using a color-management workflow, you might consider using PDF/X-3:2002.

- **PDF/X-4:2008.** Once a file has been flattened, a printer can't do much in the way of making changes to that file. More important, a printer sometimes can't trap files that have already been flattened. Although PDF/X-1a and PDF/X-3 don't allow transparency constructs in the file, the PDF/X-4 standard is based on PDF 1.5 and allows transparency. This gives the printer the ability to choose a flattener setting and to make late-stage edits. In any case, it's best to speak with your printer before using the newer PDF/X-4:2008 standard.

See "Choosing File Formats Based on Workflow" later in this chapter for additional examples of when you would want to submit a PDF file using one the standards listed here. You can find more information about the various versions of PDF/X at http://www.gwg.org/PDXFAQ.phtml.

General PDF Settings

The General panel of the Save Adobe PDF dialog box contains several important settings that determine how your PDF file is saved:

- **Preserve Illustrator Editing Capabilities.** The Preserve Illustrator Editing Capabilities option embeds a full native Illustrator file in your PDF file. This allows Illustrator to reopen and edit the file with no loss in editability. This option is turned on in the default preset, but turning this option off effectively cuts your file size in half and also reduces how long it takes to save a PDF file (**Figure 12.10**). If you want to send a file to a client for approval, for example, you can take this approach to create a smaller PDF file (which is also not as editable should they try to open it in Illustrator). If you do deselect this option, make sure to always save a copy of your file, because you won't be able to reopen the smaller PDF and edit it as a fully editable file.

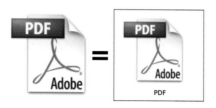

Figure 12.10 *By turning off the Preserve Illustrator Editing Capabilities option, you can create a PDF file that is smaller and suitable for posting to the web or sending via email.*

- **Embed Page Thumbnails.** With the Embed Page Thumbnails option selected, Illustrator creates thumbnails for each page. You can display these in Acrobat by choosing to view the Pages tab. Be aware that the thumbnails increase the file size somewhat, however.

- **Optimize for Fast Web View.** Selecting the Optimize for Fast Web View option enables streaming, allowing those who view the file online to view parts of the document while other parts are still loading.

- **View PDF after Saving.** It's always a good idea to take a look at a PDF on your screen to make sure it's okay before you release it to a printer or to a client. Selecting the View PDF after Saving option launches Acrobat and opens the file after the PDF file is created.

- **Create Acrobat Layers from Top-Level Layers.** If you choose to save your file with Acrobat 6 (PDF 1.5), Acrobat 7 (PDF 1.6), or Acrobat 8 (PDF 1.7) compatibility, you can have Illustrator convert all top-level layers to PDF layers. You can view a document with PDF layers in either Acrobat or the free Reader, versions 6.0 and newer (**Figure 12.11**). In addition, Acrobat layers can be turned on and off when the PDF is placed in an InDesign document.

Figure 12.11 *When a file is opened in Acrobat or Reader, the viewing of layers can be toggled on and off.*

PDF Compression Settings

The Compression panel of the Save Adobe PDF dialog box offers a variety of settings for compressing the images and art that appear in your file (**Figure 12.12**). One of the benefits of using PDF is that you can specify a variety of image settings for each need. For example, when you send a file to a client for review, you want to create a small file that transmits quickly via email and you might set all images to resample at 72 ppi. However, that same file, when transmitted to the printer for final output, needs to contain high-resolution images, which you might set to at least 300 ppi.

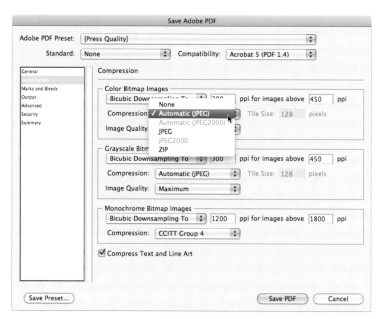

Figure 12.12 *The Compression panel of the Save Adobe PDF dialog box lets you determine which image types will be resampled, as well as choose the compression method in which to do so.*

When you create a PDF, Illustrator has the ability to resample an image. *Resampling* is a method used to change the resolution of a raster image. Although *upsampling* adds new pixels to a file, *downsampling* removes pixels from a file, resulting in a lower resolution and a smaller file size. Obviously, downsampling an image results in loss of image detail and is therefore inappropriate for final output to a printer.

- **Resampling settings.** Illustrator can apply different settings to raster images that appear in your file, according to image type and resolution. You can specify these settings for color, grayscale, and monochrome bitmap images. More importantly, you can define a threshold for when images will be resampled. The Do Not Downsample option leaves images at their native resolutions. Alternatively, you can choose from three different types of downsampling (Average, Bicubic, and Subsampling), which reduce the resolution of any raster images in your file according to the threshold settings. The first value is for the resolution to which you want images to be downsampled. The second value determines which images in your file get downsampled. For example, if you set the first value to 72 ppi and the second value to 150 ppi, then any image in your file that exceeds 150 ppi is downsampled to 72 ppi. However, if your file contains an image that's set to 100 ppi, that image is not downsampled and remains at 100 ppi because it falls below the threshold.

- **Compression and Image Quality.** In addition to resampling raster images, PDF also uses compression techniques to further reduce the size of a file. Different methods are used for compression, or you can choose None to disable compression completely (see the sidebar below).

- **Compress Text and Line Art.** To achieve smaller file sizes, select the option to compress text and line art. This uses a lossless method of compression and doesn't sacrifice quality in your file.

Compress This

Getting smaller file sizes comes at a cost. That cost is the quality of the image after it has been compressed. As we discussed in Chapter 11, "Web Design," there are two types of compression algorithms: *lossy* compression, which results in smaller files at the expense of image detail, and *lossless* compression, which doesn't make files quite as small but loses no information in the process.

When saving PDF files from Illustrator, you can choose no compression, JPEG compression, JPEG2000 compression (both JPEG compression types are lossy), or the lossless zip compression method. When using lossy compression, you can also choose an image quality setting to control how much information or detail is lost in the compression process. The Maximum setting preserves the most information in the file, while the Minimum setting sacrifices quality for a smaller file size.

PDF Marks and Bleeds Settings

NOTE The Bleed settings you specify in the Marks and Bleeds panel define the bleed box values in the resulting PDF.

The Marks and Bleeds panel of the Save Adobe PDF dialog box (**Figure 12.13**) is strikingly similar to the Marks and Bleeds panel you'll find in the Print dialog box. Here you can specify whether your PDF should have printer's marks and whether the document will have bleed space added. If you already set a bleed setting when you created your document or in the Document Setup dialog box, you can set Use Document Bleed Settings to use those values.

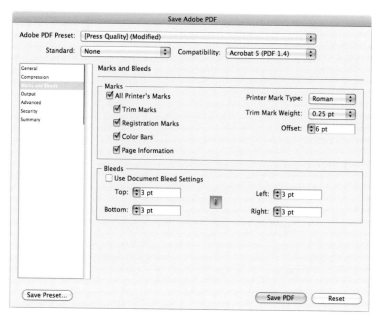

Figure 12.13 *The Marks and Bleeds panel of the Save Adobe PDF dialog box lets you create PDF files with crop marks automatically. Additionally, the Bleeds settings make it easy to turn bleed on or off depending on to whom you are sending the PDF file.*

PDF Output Settings

The Output panel of the Save Adobe PDF dialog box (**Figure 12.14**, on the next page) gives you control over what color space your PDF is saved in and whether you want to include image color management profiles in your PDF. Additionally, you can specify color management settings for files that will be saved using one of the PDF/X standards.

- **Color.** When you create a PDF file, you can specify a color conversion for the file. In the Color Conversion pop-up, you can choose No Conversion, in which case the color values and color space will remain untouched, or you can choose Convert to Destination and choose from the Destination pop-up options to convert the color values or color space using a color profile of your choice. You can also specify when Illustrator will include color profiles in the PDF file.

- **PDF/X.** When you create a PDF/X file, you must specify a color profile intent; with PDF/X-1a, this is usually set to SWOP. You can also choose to mark the file as being already trapped, which is useful in workflows where trapping may occur in the RIP. If you trapped a file in Illustrator (either manually or via a plug-in such as Esko-Graphics' DeskPack), identifying the file as already trapped prevents the file from being trapped again in the RIP.

Figure 12.14 *The Output panel of the Save Adobe PDF dialog box gives you the ability to convert all objects to a specific color space. For example, when saving a PDF/X-1a file, any linked RGB images are converted to CMYK automatically.*

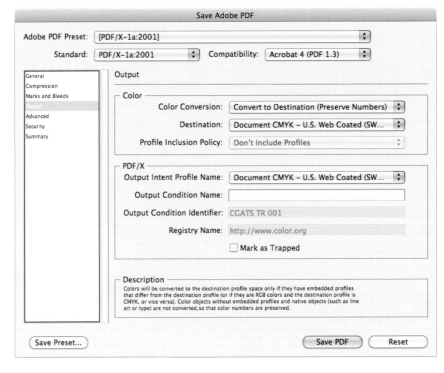

PDF Advanced Settings

The Advanced panel of the Save Adobe PDF dialog box (**Figure 12.15**) allows you to specify how fonts are embedded in your PDF file and how transparency is flattened, if necessary.

- **Fonts.** By default, Illustrator embeds subsets of fonts when saving a PDF file. A subset simply means that Illustrator includes only the parts of a font that are required to view and print the text you have in your document. If a font is protected, however, Illustrator does not embed the font. See the sidebar "Font Embedding and Permissions" for more information.

- **Overprint and Transparency Flattener Options.** If your document contains overprint settings, you can choose to preserve or discard them. Additionally, if your file contains transparency, you can choose a transparency flattener preset to control how the transparency is flattened. For more information on both overprinting and transparency, see Chapter 13. It's important to note that these two settings are applicable only when you're saving a PDF file with Acrobat 4 (PDF 1.3) compatibility because all other versions support transparency and don't require flattening.

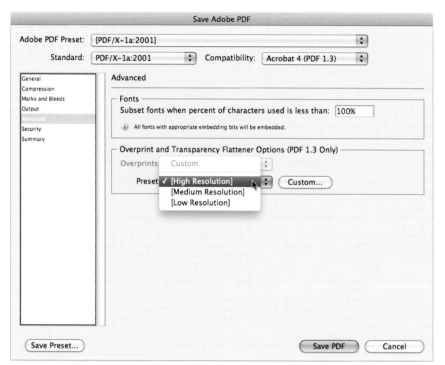

Figure 12.15 *The Advanced panel of the Save Adobe PDF dialog box allows you to specify a transparency flattener preset when saving to PDF 1.3 (all other versions support live transparency).*

Font Embedding and Permissions

Using fonts these days isn't the same as it was several years ago. Designer, meet lawyer. Lawyer, meet designer. There are some legal restrictions when it comes to using fonts, and depending on the licensing agreements that come along with the fonts you own, you may be limited in how you can use your fonts.

Generally, a font can have two kinds of embedding permissions. *Preview and Printing* permissions give the owner of the font the rights to use the font in a design and distribute the file with the font embedded so that others can view and print the document as well. *Editing* permissions give the owner the same rights as Preview and Printing permissions, but others who receive the file with the fonts embedded may also make edits and changes to the file.

Even though most fonts possess one of these two permissions (which are specified in the font licensing agreement), they usually aren't enforced in any way. A font vendor expects a user to abide by the terms specified in its license agreement. For example, a font may have Preview and Printing permissions (the more stringent of the two settings), but you may still be able to embed that font in a PDF file. This means someone using Acrobat Professional, or another product that can edit PDF files (including Illustrator), can make changes to the document, which would violate the license agreement.

(continued on next page)

Font Embedding and Permissions
(continued)

To prevent unauthorized use, some font vendors protect their fonts by specifying that their fonts can't be embedded at all. These fonts are referred to as *protected fonts*. If an Adobe application encounters such a font, the application does not embed the font in a PDF file, honoring the rights of the font vendor. Obviously, if a designer is using a protected font and wants to send a PDF file with the fonts embedded to a publication, this can pose a problem. The only solution is for the designer to contact the font vendor and request an extended license that allows the font to be embedded. Alternatively, you may be able to convert the text to outlines before saving the file.

Unfortunately, Illustrator doesn't offer any way to easily tell whether a font is protected (InDesign does). Once you create a PDF, you can open the file in Acrobat and use the Document Properties setting to make sure your fonts are embedded.

PDF Security Settings

In today's world, security has become a priority—not only in airports but with regard to electronic communications and documentation as well. One of the benefits of using PDF files is the ability to password-protect them so that you can control who can view or edit your file.

The Security panel of the Save Adobe PDF dialog box (**Figure 12.16**) allows you to specify two kinds of passwords to protect the content of your PDF file:

- **Document Open Password.** A document open password, also referred to as a *master password*, controls who can open your PDF file. If a user attempts to view the PDF, they are prompted for a password. Upon entering the password, the user is able to view the file. The file will not open if the password is incorrect.

- **Permissions Password.** A permissions password controls what a user can do with a PDF file once it is open on their screen. For example, a user who has the Professional version of Acrobat or a variety of Acrobat plug-ins, such as Enfocus PitStop, has the ability to edit a PDF file. Even if a file has a master password, once a user opens the file, they are free to do with the file as they please. By specifying a permissions password, you can restrict what a user can do with a file, even once they've opened the file in Acrobat Professional. For a detailed explanation of the different permissions settings, see the sidebar "Did You Ask for Permission?"

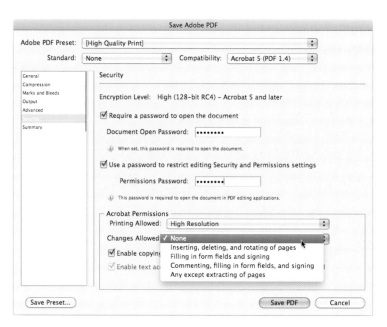

Figure 12.16 *The Security panel of the Save Adobe PDF dialog box allows you to choose a password that will restrict how your PDF file can be edited.*

Did You Ask for Permission?

The permissions settings in Illustrator give you control over the actions a user can take with your PDF file once they've opened it. You can find these options in the lower portion of the Security panel in the Save Adobe PDF dialog box:

- **Printing.** Choosing None disallows the printing of your file. Users are able to view the file in its entirety on their computer screens, but their Print command is dimmed (**Figure 12.17**). Choosing High Resolution enables full printing of the file. When using a compatibility setting of Acrobat 6 or newer, you can also choose the Low Resolution setting, which forces all pages to print only as raster images at 150 dpi.

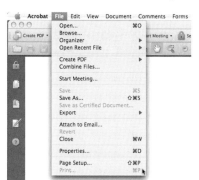

Figure 12.17 *If you use a permissions password to restrict printing, a user without the password is able to view the document but is not able to print the PDF file.*

(continued on next page)

Did You Ask for Permission?
(continued)

- **Changing/editing.** Choosing None disallows all editing of your file. Users are able to view the file in its entirety on their computer screens, but all of Acrobat's editing tools are disabled. Four additional settings restrict specific types of edits. For example, by choosing the Filling in Form Fields and Signing setting, you allow users to fill out PDF form fields and to digitally sign the file, but this setting disables all other editing features.

- **Copying.** If you want to prevent users from copying content from your PDF file and pasting that data into other applications, deselect the "Enable copying of text, images, and other content" option. However, by doing so, you may affect the accessibility of your document, especially for users who rely on screen readers to speak the content of files. These screen readers copy the text and paste the data into an application that reads the words to the user. When you select the option to enable text access to screen readers, Acrobat allows the copying of text if it senses that the application that's copying the data is a screen reader. You can also enable a user to copy the metadata from a file.

The Flex Exchange Graphic (.fxg) Format

FXG (formerly known as MXML) is an interchange format created by Adobe to move files between applications, such as Illustrator, Flash Professional, Fireworks, Flash Catalyst, and Flash Builder. The format allows both designers and developers to collaborate easily to develop graphically rich Internet experiences and applications. Since an FXG file can be saved with native data (**Figure 12.18**), designers and developers can use it to round-trip their files between traditional design applications (such as Illustrator and Flash Catalyst) and traditional developer applications (such as Flash Builder).

Figure 12.18 *FXG files can also contain native Illustrator content, allowing for round-tripping between Illustrator and the application you're placing the FXG file into.*

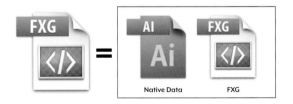

You can select several settings in the FXG Options dialog box (**Figure 12.19**):

- **Use Artboards**. In the initial Save dialog box, choose to save the file with multiple artboards left intact. If deselected, the file will be saved with all artwork on a single artboard. For details, see the sidebar "Saving and Exporting Artboards" later in this chapter.

- **Version**. At this point in time, FXG 2.0 is the only supported version.

- **Save Illustrator Private Data.** This option embeds a full native Illustrator file in your FXG file. This allows Illustrator to reopen and edit the file with no loss in editability. This option is selected by default. If you decide to deselect this option, make sure to save a copy of your file for future editability needs.

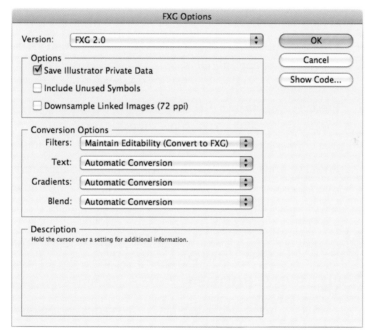

Figure 12.19 *FXG files are designed to be used by rich Internet applications.*

- **Include Unused Symbols.** Keep this option deselected (the default) if you want Illustrator to not include unused symbols in your Symbols panel. See Chapter 9, "Drawing with Efficiency," for detailed information on using symbols.

- **Downsample Linked Images (72 ppi).** If you have linked raster images in your file that are higher in resolution than 72 ppi, this option downsamples those links to 72 ppi—standard screen resolution.

- **Show Code.** This button launches a text editor, and allows you to preview the code before you save the file.

Since Illustrator can create graphics for all types of uses, including print, there could be some elements (filters, text, gradients, or blends) in your artwork that aren't supported in web applications like Flash Catalyst. Illustrator offers a variety of conversion options for handling these cases:

- **Maintain Editability (Convert to FXG).** If compatible filters exist in other applications, Illustrator will try to maintain the editability of those effects. For example, a live effect drop shadow that was applied to an object in Illustrator will be converted to the FXG equivalent of an editable drop shadow (the drop shadow would still update after the object or text was modified). Keep in mind that selecting this filter may sacrifice the preservation of the visual appearance of the artwork and text for editability.

- **Preserve Appearance (Rasterize).** If the preservation of the visual appearance of applied filters, text, and gradients is crucial, select this option to do so, at the expense of a larger file size.

- **Preserve Appearance (Create Outline).** This option preserves the appearance of your text by converting the live type to vector outlines. As a bonus, your file size will be smaller than if you rasterized the text.

- **Preserve Appearance (Expand).** To preserve the appearance of your filtered artwork, this option expands or converts into multiple vector-based objects.

The Scalable Vector Graphics (.svg, .svgz) Format

NOTE For more information on the SVG specification and SVG-enabled mobile devices, visit www.planetsvg.com.

SVG is an XML-based file format that is used primarily on the web and has recently become more popular in creating content for mobile and hand-held wireless devices. For more information about how SVG is used, refer to Chapter 11. The SVGZ format is simply the SVG format zipped (compressed).

A variety of settings are available in the SVG Options dialog box, and depending on your needs for each particular workflow, you can adjust these settings. Click the More Options button in the SVG Options dialog box to see the full list of available settings (**Figure 12.20**).

- **SVG Profiles (DTD).** This setting is akin to the version of SVG that your file is compatible with. Because SVG is an open standard, additional specifications are revised and approved. If you save an SVG file with a particular DTD, it means your file will be compatible with any device that supports that DTD. Newer specifications usually support more functionality than older ones. SVG Tiny (also referred to as SVG-t) is a subset of SVG used for displaying content on SVG-enabled cell phones. SVG Basic is a subset of SVG used for displaying content on PDAs.

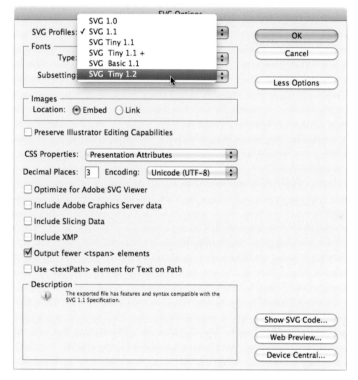

Figure 12.20 *The SVG Options dialog box offers a variety of settings that allow you to fine-tune SVG files, including a button that launches Adobe Device Central, which allows you to preview your file on a variety of handheld devices and cell phones.*

- **Fonts.** When text is present in your file, you can specify the Adobe CEF type, which results in better-looking text when your file is viewed with the Adobe SVG Viewer but may not be supported with other SVG viewers. The SVG creates more compatible text, but it's text that may not be as readable at smaller font sizes. Alternatively, you can convert all text to outlines, which increases file size.

- **Images.** When you save a file in SVG format, you can embed any images in the SVG file (making for larger but self-sufficient files), or you can choose to create smaller SVG files by using the Link option.

- **Preserve Illustrator Editing Capabilities.** The Preserve Illustrator Editing Capabilities option embeds a full native Illustrator file in your SVG file (**Figure 12.21**). This allows Illustrator to reopen and edit the file with no loss in editability. This option is deselected by default, but selecting this option effectively doubles your file size. If you leave this option deselected, make sure to always save a copy of your file because you won't be able to reopen the SVG file and edit it as a fully editable file.

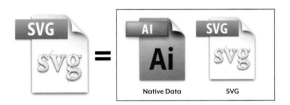

Figure 12.21 *Similar to a PDF file, Illustrator can embed a native version of the file in an SVG document to assure editability when the SVG is reopened in Illustrator.*

- **CSS Properties.** You can format SVG code in a variety of ways, and the CSS Properties options allow you to determine how object attributes are coded in the file. For the most part, these options affect the performance of your file when viewed.

- **Decimal Places.** Illustrator lets you specify how precisely vector paths are drawn. You can choose a value from 1 to 7, where higher numbers result in better-looking paths at the expense of file size and performance.

- **Encoding.** When you save an SVG file that contains text, you can specify a character encoding, including ISO-8859-1 (suitable for European languages) and 8- or 16-bit Unicode (suitable for more complex languages).

- **Optimize for Adobe SVG Viewer.** If people will be using the Adobe SVG Viewer to view your SVG files, you can select this option, which will take advantage of proprietary optimizations that exist in the Adobe SVG Viewer, including faster rendering of SVG filter effects.

- **Include Adobe Graphics Server data.** If you've defined variables in your Illustrator file (using the Variables panel), selecting this option includes those variables in the file. This enables access to variable content when the SVG file is used as a template with Adobe Graphics Server or via Java or ECMAScript otherwise.

- **Include Slicing Data.** If you've specified web slices and optimization settings in your Illustrator document (using the Slice tool or the Object > Slice > Make function), selecting this option preserves the slice information in the file, making it available to other applications.

NOTE Adobe discontinued Adobe Graphics Server in 2008, and some of the functionality has been replaced with Adobe Scene 7. For more information, visit www.adobe.com/products/scene7/creativepros.html.

- **Include XMP.** Selecting this option includes XMP metadata with the file, specified in the File > File Info dialog box. This results in a larger file size.

- **Output fewer <tspan> elements.** This option, selected by default, helps create smaller files, at the risk of text shifting slightly. If you notice errors in the way the text is displayed in your final SVG file, try deselecting this option.

- **Use <textPath> element for Text on Path.** If your document contains text on a path, you can select this option to use the <textPath> function in SVG to display that text. Otherwise, Illustrator writes each character as a separate <text> element in your file, making for a larger (although more precise) SVG file.

- **Show SVG Code and Web Preview.** Clicking either of these buttons launches a web browser and allows you to preview the code and the file itself before you save the file.

Exporting Files from Illustrator

Illustrator is a robust application that supports a wide range of file formats. Although Illustrator does a great job opening just about any graphic file format, it can also export files in different file formats for a plethora of uses. To export a file from Illustrator, choose File > Export, and then choose from one of the many formats listed in the pop-up list in the Export dialog box. Each of these formats is listed in the following sections, with descriptions of their settings as well as when you might want to use them.

Remember that when exporting, it is expected that some level of formatting or editability will be lost, so always save a native Illustrator version of your file before you export to another format.

Saving and Exporting Artboards

Just as you can create single files with multiple artboards, so can you save and export files with them as well.

Choose File > Export, and choose your desired file format. In the Export dialog box, select Use Artboards (**Figure 12.22**), and specify All or a range of artboards to export. When Range is selected, Illustrator will export separate files for each artboard specified. File names will be appended with a 01, 02, 03, and so on. If the Use Artboards option is not selected and your file contains multiple artboards, a single file will be exported with the artboards converted to a single, "conjoined" artboard (**Figure 12.23**).

Figure 12.22 *Choose to export, or not export, multiple artboards.*

Figure 12.23 *Illustrator then creates a separate file from each artboard (left) or a single file from multiple artboards (right).*

The Bitmap (.bmp) Format

Bitmaps are raster-based files that are often used in older applications. Bitmaps are is also used by some applications for displaying logos or bar codes.

When exporting a bitmap, you can choose one of three different color models: RGB, Grayscale, or Bitmap. Bitmap creates a file that contains only black-and-white pixels (**Figure 12.24**). Additionally, you can specify the resolution for your image and choose whether to antialias the art.

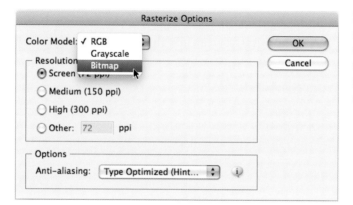

Figure 12.24 *Many applications (including Illustrator and QuarkXPress) allow you to change the color of a bitmap file that uses the Bitmap color model.*

The Targa (.tga) Format

The Targa file format is a raster-based image format used mainly in video applications. For example, you might use the Targa file format to add Illustrator artwork as masks in Adobe Premiere Pro.

When exporting a Targa file, you can choose one of two color models: RGB or Grayscale. Additionally, you can specify the resolution for your image and choose whether to antialias the art.

The Portable Network Graphic (.png) Format

The PNG file format (pronounced "ping") was originally formed as an open standard format to replace the need for the GIF image file format, because of legal complications with those who developed the compression technology used in the GIF format.

As you learned in Chapter 11, you can create PNG files from Illustrator using the Save for Web & Devices feature. However, the PNG format also appears as an export format because the Save for Web & Devices feature is hardwired at 72 ppi. To export a PNG file at any other resolution, you need to use the PNG export function.

PNG is a raster-based image format and is used for web design, icon and interface design, and general image exchange. In fact, recent Apple operating systems (Mac OS X versions 10.4, 10.5, and 10.6) create a PNG file when you take a screen capture. PNG files can support 24-bit color, but more importantly, the format also supports 256-level alpha channels for transparency, meaning you can give images soft edges that fade to transparent (unlike the GIF format, which supports one-color transparency only).

When exporting a PNG file, you can specify your image resolution as well as the background color. You can choose a transparent background, or you can choose Other to select a color from the Color Picker (**Figure 12.25**). Additionally, you can specify antialiasing and interlacing.

Figure 12.25 *You can specify any color as a background color for a PNG file, including transparency.*

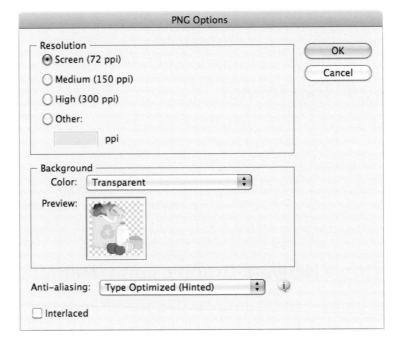

Exporting Art for Use in Microsoft Office Applications

One of the most difficult things to do is create artwork in a professional design application (such as Illustrator) and have that same artwork display and print reliably in a business application such as Microsoft PowerPoint. Finding the right file format for this workflow is difficult because JPEG images don't support transparent backgrounds and EPS files don't display well onscreen. In addition, EPS files require the use of a PostScript printer, which most business professionals do not have.

After much research, the folks on the Illustrator development team discovered that the PNG format was perfect for placing art from Illustrator into Microsoft Office documents. Because the format supports transparent backgrounds and displays beautifully on computer screens, a PNG file set to a resolution high enough to also print well results in great-looking art in Office documents.

To save time and make it easier to quickly export a file from Illustrator to use in Microsoft Office, choose File > Save for Microsoft Office. Illustrator saves your file as a PNG file set to 150 ppi with antialiasing turned on. Once you've created the PNG file, you can place it into any Microsoft Office application by choosing the Insert Picture function in Word, Excel, or PowerPoint (**Figure 12.26**).

Figure 12.26 *To place a PNG file into a Microsoft Office document, choose Insert > Picture > From File when in Word, Excel, or PowerPoint, and locate the file on your computer or server.*

Because of a bug in the Mac OSX version of Microsoft Office, transparency in a PNG file does not appear correctly at the default view setting (it does appear correctly when viewed in full-screen mode and when printed). For this reason, the Save for Microsoft Office command sets the background color to white instead of transparent. If you are placing your art into Microsoft Office for Windows, you can create a PNG with a transparent background by using the PNG Export function.

The AutoCAD Drawing (.dwg) and AutoCAD Interchange File (.dxf) Formats

TIP If you need some of the functionality that CAD applications have, you might look into the CAD tools plug-in from Hot Door, available at www.hotdoor.com.

The DWG and the DXF formats are both used for exchanging files with computer-aided design (CAD) applications. They can be especially helpful when you want to send Illustrator artwork to architects, interior designers, or industrial designers. Both formats support vector and raster elements.

When exporting a DXF or a DWG file (they both use the same export dialog box; **Figure 12.27**), you can specify the version of AutoCAD you want your file to be compatible with and the number of colors in the resulting file. If your file contains raster elements (or if vector elements need to be rasterized), you can choose to have them embedded as either bitmap or JPEG files.

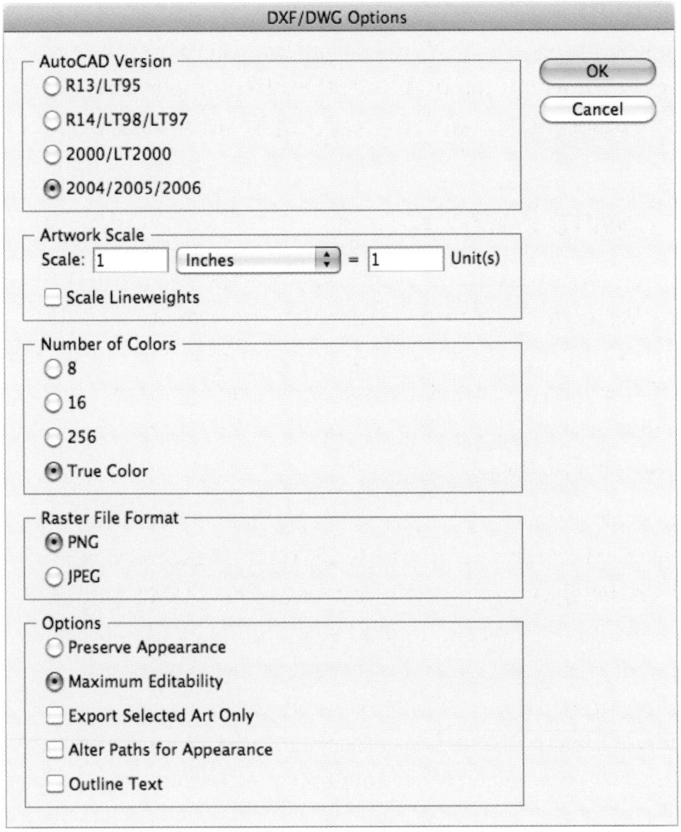

Figure 12.27 *Illustrator uses the same export options dialog box for both DXF and DWG formats.*

Additionally, you can choose to export only the artwork that you currently have selected on the artboard. Selecting Alter Paths for Appearance modifies paths, if necessary, so that they appear when opened in a CAD application. Additionally, you can outline all text to avoid the need to send fonts.

The Windows Metafile (.wmf) and Enhanced Metafile (.emf) Formats

The Windows Metafile (WMF) and Enhanced Metafile (EMF) formats were developed to move graphics between applications on the Windows platform. These two formats support both vector and raster elements but are severely limited with regard to the kinds of art they can reliably display and print (EMF is slightly better). Both formats can create only straight vector lines, not curved ones. To make up for this, curved lines appear as numerous tiny straight paths, which results in large files with many anchor points. If possible, avoid using these formats for anything other than simple artwork. You can't specify any additional options when exporting WMF or EMF files.

The Flash (.swf) Format

SWF is a popular web-based file format that supports both vectors and rasters. The Flash file format has become extremely popular because of its capability to contain interactive or animated content. You can use Illustrator to generate a SWF file that you want to upload directly to a website, use in a Flex framework rich Internet application (RIA), or even place into InDesign for creating interactive PDF files.

The SWF Options dialog box contains "just a few" options for creating the SWF files that are right for you (**Figure 12.28**, on the next page). Along the right side of the dialog box are options to save presets of SWF output settings, to preview your SWF in your default web browser, and to preview your SWF using Adobe Device Central. The SWF Options dialog box is actually split into two separate panels labeled Basic and Advanced, which you can access by clicking their respective buttons that appear underneath the Cancel button along the right side of the dialog box.

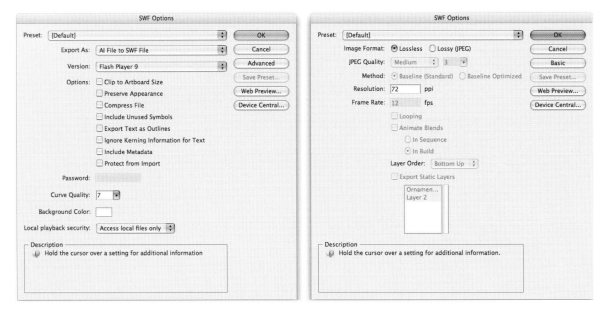

Figure 12.28 *The Flash export dialog box in Illustrator has so many options that there's a Basic button and an Advanced button that are used to toggle between two full panels.*

Basic Options

The options in the Basic panel of the SWF Options dialog box are general settings that apply to most SWF files:

- **Export As.** You can export Illustrator files in one of four ways: AI File to SWF File, which creates a single SWF file that contains all your Illustrator artwork; AI Layers to SWF Frames, where each layer is converted into a key frame, resulting in a single animated SWF file; AI Layers to SWF Files, where each layer in your Illustrator document is exported as a separate SWF file (useful when you are creating Flash scenes); and AI Layers to SWF Symbols.

- **Version.** You can export a SWF that is compatible with any available version of Flash Player. The default is Flash Player 9, which is present on more than 98 percent of computers that access the Internet.

- **Options.** A variety of general settings appear in this section. You can choose to export your SWF at the exact size of your artboard or active crop area. If your file contains artwork that may not translate to the SWF format perfectly, you can select Preserve Appearance to expand or rasterize those areas to ensure the integrity of the appearance of your art. Compressing a file will result in a smaller SWF. You can choose to include all symbols in your resulting SWF (even if they aren't used on the artboard), have your text converted to outlines, and ignore kerning that you may have applied to text. You can also choose to enclose metadata (from information you've entered using the File > File Info function) and protect the resulting SWF file from being opened in Flash by applying a password.

- **Curve Quality.** This setting controls the quality level for curved paths in the resulting SWF file.

- **Background Color.** This setting allows you to specify a background color for the SWF file.

- **Local playback security.** You can choose whether the SWF file can access local or network files only.

Advanced Options

The options found in the Advanced panel of the SWF Options dialog box are settings that apply to rasterized portions of a file and animated content:

- **Image Format.** If there is raster content in your file (or if flattening requires that content becomes rasterized), you can choose how those images are stored in your SWF file—either using a lossless format or a lossy format. If you choose the lossy format, which is JPEG, you can choose a JPEG quality and the Baseline setting. You can also choose the resolution you want your raster content to use (usually 72 ppi).

  The rest of the options in the Advanced panel of the SWF Options dialog box are specific to animated SWF content. Therefore, they are available only when choosing the AI Layers to SWF Frames option in the Export As pop-up menu in the Basic panel of the dialog box.

- **Frame Rate.** This setting controls how fast the animation plays and is measured in frames per second (although in the context of Illustrator, they are actually layers per second). A lower value will slow down the animation, while a higher value will cause the animation to play faster.

- **Looping.** Selecting this option causes the animation to repeat itself endlessly.

- **Animate Blends.** If your Illustrator file contains any blends, selecting this option will automatically animate those blends in the resulting SWF file. This setting allows you to keep blends live and editable in your Illustrator file and still get the desired animated result. Otherwise, you would have to use the Release to Layers function in your Illustrator file to manually create the content necessary to create an animation. You can choose to have blends animate either as a sequence (each frame appears individually, one after the other) or as a build (each frame appears successively, adding to the previous one).

- **Layer Order.** By default, Illustrator animates layers from the bottom up, but you can alternatively select the Top Down option.

- **Export Static Layers.** Static layers are those that appear in every frame of the animation. If you select this option, you can Command-click (Ctrl-click) any layers that you want visible throughout the entire animation. For example, if you had an animation of a bird flying across a cloudy sky, you might set the layers that contain the sky and cloud elements to export as static layers.

For an in-depth discussion of how you can create great-looking SWF files, including adding interactive hotspots and animations, refer to Chapter 11.

The Joint Photographic Experts Group (.jpg) Format

An extremely popular raster-based format, JPEG files are used mainly for exchanging photographic content and artwork. Although the JPEG format is used heavily in web design, it is also the format of choice for the electronic delivery of stock photographs and for digital cameras. One of the reasons why JPEG is used for these tasks is because the JPEG format can take advantage of compression algorithms that can dramatically reduce file size. For example, a high-resolution image that is normally 10 MB in size might be only 1 MB in size when saved as a JPEG.

However, the JPEG format uses a lossy compression algorithm, and sometimes a JPEG file may exhibit artifacts or loss in detail because of this compression (**Figure 12.29**). A lower compression setting enhances image detail, at the cost of a larger file size.

Although you can save JPEG files from the Save for Web & Devices feature in Illustrator, you can do so only at 72 ppi. Using the JPEG Export function, you can specify a custom resolution for your file, which allows you to create high-resolution files.

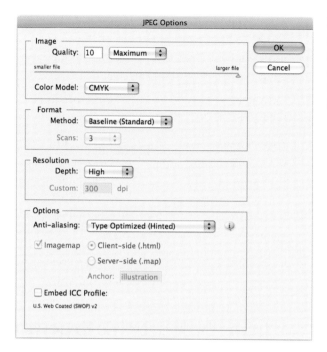

Figure 12.29 *When saving a file as a JPEG, using the Maximum setting results in a file with fewer artifacts, but doing so also results in a larger file size.*

Besides choosing an image compression level for your file, you can also specify the RGB, CMYK, or grayscale color model. Format methods determine how the image appears when viewed in a web browser. If you choose the Baseline setting, the image loads completely and is then displayed at full resolution. The Progressive setting (similar to interlacing) allows the image to appear immediately at a lower-quality setting; it then appears in full quality once the entire image is loaded (the number of scans determines how many passes are done until the final image is previewed).

Illustrator also gives you the options of antialiasing the art, embedding a color profile, and including a client-side or server-side image map. Refer to Chapter 11 for more information on how to define image maps and the differences between client-side and server-side image maps.

The Macintosh PICT (.pct) Format

Much like the WMF and EMF formats, the PICT format was developed to move files between applications on the Mac OS platform. The format supports both vector and raster elements. You can't specify any additional options when exporting a PICT file.

The Adobe Photoshop (.psd) Format

As you learned in Chapter 10, "Working with Images," you can export an Illustrator file as a Photoshop PSD file and preserve vital information. This makes it easy to start work on a design piece in Illustrator and then bring it into Photoshop to add the finishing touches. Bringing Illustrator art into Photoshop is also useful when you're creating art that you plan to use for websites. In this way, you have high-quality artwork in Illustrator that can easily be repurposed for print, and you can add rollovers and interactivity using Photoshop or even Fireworks or Flash Professional for the website.

When exporting a PSD file, you can choose between the CMYK, RGB, and grayscale color models, and you can specify a resolution for your file. If you choose to export a flat image, all Illustrator layers are flattened into a single nontransparent layer (what Photoshop calls the Background layer). Alternatively, you can select the Write Layers option that preserves layering in Illustrator where possible (**Figure 12.30**). You can also choose to preserve text and other native elements, such as compound shapes and web slices (see Chapter 10 for a complete list of the attributes that can be preserved between Illustrator and Photoshop).

Figure 12.30 *By choosing to write layers, you gain the ability to export a file that preserves live text, layers, transparency, and mask effects, and more.*

The Tagged Image File Format (.tif)

The TIFF format is widely used in graphics applications. Completely raster-based, a TIFF is a lossless image format. High-resolution files can be quite large, but image integrity is maintained. TIFF files are generally supported by print, video, and 3D-rendering applications.

When exporting a TIFF, you can choose one of three different color models: RGB, CMYK, or grayscale. Additionally, you can specify the resolution for your image and choose whether to antialias the art. Selecting the LZW Compression option results in a smaller file (the compression is lossless). You can also specify a platform-specific byte order (for better compatibility with Windows systems), and you have the ability to embed color profiles when you're working in a color-managed workflow.

The Text Format (.txt)

Sometimes you just need to export the text in a file so you can use it in another application or for another purpose that Illustrator can't handle. You can export text to be compatible with a specific platform, or you can export text in Unicode, which is platform independent.

Choosing File Formats Based on Workflow

So many different file formats exist that it's often difficult to know which one to use for each situation. Of course, every workflow demands special attention, and there are always exceptions and special cases. However, for the most part, you can follow certain rules now that you really understand what each file format is capable of doing.

Print Workflows

In print workflows, designers traditionally use page layout applications such as QuarkXPress or InDesign, using file formats such as EPS and PDF.

Traditionally, EPS is used for moving files from Illustrator into page layout applications. However, with the ability to use transparency effects in your

Illustrator files, the limitations of EPS become apparent. For example, as a designer, you know that Illustrator creates vector-based files that can be scaled infinitely because they are resolution independent. You have always been able to save a file as an EPS from Illustrator, place it into an application such as QuarkXPress, scale that artwork at will, and never worry about resolution or the quality of the resulting printout.

NOTE As of the printing of this book, the latest version of QuarkXPress, version 8, has the ability to place native Illustrator files (.ai). However, according to initial tests, Illustrator files with complex transparency do not print correctly when printed from QuarkXPress 8. The recommendation is still to use the EPS file format when placing art into QuarkXPress.

However, as you will discover in Chapter 13, the process of transparency flattening may convert some vector content in your file into raster images, which are resolution dependent. Because an EPS contains flattened information, you can't assume that an EPS file can be scaled infinitely in a QuarkXPress layout anymore. In fact, you have to think of an EPS file from Illustrator as you would an EPS file saved from Photoshop—you need to limit how much you can enlarge a graphic.

Although this is a concern only when your file contains transparency effects, keep in mind that many effects in Illustrator introduce the need for flattening (these are discussed in detail in Chapter 13).

Native Illustrator files (that contain PDF 1.5 by default) have the ability to preserve live transparency, and therefore, flattening doesn't occur. When you save your file as a native Illustrator file, you can still scale that file infinitely, after it has been placed into a page layout application. But this has a catch—you need a page layout application that can flatten that transparency when it prints your file. That means InDesign. Refer to **Table 12.2** for a list of suggested file formats, based on the page layout application you're using.

Table 12.2 *Suggested File Formats*

Application	When Transparency Is Present	When Transparency Is Not Present
QuarkXPress	EPS, Native AI (Quark Version 8), PDF/X-1a (PDF 1.3)	EPS, PDF/X-1a (PDF 1.3)
InDesign	Native AI, PDF 1.4	EPS, Native AI, PDF 1.4

Web Workflows

The choices are much easier to make for web designers. This is not because there are any fewer file types to choose from; it's mainly because the use of file types is usually dictated by the technology. For example, if you want to create animated content, you know you're using a GIF file or a SWF file.

There are some restrictions as to what kinds of formats are supported (for example, not every web browser can display SVG files), so a designer is usually at the mercy of technology when it comes to deciding on a file format.

However, much can be done to a file before a final GIF or JPEG is created. You may find it beneficial to create your artwork in Illustrator and then export it as a PSD file, which you can then edit and work on in other applications, such as Photoshop or even Fireworks or Dreamweaver.

Other Workflows

Of course, other workflows exist, including video, industrial design, architecture and engineering, fashion design, environmental design—the list goes on. With the information you now have about what each file format is used for, you should be able to develop a workflow that works for you.

Prepress and Printing 13

Nothing is more frustrating than spending hours designing the perfect piece of art only to have it come back from the printer not looking the way you expected it to look. Many times, we take printing for granted and assume that whatever we design will reproduce in print the exact way we see it on our computer screens. Achieving consistent color across multiple devices is one challenge (which good color management strategies can help control). Even more challenging are features such as transparency, live effects, and overprint settings; these can turn what seems like an ordinary print job into a weekend-long nightmare.

In reality, you need to think about printing when you first start working on a design. If you work with a printer regularly, the printer will help you figure out things in advance, including spot colors, page settings, folds, and a host of other issues. Although you certainly don't always have the luxury of knowing who the printer is before a job gets started, you can still spend a few moments at the onset of a project carefully reviewing the details; this alone can make a huge difference. Every job has its own specific requirements, and you should always feel comfortable asking an experienced printer or production artist for advice.

Whether you're a designer, a prepress operator, or a printer, this chapter is for you. This chapter discusses everything you need to know about printing files, using transparency, and using overprints—which will help you plan for the best results every time.

The artwork featured throughout this chapter comes from Sam Posnick (iStockphoto; username: sposnick).

Printing from Illustrator

Printing a file should be a straightforward experience, but it wasn't always that way in Illustrator. Prior to Illustrator CS, getting a file to print correctly often meant opening the Page Setup dialog box, the Document Setup dialog box, and the Print dialog box. When Adobe released Illustrator CS, however, it updated the Illustrator printing engine and interface and modeled them after the Print dialog box in InDesign. Ever since that version, you can go directly to the Print dialog box and control all your print specifications in one place.

Because every print job is different and has specific requirements, the contents of this chapter are organized to match the order in which print features appear in the Print dialog box. In this way, you can read the chapter now and use it as a handy reference later.

Exploring the General Print Panel

While you're designing a job, printing quick and accurate proofs to your laser or ink-jet printer is just as important as printing final output to an imagesetter. For this reason, you'll find that Adobe put many often-used settings in the General panel of the Print dialog box (**Figure 13.1**). This way, you can quickly print consistent and accurate files from Illustrator without having to dance between multiple dialog boxes or panels. At the top of the Print dialog box you'll find a pop-up to choose from predefined print presets (you'll learn more about print presets later in this chapter), a pop-up to choose which printer you want to print to (extremely useful for those who have several different printers at their disposal), and a pop-up to choose a PostScript Printer Definition (PPD) file.

TIP One of the options available in the Printer pop-up is Adobe PostScript File, which allows you to print your document as a PostScript file that can then be downloaded directly to a printer or converted to PDF using Acrobat Distiller.

A PPD file contains specific information about a printer, including media dimensions, color information, and printer-specific settings such as resolution. Illustrator makes an educated guess about the right PPD file for your selected printer, although you can override it and choose your own if you want (however, if you're not familiar with PPD files, it's best to leave this setting alone). You can choose a PPD only when an Adobe PostScript device is selected as your printer.

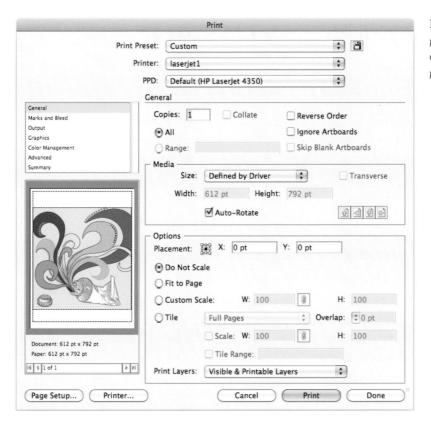

Figure 13.1 *The General panel in the Print dialog box contains the most often used print settings.*

Along the left side of the Print dialog box is a list of all the panels you can choose from to specify a range of print options. Beneath the list of panels is a print preview that gives you a better idea of what will print. But this is no ordinary print preview—it's interactive. You can drag the artwork around in the preview to determine which part of the paper the art will print on. By holding the Shift key while dragging, you can constrain movement to the X or Y axis; by double-clicking the preview, you can reset the positioning to the default. As you specify changes in the Print dialog box, such as adding trim marks, you'll see those changes appear in the preview as well.

Setting Basic Print Options

As in just about any other program, in the Print dialog box you can specify the number of copies as well as the range of pages (or artboards) you want to print. This is especially handy now that Illustrator bestows multiple artboards to its faithful users. When you specify a range of artboards, use a comma as a separation device and a hyphen to indicate a continuous string

NOTE The items we've discussed to this point appear across the top and along the left side of the Print dialog box and are always visible no matter which panel of the dialog box is active.

of artboards. For example, you can specify a range of 1-3, 6, which will print artboards 1, 2, 3, and 6 (**Figure 13.2**).

Figure 13.2 *If your document contains multiple artboards, you can click the left and right arrows under the preview to view how each page will print.*

In addition to page range, you can specify the following options when printing your artboards:

- **Reverse Order.** This option prints your last artboard first and your first artboard last.

- **Ignore Artboards.** If you do not select this option, Illustrator will print each of the artboards in your document. If you select this option, Illustrator will not print separate pages for each artboard. Instead, Illustrator will treat all artwork as one single large artboard (determined by the total bounding area of all the art), as shown in **Figure 13.3**.

Figure 13.3 *You can choose to print each artboard separately or ignore artboards altogether.*

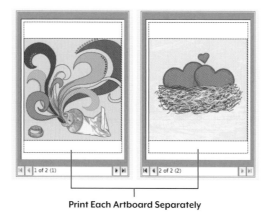

Print Each Artboard Separately

Ignore Artboards

- **Skip Blank Artboards.** If you have artboards that haven't been filled with artwork yet, save paper by selecting this option.

In the Media section of the dialog box, you can specify the size of the paper on which you want to print. The items that appear in this pop-up menu are defined by the PPD file that is chosen for your printer. If your printer supports it, you'll also have the ability to define custom media sizes; being able to do so is extremely useful with large-format ink-jet printers or for printing to imagesetters or platesetters. Checking the Auto-Rotate option will automatically print pages at their correct orientation, which is perfect for documents that contain artboards with both landscape and portrait settings. Additionally, you can choose an orientation to flip a page on its side. Changing the orientation can be extremely important when printers want to choose which side of a sheet the press will grip. It can also be useful when printing to a large-format printer that uses rolls of paper, enabling you to save paper by positioning your document to use the longer side of the roll.

You can use the Print Layers pop-up menu to specify which kinds of layers will or won't print: Visible & Printable Layers, Visible Layers, or All Layers. Additionally, you can set a custom scale size at which to print your file. The Do Not Scale option prints your file at actual size, the Fit to Page option reduces or enlarges your artwork so that it fills the entire size of the output media, and the Custom Scale setting lets you specify any scale size for the height or the width. The Placement option lets you reposition your artwork on the artboard either by entering values in the X and Y fields or by manually dragging your artwork in the preview window.

Using Page Tiling

Page tiling was initially added to Illustrator to let users print a single large file across several smaller pages. This allowed a designer to assemble a large document at the actual size using a printer with smaller media sizes. However, over the years, designers learned to use this feature to create a single large artboard, using the tiled areas as a substitute for multiple pages. For example, setting up a document at 11 by 17 inches with page tiling would result in two 8.5-by-11-inch pages. Now, of course, with multiple artboards, this workaround is unnecessary.

You can now choose from two page tiling settings (**Figure 13.4**):

TIP When you're using Tile Full Pages or Tile Imageable Areas, each tile is assigned a number, and you can specify which tiles you want to print by entering a tile number in the Page Range field in the General panel of the Print dialog box.

- **Tile Full Pages.** The Tile Full Pages option divides a single artboard into multiple sections, or *tiles*. Each tile matches the media size you choose in the General panel of the Print dialog box, and Illustrator creates as many of those tiles as necessary to cover the entire document. Tile Full Pages also allows you to specify an Overlap value in case your printer doesn't print to the edge of each sheet.

- **Tile Imageable Areas.** The Tile Imageable Areas option divides one artboard into multiple tiles. Tiles match the media size you choose in the General panel of the Print dialog box where possible, and Illustrator creates custom-sized tiles as necessary to tile the entire document.

To tile a document with multiple artboards, you must select the Ignore Artboards option.

Figure 13.4 *Tiling enables you to print large artwork on smaller sheets of paper that you can then assemble manually.*

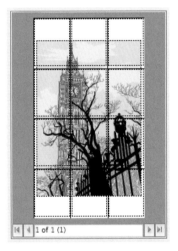

Because tiling is something you might want to set in your document before you even start working, be aware of the Done button at the bottom of the Print dialog box. Clicking Done keeps the settings you've made in the Print dialog box and returns you to the document for further editing and designing without actually printing the file. Although it may seem odd to open the Print dialog box to specify tiling settings, remember that the main reason for tiling in Illustrator is specific to printing.

Exploring the Marks and Bleed Print Panel

When printing a page for final output, you need to add page marks and bleeds to help printers print the job correctly on press. *Trim marks* tell a printer where to cut the paper, *registration marks* help a printer align each separated plate correctly, *color bars* help a printer calibrate color correctly on press, and *page information* makes it possible for printers to easily identify each separated plate (**Figure 13.5**).

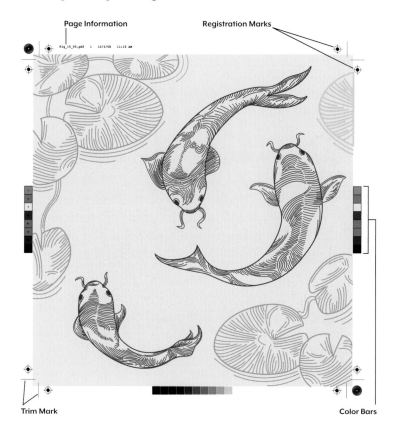

Figure 13.5 *A printer uses a variety of printer marks to help ensure that the job prints correctly.*

Of course, you don't always need all this information on each printout, so you choose them individually (for example, on a one-color job, registration marks aren't necessary). Additionally, you can choose between Roman- and Japanese-style trim marks. The trim mark weight determines the width of the strokes used to create trim marks, and the offset determines how far from the page the trim marks will appear.

When you have artwork that extends beyond the boundary of a page, you can specify a bleed setting to ensure that the printable area of the page

NOTE Page marks print outside the margins of the artboard (or wherever you've defined a crop area), so you need to make sure the media size you've chosen in the General panel of the Print dialog box is large enough to include the page marks. If you select the Fit to Page option, Illustrator scales the entire document to ensure that the trim marks print on the chosen page.

includes the extra bleed area. When the bleed settings are set to zero, even if you've extended artwork beyond the boundary of the artboard, the art clips to the edge of the artboard. Additionally, if you specify a bleed setting, you'll need to print to a paper size large enough to display the page size and the bleed as well. For more information on bleeds, see the sidebar "Adding Bleed" in Chapter 1, "Creating and Managing Documents." If you've already specified a bleed setting in the New Document or Document Setup dialog box, you can select Use Document Bleed Settings to apply those settings here.

Exploring the Output Print Panel

The Output panel in the Print dialog box is a prepress operator's dream come true. With the ability to specify color separations and control the behavior of inks, a print service provider can output Illustrator files with confidence.

Illustrator supports three printing modes, each of which is used for a different workflow (**Figure 13.6**):

> **NOTE** A raster image processor is the software in a printer, imagesetter, or platesetter that converts all art into dots so that it can be printed.

- **Composite.** When you choose the Composite setting, Illustrator sends a single composite of the artwork, with all colors appearing on the same page, to the printer or raster image processor (RIP). This is the setting you would use to create any kind of black-and-white or grayscale printout, as well as any color proof printout.

- **Separations (Host-Based).** When you choose the Separations (Host-Based) setting, Illustrator (the host) separates the artwork into the required number of plates (specified in the Document Ink Options settings mentioned shortly) and sends each plate to the printer or RIP as a separate page. This is the setting you use if you want to proof color-separated artwork. A prepress operator or printer also uses this setting to create final film or plates from your artwork.

- **In-RIP Separations.** When you choose the In-RIP Separations setting, Illustrator sends a single composite of the artwork to the RIP so that the RIP can perform the color separation instead of Illustrator. All the Document Ink Options and separation-specific settings become available so you can still control the inks that will print on the composite. This is the setting you use to take advantage of proprietary trapping, screening, and separations software present in your RIP.

Figure 13.6 *Printing a composite is perfect for proofing (top). Printing separations is required for printing colors on a printing press (four underlying pages).*

Specifying Color Separations

If you choose either of the two separations print modes, you can specify additional options for how the color separations will print.

You can choose to print with the right reading emulsion up or down, and you can choose whether to print a positive or negative image. You'll notice that as you choose these settings, the interactive print preview updates to show you how the art will print. You can also choose a printer resolution; these settings are specific to the printer to which you've to print. This information comes from the PPD file chosen for your printer or RIP.

If your file contains spot colors, you can convert them all to separate as process colors by selecting the Convert All Spot Colors to Process option. This option is even available when you're printing composite proofs.

When you select the Overprint Black option, all objects that are colored 100% K overprint. See "Understanding Overprints" later in this chapter for more information about overprinting.

Previewing Separations Before You Print

The great news is that Illustrator has a Separations Preview panel. The bad news is that it's not much more than a bare-bones implementation. Like the panels found in InDesign and Acrobat, the Separations Preview panel in Illustrator enables you to preview individual color separations for both process and spot colors (**Figure 13.8**) onscreen. Choose Window > Separations Preview to open the panel, and then select Overprint Preview to turn the feature on. Then, simply click the display or hide icon (eye) of your desired color to view or hide that plate. However, that's where the similarities stop. Illustrator doesn't "sense" what colors are actually being used in the document. For example, if you add five Pantone spot colors to your file but use only one, all five are listed in the Separations Preview panel, even though you didn't use the other four. In addition, you do not have options for viewing ink coverage percentages, areas with varnishes, and other valuable print settings that you find in the Separations Preview panels in InDesign and Acrobat.

In the Document Ink Options section of the Output panel, you can specify which plates are sent to the printer and which settings each plate uses (**Figure 13.7**). Colors that appear with a printer icon on the far left print. To prevent an ink color from printing, click the printer icon to remove it. Inks that appear with a four-color icon separate as process colors. Inks that appear with a solid color icon print to their own plates as a spot (custom) color. Clicking a solid color icon causes just that color to separate as a process color. Additionally, you can specify custom Frequency, Angle, and Dot Shape settings for each ink.

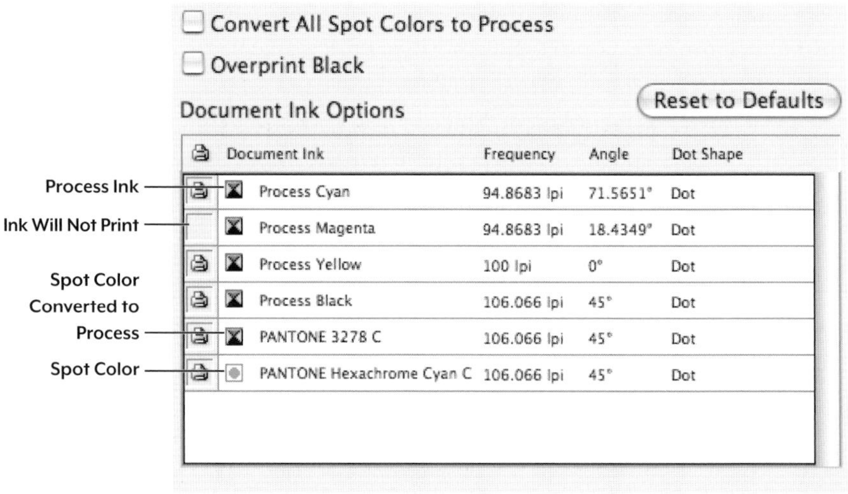

Figure 13.7 *The different icons that display in the Document Ink Options section of the Output panel indicate how the inks print.*

Previewing Separations Before You Print

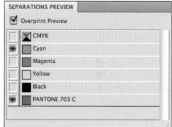

Figure 13.8 *The Separations Preview panel lets you view each color plate onscreen.*

Exploring the Graphics Print Panel

The settings in the Graphics panel of the Print dialog box are mainly for specifying options for your print device.

Prior to the release of Illustrator CS, the Document Setup dialog box contained an Object Resolution setting that determined the flatness setting for Bézier paths at output time. In CS versions of Illustrator the flatness setting is set by default, based on information from the selected PPD file. You can override this setting and use the slider to sacrifice path quality for print performance (although it's best to leave this setting alone).

By default, Illustrator downloads subsets of fonts to the printer when you print a file. *Downloading a subset* simply means that Illustrator sends only the parts of a font that are required to print the text in your document. For example, if you have the word *me* in your document, Illustrator sends only the letters *m* and *e* to the printer instead of the entire font (this practice speeds up print times). You can override this behavior and choose Complete, which forces Illustrator to download the entire font to the printer at print time. Alternatively, you can choose not to download any fonts at all. You choose this option if you have fonts installed in your printer (some printers can contain hard drives and store fonts internally).

TIP If you have prob-
lems printing Illustrator
files to older print devices, try
selecting the Compatible
Gradient and Gradient Mesh
Printing options.

By default, Illustrator chooses a PostScript language level that your selected printer will support. LanguageLevel 3 PostScript can print documents with transparency more reliably, and it contains smooth shading technology that helps prevent banding from appearing in gradients. You can also choose to send data to the printer in ASCII or in the default binary format.

As discussed in Chapter 7, "Working with Live Effects," the resolution at which live effects are rasterized is determined by the setting in the Document Raster Effects Settings dialog box. Here in the Graphics panel of the Print dialog box, Illustrator displays the current setting in that dialog box, allowing you to double-check to make sure the setting is indeed correct for printing (**Figure 13.9**). Illustrator won't allow you to change the setting from the Print dialog box because changing the resolution setting may change the appearance of your artwork. To change the resolution setting, click the Done button in the Print dialog box, and choose Effect > Document Raster Effects Settings. You can then return to the Print dialog box to print your file.

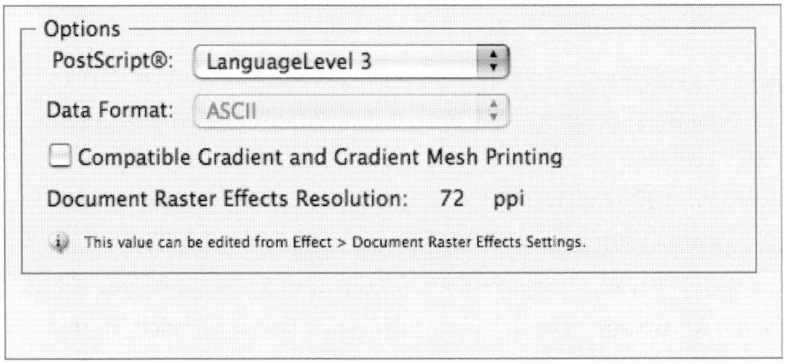

Figure 13.9 *Although you can't change the Document Raster Effects Resolution setting from the Print dialog box, the Graphics panel does alert you to the current setting in case you need to make a change.*

Exploring the Color Management Print Panel

The topic of color management really requires a book of its own. In fact, if you really want to learn everything there is to know about color management, you should check out *Real World Color Management, Second Edition,* by Bruce Fraser, Chris Murphy, and Fred Bunting (Peachpit Press, 2005).

However, within the scope of the book you are reading now are some brief explanations for the settings found in the Color Management panel of the Print dialog box:

- **Document Profile.** The Document Profile setting displays the color profile that is currently embedded (or assumed) in the file. If you didn't manually choose one, the profile you see here is the profile that is chosen in the Color Settings dialog box.

- **Color Handling.** The Color Handling setting allows you to determine whether Illustrator will perform any necessary color adjustments (based on the chosen printer profile) or whether your printer will handle any required conversion on its own. Unless you are working within a proprietary workflow system, you should always let Illustrator determine colors, not the printer.

- **Printer Profile.** When the Color Handling option is set to Let Illustrator Determine Colors, the Printer Profile setting lets you specify a profile for your printer. This gives Illustrator the information it needs to change colors so they look correct on your printer. If the Color Handling option is set to Let PostScript Printer Determine Colors, the Printer Profile setting is not applicable.

- **Rendering Intent.** If some colors in your document cannot be reproduced on a given output device, the colors are considered *out of gamut* and must be converted to colors that will reproduce on the output device. There are different methods for converting these colors, and the Rendering Intent setting determines the method used. The most commonly used method, Relative Colorimetric, moves out-of-gamut colors to the closest possible color that will print on the device. It also adjusts other colors so that colors appear to be accurate. The Absolute Colorimetric setting adjusts only out-of-gamut colors and may result in *posterization*, where many shades of similar colors are used. The Perceptual method shifts colors so that they appear correct relative to each other, but it may not represent colors as being the most accurate match to the original values. The Saturation method enhances colors and makes them more vibrant and most suitable for business presentations where bright colors are more important than accurate colors.

- **Preserve CMYK Numbers.** The Preserve CMYK Numbers setting is active only when Color Handling is set to the Let PostScript Printer Determine Colors option. With Preserve CMYK Numbers active, color values remain untouched in native artwork and text components.

Exploring the Advanced Print Panel

The Advanced panel in the Print dialog box gives you control over important settings such as overprinting and transparency flattening.

If your document contains overprint settings, you can choose from one of three settings to control overprint behavior:

- **Preserve.** The Preserve option leaves all overprints intact in your file.

- **Discard.** The Discard option strips your file of any overprint commands. Those who have proprietary production systems or advanced trapping software in their RIPs will find this option useful. Rather than use a designer's overprint settings, the trapping software applies and determines all overprint behavior.

- **Simulate.** The Simulate option, available only when printing composite proofs, simulates overprints in the printout, giving the correct appearance of the final output in the proof.

If your document contains transparency, you can choose from a list of predefined transparency flattener presets. Illustrator ships with three presets called Low Resolution, Medium Resolution, and High Resolution, but you can also define your own custom option for your particular print session by choosing Edit > Transparency Flattener Presets. For detailed information about what these settings are used for and what the differences between them are, see the section "Learning the Truth About Transparency," below.

Defining Print Presets

As you've undoubtedly seen, the Print dialog box in Illustrator contains a plethora of settings, and going through each panel to make sure the settings are correct is an exercise in patience. *Print presets* allow you to capture all

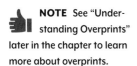

NOTE The Print as Bitmap option is available for non-PostScript printers only and rasterizes all artwork in your file for printing.

NOTE See "Understanding Overprints" later in the chapter to learn more about overprints.

NOTE If you delete your application preferences, you won't lose your saved print presets.

the options set in the different Print dialog box panels so that you can easily retrieve those settings at any time. To create a print preset, click the Save Preset button (the disk icon) at the top right of the Print dialog box; to manage your presets, choose Edit > Print Presets. Print presets are saved in XML and are cross-platform, so you can import and export them and distribute them among others.

Learning the Truth About Transparency

Illustrator contains several features that use transparency, including the ability to specify blending modes and opacity masks with the Transparency panel and via effects such as Feather and Drop Shadow. Transparency as a feature in Illustrator (and InDesign as well) requires closer attention when it comes to printing documents. In fact, Illustrator, InDesign, and Adobe Acrobat all use the same methods to print with transparency, so the concepts you learn here apply to all those applications as well.

You may have heard that printing with transparency is problematic, but a lot has changed since transparency was first introduced in Illustrator 9. Once you understand what happens to a file with transparency and you learn about a few simple settings, you won't have to worry about printing issues when you're using transparency features.

In truth, transparency has always been around—in raster form—in Photoshop. The only difference now is that you can apply these effects in vector form and still edit them late in your workflow. At the end of the day, these transparency effects will become rasterized, leaving you with the same result as if you had done everything in Photoshop. In any case, let's take a closer look at what transparency is and how it works.

Understanding Transparency Flattening

Let's start with a simple fact: PostScript doesn't understand transparency. As you probably know, PostScript is the language that printers and RIPs speak. Native transparency is understood only by PDF language version 1.4 or newer (first present in Acrobat 5 and Illustrator 9).

NOTE If you've used Photoshop before, you may be familiar with the term *flattening*, which combines all layers in a document. Although similar in concept, transparency flattening is different.

To print objects with transparency, Illustrator must "translate" any transparent artwork into a language that PostScript understands. This translation process is called *transparency flattening*.

The process of flattening is simple, and Illustrator follows two cardinal rules when performing flattening on a file:

1. All transparency in the file must be removed.

2. While performing rule #1, the appearance of the file cannot change.

Both of these rules are followed during the flattening process, with no exception. Obviously, all transparency has to be removed because PostScript doesn't know what transparency is. Additionally, if removing the transparency would result in your file changing in appearance, that would mean you could design something in Illustrator that couldn't be printed, which doesn't make sense either. If you think about it, if you're removing transparency from the file and you're also keeping the visual appearance of the object, something has to give, and that something is the editability of your file. Let's take a look at an example of this.

Flattening Artwork

Let's try an example of flattening:

1. Draw two different-colored circles, one overlapping the other.

2. Set the top circle to Multiply (**Figure 13.10**).

   The nice feature of transparency is that you can move the top circle around or change its color, and any overlapping areas will simply multiply. The problem is that PostScript doesn't know what transparency is and doesn't know how to print that overlapping area, so transparency flattening is required.

Figure 13.10 *By setting the top circle to the Multiply blending mode, you can see through it to the circle below, even with Opacity set to 100%.*

3. Select both circles, choose Object > Flatten Transparency, and click OK (don't worry about the dialog box, which we'll get to later).

    The file is now flattened. Does it look any different? It can't, because of rule #2, but the file now no longer contains any transparency and can be printed on a PostScript device. The difference is that the file is no longer editable as it was before it was flattened. Upon selecting the circles, you'll find that the two transparent circles have now been broken up into three individual opaque shapes (**Figure 13.11**).

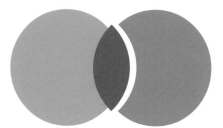

*Figure 13.11 Once the objects are flattened, the artwork is split up into individual opaque pieces, called **atomic regions**.*

This flattening process happens every time you print something with transparency. However, the flattening happens in the print stream, not to your actual Illustrator file. When you choose to print a file, Illustrator flattens a copy of your file and sends the flattened file to the printer, while leaving your document intact. It wouldn't be good if simply printing a file rendered it uneditable. In our example, we specifically flattened the file using the flatten transparency function to see the results, but under normal circumstances, you would not flatten the transparency manually—Illustrator would do that for you automatically at print time.

So, when you print a file with transparency, this flattening process occurs so that a PostScript printer can print the file correctly, and this process happens on the way to the printer, so your Illustrator file is not affected in any way.

The example of the two overlapping circles is a simple case of flattening. But other examples can display certain side effects. Let's explore such a case.

NOTE Flattening also happens whenever you save or export your file to a format that doesn't understand transparency. For example, EPS (which is PostScript) and PDF 1.3 do not support transparency.

Flattening with Rasterization

Let's create another example:

1. As in the previous example, create two overlapping circles.

2. Set the top circle to Multiply.

3. Fill each circle with a linear gradient, but in one of the circles, apply the gradient on a 45-degree angle.

The result is two circles with gradients, but the area in which these two shapes overlap appears as two gradients traveling in different directions (**Figure 13.12**).

Figure 13.12 *This figure shows two overlapping circles, each filled with a gradient on a different angle.*

When this file is flattened, you know that the result will be three separate shapes as in the previous example; however, this example is a bit different. Although gradients can be preserved in vector form, there's no way to describe a crisscross gradient, like you see in the overlapping area, as a vector. Because of rule #2, Illustrator is not allowed to change the appearance of your file during flattening, so the only course of action Illustrator can take is to turn that overlapping area into a raster image.

4. Select both circles, choose Object > Flatten Transparency, and click OK.

    You'll find that although the file looks the same, it now consists of two vector shapes and a raster image in the middle. Illustrator creates a vector mask for the middle shape so that the file will print correctly (raster images are always rectangular in shape). It's important to point out that Illustrator didn't raster the entire file; it merely rasterized the portion of the file that could not be preserved in vector form (**Figure 13.13**).

Figure 13.13 *Where appearance can't be preserved in vector form, Illustrator converts parts of a file into a raster.*

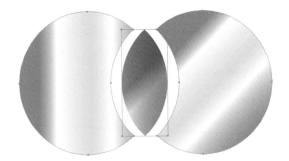

At this point, a question should be forming in your mind: If part of the file is now a raster image, what is the resolution of that raster? Patience, young Padawan; we'll get to that soon. Here's a review of what you've learned to this point:

- Transparency flattening is required to correctly print a file with transparency to a PostScript device.

- Transparency flattening happens automatically, in the print stream, when you print a file with transparency from Illustrator, InDesign, Acrobat, or Adobe Reader.

- Transparency flattening may cause certain parts of a vector file to become rasterized to prevent a file from changing in appearance.

Using the Two Levels of Rasterization

In the previous example, where two vector shapes resulted in a portion of that file becoming rasterized, Illustrator had no choice but to rasterize the middle region because there was simply no other way to preserve the appearance in vector form. This is one level of rasterization.

However, in some cases a second level of rasterization may occur, even if the appearance of a file could be preserved in vector form. Before printing a file, Illustrator analyzes the entire document and looks for *complex regions* containing many overlapping objects (which would result in a large number of atomic regions). Illustrator may then choose to rasterize those complex regions for performance reasons. Although we've been trained to think vector objects are simpler than their bitmapped counterparts, try to imagine an Illustrator graphic filled with many overlapping objects with transparency applied (**Figure 13.14**, on the next page). Although it may seem like only several objects at first glance, once those objects are broken up into atomic regions, you may be looking at thousands of vector shapes, which can take a long time to process and print (**Figure 13.15**, on the next page). In those cases, Illustrator can save precious RIP and processing time by rasterizing these complex regions.

Figure 13.14 *Using the Symbol Sprayer tool, you can easily create a file that contains many overlapping shapes. You can also make some of these symbols transparent with the same tool.*

Figure 13.15 *Even though you may have started with a small number of objects, the resulting number of atomic regions can be extremely large because of flattening.*

As far as the first level of rasterization goes, you really have no choice but to allow Illustrator to rasterize objects where it needs to do so. What you *can* do, however, is learn how to build files that work around this issue (see "Understanding Object Stacking Order and Transparency Flattening" later in this chapter). With regard to the second level of rasterization, you can control how liberal Illustrator is when looking for complex regions. In fact, you can even disable this second level of rasterization altogether. Finally, with either level of rasterization, Illustrator always gives you total control over *how* these areas are rasterized.

Understanding the Transparency Flattener Settings

As mentioned earlier in this chapter, Illustrator has three transparency flattener presets that you can choose from in the Advanced panel of the Print dialog box. These settings control how files with transparency are flattened at print time. To access these settings, choose Edit > Transparency Flattener Presets, and click the New button to define a new preset. Let's explore the settings in the Transparency Flattener Preset Options dialog box (**Figure 13.16**).

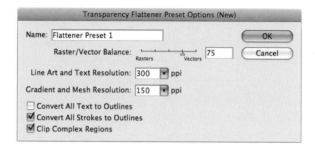

Figure 13.16 *You can define your own custom flattener settings, or your printer or service provider can define them for you.*

- **Raster/Vector Balance.** This slider is what controls how liberal Illustrator is when looking for complex regions to rasterize (what we defined previously as the second level of rasterization). A number closer to zero (0) gives Illustrator more freedom to rasterize at will, resulting in faster print times. Moving the slider closer to 100 results in fewer rasterized areas but longer print times. At the 100 setting, Illustrator does not rasterize *any* parts of the file for performance reasons, effectively disabling the second level of rasterization. The High Resolution flattener preset uses this setting. In cases where files are taking extremely long to print (or crashing the RIP altogether), adjusting this slider to a slightly lower setting helps.

- **Line Art and Text Resolution.** In cases where Illustrator is going to rasterize line art or text, you can specify a resolution that results in good-looking, sharp output. You'll notice that the High Resolution flattener setting specifies a resolution of 1200 ppi, ensuring that text elements and vector objects still have nice, clean, sharp edges in final output.

- **Gradient and Mesh Resolution.** Because gradients and meshes are continuous tones in nature, they don't require a resolution as high as line art or text. In fact, anything twice your line screen is probably getting thrown out anyway. Therefore, Illustrator uses this setting to rasterize elements that can afford to be set at a lower resolution. You'll notice that the High Resolution flattener preset uses a value of 300 ppi.

NOTE The two resolution settings in the flattener controls are used whenever vector objects are forced to become rasters during the flattening process. However, live effects, such as Feather and Drop Shadow, use the Document Raster Effects Resolution setting to determine their resolutions.

- **Convert All Text to Outlines.** In cases where text is going to be rasterized, chances are that the rasterized text looks a bit chunkier than regular vector text. To compensate for this, you can turn on this option to convert all text to outlines, giving a consistent chunkier look to all of your text. If you use the method described later in this chapter to move text onto its own layer, you'll rarely need to concern yourself with this setting.

- **Convert All Strokes to Outlines.** Similar to the previous setting, this compensates for disparities between vector and rasterized strokes by converting all strokes to outlines.

- **Clip Complex Regions.** We mentioned that Illustrator can look for complex areas of a file and rasterize them for performance reasons. However, we know that raster images are always rectangular in shape, which means it's possible for "innocent" parts of your file to become rasterized simply because they fall into the rectangular bounding box of the area that is complex. More often than not, this results in *stitching*, or noticeable boxes and color shifts. The Clip Complex Regions option avoids this issue by creating a clipping mask around any rasterized complex region (so the rectangular-shaped raster is masked by the vector outline of the object). As you can probably understand, this makes for even more complex files and can result in longer print times as well. This option is turned on by default but isn't applicable in the High Resolution preset because no complex regions are rasterized at all with that setting (because it has a Raster/Vector Balance setting of 100).

Understanding Object Stacking Order and Transparency Flattening

When rasterization occurs during transparency flattening, the last thing you want to see turning into a raster is text. That's because you always want text to be clean and sharp in your printouts. Even at the High Resolution setting, where text is rasterized at 1200 ppi, that resolution is still less than half of what most imagesetters set text with—usually upward of 2400 ppi.

Although it's true that under certain circumstances rasterization must occur in order to print a file and maintain its appearance, the way you build your files can affect how often this happens. Let's look at a simple example that clarifies this:

1. Draw a circle, and add a drop shadow to it by choosing Effect > Stylize > Drop Shadow.

As you learned in Chapter 8, "Working with Typography," the Drop Shadow effect is a raster-based effect, and when transparency is flattened, the drop shadow becomes rasterized.

2. Switch to the Type tool, create some text, and position the text near the drop shadow (**Figure 13.17**).

Figure 13.17 *Placing text near an object is common, especially when you're adding captions or credit text near photographs.*

3. With the text still selected, choose Object > Arrange > Send to Back.

4. Now select both the circle and the text, choose Object > Flatten Transparency, and click OK.

Upon close inspection, you'll see that a portion of the text was rasterized. This happened because the text was below the drop shadow in the stacking order, and to maintain the file's appearance when the drop shadow was rasterized, Illustrator had to include part of the text in the drop shadow's bounding area (**Figure 13.18**).

Figure 13.18 *To maintain the appearance of the file, Illustrator rasterized the text that was behind the drop shadow.*

5. Choose Edit > Undo to go back to the version before you applied the Flatten Transparency function, and select the text object.

6.   Choose Object > Arrange > Bring to Front.

7.   Select the circle and the text, choose Object > Flatten Transparency, and click OK.

In this case, the text, which was above the drop shadow in the stacking order, was not affected at all and was not rasterized (**Figure 13.19**).

Figure 13.19 *If the text appears above the shadow in the stacking order, the text is not rasterized during flattening.*

When using transparency features in Illustrator (or InDesign, for that matter), it's important to make sure that text always appears *above* objects with transparency to avoid unwanted rasterized text issues. Of course, some designs call for text to appear beneath transparent objects, and in those cases, you don't have much of a choice.

Does My File Contain Transparency?

Not every document needs flattening—only those with transparency in them. The tricky part is that transparency can be introduced into an Illustrator document in several ways:

•   You apply a blending mode or an Opacity value other than 100% in the Transparency panel.

•   You apply the Effect > Stylize > Drop Shadow feature.

•   You apply the Effect > Stylize > Feather feature.

•   You apply the Effect > Stylize > Outer Glow feature.

•   You apply the Effect > Stylize > Inner Glow feature.

•   You apply any "below-the-line" Photoshop effect from the Effect menu.

•   You place a PDF file that contains transparency.

- You place a native Photoshop file or layered TIFF that contains transparency.

- You apply a Bristle brush stroke that contains a paint opacity value of less than 100 percent.

It would be helpful to know whether your document uses transparency or even will require either of the two levels of rasterization discussed earlier. You can use the Flattener Preview panel (Window > Flattener Preview) to tell whether a document has transparency effects in it, as well as to preview areas that will become rasterized in the flattening process.

By clicking the Refresh button in the panel, Illustrator highlights specific areas in your file in red, indicating where rasterization will occur. You can enlarge the panel to see a larger image, and you can also click inside the preview area of the panel to zoom in closer to see more detail. From the Highlight pop-up menu, you can choose from a variety of items that Illustrator will preview. If all the items listed in your Highlight pop-up are dim, that indicates your file doesn't have transparency present, and no flattening is necessary to print your file (**Figure 13.20**, on the next page). For example, when you choose Transparent Objects, Illustrator shows you where all objects that use transparency are on your page—although those regions may not necessarily become rasterized. We also mentioned earlier that Illustrator looks for complex areas of a document; you can see where those areas are by choosing Rasterized Complex Regions in the pop-up menu (**Figure 13.21**, on the next page). Additionally, the All Affected Objects option shows you all the objects that may not be transparent themselves but that interact with transparency in some way. (Like with the example we mentioned earlier with the drop shadow and the text, the text itself doesn't have transparency applied to it, but if the text appears below the drop shadow, the text must become rasterized to preserve the appearance.)

To take advantage of all that the Flattener Preview panel can offer, adjust the different flattener settings, and preview the results—making changes or adjustments where necessary—before you actually print the file. As an aside, InDesign and Acrobat Pro also contain a similar Flattener Preview panel and identical flattener settings (in fact, it's the same underlying code).

Figure 13.20 *If your file contains no transparency, you don't have to worry about the effects of flattening.*

Figure 13.21 *You can use the Flattener Preview panel to identify areas that Illustrator deems as complex regions, giving you a heads up for what areas will be rasterized.*

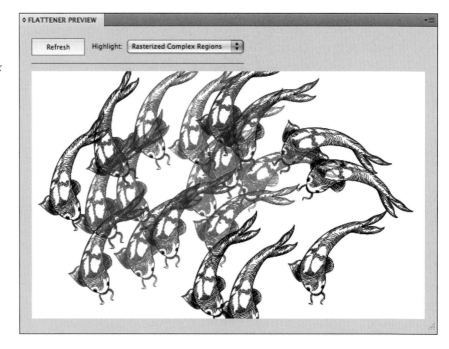

What Kind of RIP Are You Using?

To throw yet another variable into the mix, the kind of printer or RIP you use also affects your results. Any Adobe PostScript LanguageLevel 3 device should be able to handle transparency without issue. Specifically, PostScript version 3015 (which appears in the latest versions of RIPs) can process files that have been flattened. It's important to remember that flattening has to occur for any RIP to understand how to print transparency. If your RIP can process PDF files, that doesn't necessarily mean it can process PDF files with transparency in them. If you're in doubt, check with your RIP manufacturer to find out whether transparency flattening can occur inside the RIP or whether you need to print files from an Adobe application to flatten them.

Some older print devices are confused by the effects of flattening. For example, a Scitex Brisque RIP (since acquired by Creo and now Kodak) looks at jobs that are printing and splits up the vector and raster elements onto two "layers." The rasterized content prints on a continuous tone (CT) layer at a lower resolution (such as 300 dpi), and line art prints on a separate vector layer at a much higher resolution (such as 2400 dpi). Because flattening could cause a vector object to be rasterized, the RIP sees that raster only as a CT image and prints it at the lower resolution. This might cause text that is rasterized to print with noticeably jagged edges. There's an update available for Brisque RIPs to address this issue, but that doesn't automatically mean everyone who owns a Brisque has installed the update (or knows it exists).

Rampage RIPs experience similar issues, although turning off the dual-mode setting addresses them.

The best advice in any case is to talk with your printer. For any big job, most printers will be happy to run a test file for you to make sure everything will print correctly. Taking advantage of these opportunities will surely save you headaches when press deadlines loom. Adobe also has free specialized training materials for print service providers if your printer needs more information (online at http://www.adobe.com/print).

Printing with Confidence

You can avoid accidents by learning to anticipate possible problems. Now that you're aware of how transparency works, here are a few ways to ensure that you get the results you expect when you're printing from Illustrator:

- Use the right flattener presets—Low Resolution, Medium Resolution, and High Resolution. For quick proofs to your laser printer, you can use the Low Resolution or Medium Resolution setting, but when you're printing to a high-end proofer or imagesetter, use the High Resolution setting. You'll find the Transparency Flattener settings in the Advanced panel of the Print dialog box.

- To avoid text becoming rasterized, create a new layer in your Illustrator file, and place all your text on that layer. As long as you keep that text layer as the top layer in your document, you won't have to worry about chunky or pixelated text because of rasterization.

- A potential problem is that even if you, as a designer, are aware of transparency, plenty of printers aren't. If you are sending a file and aren't sure who will be printing it or what they will be using to print it, you might consider sending the file as a PDF/X-1a file. See Chapter 12, "Saving and Exporting Files," for more information about PDF/X.

If you'd like an easy way to remember the important steps to get great results when printing, a small transparency checklist (**Figure 13.22**, courtesy of Design Responsibly), is available when you register at www.peachpit.com/rwillcs5.

Figure 13.22 *The transparency checklist offers a few quick reminders to help ensure your file prints correctly.*

Designing with transparency allows you to design creations that were previously prohibitive and difficult to implement, thus allowing you to save valuable time while being even more creative. Now that you know how transparency works and what's necessary to use it in your workflow, give it a test drive. You'll be happy you did.

Understanding Overprints

Hang around a print shop long enough, and you'll hear the term *overprint*. In the world of prepress, overprinting is a way to control how color separated plates interact with each other. A printing press imprints each color on a piece of paper, one after the other, as it runs through the press. Because of this process, you need to consider certain issues when making color separations.

For example, say you design some blue text over a yellow background. When those colors are separated and printed on press, the blue and yellow mix, resulting in green text on a yellow background. Therefore, under normal conditions, when pages are separated, color that appears underneath other objects is removed so that the color on top is unaffected. In this example, the blue text removes, or *knocks out*, the yellow background underneath it, allowing the blue to appear correctly when printed.

Overprinting, however, is a method of overriding a knockout and forcing overlapping colors to mix on press. In our example, setting the blue text to overprint means that the yellow background still appears behind it, and the result on press is green text on a yellow background (**Figure 13.23**).

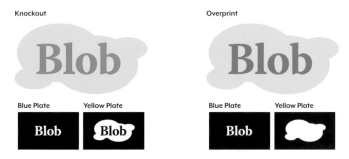

Figure 13.23 *The text on the left, by default, knocks out the background behind it. The text on the right is set to overprint, and the background behind it is unaffected.*

Why Overprint?

You'd want to apply an overprint when you specifically want to mix colors on press. Some designers who work with low-budget jobs that print in two or three spot colors can simulate other colors by mixing those spot colors. Before transparency rolled around, designers would also specify overprints to simulate objects being transparent; you could also simulate shadows or shading by overprinting with black over other elements.

Overprinting is also essential when you're creating plates for custom dyes and varnishes. For example, if you want to create a spot varnish for a particular photo, you need to create a spot color called Varnish and set it to overprint, because this allows the photo that appears beneath it to print (otherwise, the varnish knocks out the photo).

You can easily specify overprinting from the Attributes panel (Window > Attributes). With an object selected, you can force the fill, the stroke, or both to overprint. Remember that Illustrator also allows you to specify whether a stroke is painted in the centerline, inside, or outside a path, and you should be aware that if you overprint a stroke that's on the inside or the centerline of a path, the stroke also overprints the fill of that object.

Trapped in a Corner

Those who work in packaging use overprints all the time to create *traps*—colors that share borders with other colors that overlap slightly. This is because commonly used package materials and the printing processes used (called *flexographic printing*, or *flexo*) don't always result in perfect printing. Remember that the requirements for printing a couple hundred brochures and printing several million containers of milk can be quite different. The next time you see a bag of potato chips or a bottle of soda, take a close look at the label; you'll be able to see the overprint traps. These are usually created in Illustrator by setting just the stroke to overprint.

Handling the Limitations of Overprints

Let's get technical for a moment. You'll encounter some limitations when it comes to using overprints. First, whereas one color plate can overprint another, an overprint cannot overprint its own plate. For example, if you have a color that contains cyan and you set it to overprint over a background that contains cyan, you won't get an overprint on the cyan plate.

Second, sometimes users specify overprinting for objects colored white. Usually, white is always a knockout (because it lets the white paper show through), and setting a white object to overprint would kind of defeat the purpose. However, these things do happen accidentally. You might have a logo that you created that's colored black and that you've set to overprint. Then you might come upon a situation where you need a reverse (white) version of the logo, so you might just open the file, color it white, and save it with a different name, forgetting that you set the fill to overprint. This would most likely result in the file not printing properly, because either the white overprints (making it entirely transparent) or the RIP doesn't process the file correctly.

Previewing Overprints

Because overprints are really PostScript commands that you use when you're printing color separations, you'll always have a problem with displaying overprints onscreen or when you're printing composite proofs to show a client. In the past, the only real way to proof overprints was by printing separations and creating a matchprint proof or by investing in expensive prepress plug-ins. More often than not, a designer would show a proof to a client and say, "It won't look like this when it's actually printed." If only there were a better way...

Illustrator offers that better way. By choosing View > Overprint Preview, you can actually see on your monitor what the effects of overprint commands are. Additionally, in the Output panel of the Print dialog box, the Simulate Overprint option, when activated, prints composites as they will look with overprints applied. This is perfect for showing clients exactly what they are going to get. The Simulate Overprint option is also available in the Advanced panel of the PDF dialog box, so you can even show your client an accurate proof via PDF. You disable Simulate Overprint when you choose to print separations—it's available only when you're printing composites.

Although overprints are useful (and essential in some workflows), our advice is to talk to your printer before you use them, because some printers prefer to specify overprints themselves.

Handling Transparency Effects That Disappear or Print as White Boxes

Has the following scenario ever happened to you?

You create some artwork that contains two spot colors (let's say Pantone Blue 072 and Red 032). The logo has a drop shadow behind it, and you've correctly set the Illustrator Drop Shadow effect to use the Blue 072 spot color, not black. On the Illustrator artboard, the logo appears correctly against the spot color background (**Figure 13.24**).

Figure 13.24 *In Illustrator, the Drop Shadow effect appears correctly against the spot color background.*

Then you save the art as a PDF/X-1a file because it will be used in an ad and you want to make sure it will print correctly. Or you save your document using Acrobat 4 (PDF 1.3) compatibility. Alternatively, you save your file as an EPS file because maybe you're required to place this logo into a QuarkXPress document. The point here to focus on is that you're saving your file to a flattened format.

The "problem" is that when you open the PDF in Acrobat or Reader, or when you place the file into QuarkXPress or InDesign and print the file to your laser or ink-jet printer, it comes out looking incorrect—either the drop shadow disappears completely (**Figure 13.25**) or a white box appears where the transparent effect should blend into the background (**Figure 13.26**).

Figure 13.25 *When saving the file from Illustrator and viewing or printing the art outside of Illustrator, a white box appears around the transparency effect.*

Figure 13.26 *When saving the file from Illustrator and viewing or printing the art outside of Illustrator, the transparency effect seems to disappear.*

NOTE Some RIPs have built-in settings to ignore overprints in files and instead use their own settings for overprints. This often results in output that isn't desirable. You can easily fix these issues by instructing the RIP to honor the overprints in your files. For example, Rampage RIPs have a setting called Preserve Application Overprint that, when activated, results in perfect output.

The key items to focus on here are that you have used a transparent effect and you've used a spot color. Now, you'll know what's happening and what the solution is.

When you have a transparent effect, the result is a mixture of the inks. In this case, the shadow, which is Pantone Blue 072, blends right into the Red 032 background. By default, when one color sits on top of another color, a knockout occurs, as we discussed earlier in this chapter. In other words, the area beneath the top shape is removed from the lower object. Otherwise, the top color will print on top of the bottom color when the paper is run through the printing press, causing the two inks to mix. In the case of the red and blue colors, the result would be purple in appearance. However, in this case, where you *want* the drop shadow to blend into the background on press, you have to override that knockout by specifying an overprint.

The thing is, Illustrator already knows this, so no action is required on your part. When you print your file from Illustrator, all these settings are done automatically, so your file looks great when you print it—either as a composite or as separations. The same applies when you save your file from Illustrator as a native Illustrator file and place it into InDesign or when you create a PDF with Acrobat 5 compatibility (PDF 1.4) or newer.

But when you save your file to a format that doesn't support transparency, Illustrator has to flatten the transparency. And in that process, Illustrator realizes that in order to preserve the spot colors so that they print in separations correctly, the drop shadow must be set to overprint the background color (in Illustrator CS4 and CS5, the spot color is set to overprint instead).

The problem is that overprint commands are honored only when you print your file as separations. When you are previewing your document onscreen or when you are printing a composite proof of your file, the overprint commands aren't used, and either the result will be white where overprinting should occur or the transparency effect will simply disappear. The file will print correctly when you print as separations, because, at that time, the overprints are honored (as they should be).

This issue is easy to solve in InDesign, Acrobat, or Reader:

- In InDesign, choose View > Overprint Preview. This will allow you to view overprints on your screen. When printing composite proofs, select the Simulate Overprints box in the Output panel of the Print dialog box to get the correct appearance in your printouts.

- In Acrobat or Reader, choose Always in the Use Overprint Preview popup menu (in the Page Display panel in Preferences) to view the file correctly on your screen. When printing composite proofs, choose Print, and then click the Advanced button. Then select the Simulate Overprinting box in the Output section of the dialog box. The file will then print with the correct appearance.

TIP If you're using QuarkXPress (at least up through version 8.0) you really don't have an option, because that program doesn't allow you to simulate overprint commands when printing composite proofs. One workaround is to create two versions of your file: one that uses spot colors that will separate correctly when you print separations and another version where you've converted your spot colors to process colors. When you convert to process colors, you don't need the overprints, and the file will print with the correct appearance on a composite proof.

Application Preferences

Illustrator has many different settings, or *preferences*, that control the program's behavior. You can find these settings on the 12 panels of the Preferences dialog box. On Mac OS, you can open the Preferences dialog box by choosing Application > Preferences or by pressing Command-K. On Windows, you can open the Preferences dialog box by choosing Edit > Preferences or by pressing Ctrl-K.

In general, the preferences in Illustrator are application-based, meaning they aren't saved in each Illustrator document but rather in Illustrator's application preferences file (see "The Illustrator Preferences File"). This means if you open an Illustrator file that was created on another computer with different preferences, your own preferences don't change.

The Illustrator Preferences File

Each time you quit or close Illustrator, it writes the latest preferences you've specified along with information about which panels are open and their locations on your screen.

When things go awry in Illustrator (frequent crashing, missing tools or panels, and so on), the culprit can often be a corrupted preferences file. In such cases, the cure is to delete the preferences file (when no preferences file is present at launch time, Illustrator generates a new one).

You can delete the preferences file by pressing Command-Option-Shift (Ctrl-Alt-Shift) while launching Illustrator. Keep the keys pressed until you see the splash screen appear. Alternatively, you can manually delete the file, which you can find in the following location:

Mac OS: Username/Library/Preferences/Adobe Illustrator CS5 Settings/ en_US/Adobe Illustrator Prefs

Windows: Documents and Settings\Username\Application Data\Adobe\ Adobe Illustrator CS5 Settings\en_US\AIPrefs

If you make many changes to your preferences, you'll lose those changes when you delete your preferences file. For this reason, you might consider making a copy of your file for safekeeping, after you've changed your preferences. If you ever need to delete the preferences file, simply use the copy you've created. If you're really brave, you can also manually edit the file in just about any text editor.

The General Panel

The General panel of Preferences is pretty much a melting pot of settings (**Figure A.1**). These settings are also the ones that affect the behavior of Illustrator the most.

Figure A.1 *The General panel in Preferences offers quick access to settings such as Keyboard Increment.*

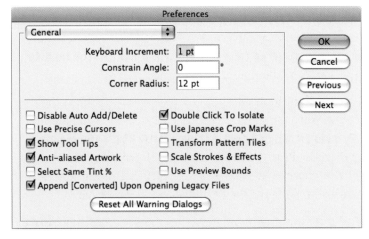

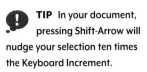

TIP In your document, pressing Shift-Arrow will nudge your selection ten times the Keyboard Increment.

Keyboard Increment. When moving artwork around on your screen, using the mouse or even a pressure-sensitive pen doesn't always give you the control you need. The Keyboard Increment setting determines the distance a selected object moves when you tap any of the four arrow keys on your keyboard. Some call this the *nudge amount*. Don't be fooled into thinking that this setting should always be as small as possible. When you're working with a grid or in scale (designing floor plans, schematics, and so on), it can be extremely helpful to set your keyboard increment to a specific value (such as .25 inch). In this way, you can easily tap an arrow two times and know you've moved the object exactly .5 inch. It's no coincidence that when you open the Preferences dialog box, the Keyboard Increment value is highlighted. Power users know they can quickly press Command-K (Ctrl-K), enter a value, press Enter, and then nudge their objects precisely.

Constrain Angle. When you draw objects in Illustrator, the objects are aligned to the Constrain Angle setting, which is normally set to 0 degrees. However, sometimes you'll want to draw your document on a specific angle. Changing the Constrain Angle preference affects all tools and modifier keys in Illustrator.

Corner Radius. When you're creating a shape with the Rounded Rectangle tool, this setting defines the default corner radius for the rounded corners. This preference sets the default behavior, which you can easily override on a per-object basis in the Rounded Rectangle tool dialog box.

Disable Auto Add/Delete. Illustrator tries its best to help you get your work done, but sometimes its overzealousness gets in the way. By default, when you move your pointer over an existing path with the Pen tool, Illustrator thinks you want to add a point to the existing path and conveniently switches to the Add Anchor Point tool. This is great, unless, of course, you wanted to start drawing a new path with the Pen tool. Turning this preference on politely tells Illustrator, "Thanks but no thanks."

Use Precise Cursors. Some tool icons in Illustrator are cute, such as the Symbol Sprayer and Warp tools, but they can be hard to position precisely. Even with the Pen tool, it can be hard to know exactly where the real tip of the pointer is. When Use Precise Cursors is active, all pointers are replaced by a simple X icon, which clearly defines the spot you're clicking. You can toggle this setting by pressing the Caps Lock key on your keyboard.

Show Tool Tips. Illustrator has a lot of icons—tiny chicklet icons, as we like to call them. Sometimes it's hard to know what a tool or button is just by look-ing at it, so if you hold your pointer over the icon for a second, a little window pops up identifying the name of the feature. These are called *tool tips*, and they are turned on by default. Although they are helpful, some people think they get in the way, which is why this preference lets you disable tool tips.

Anti-aliased Artwork. Computer screens are low-resolution devices (generally between 72 and 130 ppi), so artwork may appear jagged onscreen. This is especially true with the sharp vector shapes you create with Illustrator. Although the files print fine, looking at jagged artwork all day may cause eyestrain and doesn't accurately display the way the graphics will eventually print. This option (on by default) applies antialiasing to the Preview mode so your art onscreen appears clean and smooth. Antialiasing is always turned off in Outline view mode. Note that this setting affects how the art appears onscreen in Illustrator only and does not affect how the art prints.

Select Same Tint %. Illustrator has a feature that allows you to select all objects that are filled or stroked with the same color. When you use this feature, all objects filled with tint percentages of that same color are also selected. The Select Same Tint % preference setting selects only those objects that are filled with the same tint percentages of that color (resulting in fewer objects being selected).

Append [Converted] Upon Opening Legacy Files. When you open files that were created in previous versions of Illustrator (what Illustrator refers to as *legacy files*), you may have to adjust text objects. To prevent you from accidentally overwriting your original files, Illustrator tacks on the word *[converted]* to your file name when it opens legacy files. For more information about text and legacy files, see Chapter 8, "Working with Typography."

Double Click To Isolate. On by default, this option makes it possible to double-click an object to isolate it for editing. With this option turned off, you can still isolate a selection, but you have to either select Enter Isolation Mode from the panel menu in the Layers panel or click the Isolate Selected Object icon on the Control panel.

Use Japanese Crop Marks. Illustrator allows you to create simple crop marks automatically by choosing Effect > Crop Marks or Object > Create Trim Marks. If you want something more than the standard marks, you can turn on this preference. At the very least, people who see your files will know you're serious about crop marks.

Transform Pattern Tiles. When you apply transformations (such as Scale or Rotate) to objects that are filled with patterns, the default behavior is that only the shape is transformed, not the pattern fill. Turning this preference on changes the default behavior so that pattern fills are transformed as well. Note that this preference sets the default behavior, which you can easily override as you need to by using the setting in the Scale tool dialog box or by pressing the tilde key (~) during a manual transform function.

Scale Strokes & Effects. Similar to patterns, when you apply scale transformations to objects that have strokes or effects applied, by default only the shape is transformed, not the strokes or the effects. Turning this preference on changes the default behavior so that strokes and effects are transformed as well. This preference sets the default behavior, which you can easily override as you need to by using the setting in the Scale tool dialog box.

Use Preview Bounds. One of the benefits of using Illustrator is that you can be extremely precise when drawing objects. The Control, Transform, and Info panels all provide exact feedback on coordinates, positioning, sizing, and more. By default, these panels use the actual vector path to determine these numbers, not the visual boundaries of the object. For example, you may have a shape that has a thick stroke or a scale effect applied to it, which is not represented in the value you see in the Transform panel. With the Use Preview Bounds preference activated, all panels use the visual boundary of a file as the value, not the underlying vector path.

Reset All Warning Dialogs. With daily use of Illustrator, you'll encounter a variety of warning dialog boxes. Sometimes these are helpful, and sometimes they can be quite annoying and you'll wish bad things upon them. You'll find that most of them contain a "Don't show again" check box, which you can use to tell Illustrator that a simple beep would be just fine, thank you. Clicking Reset All Warning Dialogs brings back any warning dialog boxes that you asked Illustrator not to show again.

The Selection & Anchor Display Panel

If you're having trouble selecting individual anchor points or if you are coming from Macromedia FreeHand and are used to seeing anchor points and control handles displayed a bit differently, the Selection & Anchor Display panel in Preferences is for you (**Figure A.2**, on the next page). The Object Selection by Path Only setting, which at one time appeared in the General panel, now appears here.

Figure A.2 *The Selection & Anchor Display panel in Preferences enables you to control settings used when you select and edit paths.*

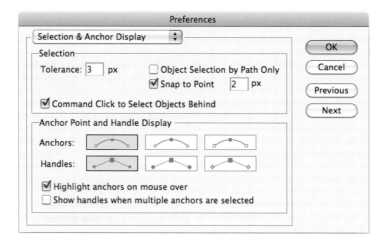

Tolerance. The Tolerance setting determines how close your pointer has to be to an object in order to select it. Using a lower number means you'll have to position your pointer perfectly in order to make a selection (good for very precise work where there are many anchor points within a small area), while higher numbers allow for faster and easier selections.

Object Selection by Path Only. When working in Preview mode, Illustrator allows you to select an object by clicking its path or anywhere within its fill area (if it has a fill attribute applied). Sometimes—especially when you're working with complex artwork—this behavior makes it difficult to select objects. Turning this preference on allows you to select objects only by clicking their paths, not their fills.

Snap to Point. As you drag objects around the page, you'll notice that your pointer snaps to the anchor points of other objects and to guides as well. The Snap to Point value determines how close your pointer has to be to another object in order for it to snap to it.

Command-Click to Select Objects Behind. On by default, this setting makes it possible to select objects that are beneath other objects in the stacking order. Where you have multiple objects that overlap each other, you can press and hold the Command (Ctrl) key while clicking with the Selection or Direct Selection tool. Each successive click selects the next object beneath the cursor in the stacking order.

Anchors. Illustrator offers three ways to display anchor points. The difference between each size may be subtle here, but this setting can help make Illustrator seem more familiar to FreeHand users.

Handles. Illustrator offers three different ways to display control handles. The difference between each of the three may be subtle, but this setting can mean all the difference to those who might be used to seeing handles in a different way, as in FreeHand.

Highlight anchors on mouse over. On by default, this setting highlights anchor points as you mouse over them. This happens even if the objects are not selected. They can be either very helpful, such as when you're editing paths, or very annoying, which explains the preference setting.

Show handles when multiple anchors are selected. In previous versions of Illustrator, you were able to see only the control handles of one anchor point or path segment at a time. With this preference turned on, you can view control handles even with multiple anchor points selected. Note that you edit only one control handle at a time.

The Type Panel

Illustrator has a variety of preference settings that apply specifically to working with typography and text (**Figure A.3**).

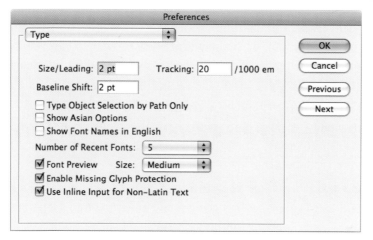

Figure A.3 *The Type panel in Preferences enables you to activate the WYSIWYG (what you see is what you get) Font menu.*

Keyboard shortcut increments. Keyboard shortcut junkies know they can perform a variety of tasks without ever reaching for the mouse. This is never more helpful than when you are working with type, when your hands are already on the keyboard. You can set the keyboard increments for changing size/leading, baseline shift, and tracking here.

Type Object Selection by Path Only. Similar to the Object Selection by Path Only setting, this one refers to text objects. With this preference on, you can select a text object by clicking only its baseline.

Show Asian Options. Illustrator is extremely popular in Japan and in other Asian countries; therefore, it has some features, such as Warichu, Kinsoku, Mojikumi, Tsume, Aki, and composite fonts, that are used specifically in those locales. These features are hidden from view by default, but turning this preference on makes them visible in the user interface.

Show Font Names in English. When working with foreign or non-English fonts, you can use this option to specify that the fonts are listed in the Font menu using their English names.

Number of Recent Fonts. As you work, Illustrator takes note of the fonts you use and lists them at the top of your Font menu. When you have hundreds of fonts installed, this makes it easier to find a particular font than scrolling through the entire list. You can have Illustrator track up to 15 of the most recent fonts you've used. If you need more than 15 recent fonts in one project, you might want to look into taking a course in graphic design.

Font Preview. Illustrator has a WYSIWYG Font menu that allows you to preview what each font looks like as you scroll through the menu. You can choose between Small, Medium, and Large preview sizes. There is a slight performance hit that comes with using this feature, and this preference setting can enable or disable the preview altogether. One valuable aspect of the font preview is that it also displays an icon indicating whether a font is TrueType, PostScript, Multiple Master, or OpenType.

Enable Missing Glyph Protection. Turning this setting on gives Illustrator the ability to substitute a glyph or a character where the desired glyph is not available (because either the current font or the font you just switched to doesn't support that glyph).

Use Inline Input for Non-Latin Text. Some operating systems support non-Latin languages by forcing you to enter text into a separate system-level dialog box. Enabling this option lets you set such text directly in Illustrator.

The Units Panel

Illustrator not only speaks different languages, but it also can work with various measurement systems. The settings you specify in the Units panel affect the values you see displayed in panels and dialog boxes throughout Illustrator (**Figure A.4**).

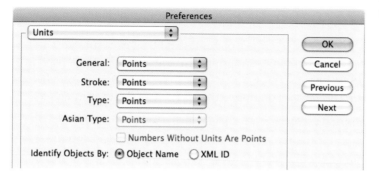

Units. These preferences let you specify default measurements for general items (rulers and coordinates, sizes and values for objects and drawing tools, and so on), stroke width and dash settings, and Roman and Asian type specifications (size, leading, and so on). Note that these are all used to set the default measurements in Illustrator, but at any time you can always enter a value to have Illustrator do the conversion for you. So if your document is set to inches, you can still specify a **4p9** rectangle (see the next paragraph for information about such measurements).

Numbers Without Units Are Points. When you're using picas and points, the standard notation is to enter the number of picas, the letter *p*, and the number of points (such as 12p6). If your value is only points, you enter something like **p6** to indicate 6 points instead. With this option turned on, simply typing **6** means 6 points (as opposed to 6 picas).

Identify Objects By. Illustrator has the ability to generate templates with XML-based variables, which are useful for generating graphics files automatically using scripts or the Adobe Graphics Server (a separate server-based product). Some of these templates require that all variables be defined using valid XML names. By default, Illustrator uses the object name to define variables, but you can specify that Illustrator should use valid XML IDs instead.

The Guides & Grid Panel

Illustrator allows you to define guides, which you drag out from either the horizontal ruler or the vertical ruler (View > Show Rulers). These guides act like magnets, helping you draw or position elements on your page. In reality, you can turn any vector shape into a guide by selecting it and choosing View > Guides > Make Guides. Additionally, Illustrator has a grid feature that makes your artboard appear almost as if it were a sheet of graph paper. Objects can snap to this grid, making it easy to visually align items in a layout.

You set the appearance of guides and the grid using the Guides & Grid panel in Preferences (**Figure A.5**). Some people prefer solid lines for guides, whereas others prefer dotted lines. You can also choose the color used for the guides. Additionally, you can set the number of grid lines and subdivisions that appear in the grid, which could be useful for artists or architects who normally work in scale. The Show Pixel Grid option is great for Web designers who want to view their artwork on a pixel-by-pixel basis. When activated, the pixel grid appears when your zoom level is higher than 600%.

Figure A.5 *The Guides & Grid panel in Preferences lets you change the color and appearance of grid lines.*

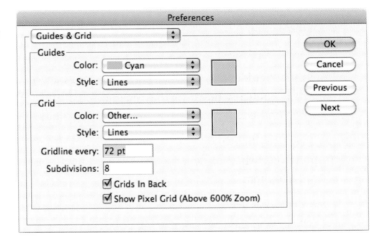

The Smart Guides Panel

In addition to normal guides, Illustrator has a useful feature called *smart guides*, which offer a variety of pointer feedback options as you work. You activate this feature by choosing View > Smart Guides. The Smart Guides panel allows you to control the feature's behavior (**Figure A.6**).

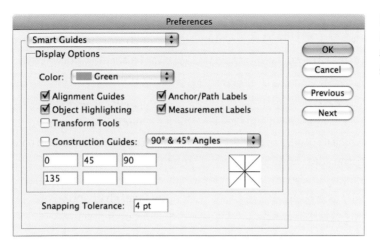

Figure A.6 *The Smart Guides panel controls the settings for the useful smart guides feature.*

Aside from choosing the color in which smart guides appear, the Display Options section of the Smart Guides preferences panel lets you enable or disable any of the six kinds of smart guides.

Alignment Guides. Alignment guides appear when you move your cursor; they help you align objects in context while drawing, moving, or editing objects. In this way, you don't have to perform additional align functions.

Object Highlighting. Object highlighting identifies the underlying Bézier paths or original text or artwork when you mouse over objects that have live effects or envelopes applied to them.

Transform Tools. Transform tools are guides that appear when using any of transform functions in Illustrator, such as Rotate or Scale.

Construction Guides. Construction guides appear as you're drawing new shapes and identifying similar planes or angles with other objects. You can specify which angles are identified using the pop-up list, or you can choose Custom Angles and specify up to six custom angles.

Anchor/Path Labels. Anchor/path labels identify anchor points and paths as you mouse over them.

Measurement Labels. Measurement labels help you identify the dimensions of objects as you draw them.

The Snapping Tolerance setting at the bottom of the panel allows you to specify how close your cursor needs to be to an object for smart guides to kick in. Smart guides are covered in detail in Chapter 1, "Creating and Managing Documents."

The Slices Panel

When creating art for the web, you can use web slicing to assist in optimizing your images. In Preferences, you can define how these slices are indicated on the Illustrator artboard. The Slices panel offers settings for how the slice regions are displayed on your screen (**Figure A.7**).

Figure A.7 *The Slices preferences panel.*

The Hyphenation Panel

Straightforward in its implementation, the Hyphenation panel in Preferences allows you to choose the default language (which you can override by using the pop-up list in the Character panel) and hyphenation exceptions; it also allows you to add new words to the dictionary (**Figure A.8**).

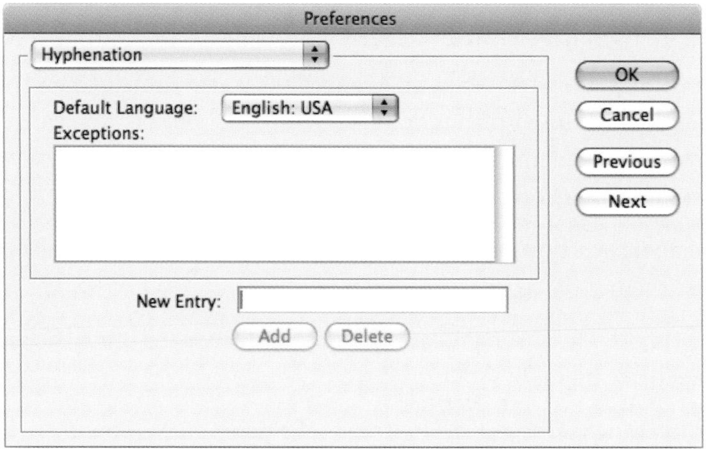

Figure A.8 *The Hyphenation panel in Preferences lets you add new words to the dictionary in Illustrator for better hyphenation.*

The Plug-ins & Scratch Disks Panel

From an architectural standpoint, Illustrator has a core engine, and the rest of the application is built using plug-ins, which are stored in the Plug-ins folder. Third-party plug-ins such as MAPublisher and CADtools are also stored in this folder. The Additional Plug-ins Folder option in the Plug-Ins & Scratch Disks panel of Preferences allows you to also specify additional folders where plug-ins might be stored (**Figure A.9**).

Figure A.9 *The Plug-ins & Scratch Disks panel in Preferences lets you specify multiple disks for memory-intensive operations.*

Just as you did in math class, Illustrator uses a scratch pad to save work while performing normal functions. Sometimes, in really complex files, Illustrator may need a lot of space. You can specify a hard drive or volume that Illustrator should use as a scratch disk to perform these functions. By default, your startup disk is your scratch disk, but you can change to a disk with more free space if you'd like. You can also specify a second scratch disk should Illustrator ever run out of room on the first one.

The User Interface Panel

Illustrator contains a panel-based user interface that is consistent with other components of the Creative Suite family. The User Interface panel in Preferences lets you configure how the user interface looks and how it works when you use it (**Figure A.10**, on the next page).

Figure A.10 *The User Interface panel in Preferences lets you control settings for how the Illustrator interface looks and works.*

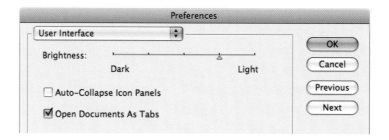

Brightness. Some people work in a brightly lit studio, while others work in dark or dimly lit rooms. People who do certain types of work, such as video or prepress production, may prefer to work in darker environments so that they can better focus on their work. In these dark environments, the panels in the interface can be bright enough to be a distraction. To allow these users to better focus on the art on their screens, the user interface has a Brightness slider. Sliding the triangle to the right will make the backgrounds in the panels brighter; sliding the triangle to the left will result in a dark gray background in the panels.

Auto-Collapse Icon Panels. When a panel is collapsed, you can click its icon to open the panel as you need it. With the Auto-Collapse Icon Panels setting turned on, a panel will return to its collapsed, iconic state after you've clicked elsewhere on your screen. Turning the setting off means a panel will stay open and return to its collapsed, iconic state only if you click its icon again.

Open Documents As Tabs. The user interface in Illustrator allows documents to be displayed as individual windows or as tabs in a single overall window. This setting lets you enable or disable the tabs feature.

The File Handling & Clipboard Panel

The File Handling & Clipboard panel includes settings for how Illustrator handles certain files as well as settings for how art is copied to the clipboard for pasting into other applications (**Figure A.11**).

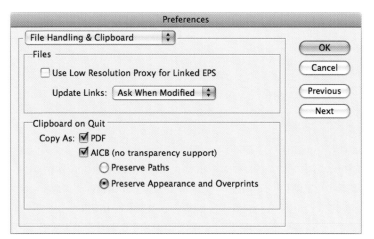

Figure A.11 *The File Handling & Clipboard panel in Preferences allows you to determine how graphics are copied and pasted into other applications.*

Use Low Resolution Proxy for Linked EPS. When you place-link an EPS file into Illustrator, whether it is a Photoshop EPS file or any other type, the preview that's displayed onscreen can be either the low-resolution preview that's embedded in the EPS file or a high-resolution version that Illustrator parses from the PostScript data in the actual EPS file. By default, Illustrator ships with this preference setting turned off, so a high-resolution file is used, resulting in a much better-looking preview on your screen. In addition, this high-resolution data is used when exporting your file in pixel-based formats (PSD, TFF, JPEG); however, screen redraw is slower, and the file size increases. On a separate note, when you're using the Live Trace feature with place-linked EPS files, the resolution of the image that Live Trace can detect depends on this setting as well. When the option is selected, Live Trace sees the 72 ppi preview file and traces that. By turning this setting off, Live Trace can detect the full resolution of the file and use it to trace the image.

Update Links. When you place-link a file into Illustrator, the Links panel maintains the link information about that file. Because the file is external, you can edit that file easily by using the Edit Original feature, found in either the Links panel or the Control panel. When the default Ask When Modified setting is used, if you edit a linked file outside Illustrator and return to the Illustrator document, you'll get a dialog box telling you that the file was updated, with an option to update the link. Alternatively, you can choose to manually update links yourself through the Links panel, or you can set Illustrator to automatically update all links as they happen.

Clipboard on Quit. Today's modern operating systems use an efficient method to copy and paste data using the system's clipboard, called *promising*.

Rather than copy art in a variety of formats to the clipboard (which would take time), applications promise to deliver art when pasted. Then, when you paste the art, the operating system goes back to the application you copied from and gets the data. The problem is, if you've quit the program since you performed the copy function, the operating system can't fulfill its promise. So when you quit an application, it copies whatever was promised to the clipboard (which explains why sometimes it takes a while for an application to actually quit). The Clipboard on Quit preference allows you to determine which file formats are used to copy art to the clipboard when you quit Illustrator. By default, both the PDF and the Adobe Illustrator Clip Board (AICB) options are selected, which gives you the most options. Unless you have a specific reason, we suggest you leave both of these selected at all times. In general, the PDF option supports native transparency and is PDF 1.6, whereas the AICB is flattened data and is PostScript.

The Appearance of Black Panel

In an effort to display graphics on your screen or proofs that closely match what you will see on a printed sheet, Illustrator includes a setting specifically for how the color black is displayed or printed (**Figure A.12**). You can choose to have your blacks display accurately, in which case black will appear closer to a dark gray color (closer to what you might see on newsprint), or you can choose to display rich blacks, in which case your blacks will be much darker. Note that these settings are not color management settings and don't affect your final separated output. These settings affect only your screen display or output to an RGB device.

Figure A.12 *The Appearance of Black panel in Preferences allows you to achieve more accurate color results on your screen.*

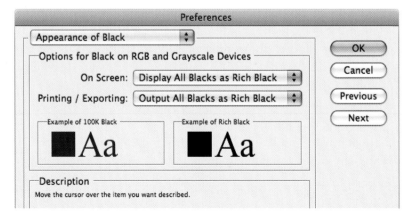

Index